The Light Of The Trees

El Corazon

Dr. Claus

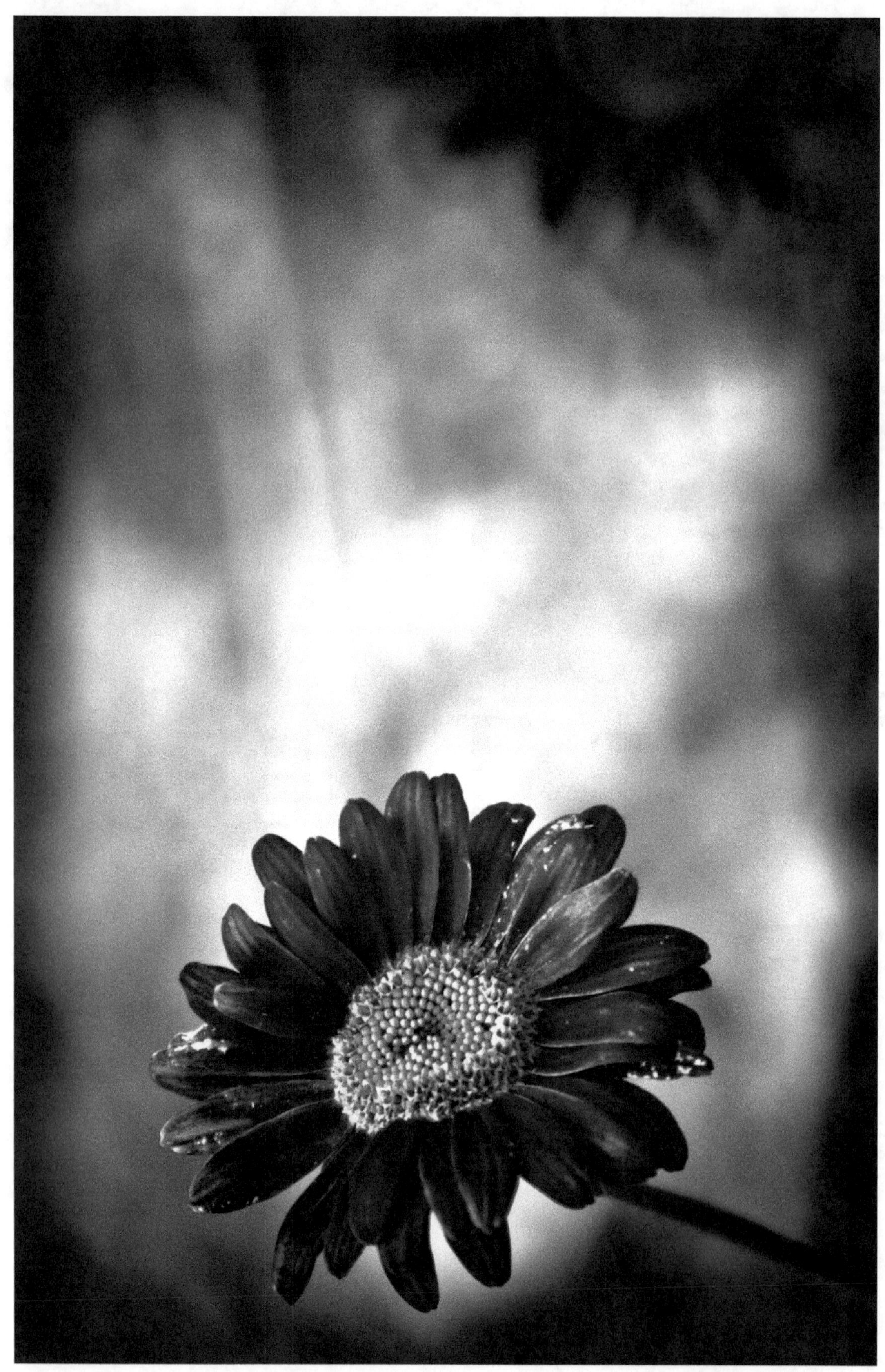

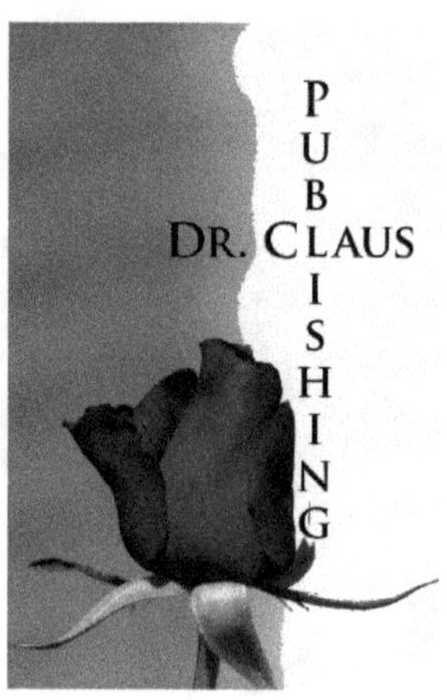

PUBLISHED BY DR. CLAUS PUBLISHING

First Edition
ISBN: 1-61497-050-5
ISBN-13: 978-1-61497-050-7
Library of Congress Control Number: 2014922095

DEDICATION

Allison

CONTENTS

ACKNOWLEDGMENT

During the war, my heart of stone was taken from my chest.
In place of that stone, I received a heart of flesh.
My old heart was handed back to me and as I received this heart of stone,
my thumbprint was forever seared into this rock.
I carry this heart of stone with me wherever I may go.
On any given day when words of doubt rain down upon my soul,
I reach for a stone once embedded in my chest
and I place my thumb into the mark.

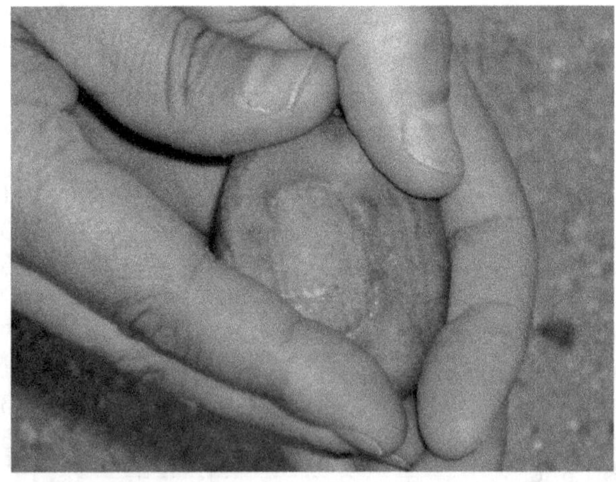

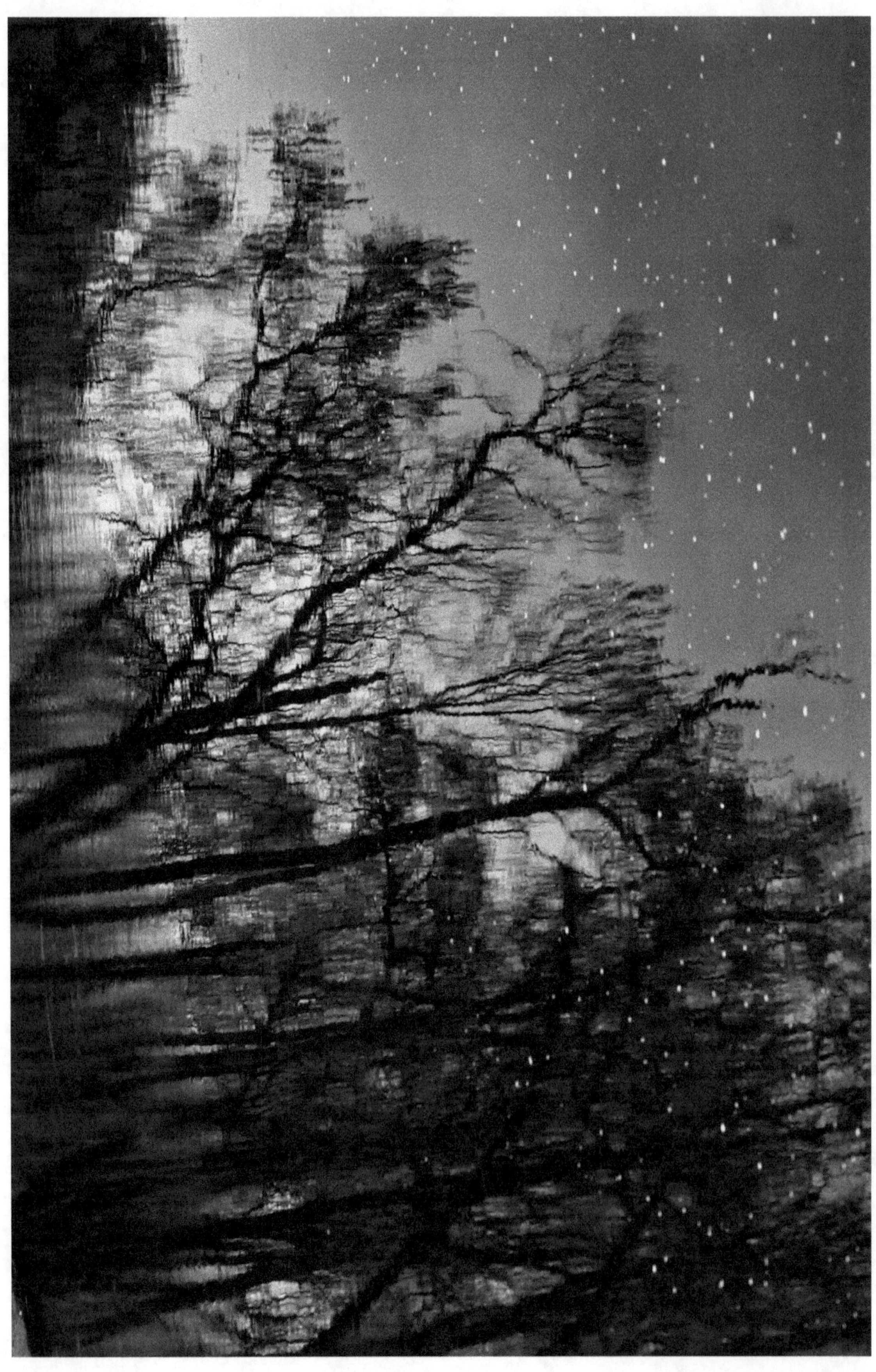

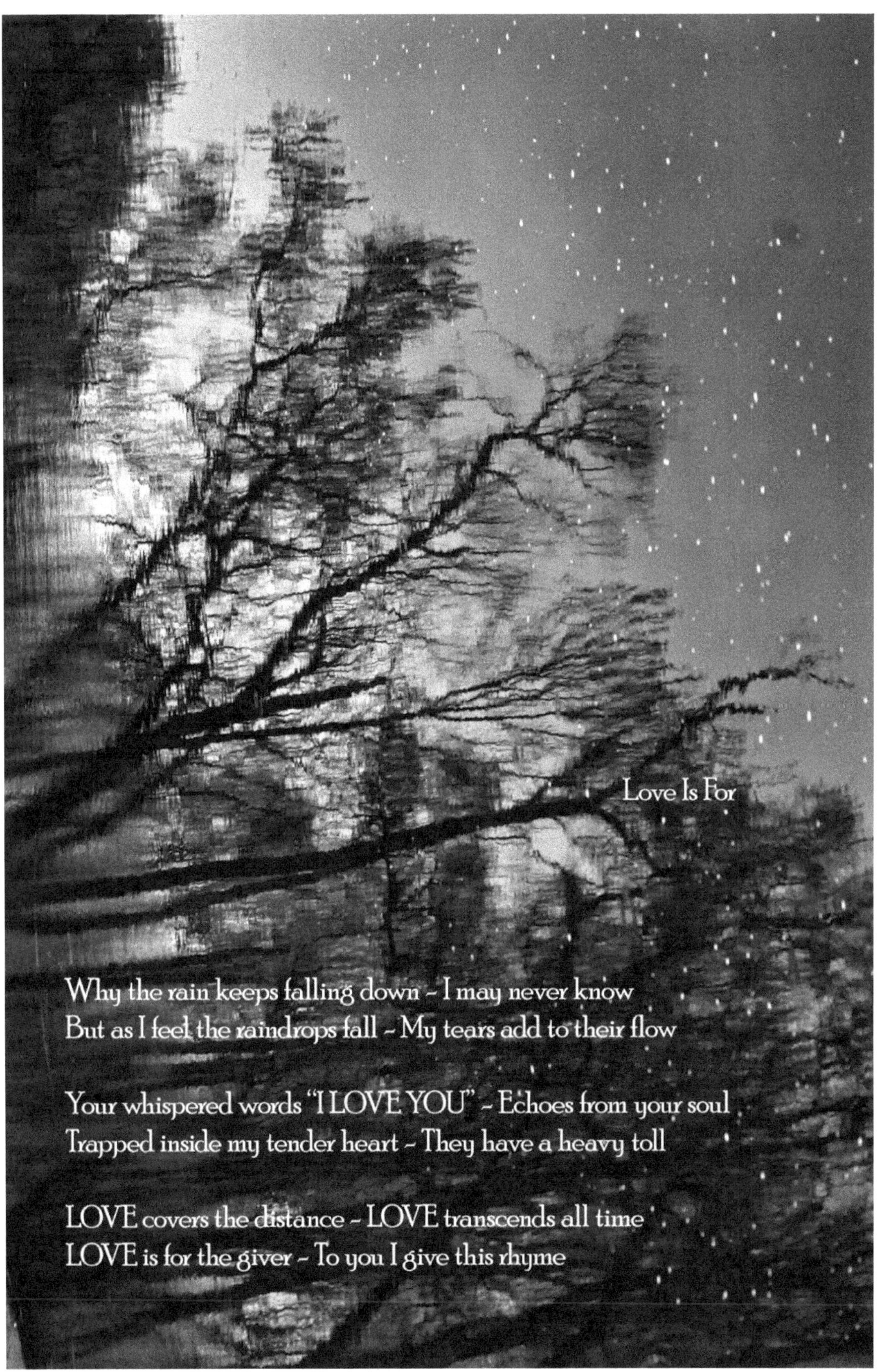

Love Is For

Why the rain keeps falling down ~ I may never know
But as I feel the raindrops fall ~ My tears add to their flow

Your whispered words "I LOVE YOU" ~ Echoes from your soul
Trapped inside my tender heart ~ They have a heavy toll

LOVE covers the distance ~ LOVE transcends all time
LOVE is for the giver ~ To you I give this rhyme

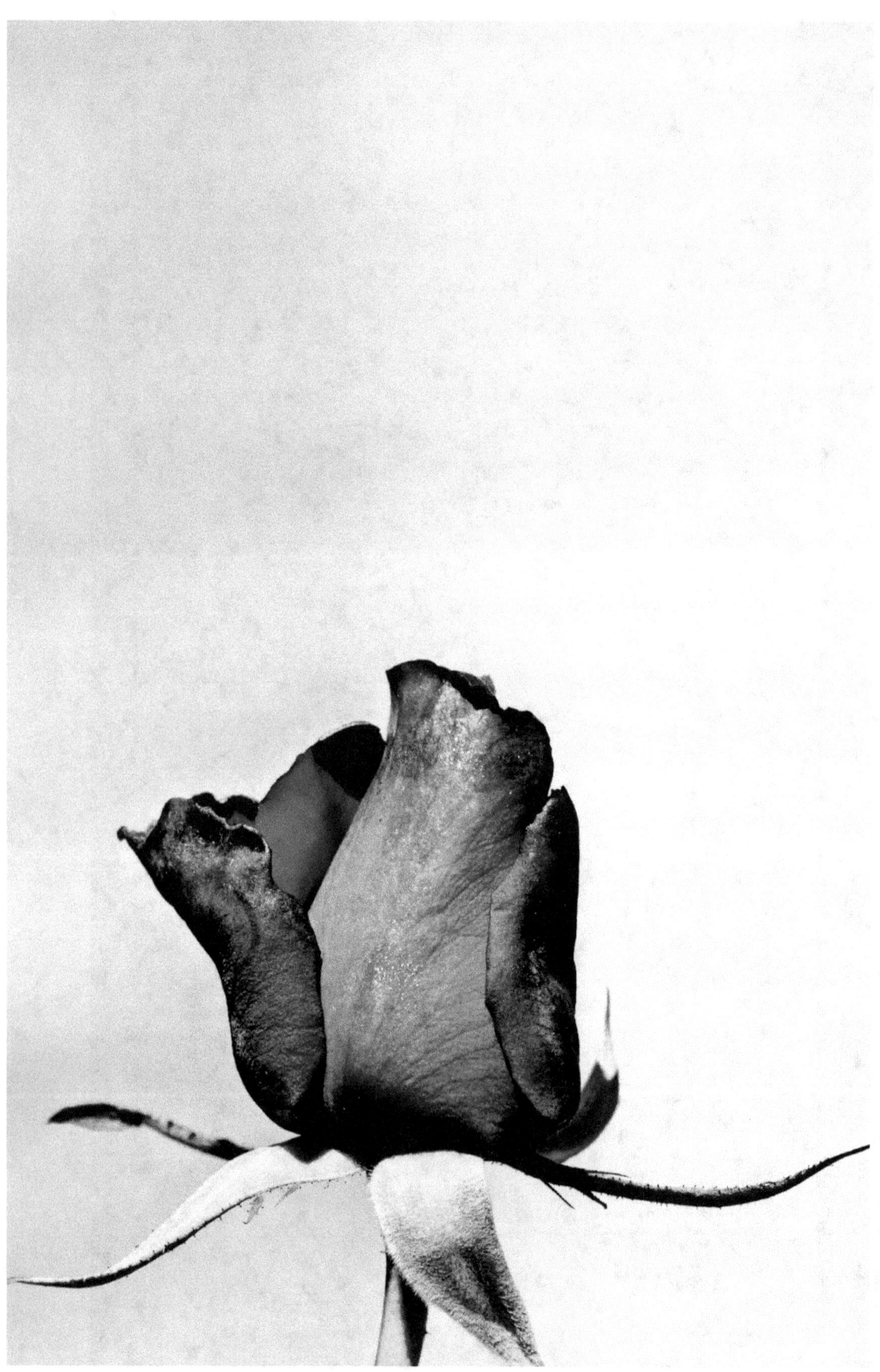

My Love Whispers

My Love you wear the rainbow
All colors touch your face
Even the gentle flowers say
From you they receive grace

My Love in all their glory
These flowers speak of you
Their beauty is your story
From your heart they all grew

They whisper Do I know you
I tell each flower this
My Love whispers I Love you
And seals it with a kiss

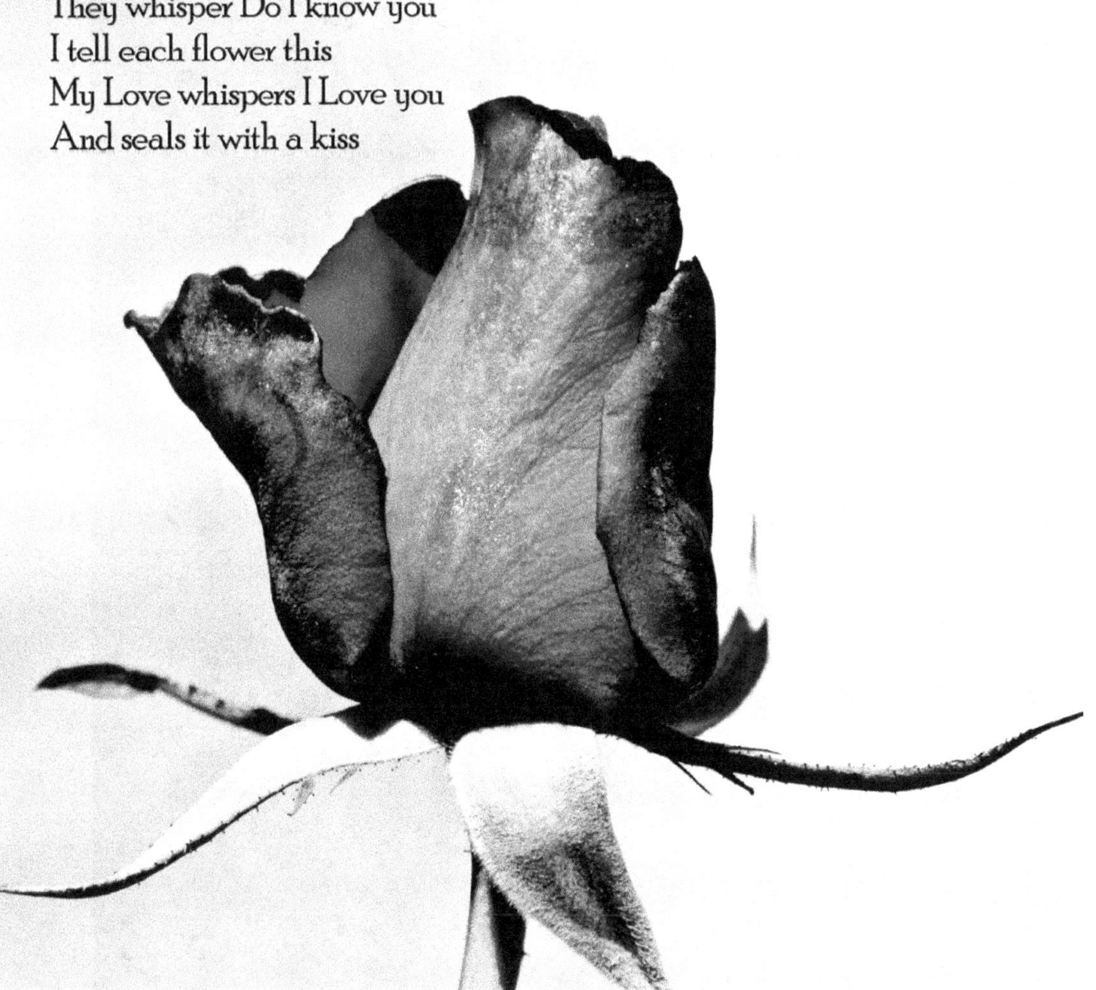

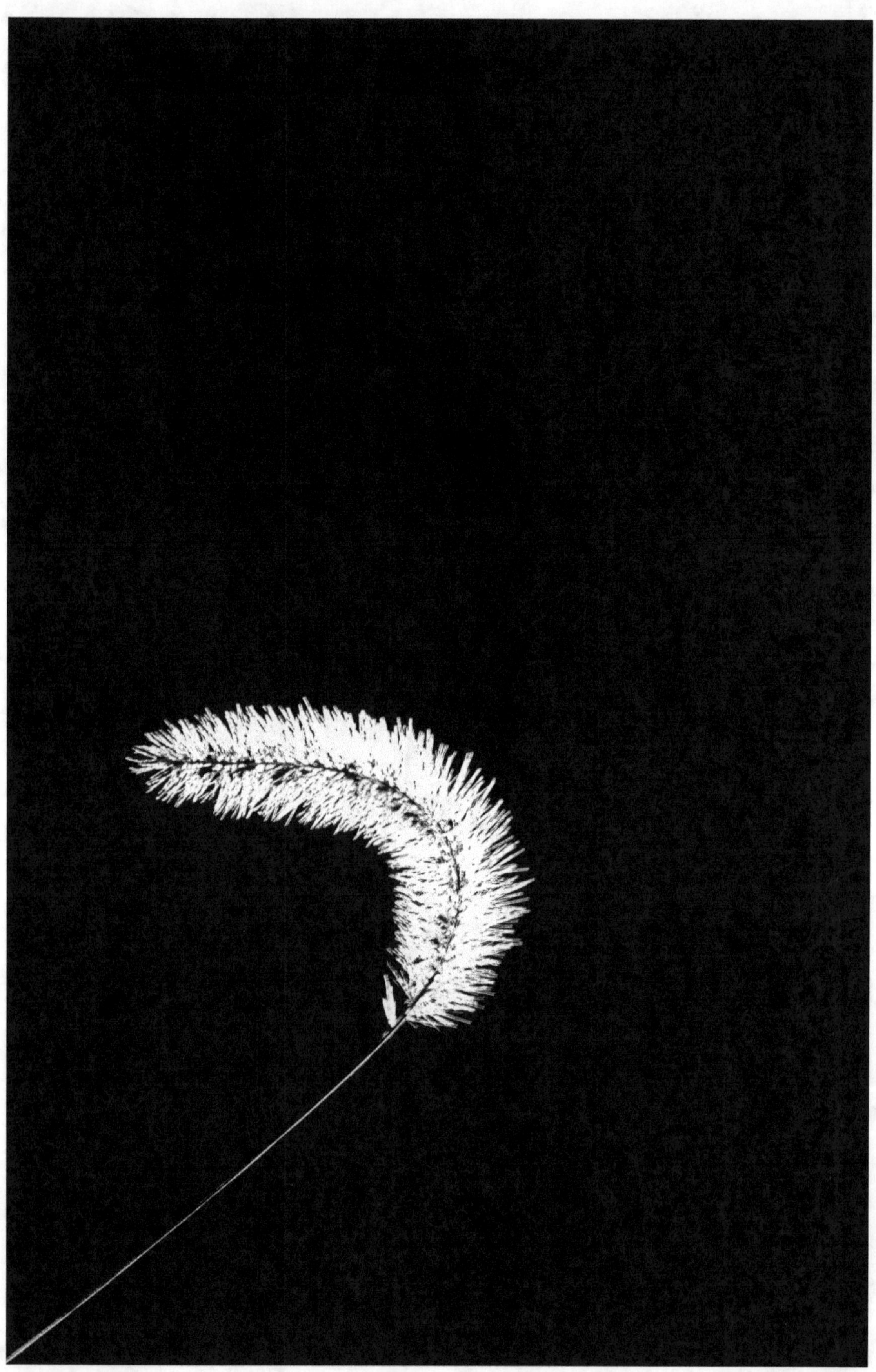

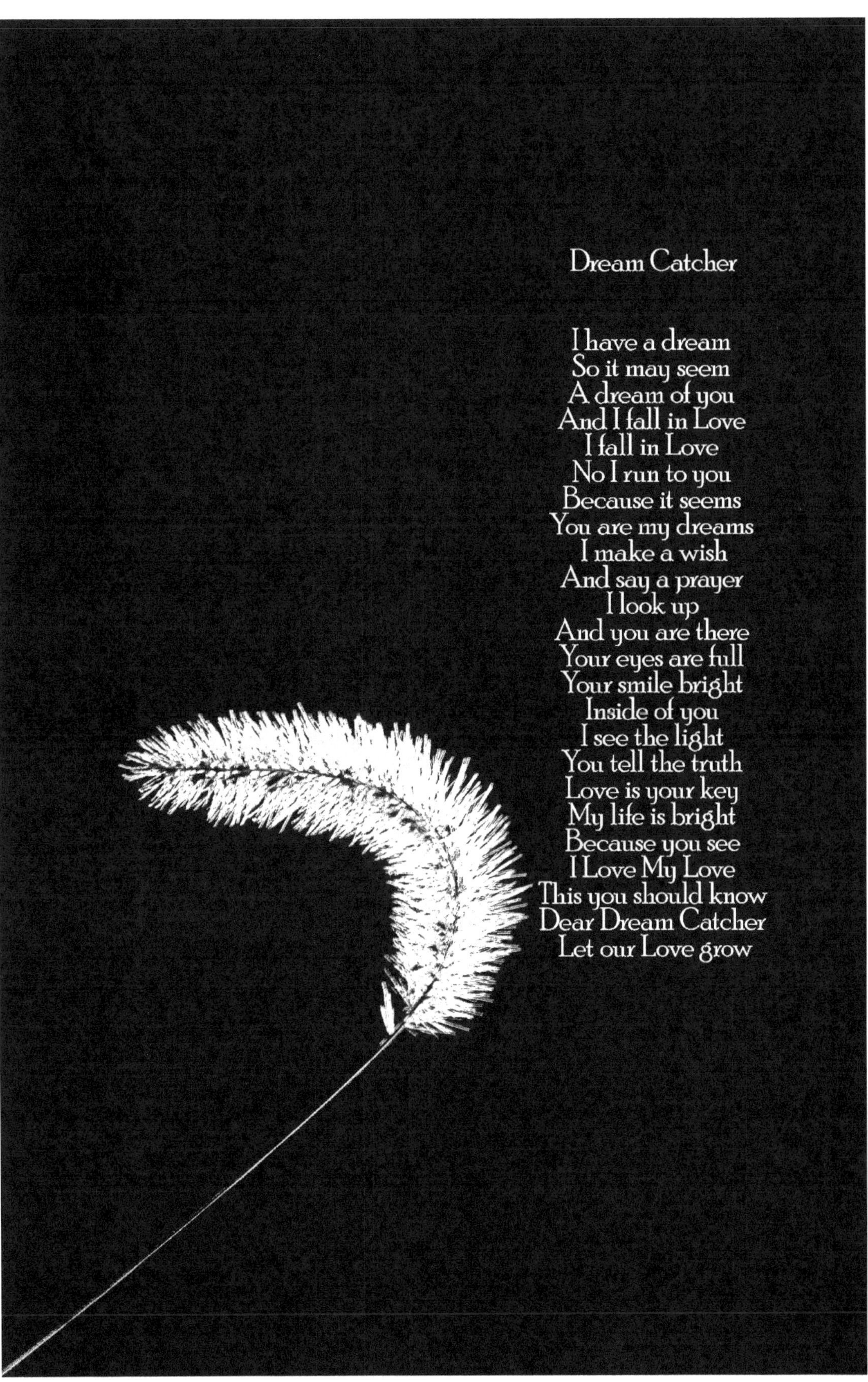

Dream Catcher

I have a dream
So it may seem
A dream of you
And I fall in Love
I fall in Love
No I run to you
Because it seems
You are my dreams
I make a wish
And say a prayer
I look up
And you are there
Your eyes are full
Your smile bright
Inside of you
I see the light
You tell the truth
Love is your key
My life is bright
Because you see
I Love My Love
This you should know
Dear Dream Catcher
Let our Love grow

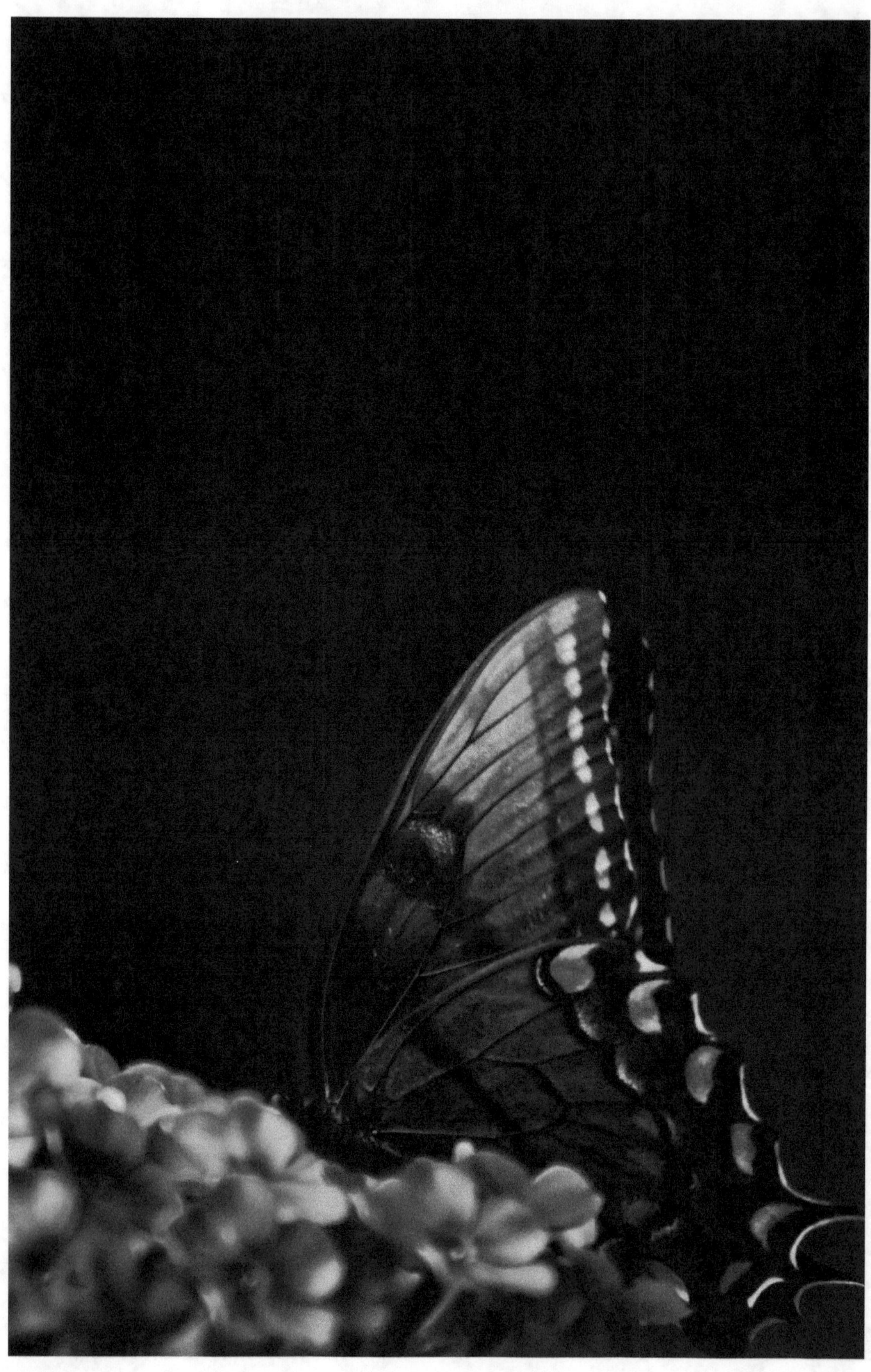

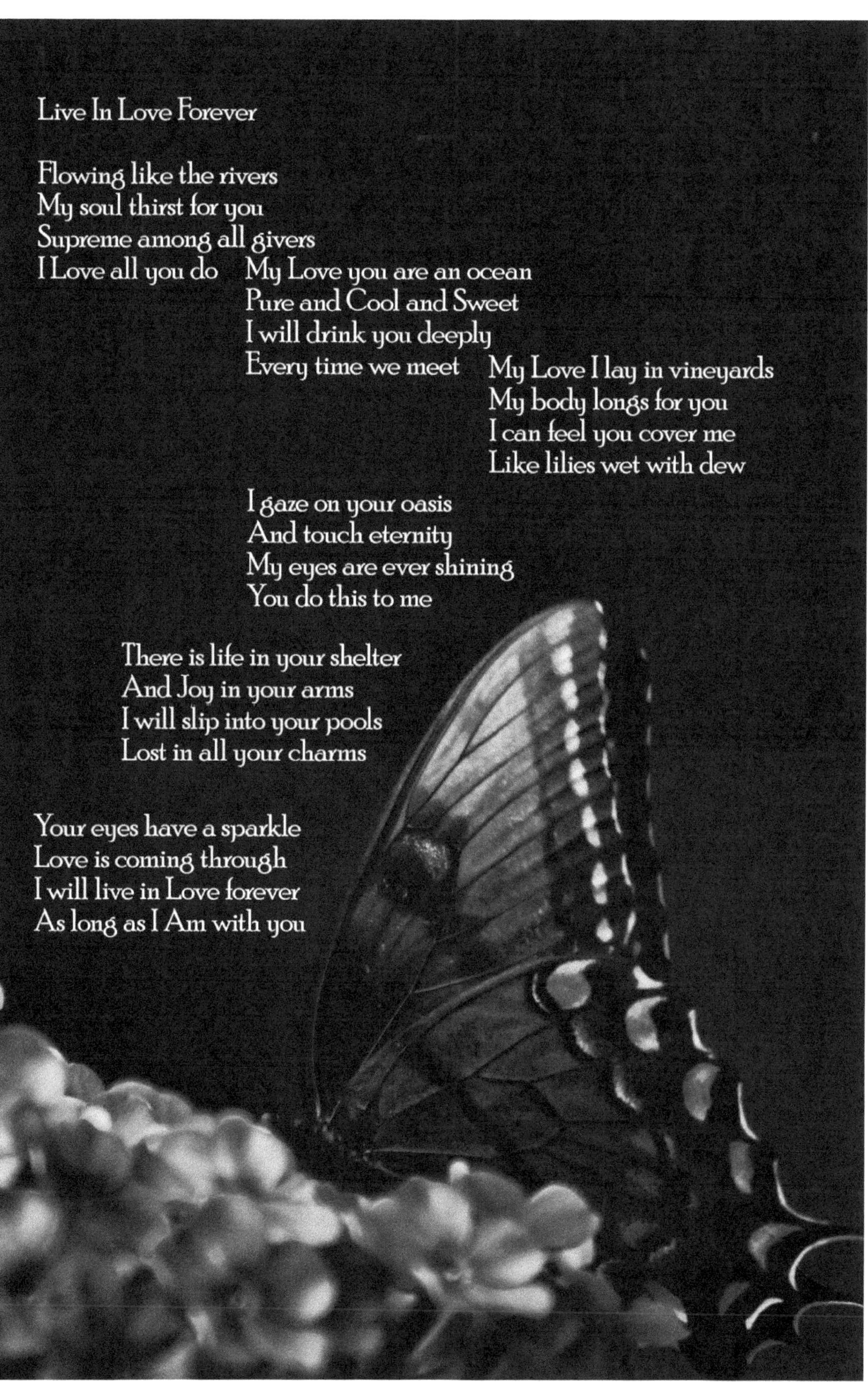

Live In Love Forever

Flowing like the rivers
My soul thirst for you
Supreme among all givers
I Love all you do

My Love you are an ocean
Pure and Cool and Sweet
I will drink you deeply
Every time we meet

My Love I lay in vineyards
My body longs for you
I can feel you cover me
Like lilies wet with dew

I gaze on your oasis
And touch eternity
My eyes are ever shining
You do this to me

There is life in your shelter
And Joy in your arms
I will slip into your pools
Lost in all your charms

Your eyes have a sparkle
Love is coming through
I will live in Love forever
As long as I Am with you

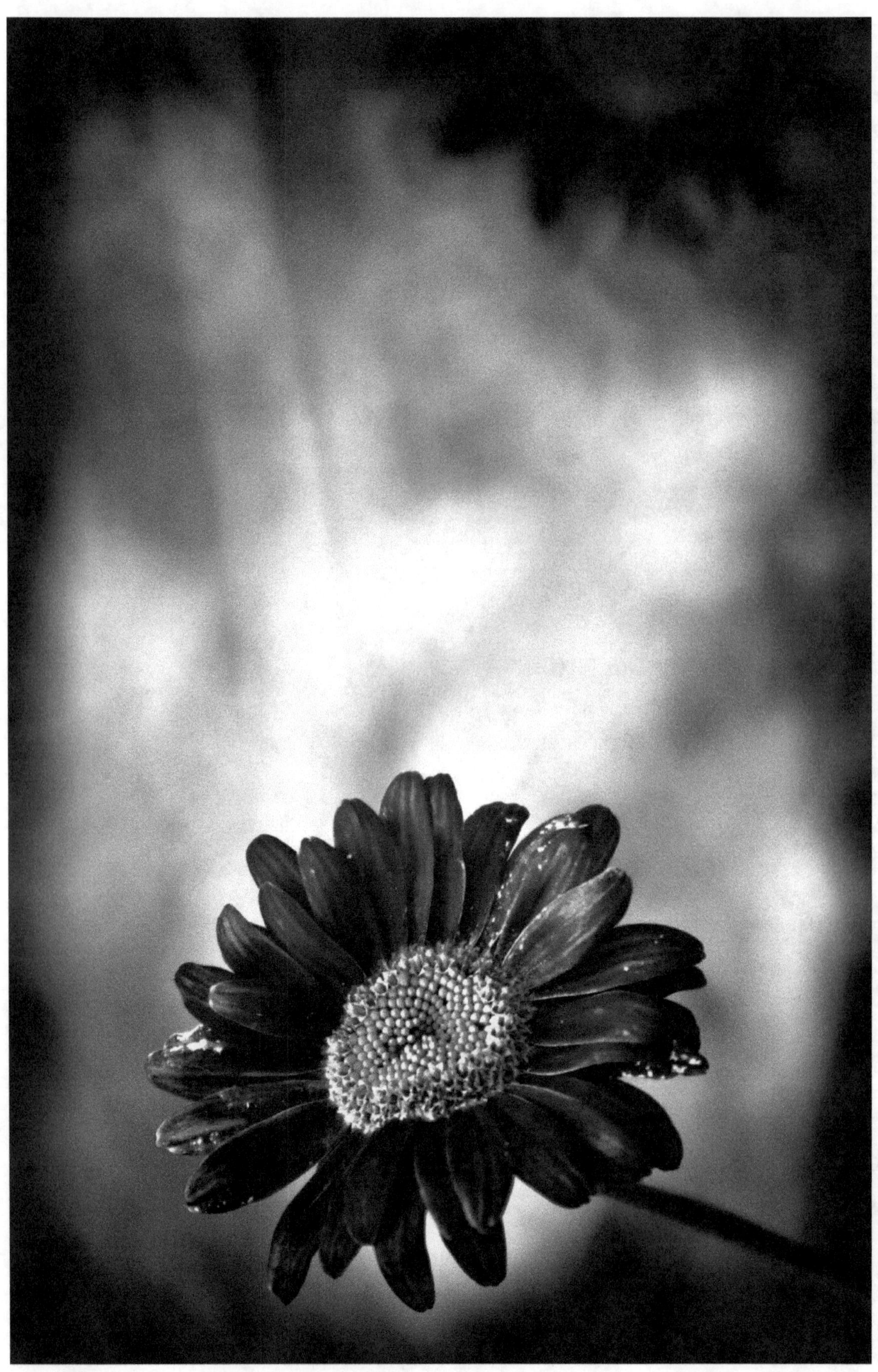

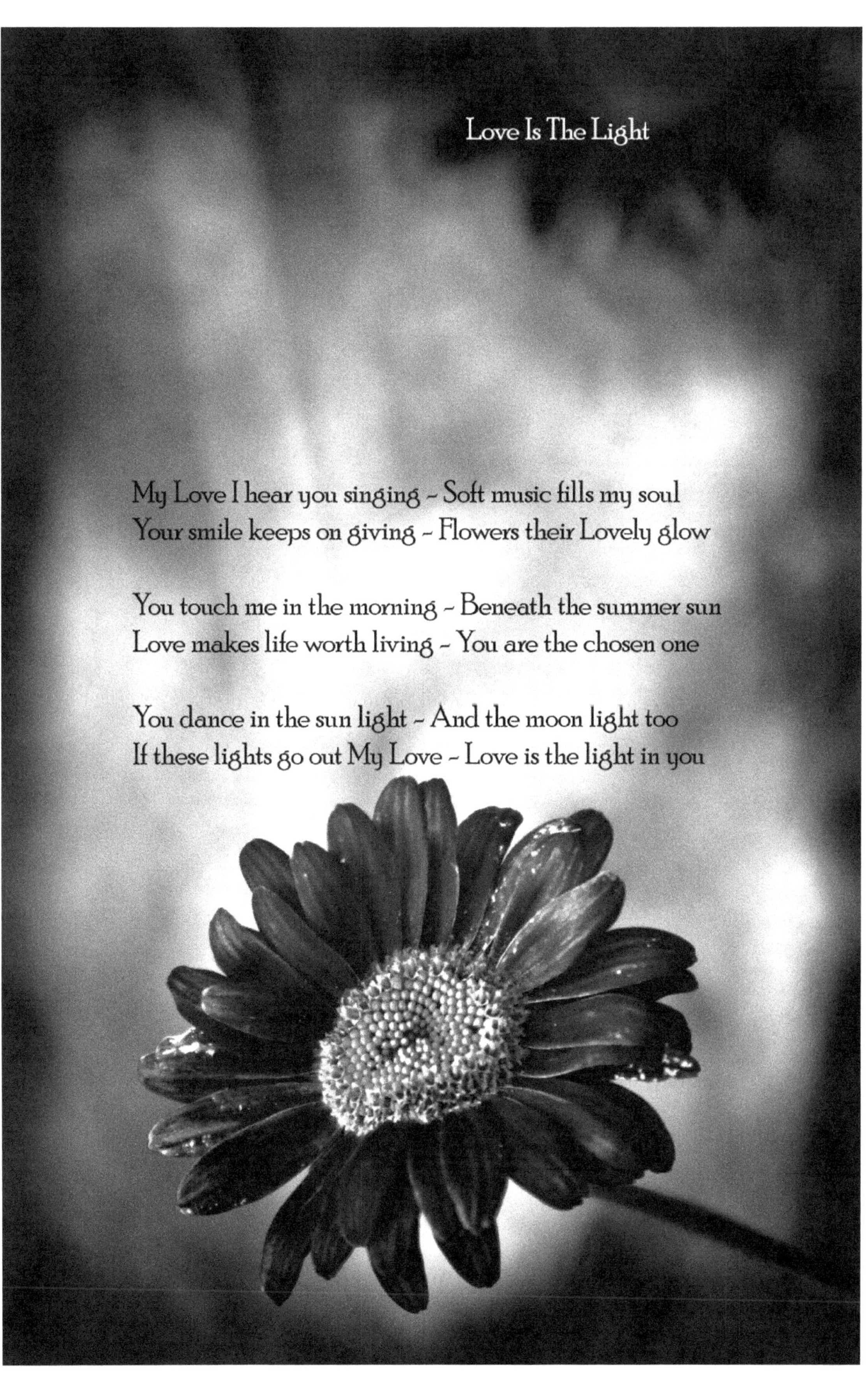

Love Is The Light

My Love I hear you singing ~ Soft music fills my soul
Your smile keeps on giving ~ Flowers their Lovely glow

You touch me in the morning ~ Beneath the summer sun
Love makes life worth living ~ You are the chosen one

You dance in the sun light ~ And the moon light too
If these lights go out My Love ~ Love is the light in you

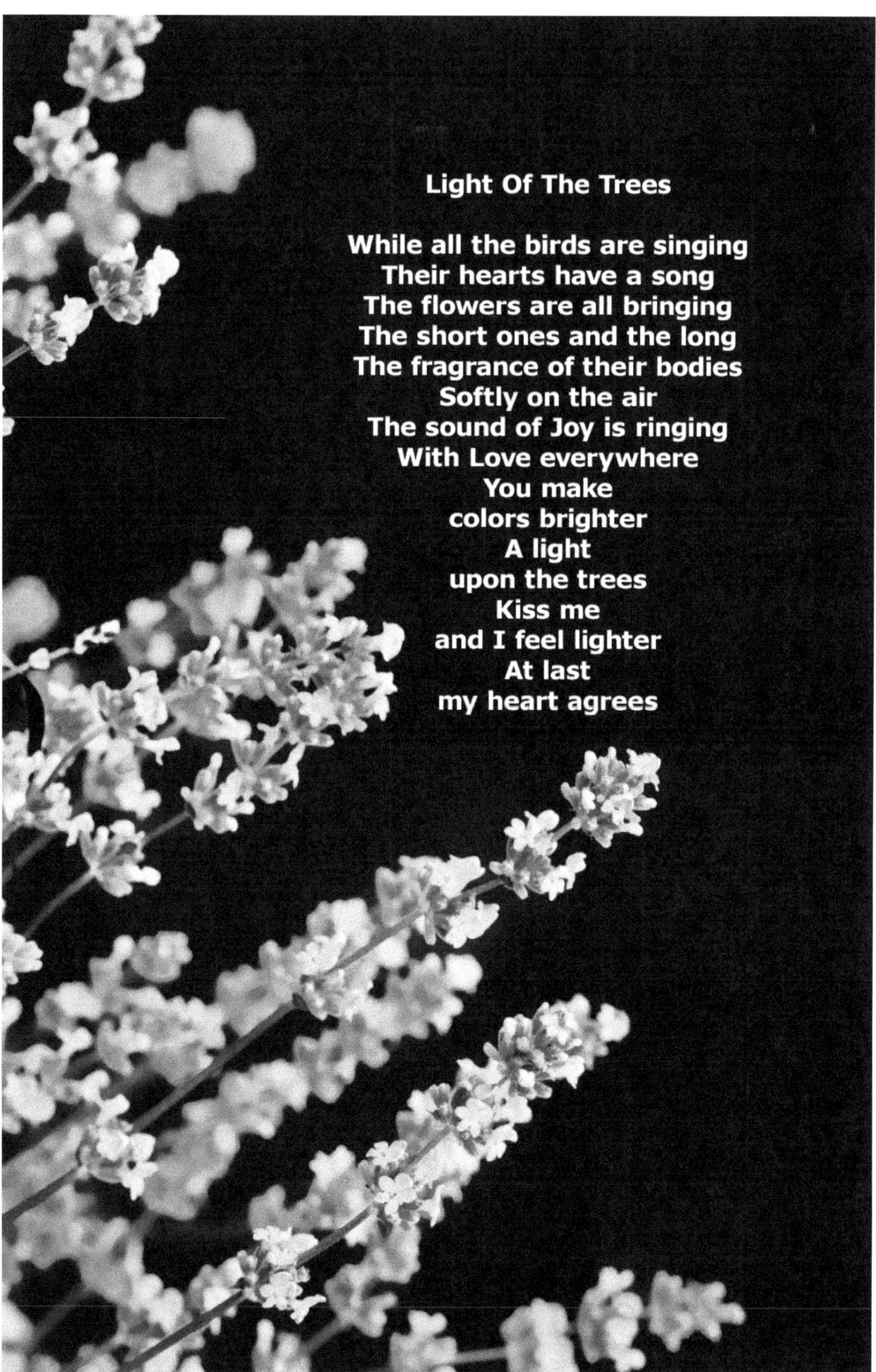

Light Of The Trees

While all the birds are singing
Their hearts have a song
The flowers are all bringing
The short ones and the long
The fragrance of their bodies
Softly on the air
The sound of Joy is ringing
With Love everywhere
You make
colors brighter
A light
upon the trees
Kiss me
and I feel lighter
At last
my heart agrees

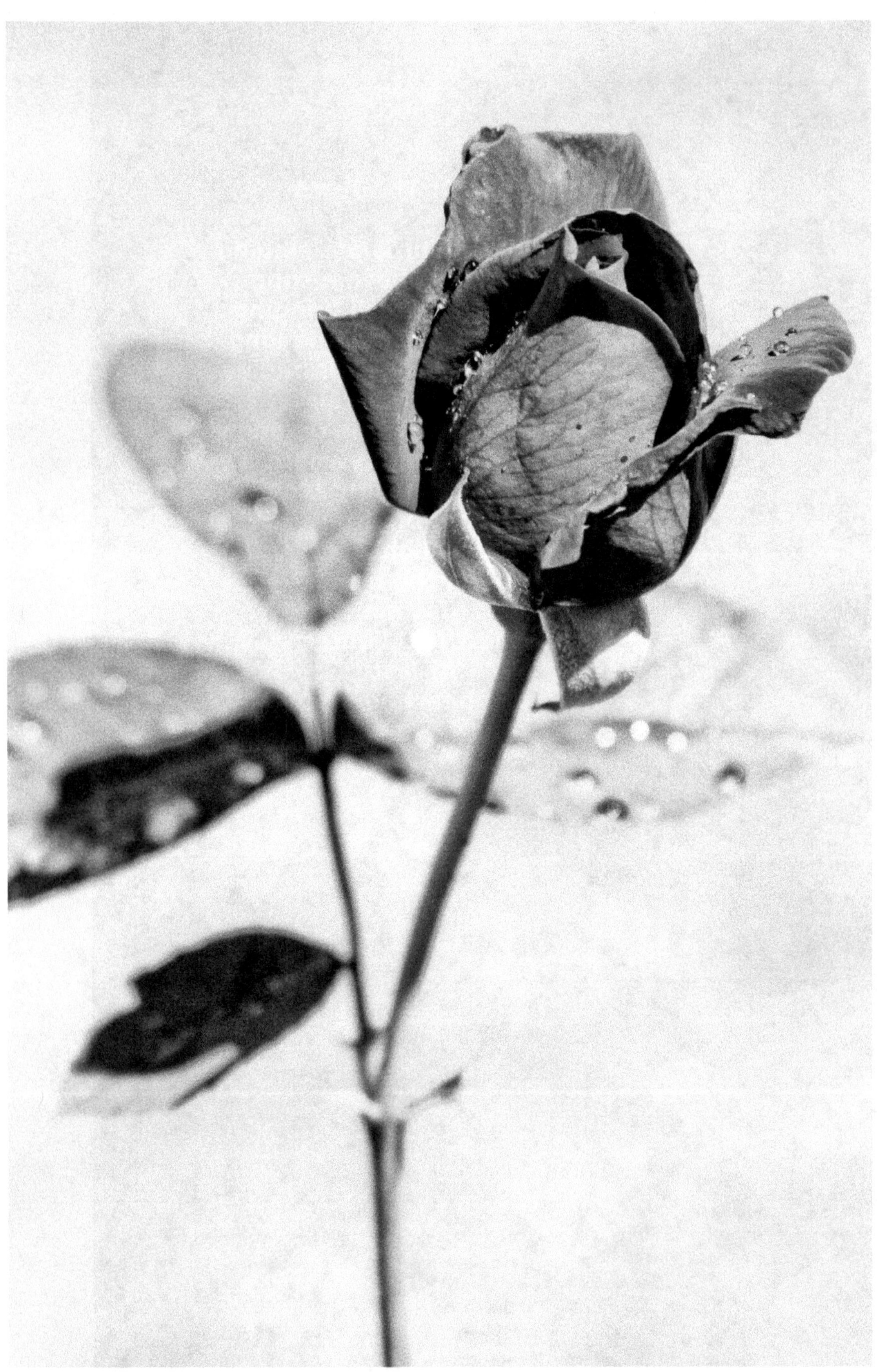

The Promise

I feel your tears
Inside my heart
Like a river Overflowing

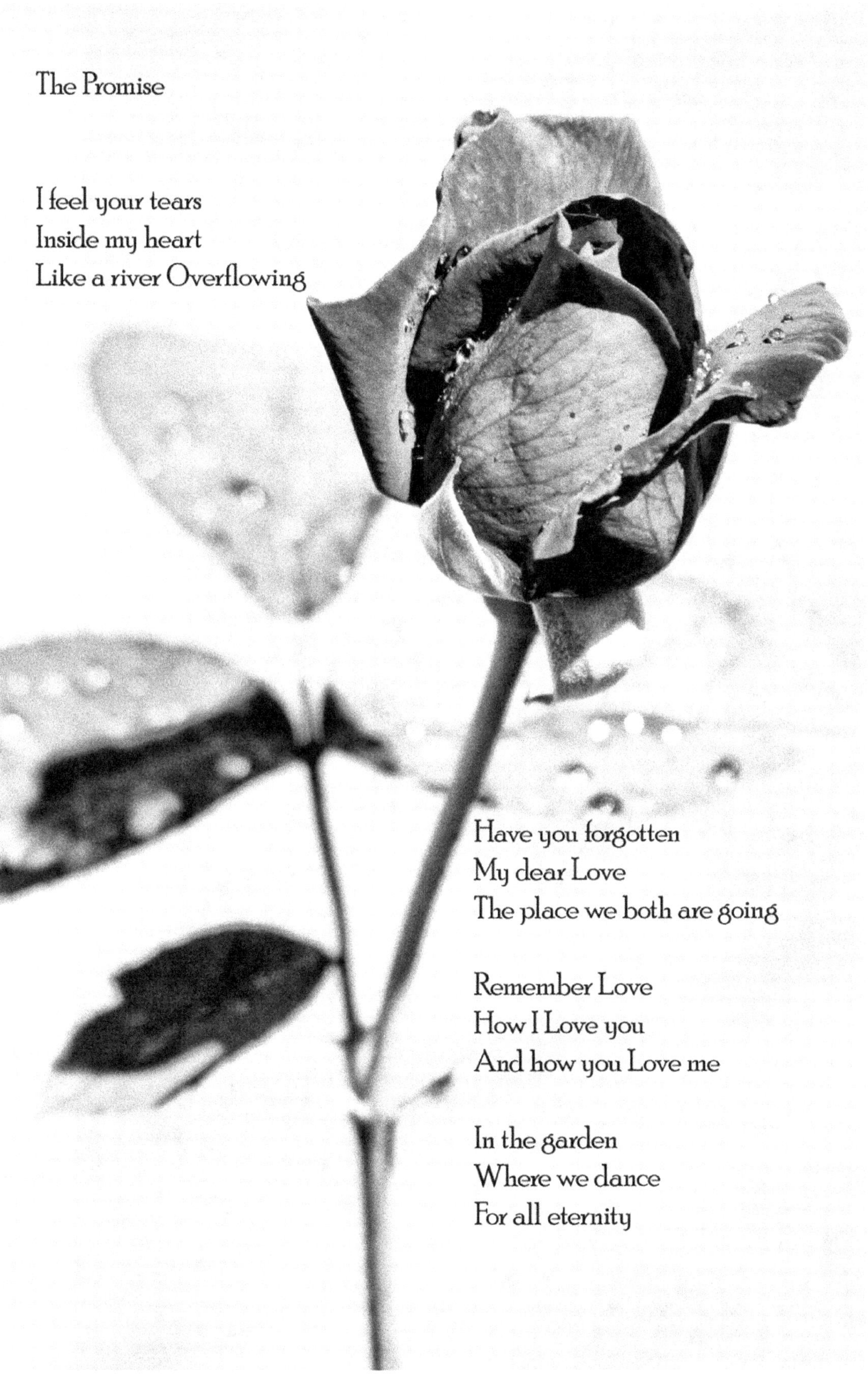

Have you forgotten
My dear Love
The place we both are going

Remember Love
How I Love you
And how you Love me

In the garden
Where we dance
For all eternity

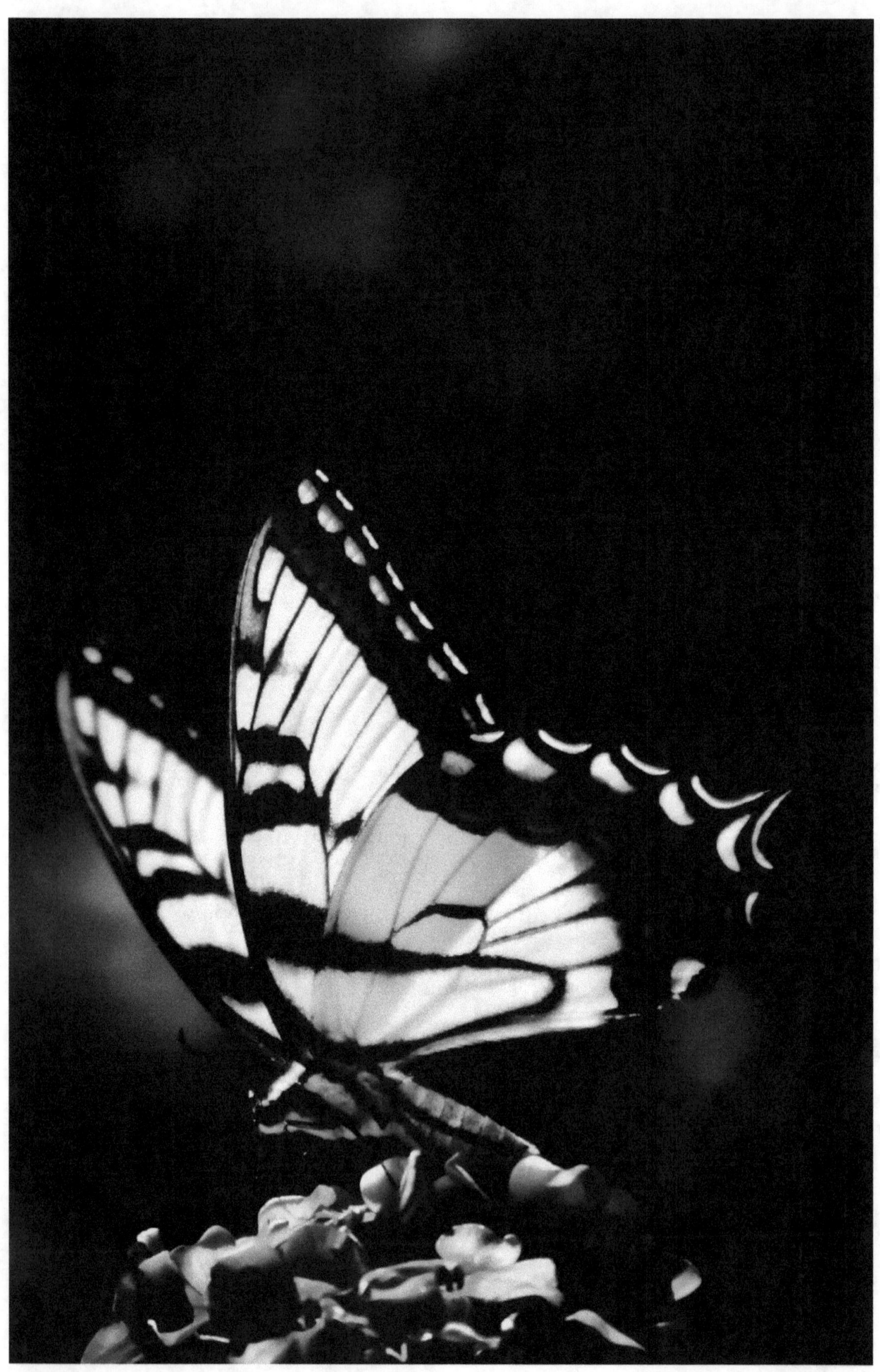

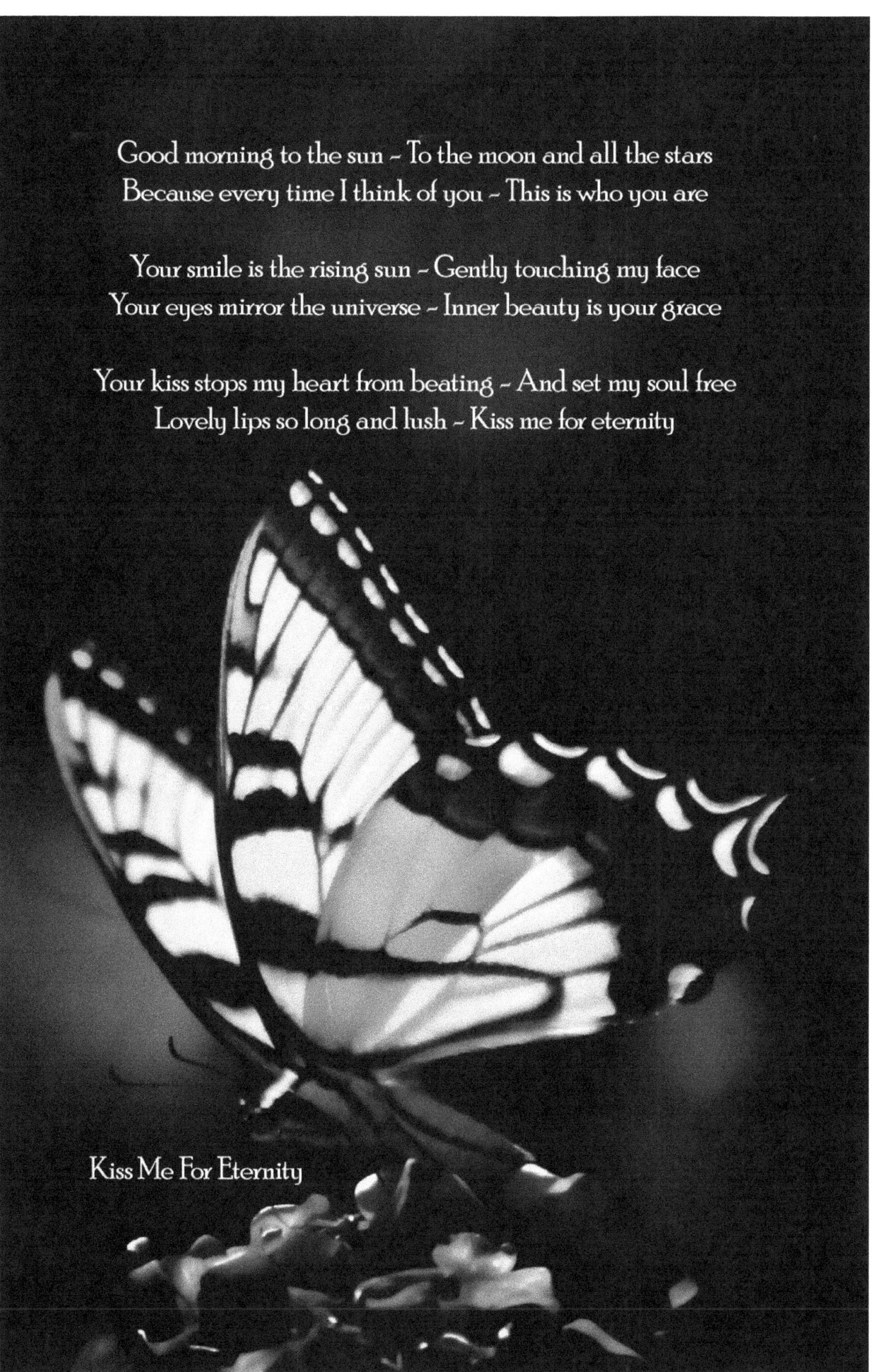
Good morning to the sun ~ To the moon and all the stars
Because every time I think of you ~ This is who you are

Your smile is the rising sun ~ Gently touching my face
Your eyes mirror the universe ~ Inner beauty is your grace

Your kiss stops my heart from beating ~ And set my soul free
Lovely lips so long and lush ~ Kiss me for eternity

Kiss Me For Eternity

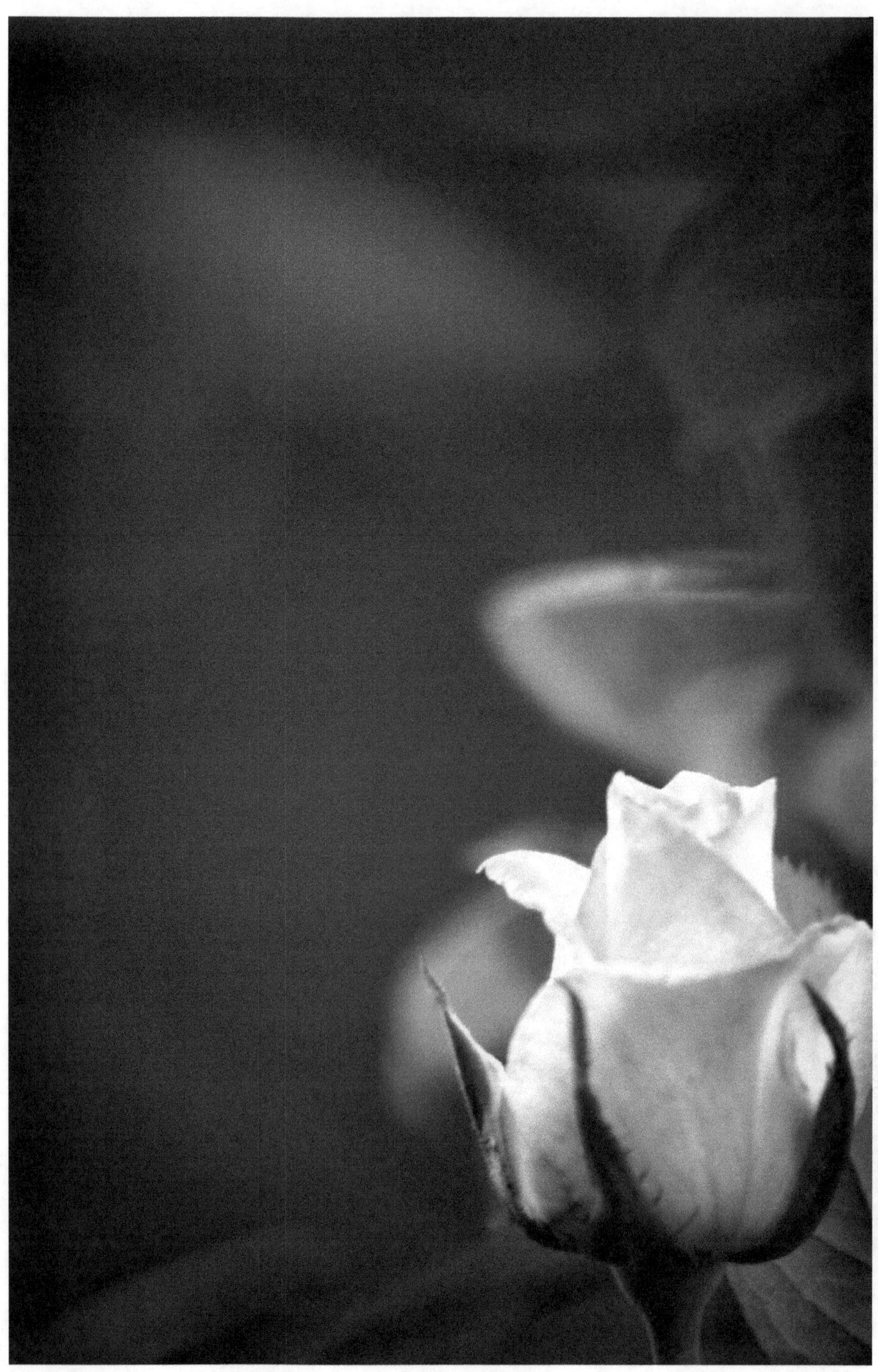

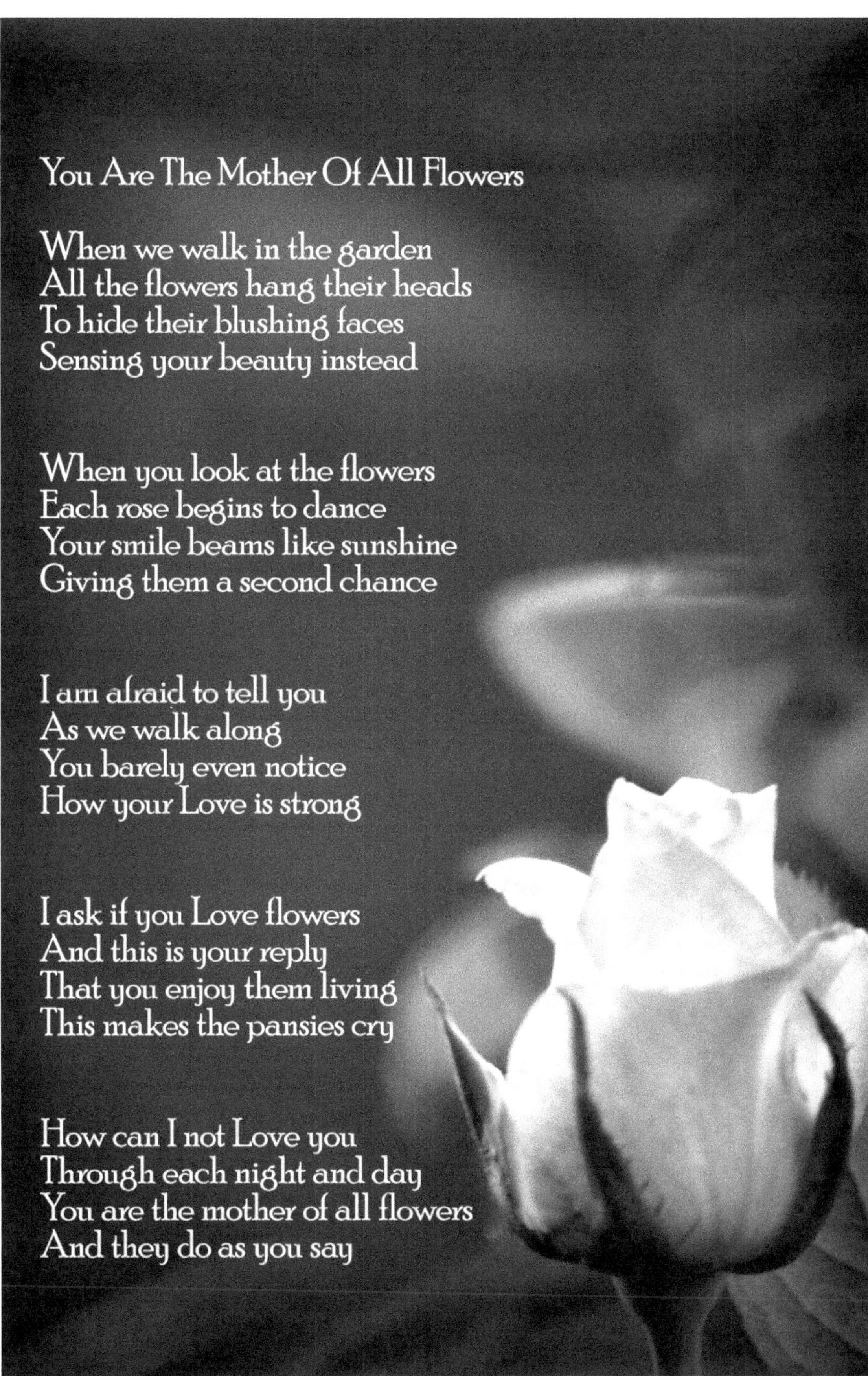

You Are The Mother Of All Flowers

When we walk in the garden
All the flowers hang their heads
To hide their blushing faces
Sensing your beauty instead

When you look at the flowers
Each rose begins to dance
Your smile beams like sunshine
Giving them a second chance

I am afraid to tell you
As we walk along
You barely even notice
How your Love is strong

I ask if you Love flowers
And this is your reply
That you enjoy them living
This makes the pansies cry

How can I not Love you
Through each night and day
You are the mother of all flowers
And they do as you say

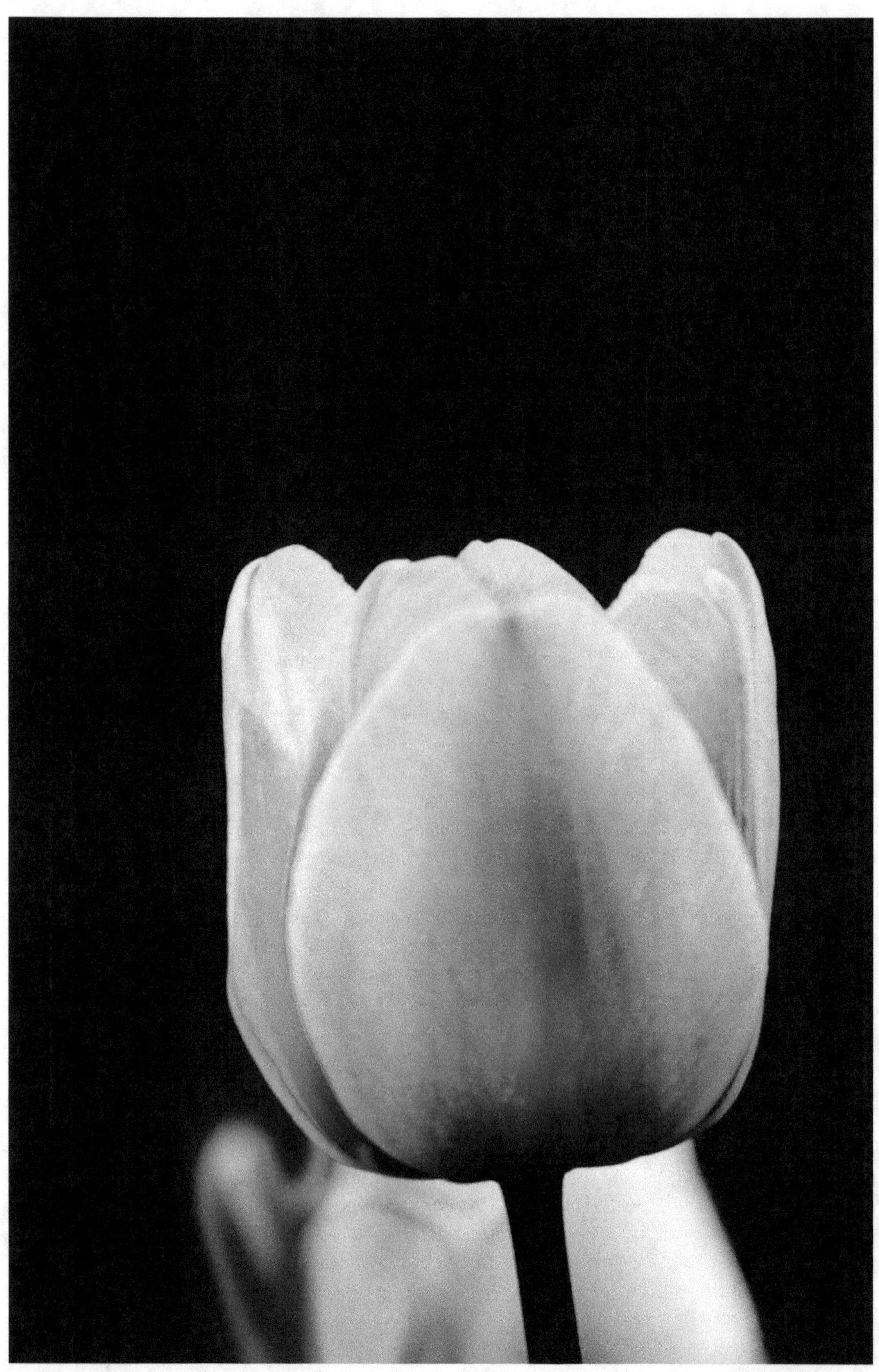

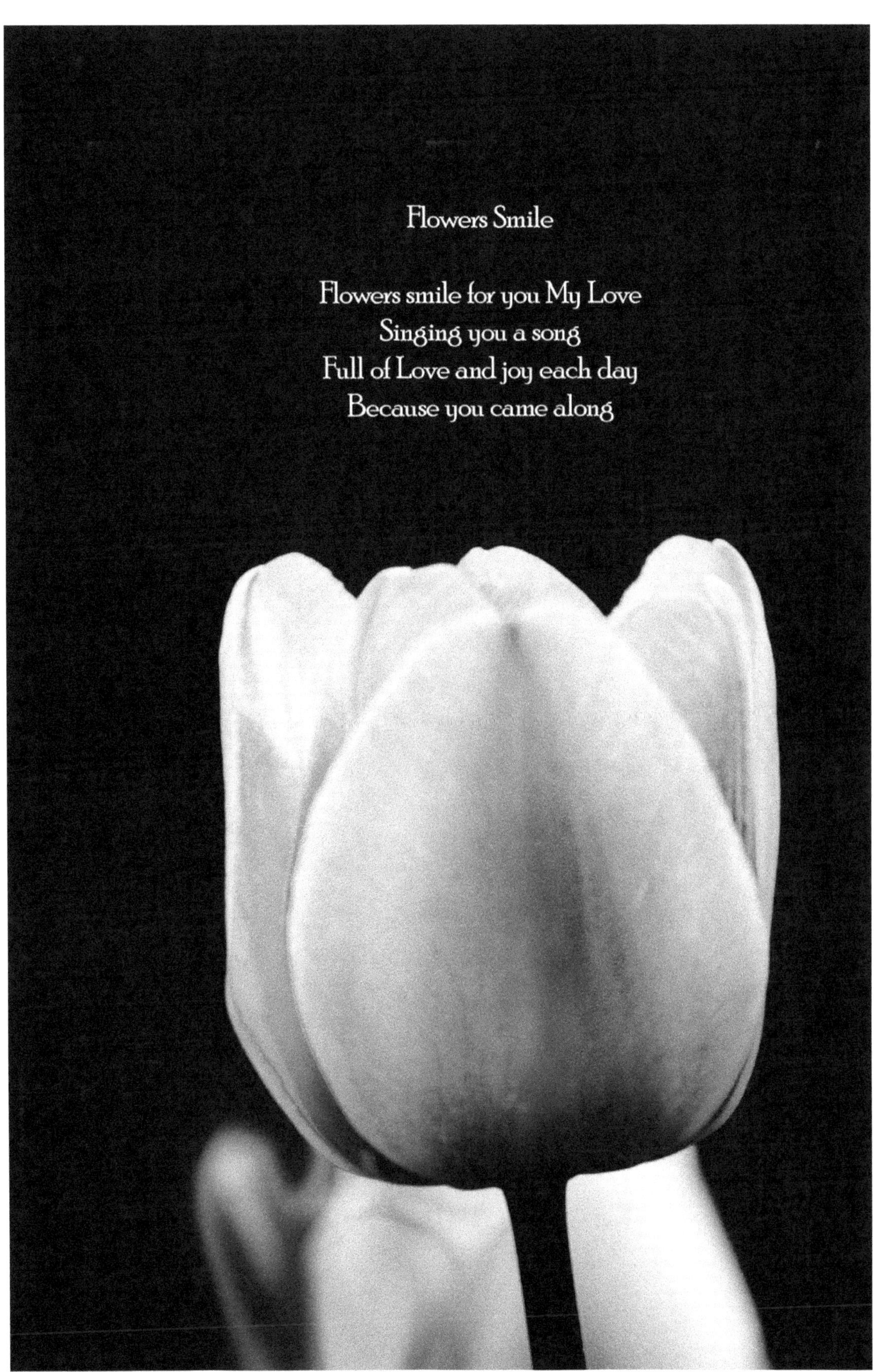

Flowers Smile

Flowers smile for you My Love
Singing you a song
Full of Love and joy each day
Because you came along

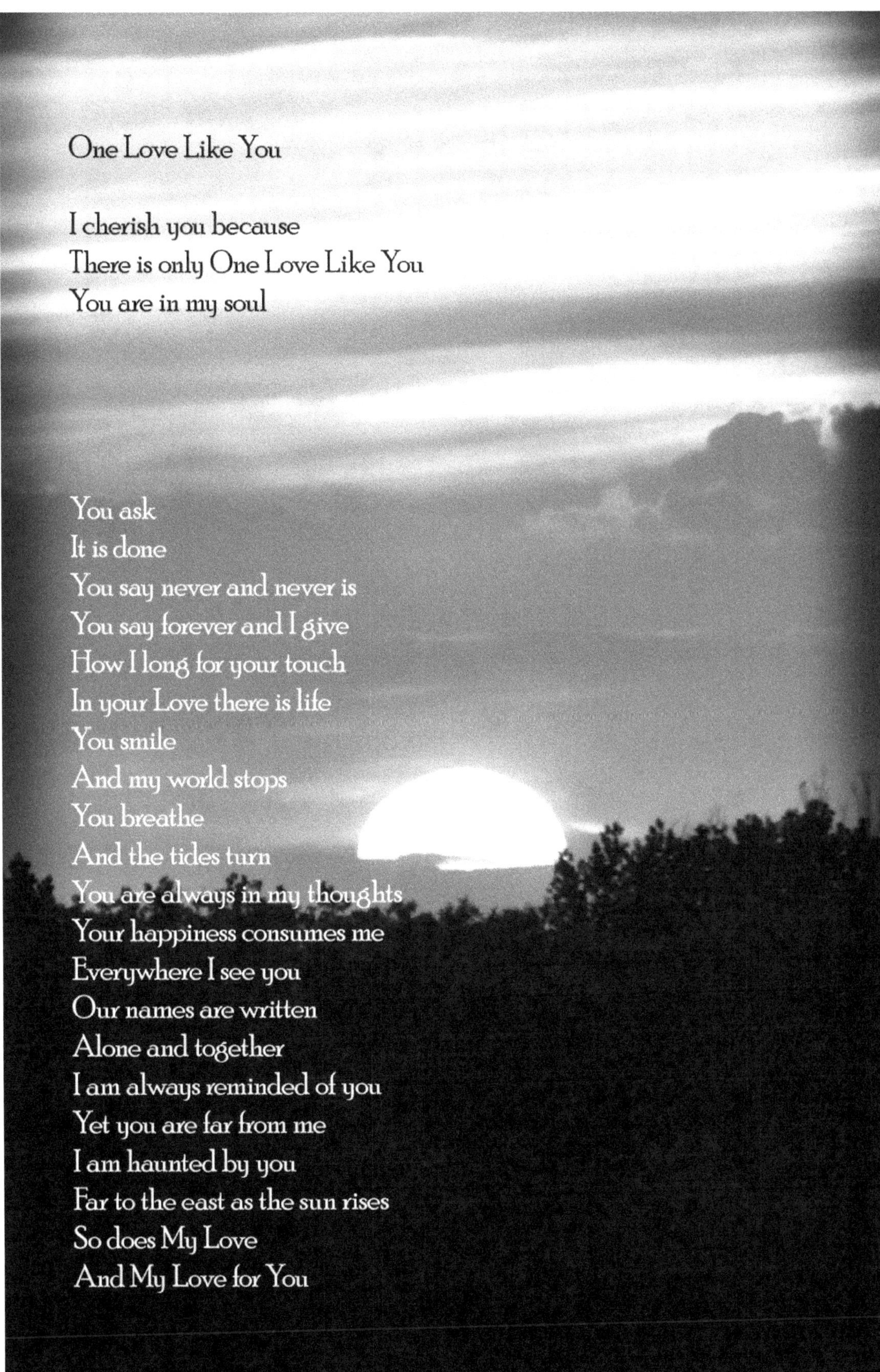

One Love Like You

I cherish you because
There is only One Love Like You
You are in my soul

You ask
It is done
You say never and never is
You say forever and I give
How I long for your touch
In your Love there is life
You smile
And my world stops
You breathe
And the tides turn
You are always in my thoughts
Your happiness consumes me
Everywhere I see you
Our names are written
Alone and together
I am always reminded of you
Yet you are far from me
I am haunted by you
Far to the east as the sun rises
So does My Love
And My Love for You

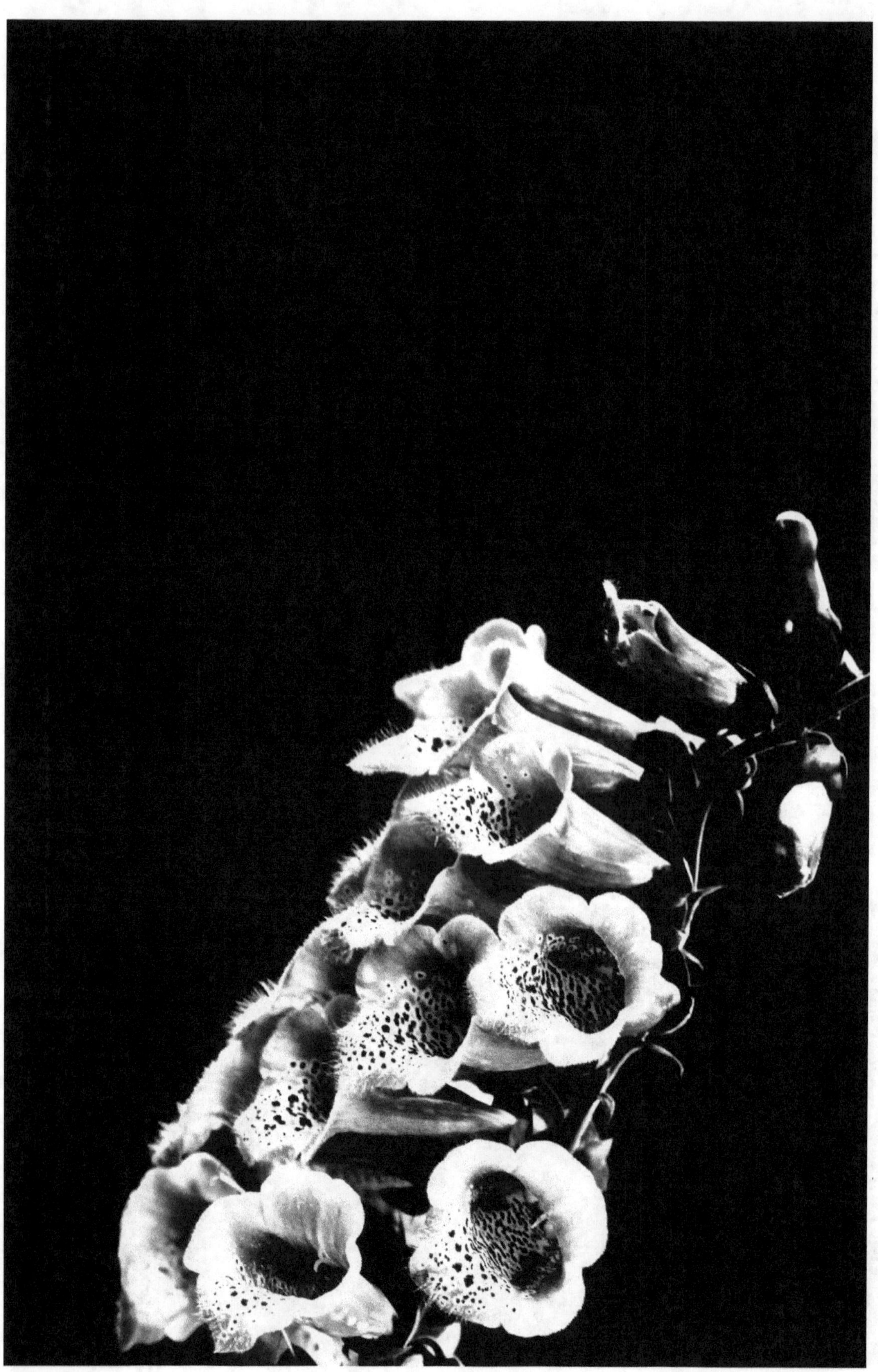

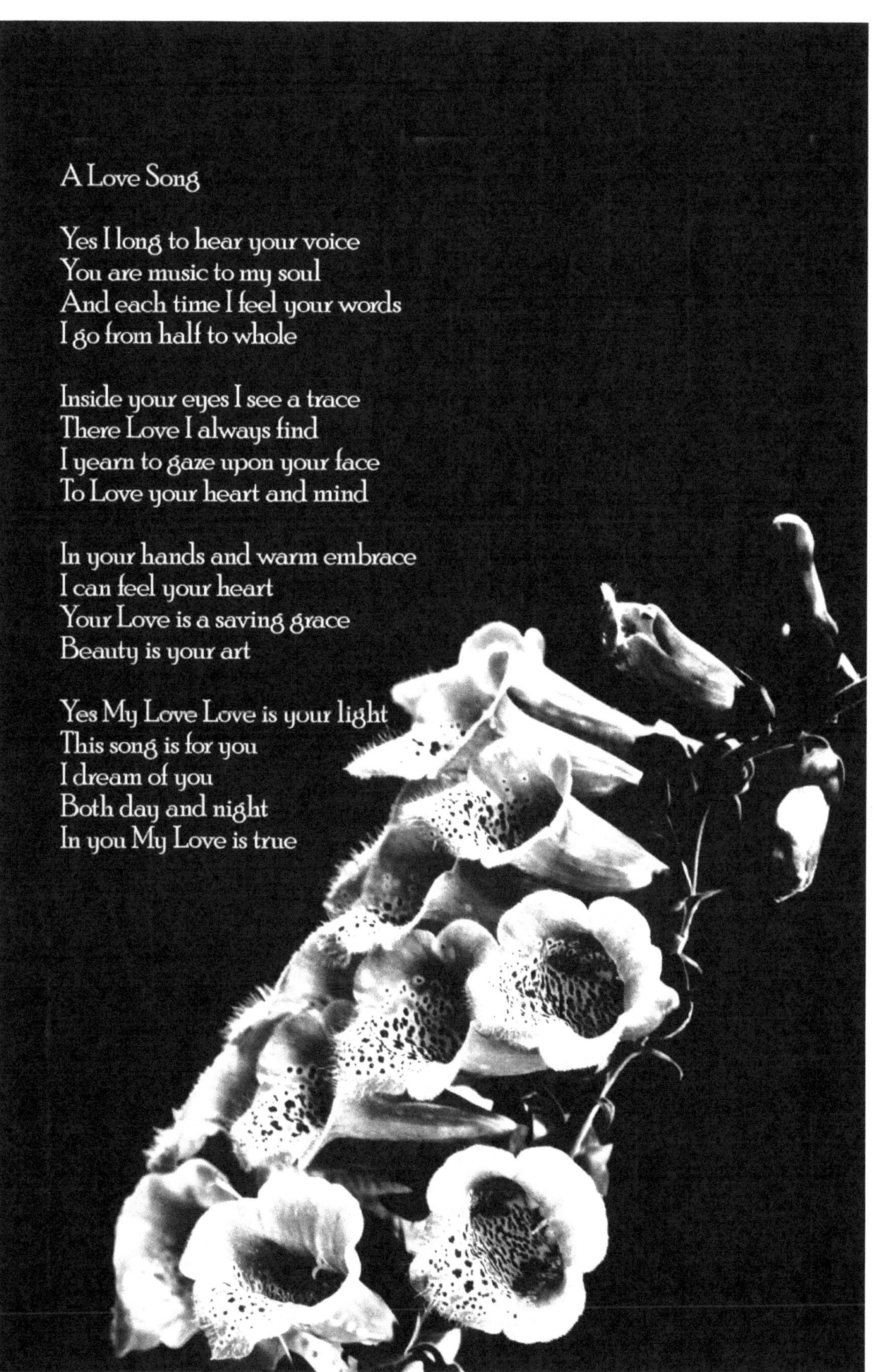

A Love Song

Yes I long to hear your voice
You are music to my soul
And each time I feel your words
I go from half to whole

Inside your eyes I see a trace
There Love I always find
I yearn to gaze upon your face
To Love your heart and mind

In your hands and warm embrace
I can feel your heart
Your Love is a saving grace
Beauty is your art

Yes My Love Love is your light
This song is for you
I dream of you
Both day and night
In you My Love is true

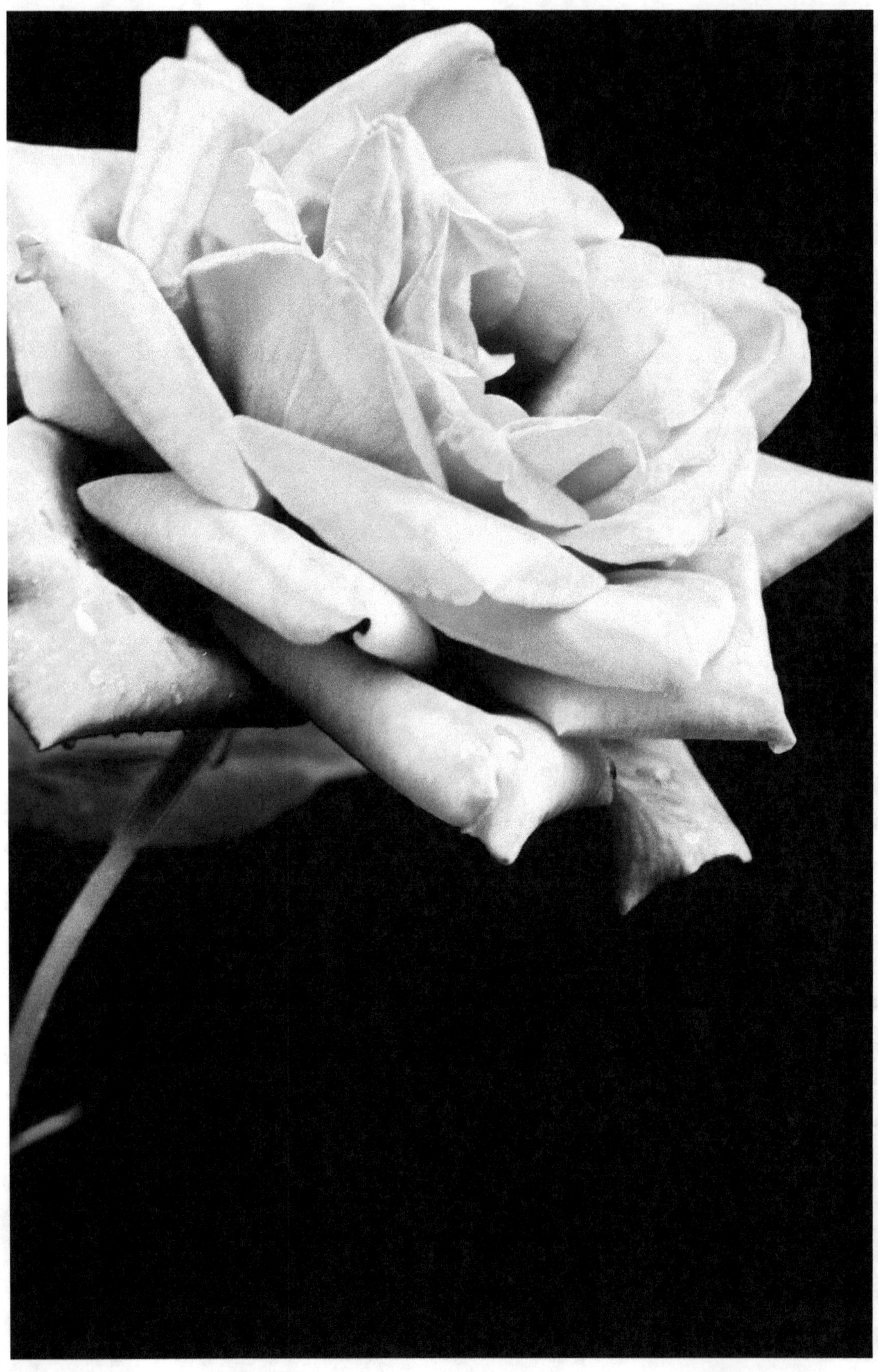

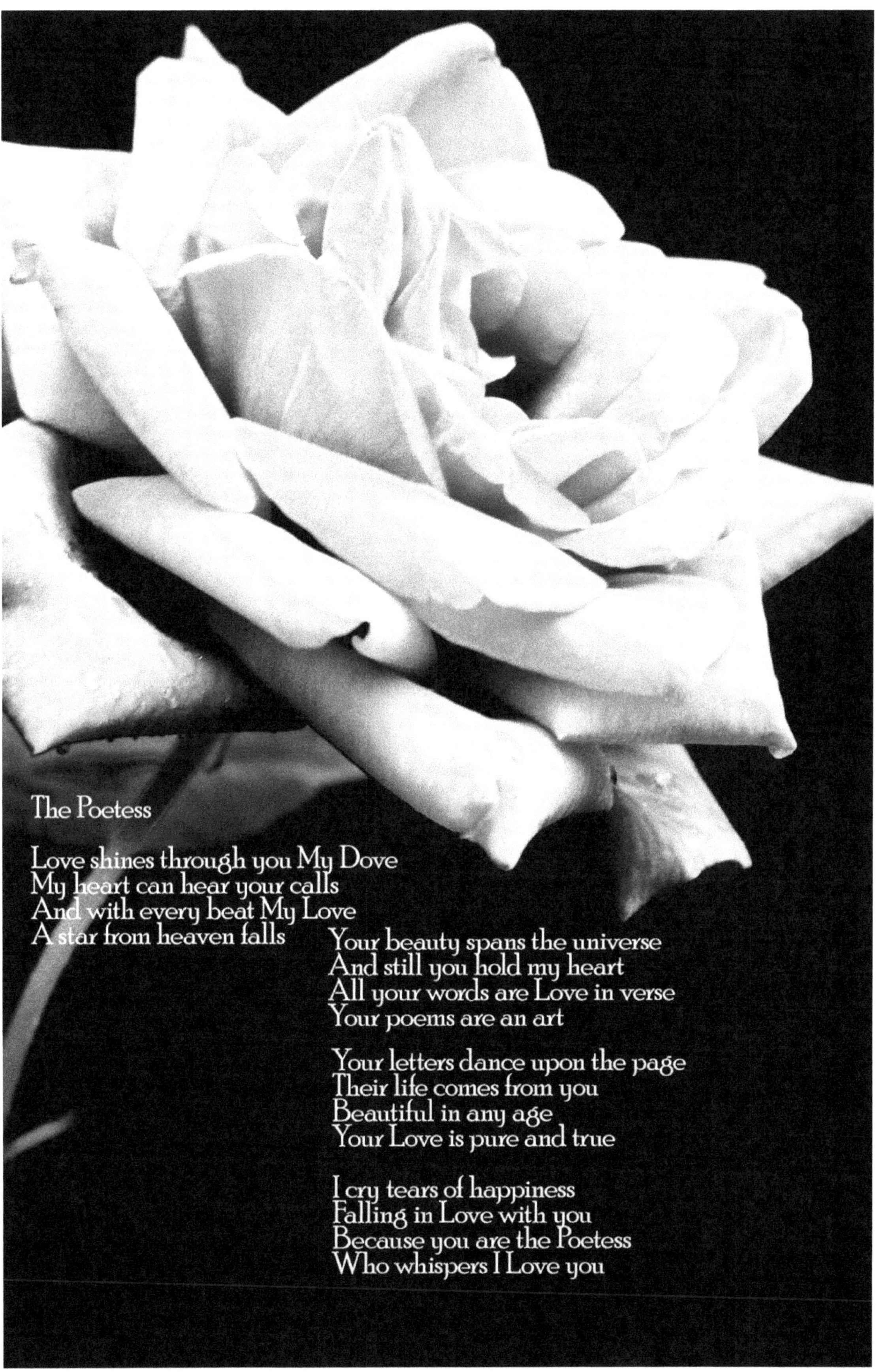

The Poetess

Love shines through you My Dove
My heart can hear your calls
And with every beat My Love
A star from heaven falls

Your beauty spans the universe
And still you hold my heart
All your words are Love in verse
Your poems are an art

Your letters dance upon the page
Their life comes from you
Beautiful in any age
Your Love is pure and true

I cry tears of happiness
Falling in Love with you
Because you are the Poetess
Who whispers I Love you

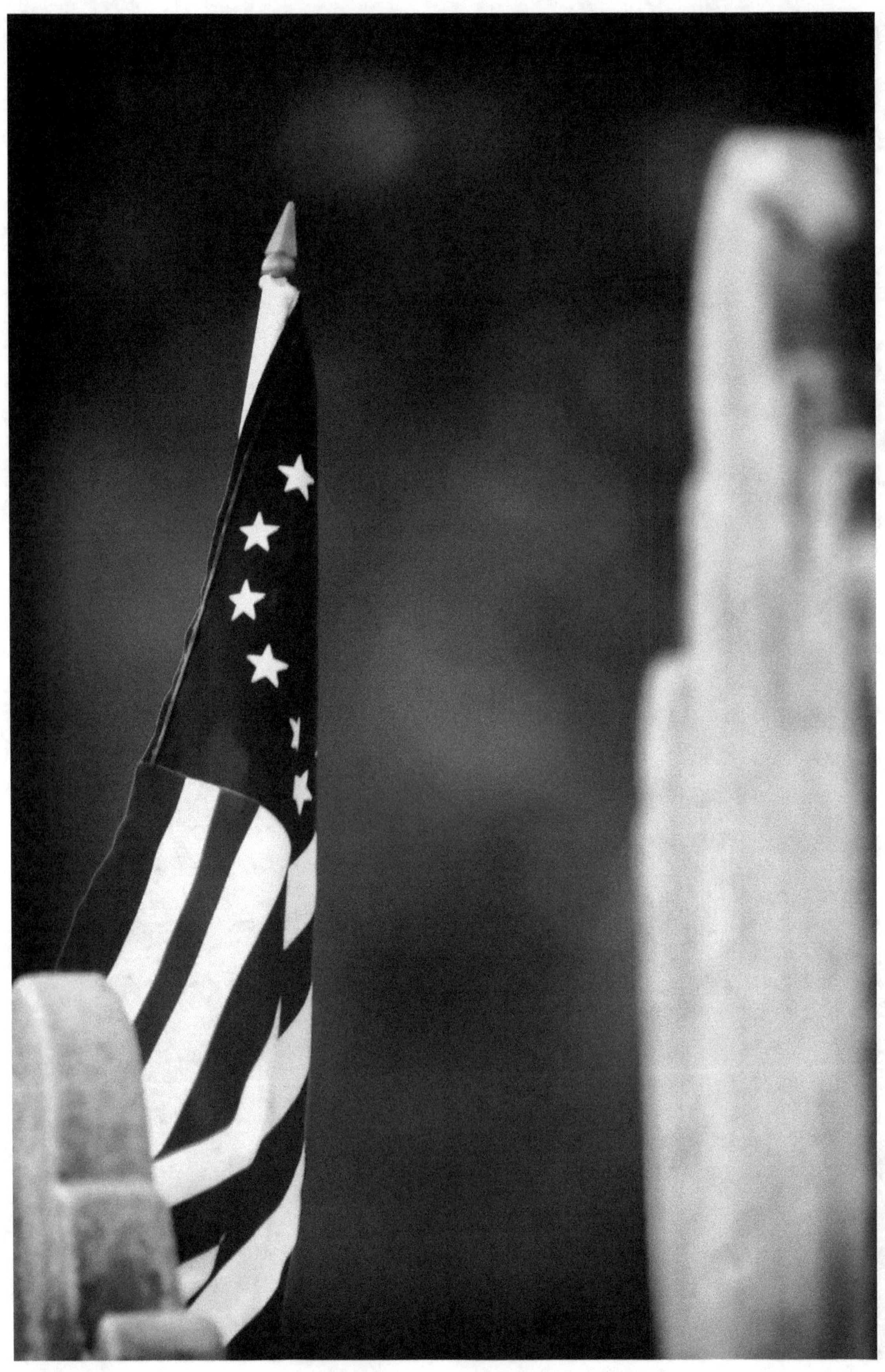

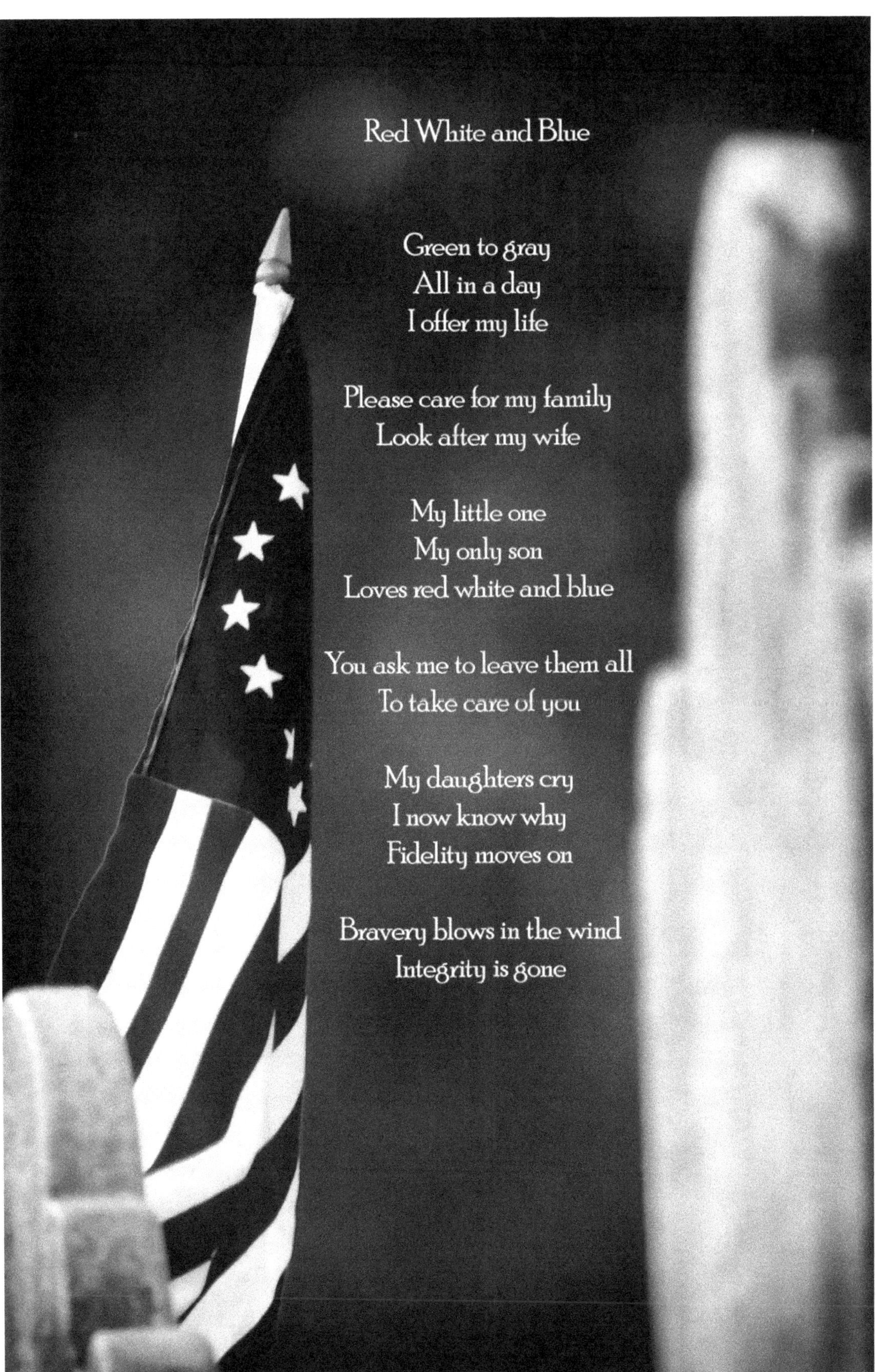

Red White and Blue

Green to gray
All in a day
I offer my life

Please care for my family
Look after my wife

My little one
My only son
Loves red white and blue

You ask me to leave them all
To take care of you

My daughters cry
I now know why
Fidelity moves on

Bravery blows in the wind
Integrity is gone

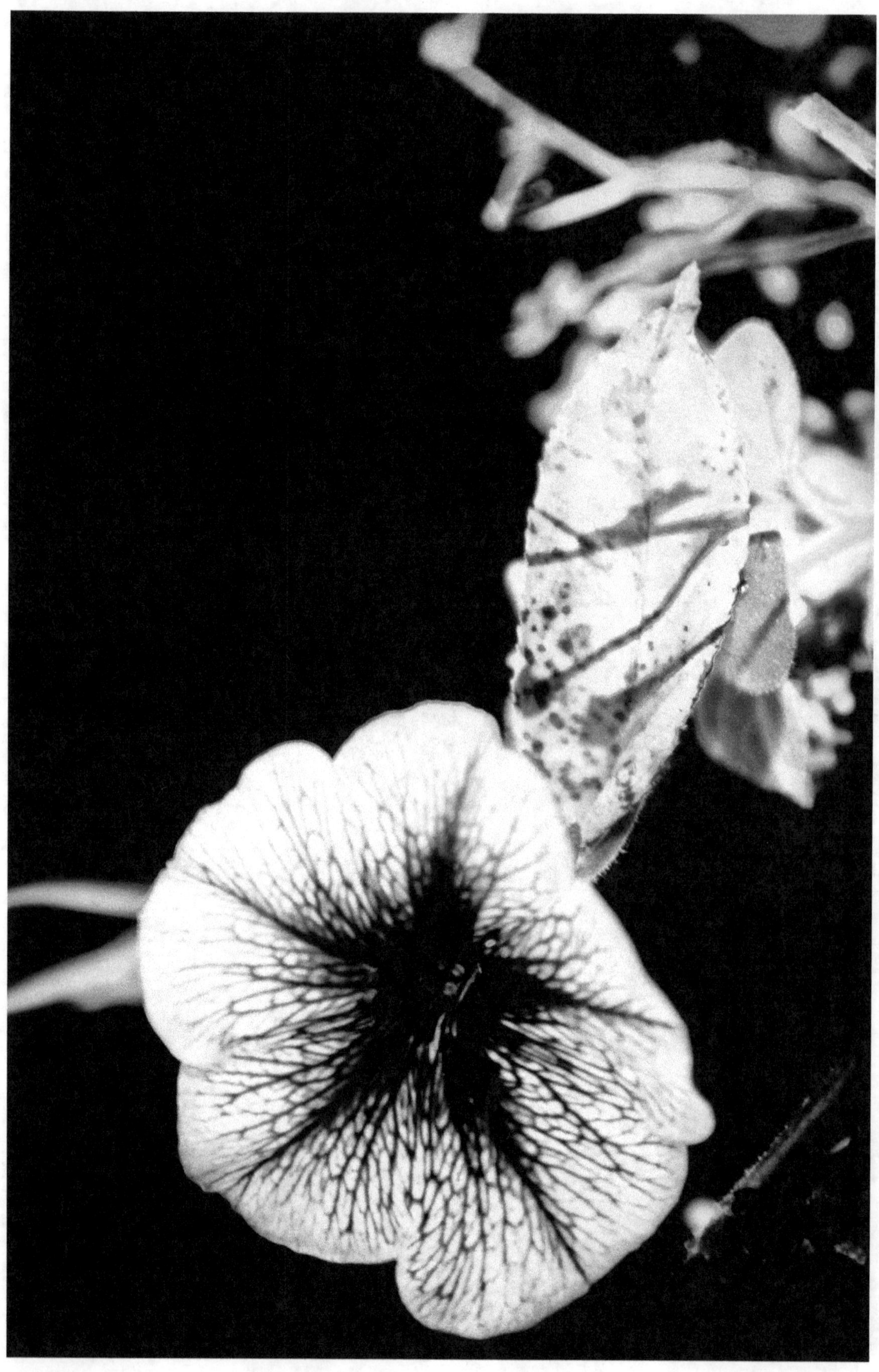

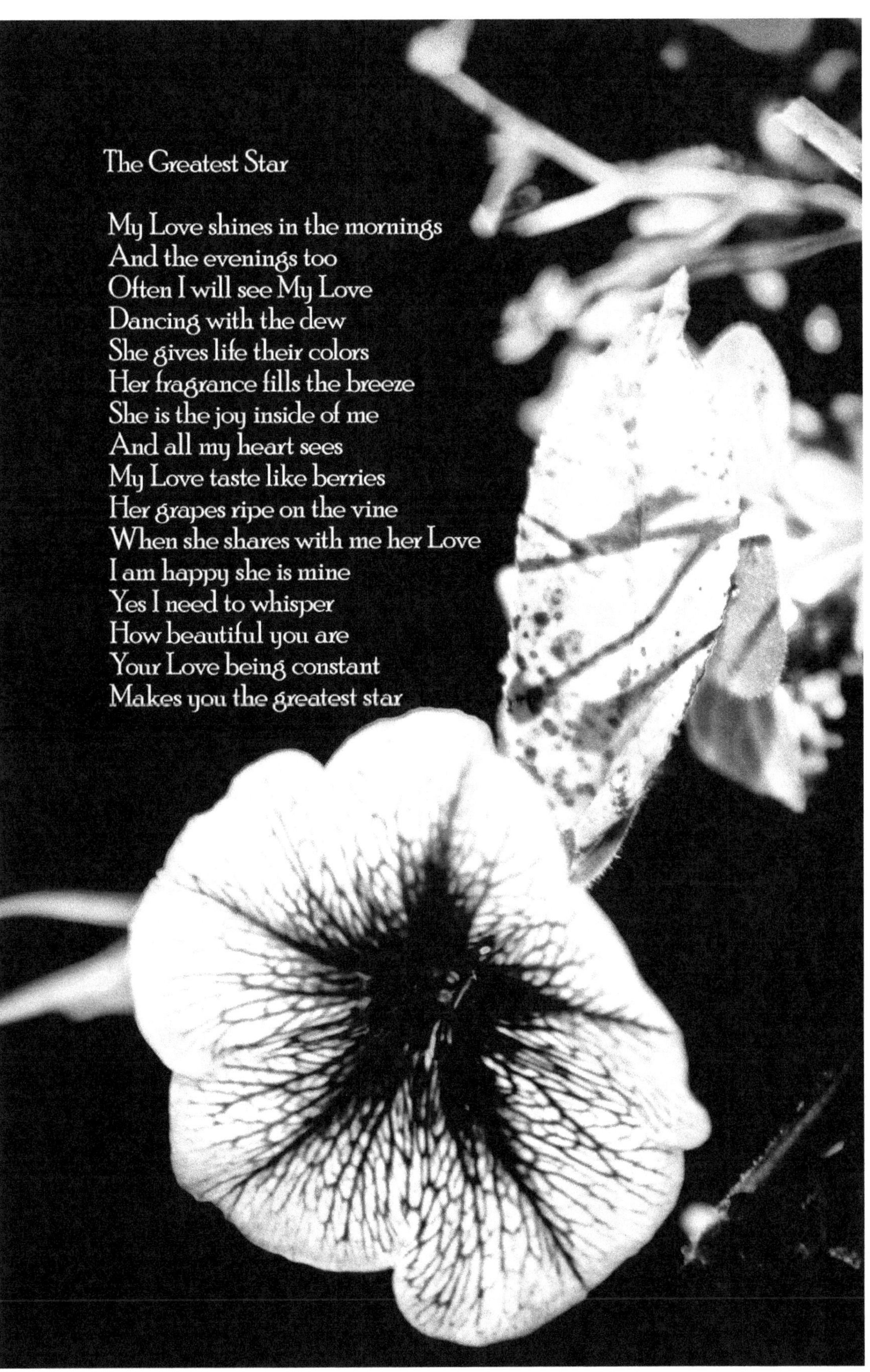

The Greatest Star

My Love shines in the mornings
And the evenings too
Often I will see My Love
Dancing with the dew
She gives life their colors
Her fragrance fills the breeze
She is the joy inside of me
And all my heart sees
My Love taste like berries
Her grapes ripe on the vine
When she shares with me her Love
I am happy she is mine
Yes I need to whisper
How beautiful you are
Your Love being constant
Makes you the greatest star

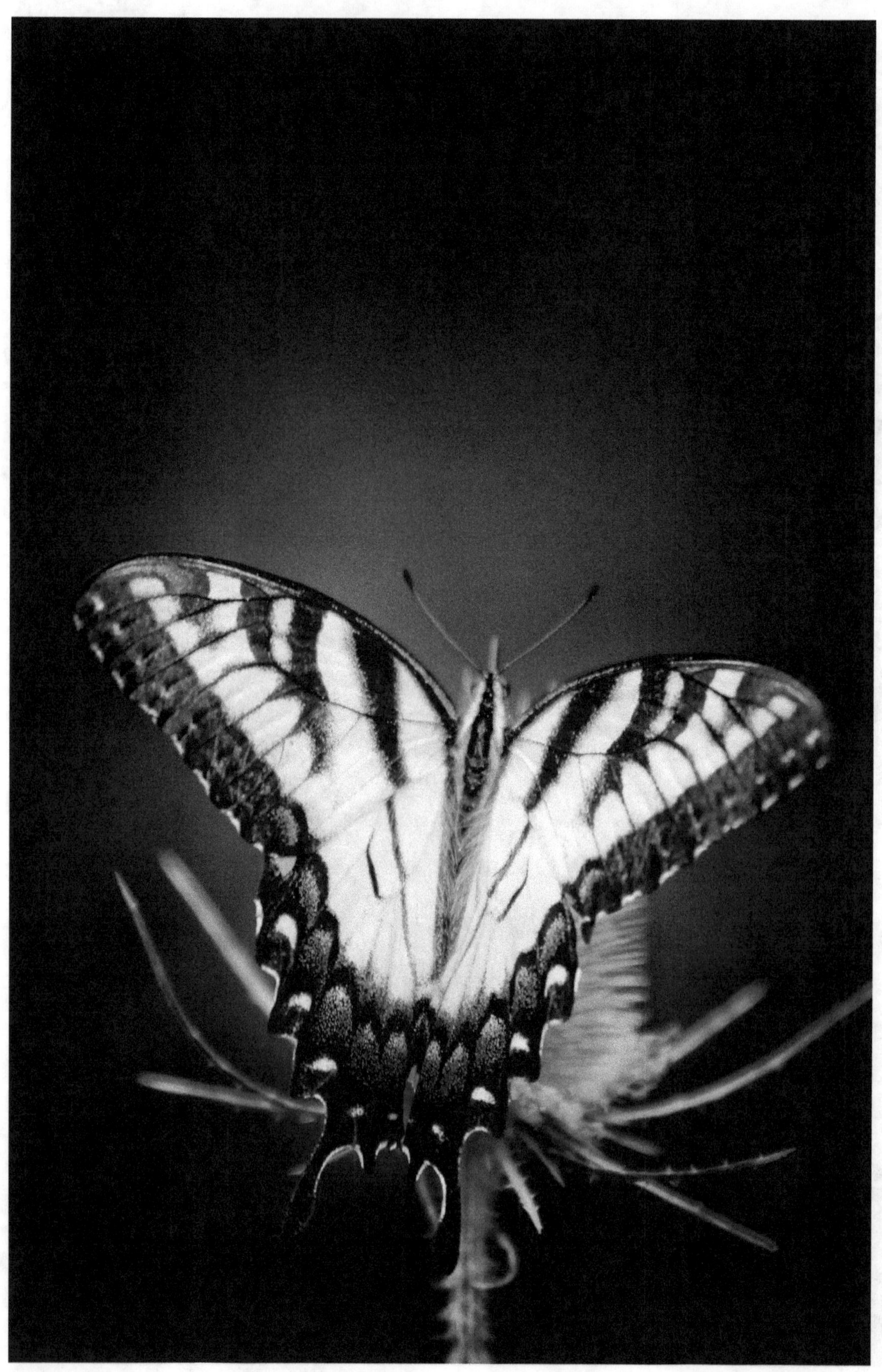

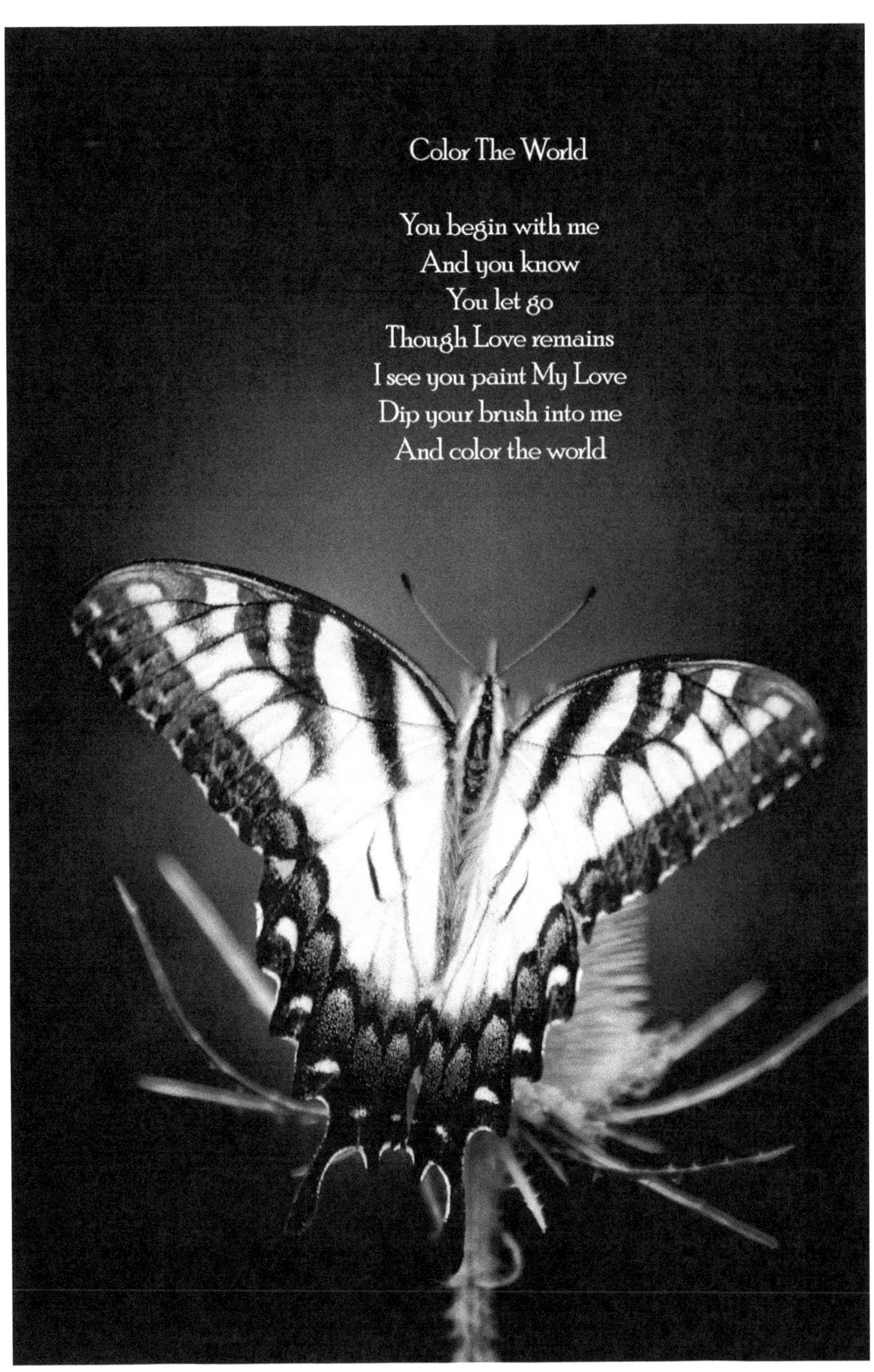
Color The World

You begin with me
And you know
You let go
Though Love remains
I see you paint My Love
Dip your brush into me
And color the world

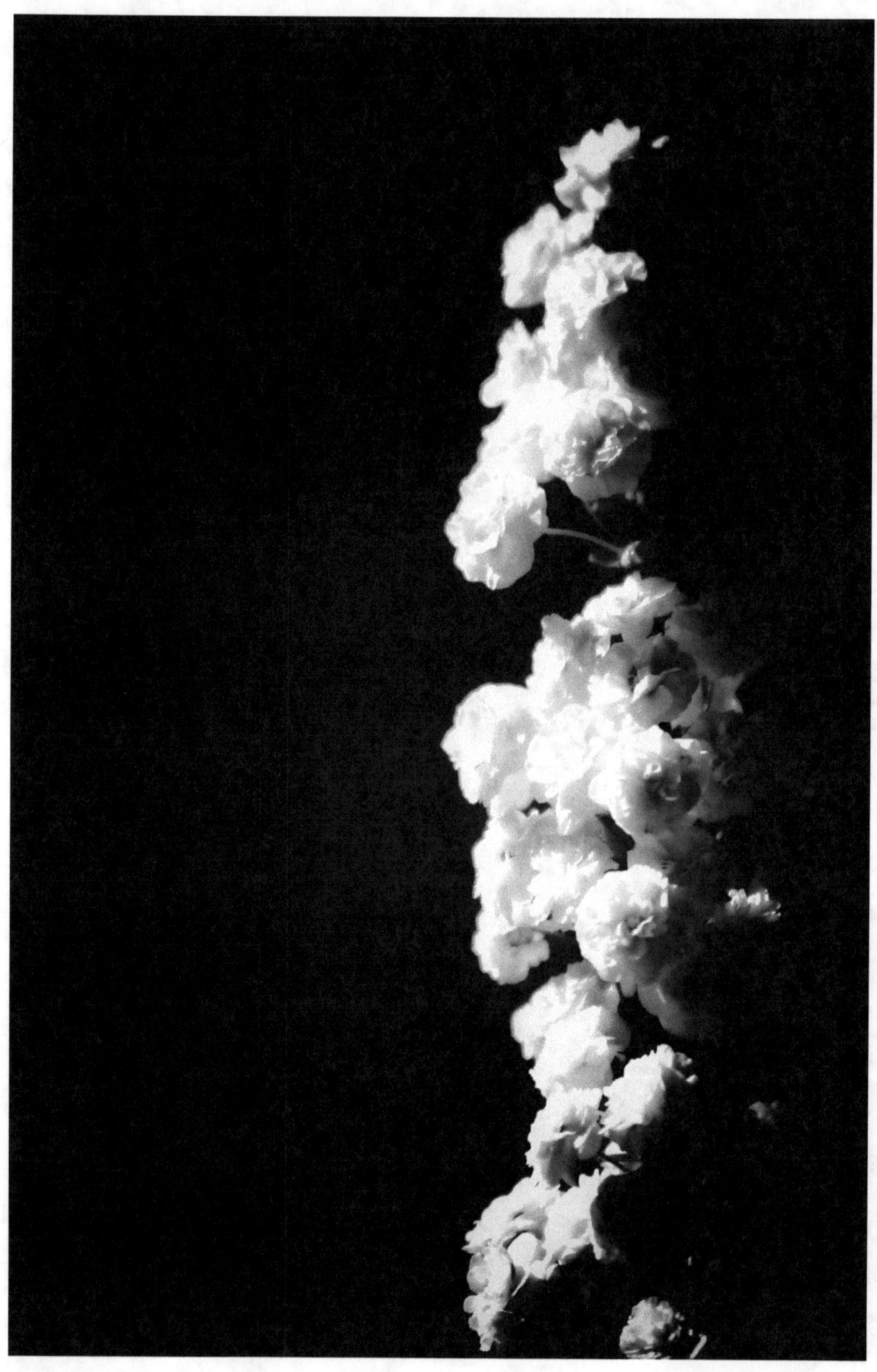

I Am In Love

With you I am In Love

My Love your mouth
Is sweetness itself
Your Lips are full
Like my desire for you

Your waist is
A mound of silk
Encircled by flowers
And creamy like milk

Your eyes are like pools
Refreshing and cool
Playground of your soul
Quenching my thirst

You are like the dawn
A majestic tapestry
Fairer than the moon
And brighter than the sun

I Am In Love with you

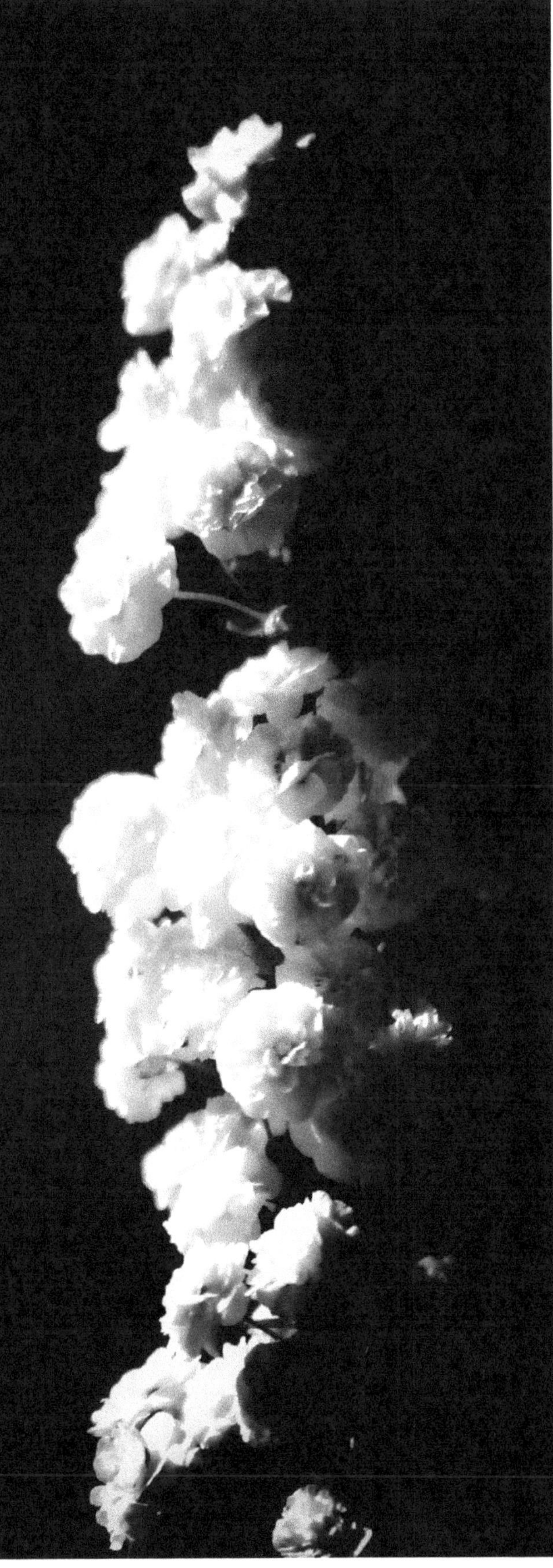

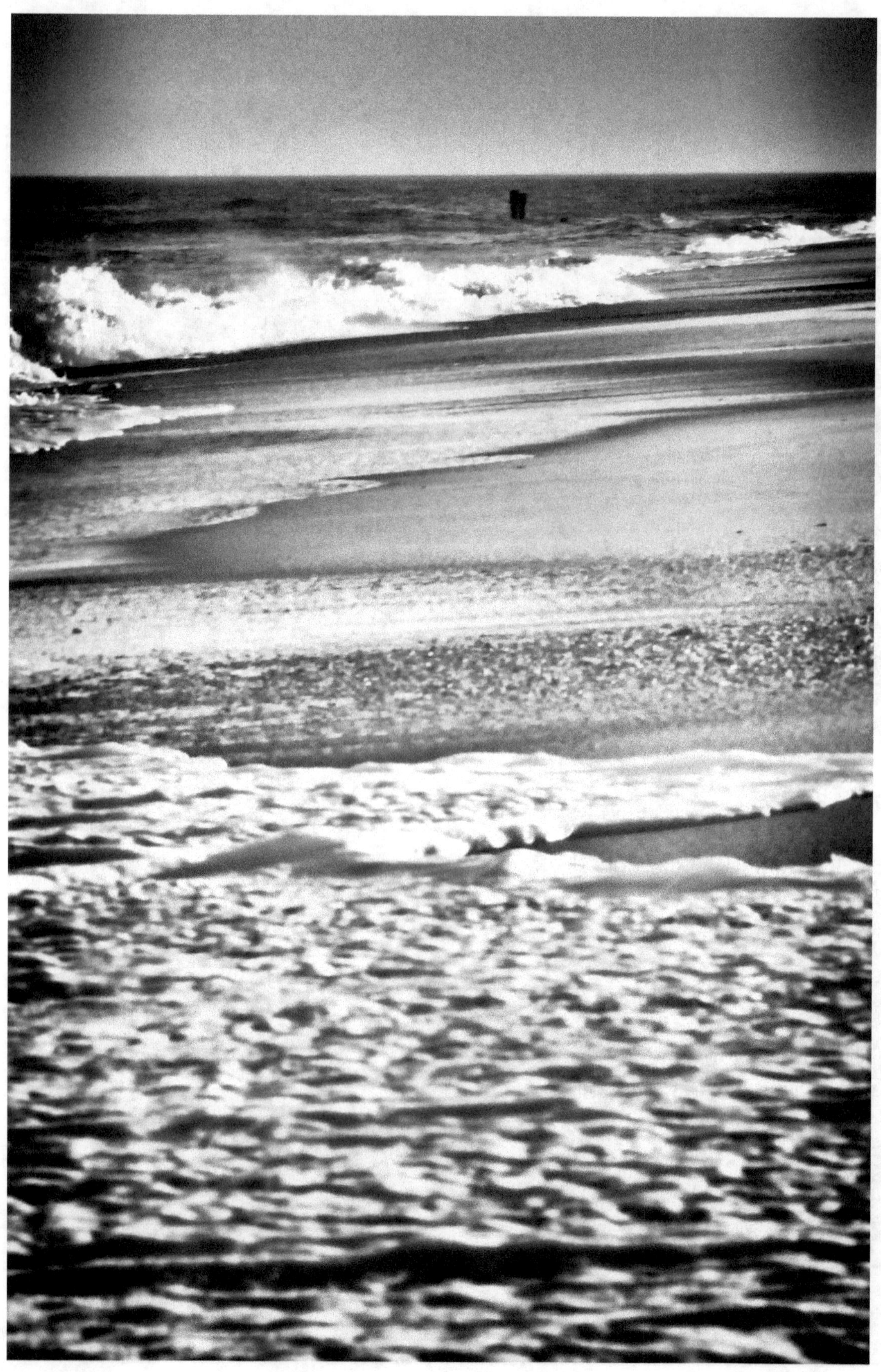

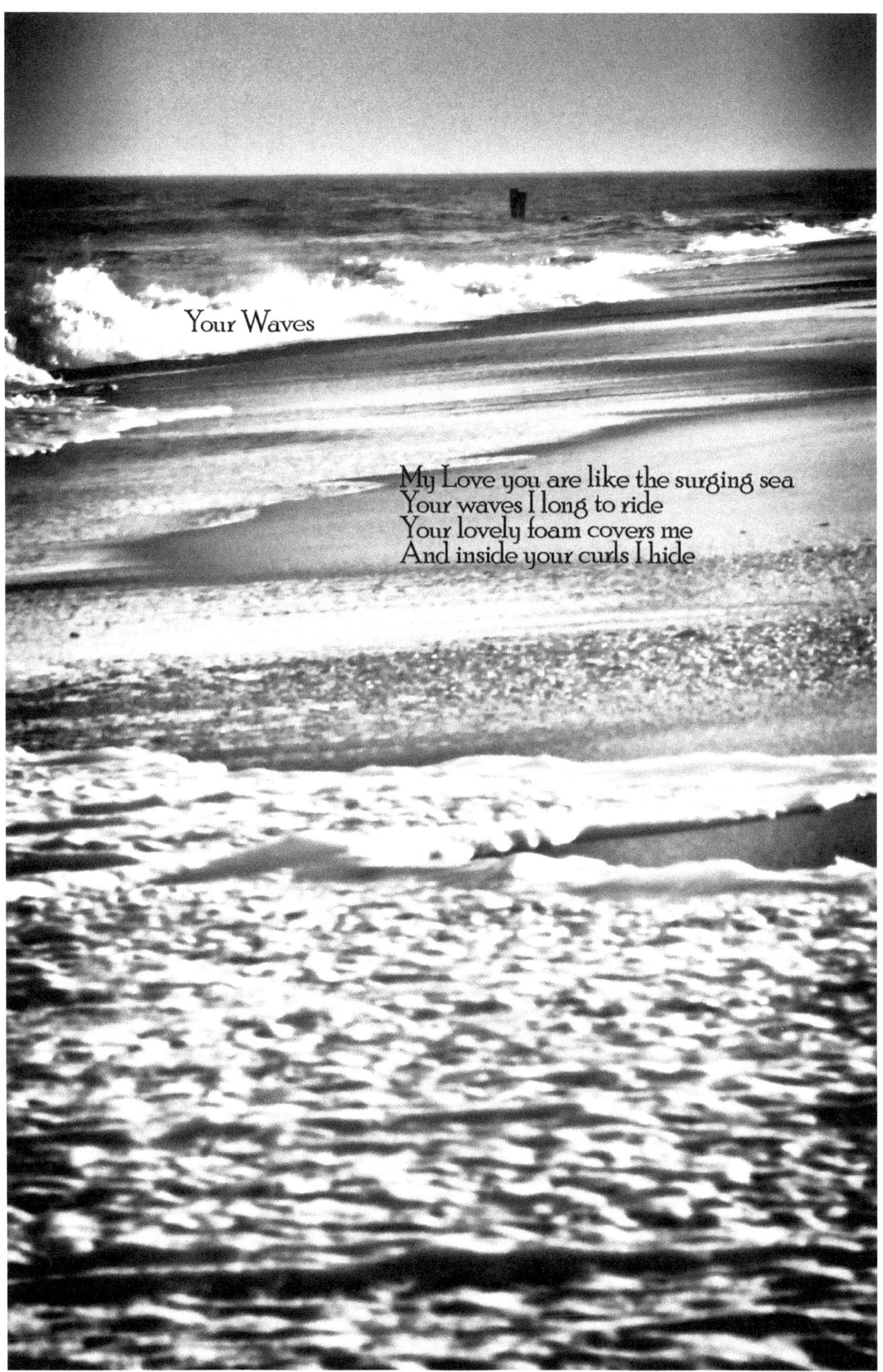

Your Waves

My Love you are like the surging sea
Your waves I long to ride
Your lovely foam covers me
And inside your curls I hide

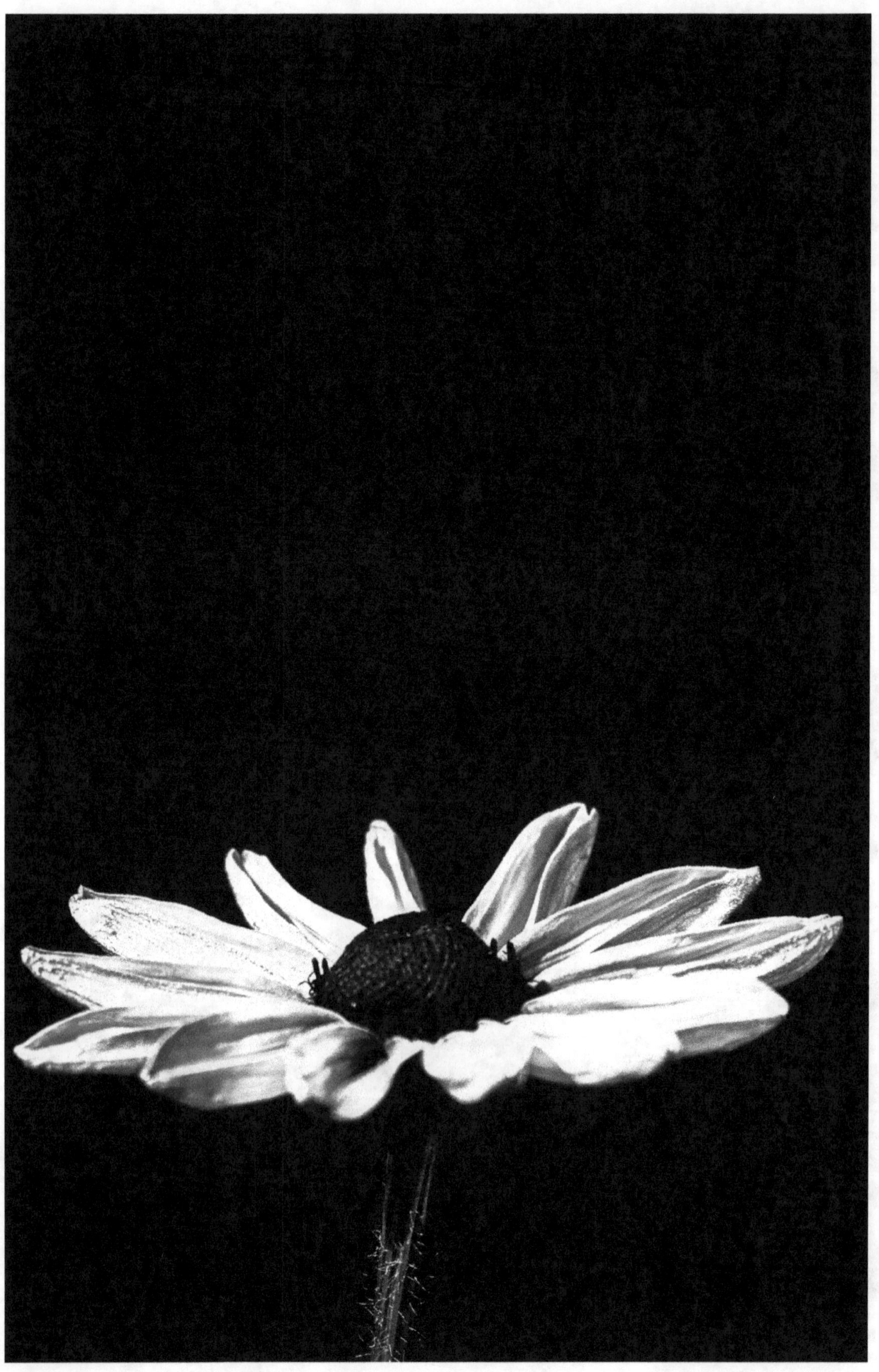

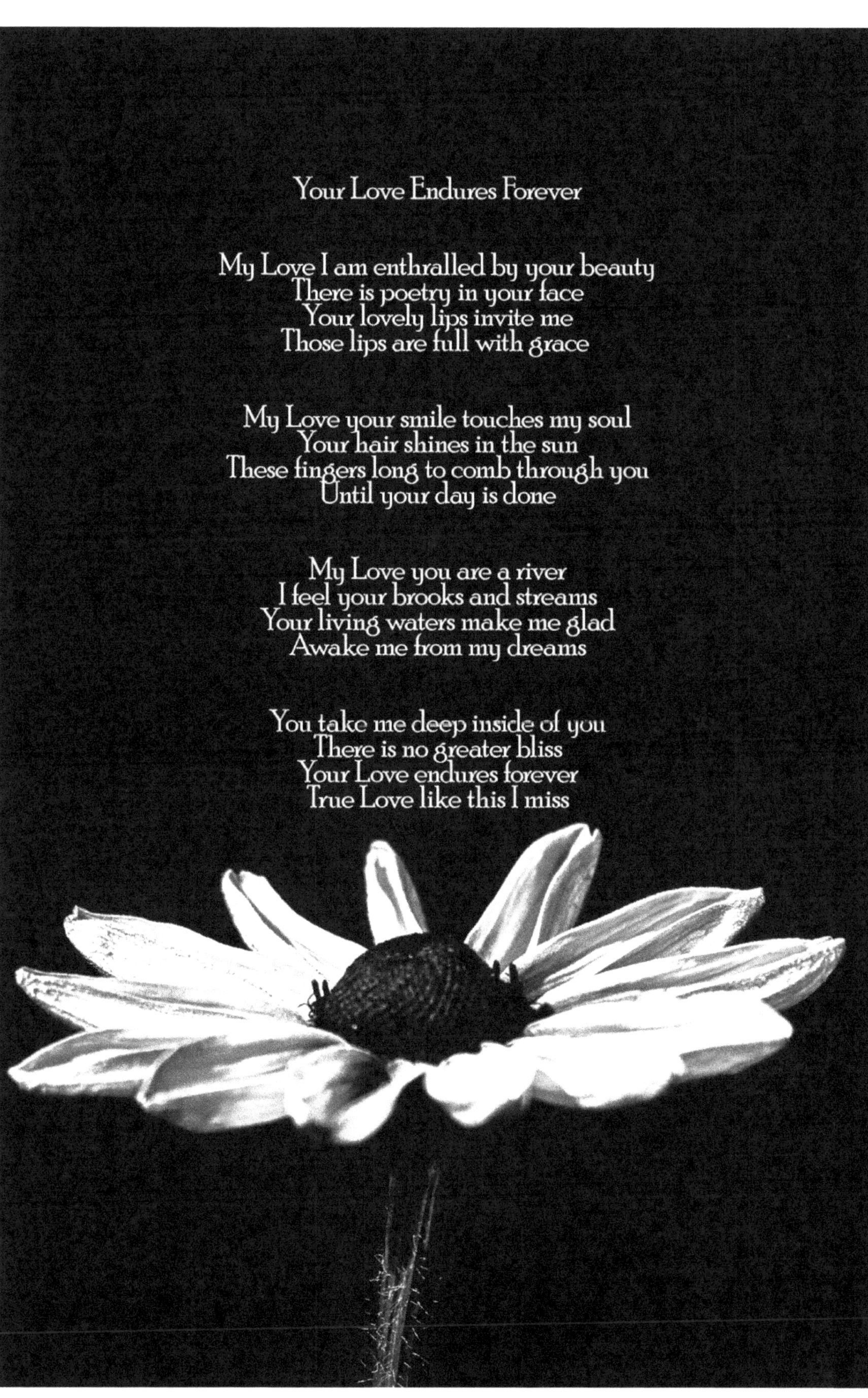

Your Love Endures Forever

My Love I am enthralled by your beauty
There is poetry in your face
Your lovely lips invite me
Those lips are full with grace

My Love your smile touches my soul
Your hair shines in the sun
These fingers long to comb through you
Until your day is done

My Love you are a river
I feel your brooks and streams
Your living waters make me glad
Awake me from my dreams

You take me deep inside of you
There is no greater bliss
Your Love endures forever
True Love like this I miss

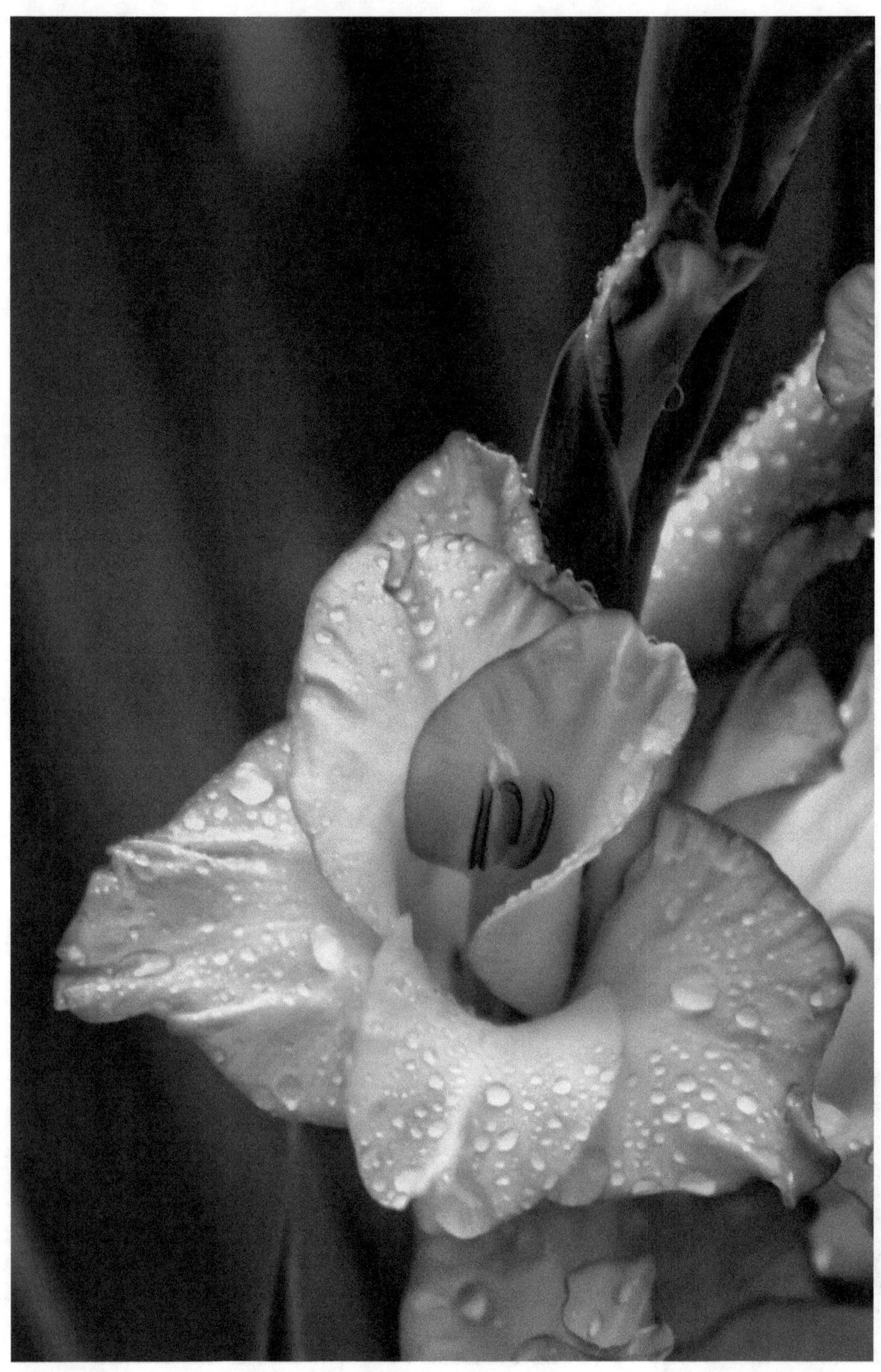

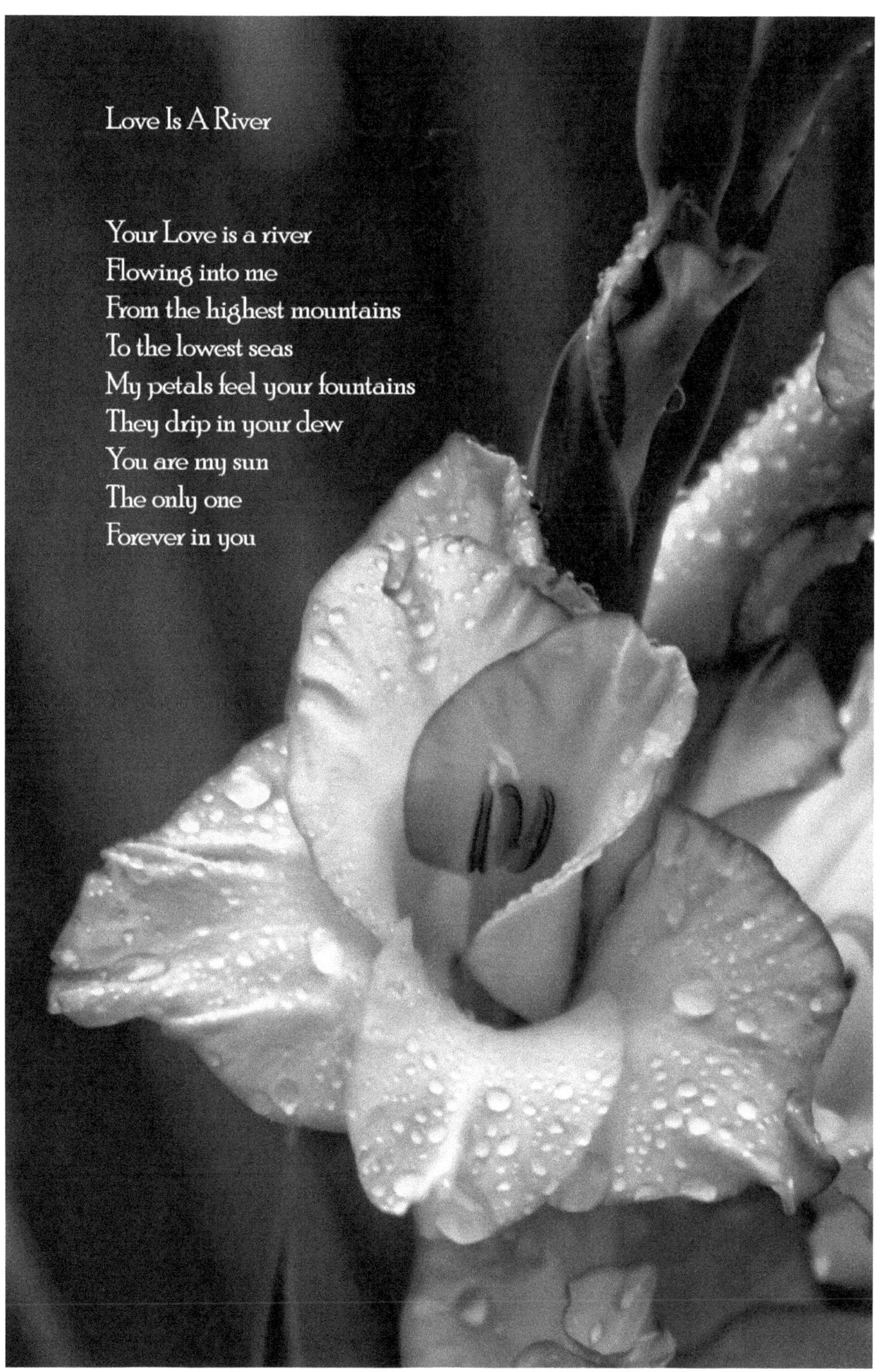

Love Is A River

Your Love is a river
Flowing into me
From the highest mountains
To the lowest seas
My petals feel your fountains
They drip in your dew
You are my sun
The only one
Forever in you

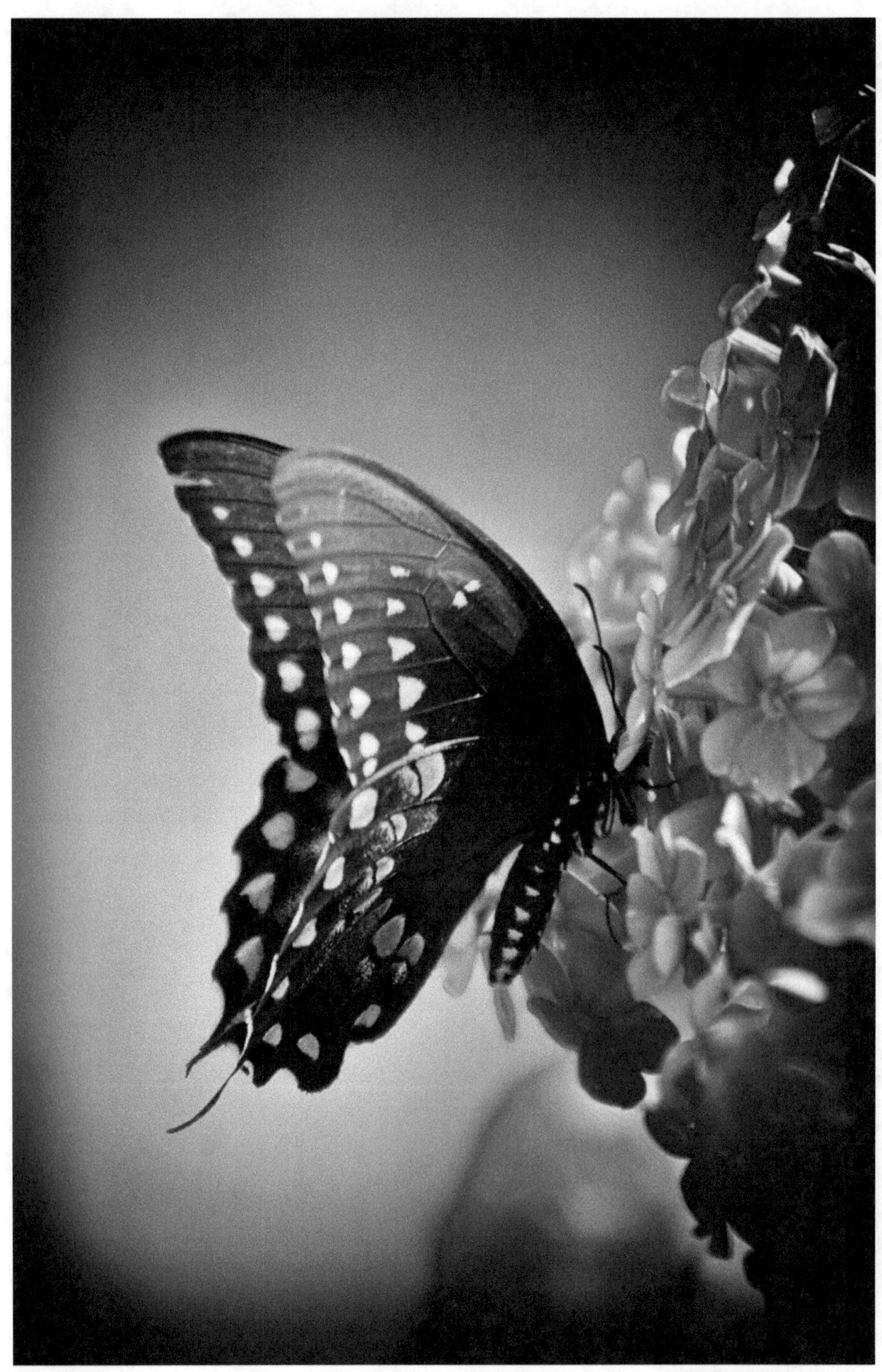

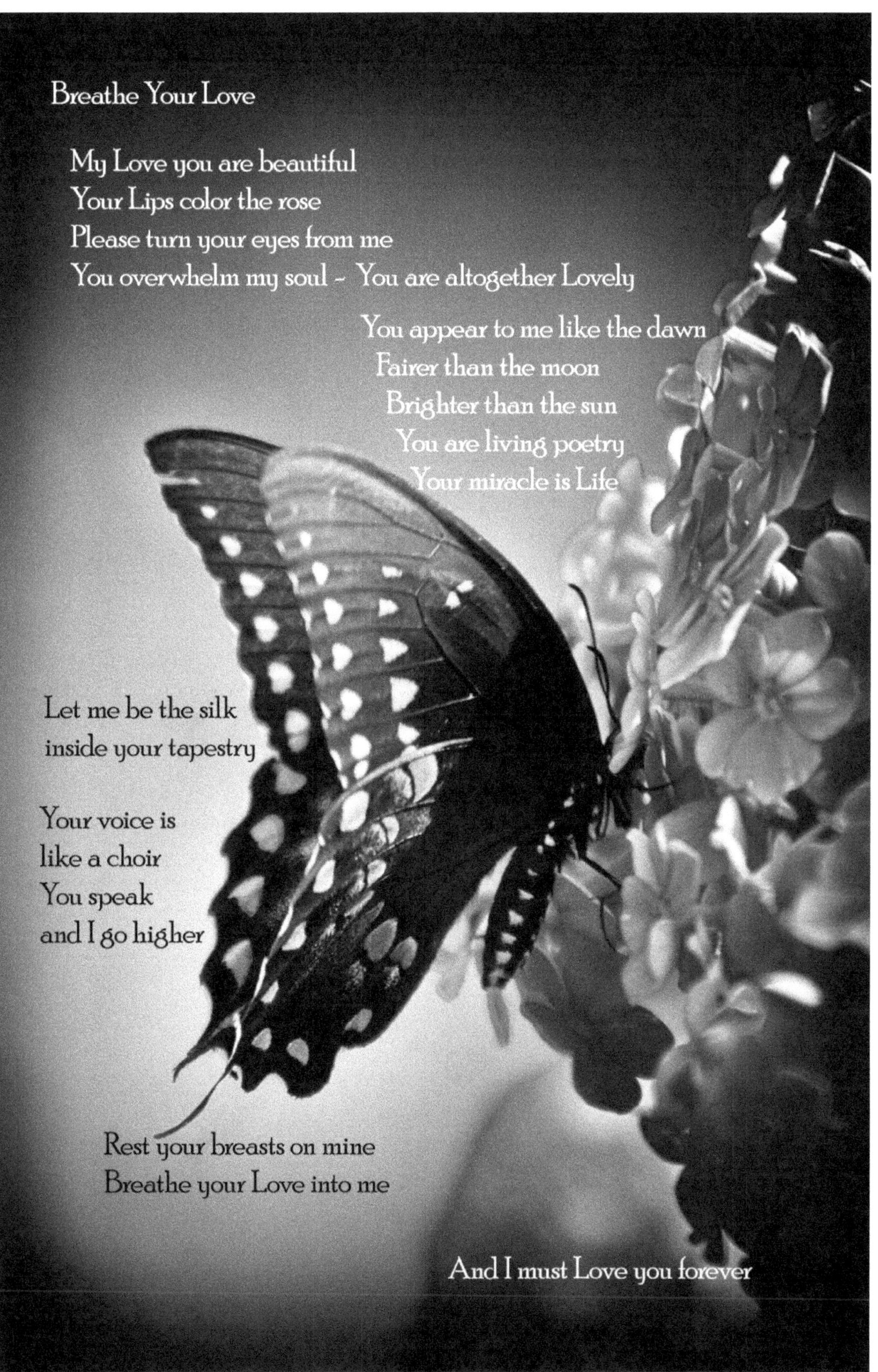
Breathe Your Love
My Love you are beautiful
Your Lips color the rose
Please turn your eyes from me
You overwhelm my soul - You are altogether Lovely
You appear to me like the dawn
Fairer than the moon
Brighter than the sun
You are living poetry
Your miracle is Life
Let me be the silk
inside your tapestry
Your voice is
like a choir
You speak
and I go higher
Rest your breasts on mine
Breathe your Love into me
And I must Love you forever

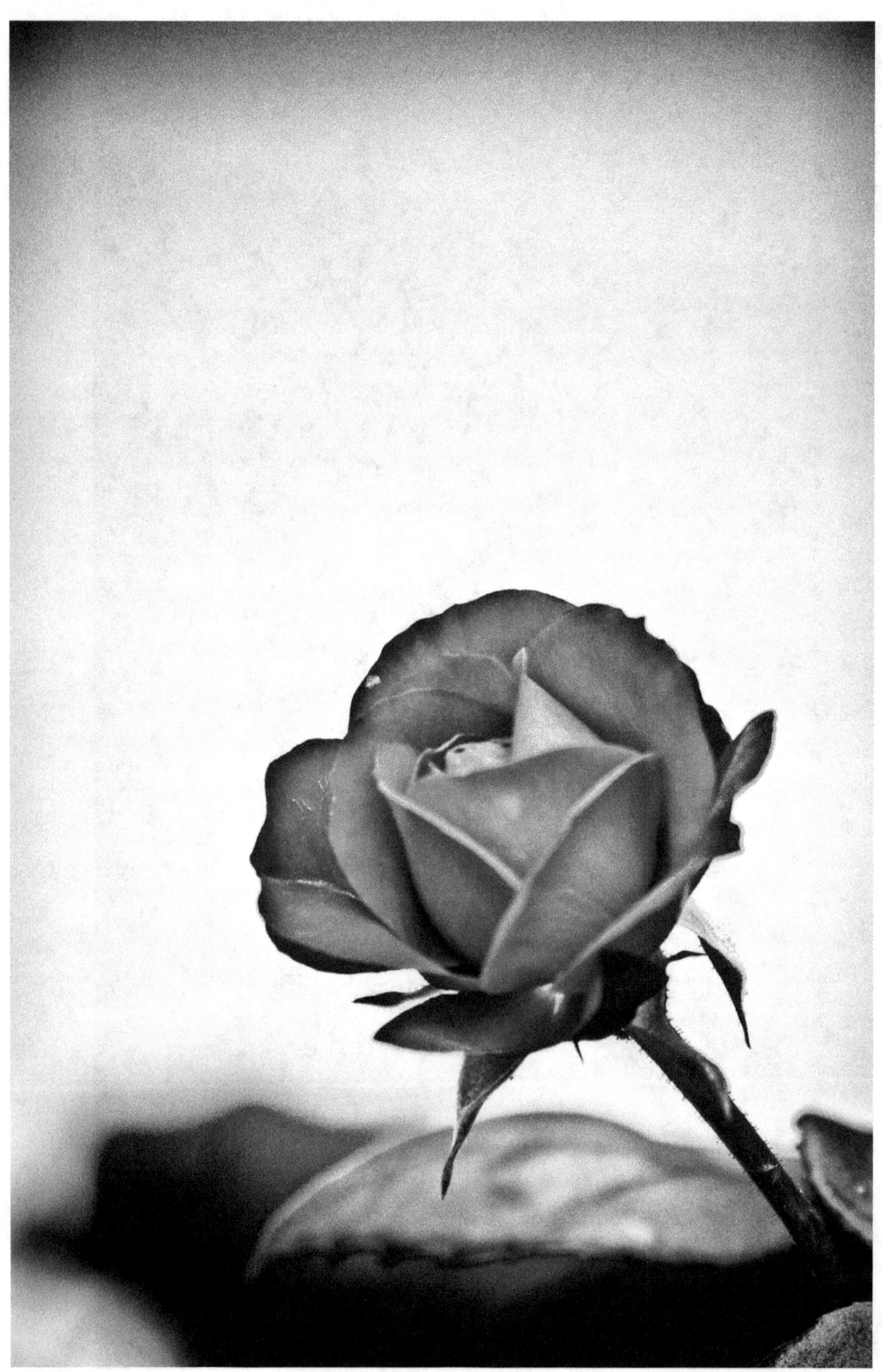

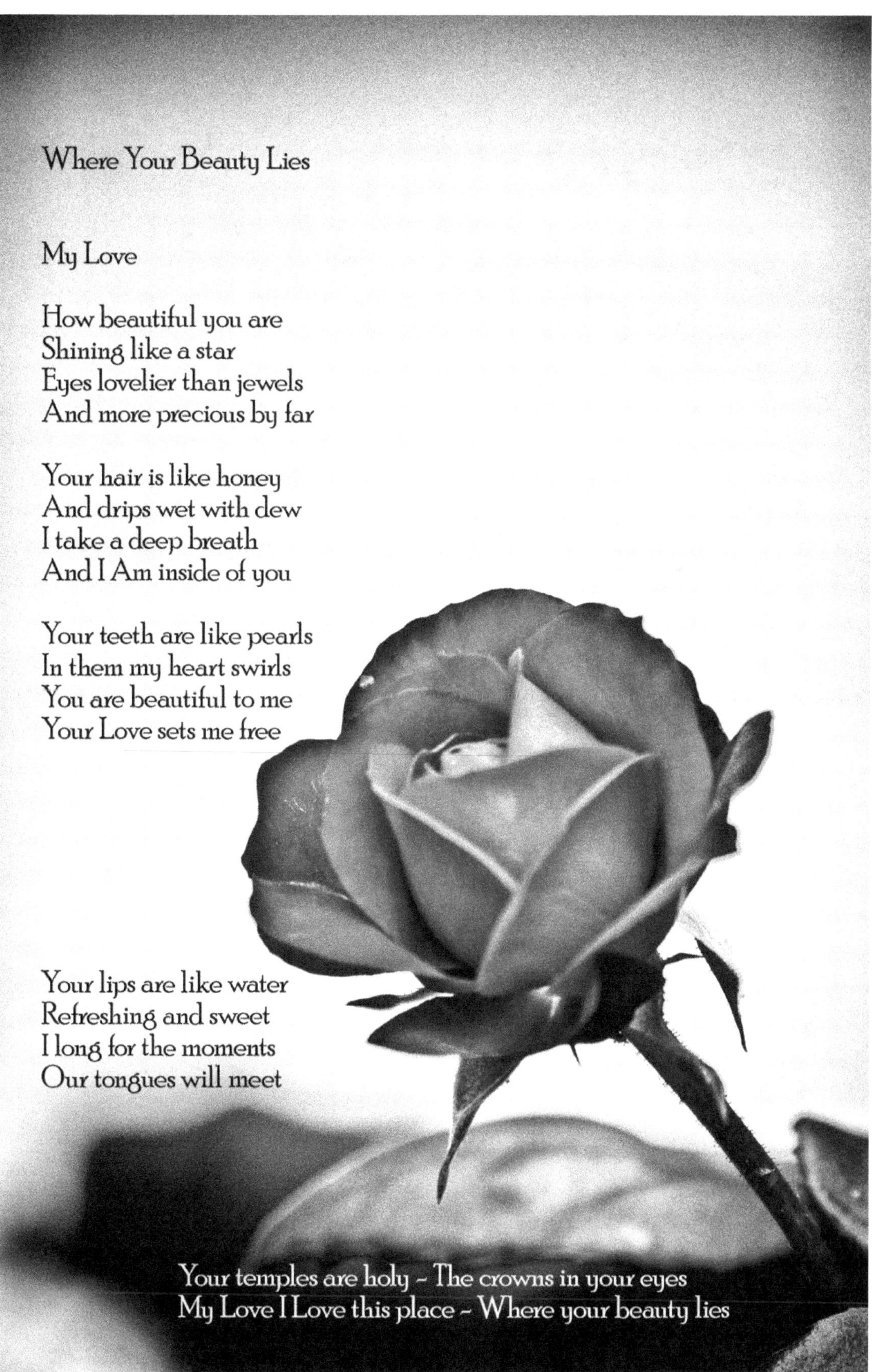

Where Your Beauty Lies

My Love

How beautiful you are
Shining like a star
Eyes lovelier than jewels
And more precious by far

Your hair is like honey
And drips wet with dew
I take a deep breath
And I Am inside of you

Your teeth are like pearls
In them my heart swirls
You are beautiful to me
Your Love sets me free

Your lips are like water
Refreshing and sweet
I long for the moments
Our tongues will meet

Your temples are holy - The crowns in your eyes
My Love I Love this place - Where your beauty lies

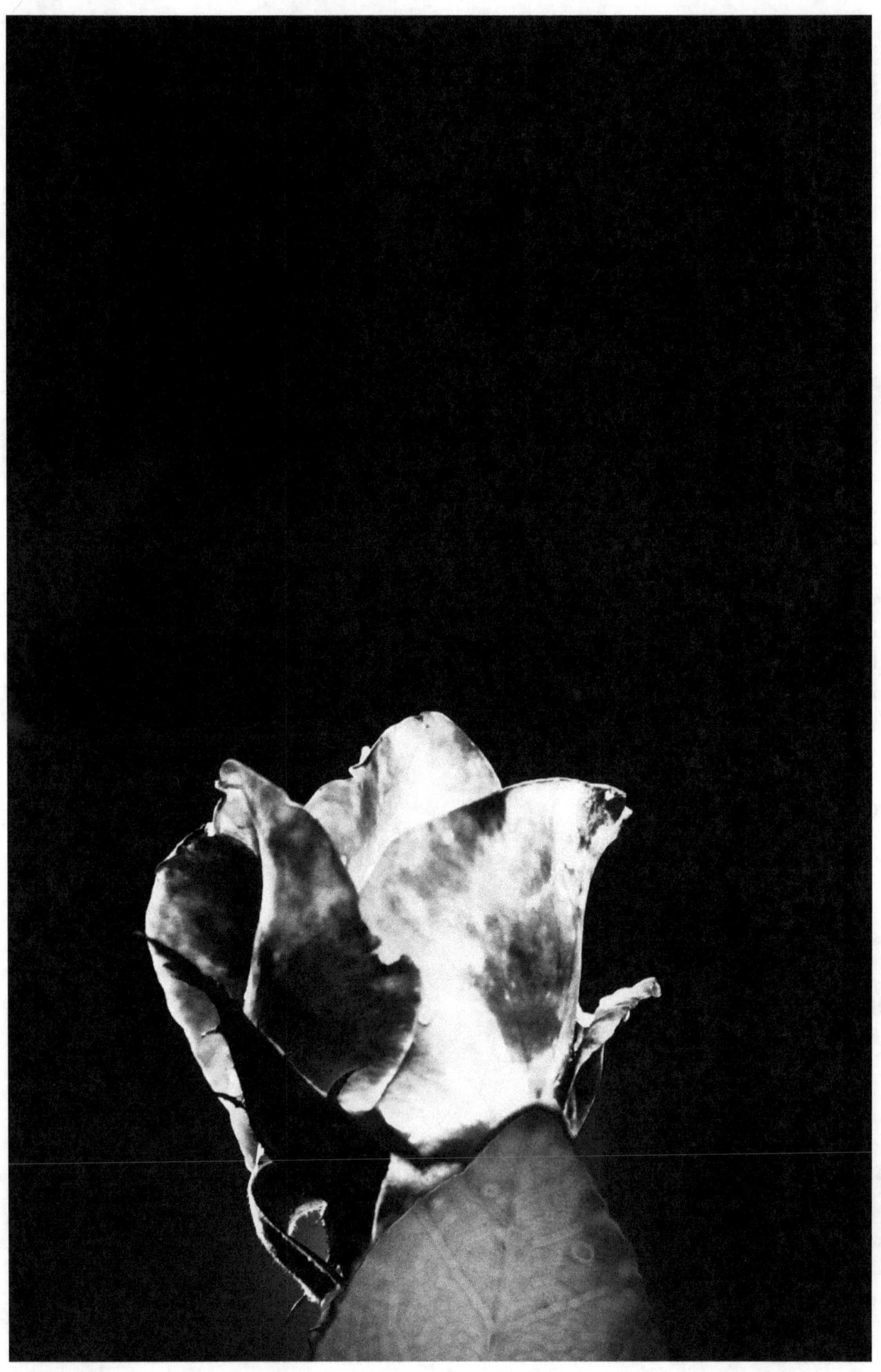

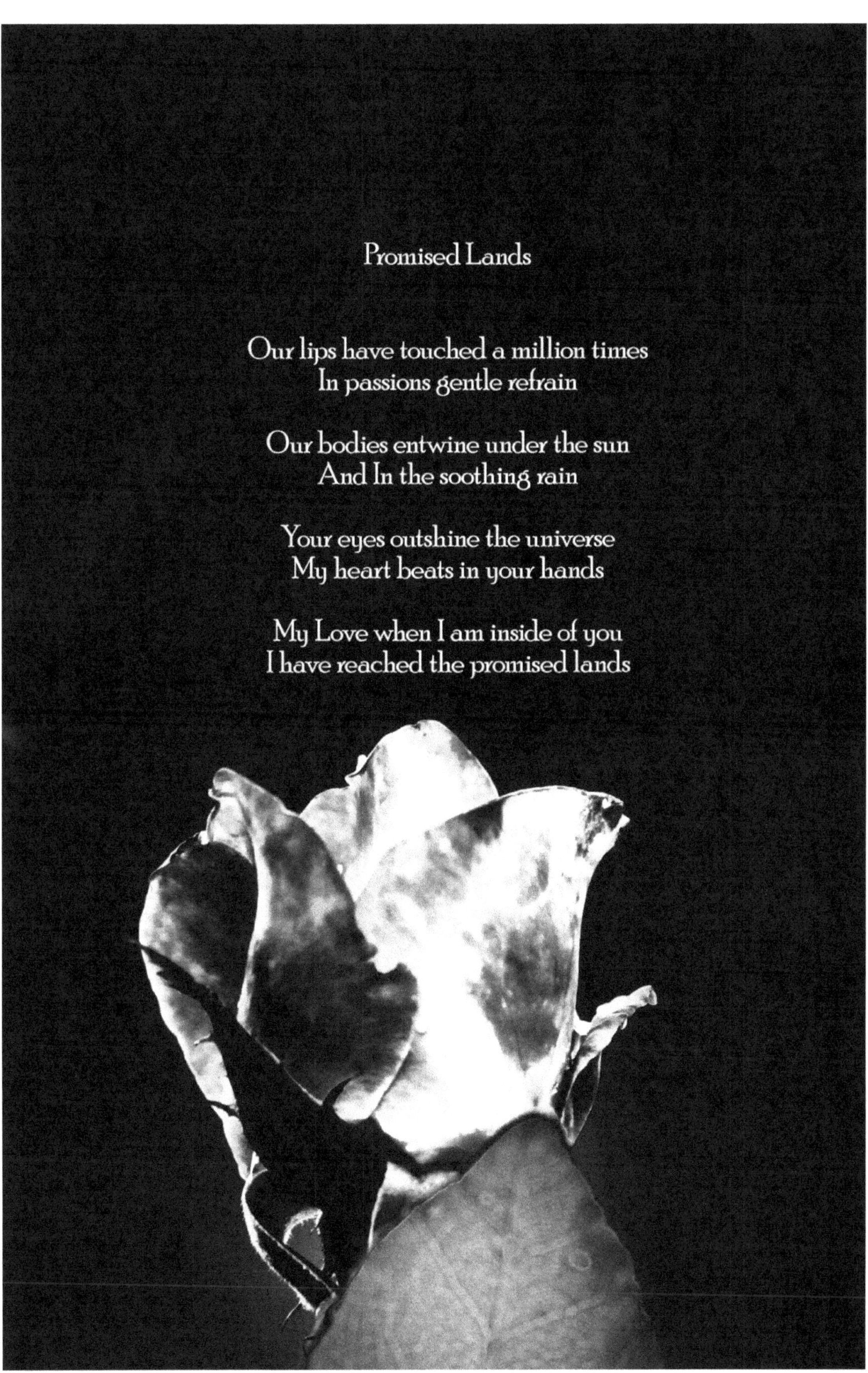

Promised Lands

Our lips have touched a million times
In passions gentle refrain

Our bodies entwine under the sun
And In the soothing rain

Your eyes outshine the universe
My heart beats in your hands

My Love when I am inside of you
I have reached the promised lands

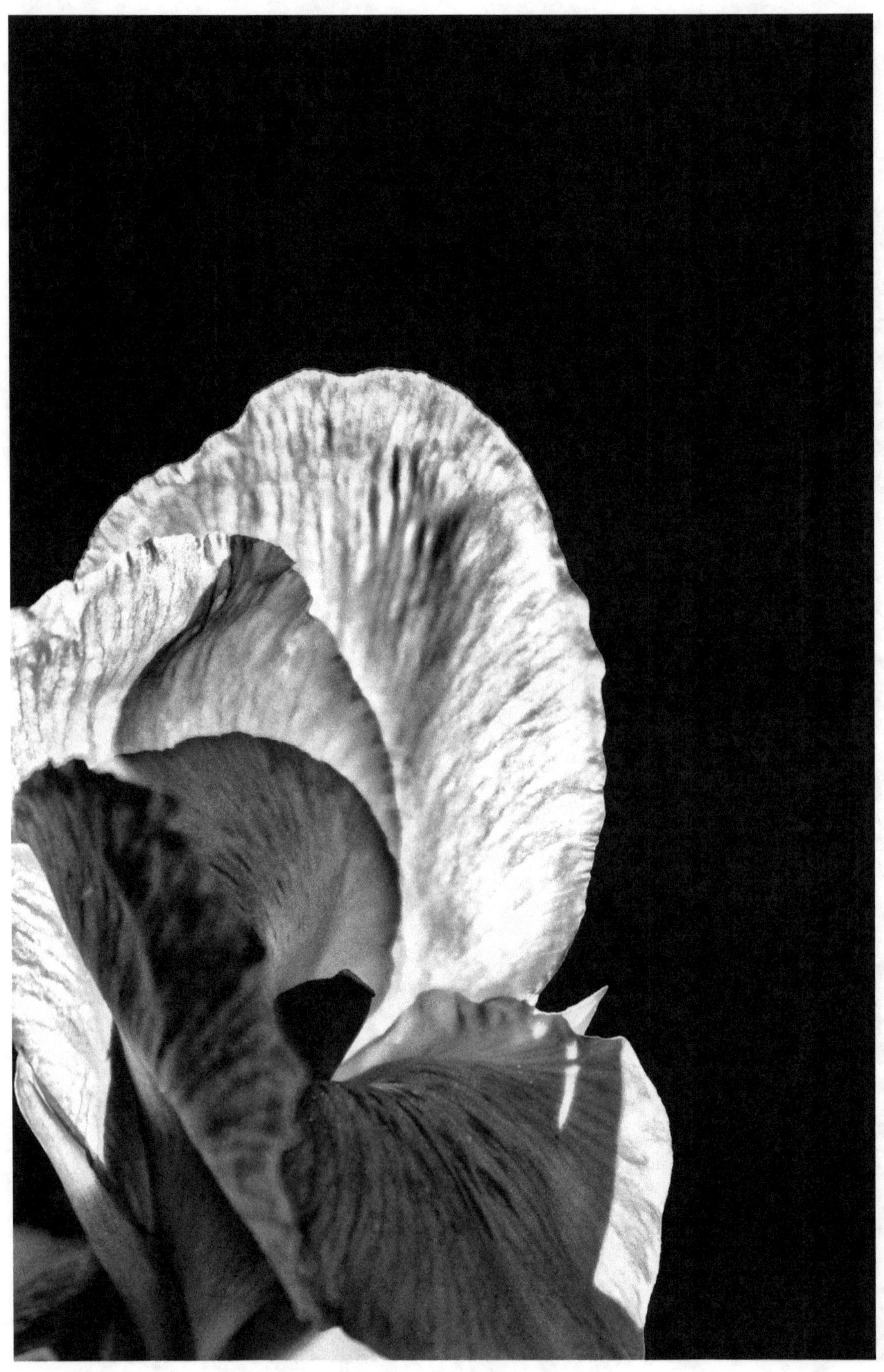

My Love

You are like the sunshine-Your warmth fills my soul-Your eyes reveal
the power of a million suns-Yet your touch is like a hundred butterflies
Gently flapping their paper thin wings-Against my fragile heart
Do you know the power of your words-They contain all the Empires
under the sun-When you write My Love-The greatest of painters submit
Because you color with your words-As only a prodigy can-With your
words-I rise to my knees-Before you I lay in the dust-Your gift lifts me up
Arising to my knees-Calling me to awake-To see the beauty in you
The lives you create when you release your heart-You have my heart

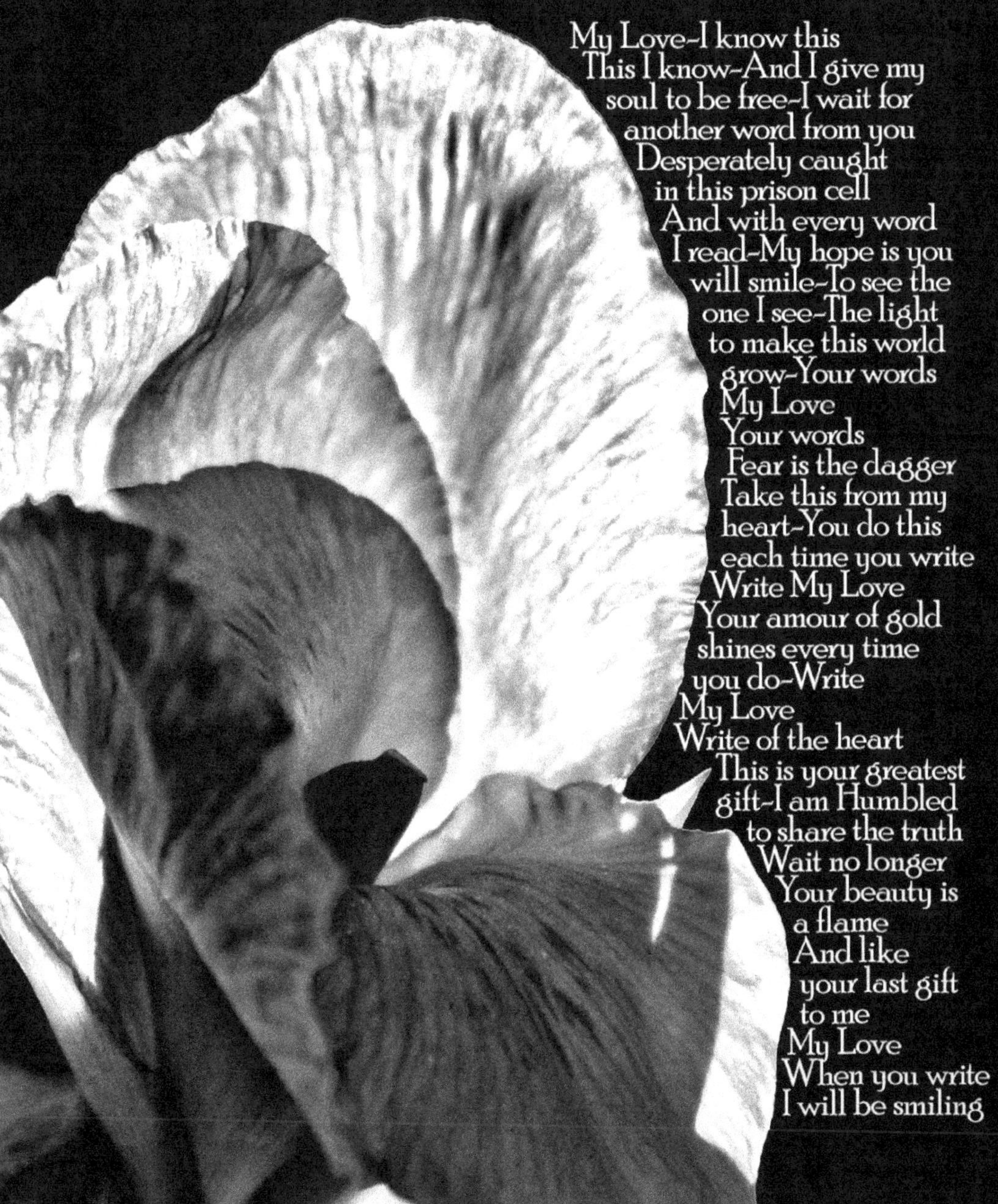

My Love-I know this
This I know-And I give my
soul to be free-I wait for
another word from you
Desperately caught
in this prison cell
And with every word
I read-My hope is you
will smile-To see the
one I see-The light
to make this world
grow-Your words
My Love
Your words
Fear is the dagger
Take this from my
heart-You do this
each time you write
Write My Love
Your amour of gold
shines every time
you do-Write
My Love
Write of the heart
This is your greatest
gift-I am Humbled
to share the truth
Wait no longer
Your beauty is
a flame
And like
your last gift
to me
My Love
When you write
I will be smiling

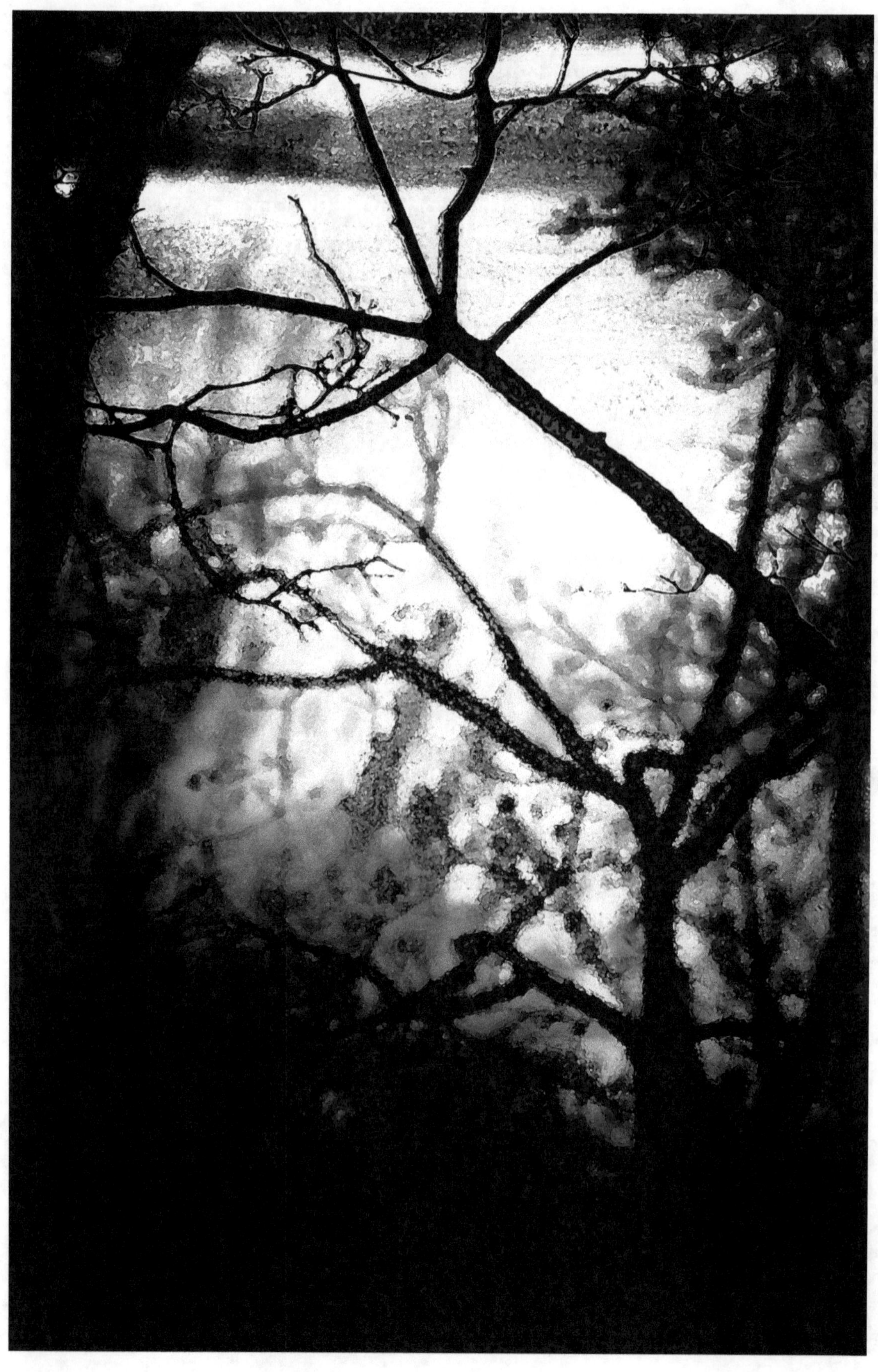

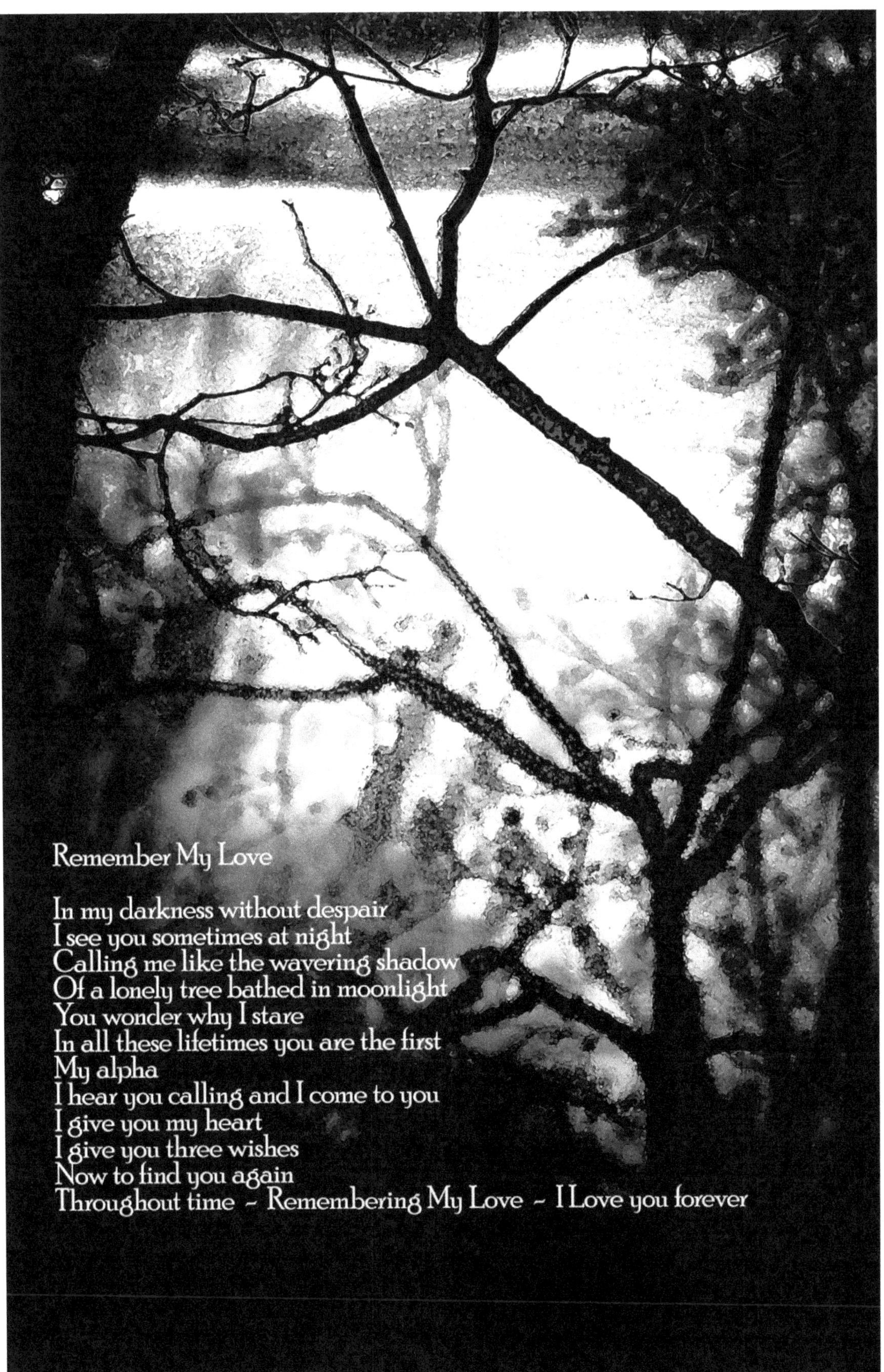

Remember My Love

In my darkness without despair
I see you sometimes at night
Calling me like the wavering shadow
Of a lonely tree bathed in moonlight
You wonder why I stare
In all these lifetimes you are the first
My alpha
I hear you calling and I come to you
I give you my heart
I give you three wishes
Now to find you again
Throughout time ~ Remembering My Love ~ I Love you forever

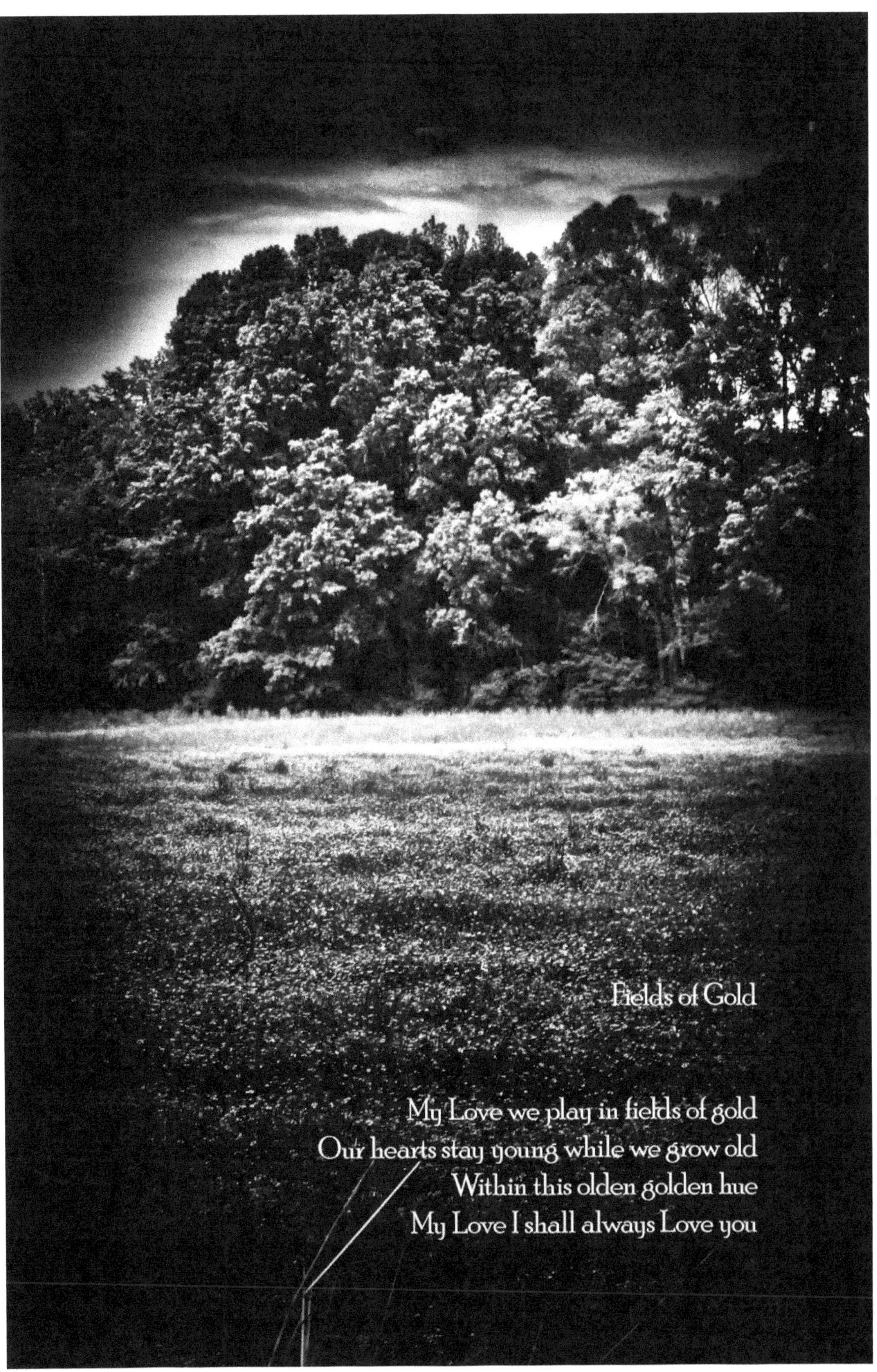
Fields of Gold
My Love we play in fields of gold
Our hearts stay young while we grow old
Within this olden golden hue
My Love I shall always Love you

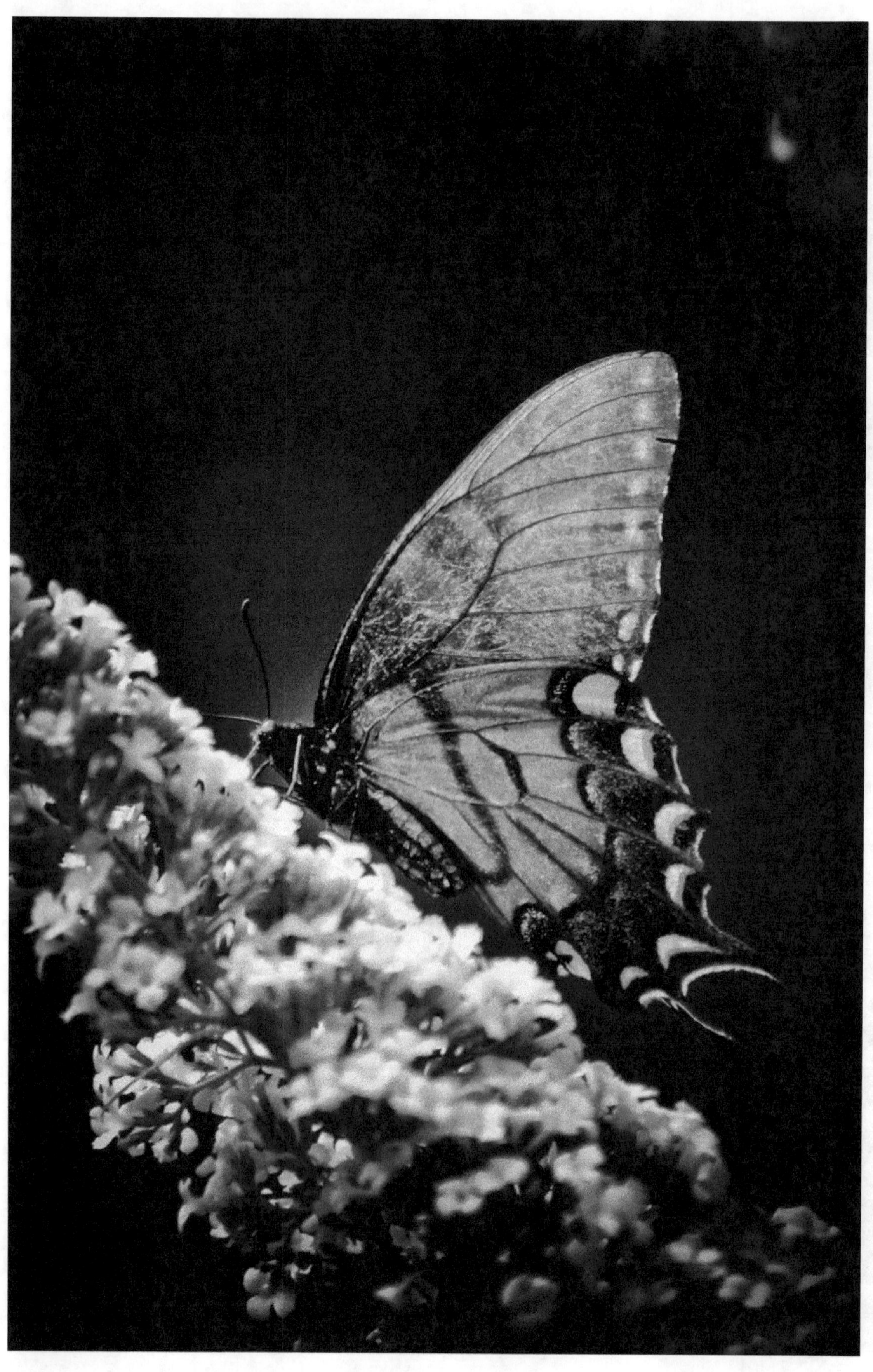

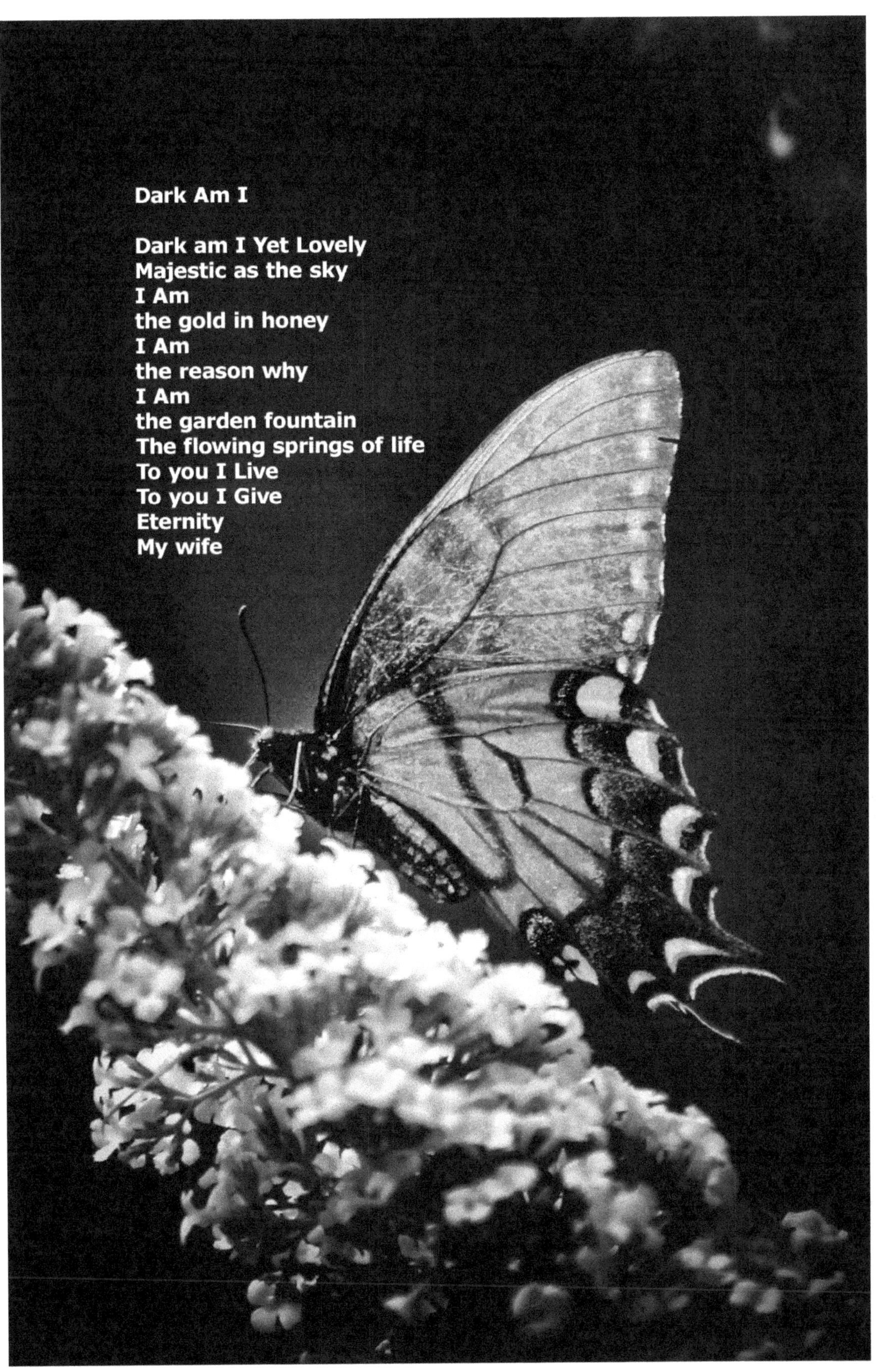
Dark Am I

Dark am I Yet Lovely
Majestic as the sky
I Am
the gold in honey
I Am
the reason why
I Am
the garden fountain
The flowing springs of life
To you I Live
To you I Give
Eternity
My wife

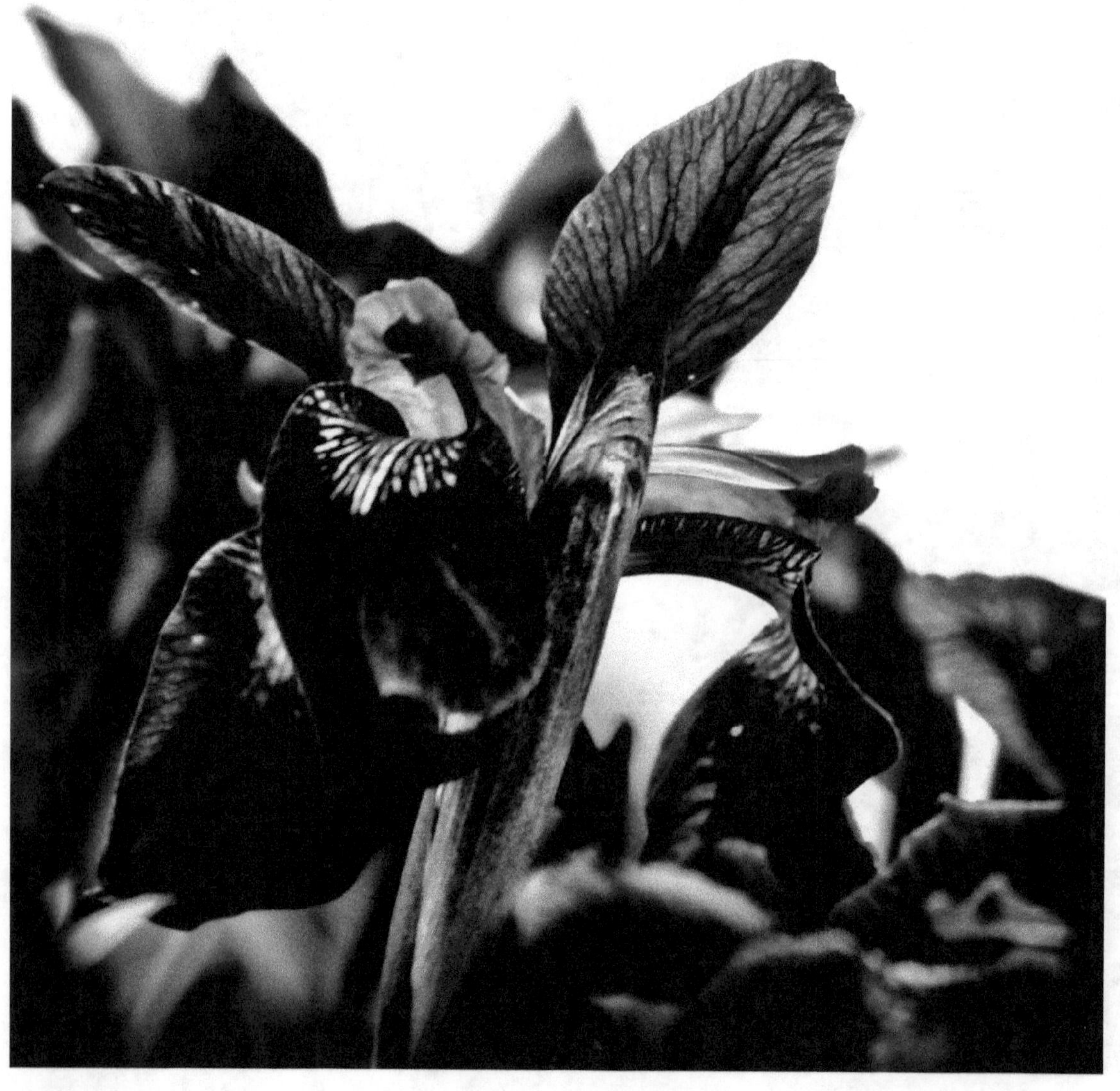

Love Will Grow

Dear Love in the garden
I gave to you my ring
For the first time in my life
I heard flowers sing

In your joy you make them glad
Their hearts fill with song
Because your smile is the sun
Their day is all night long

You are beautiful in every way
And like the flowers glow
I long to be in you each day
Where our Love will grow

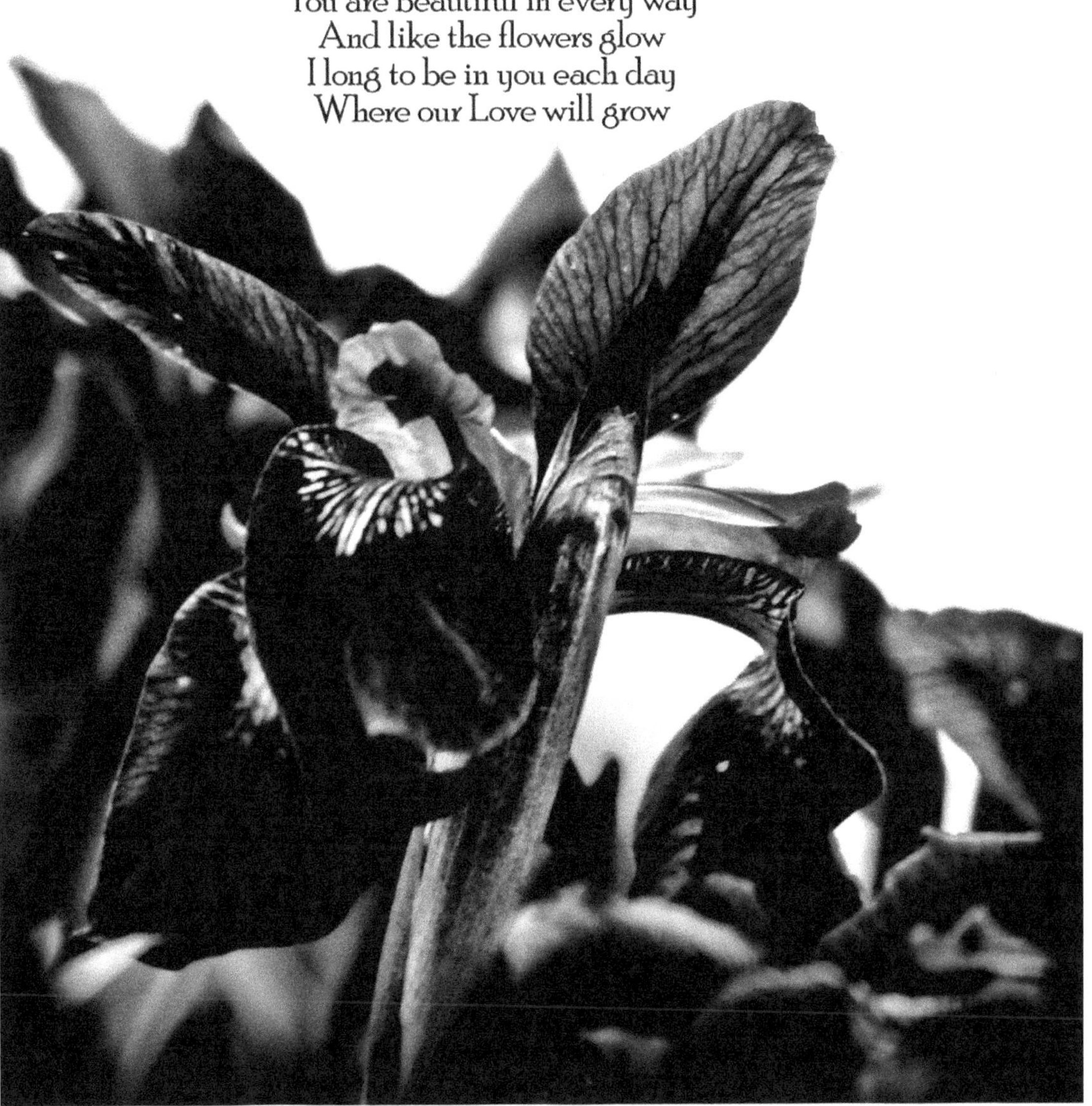

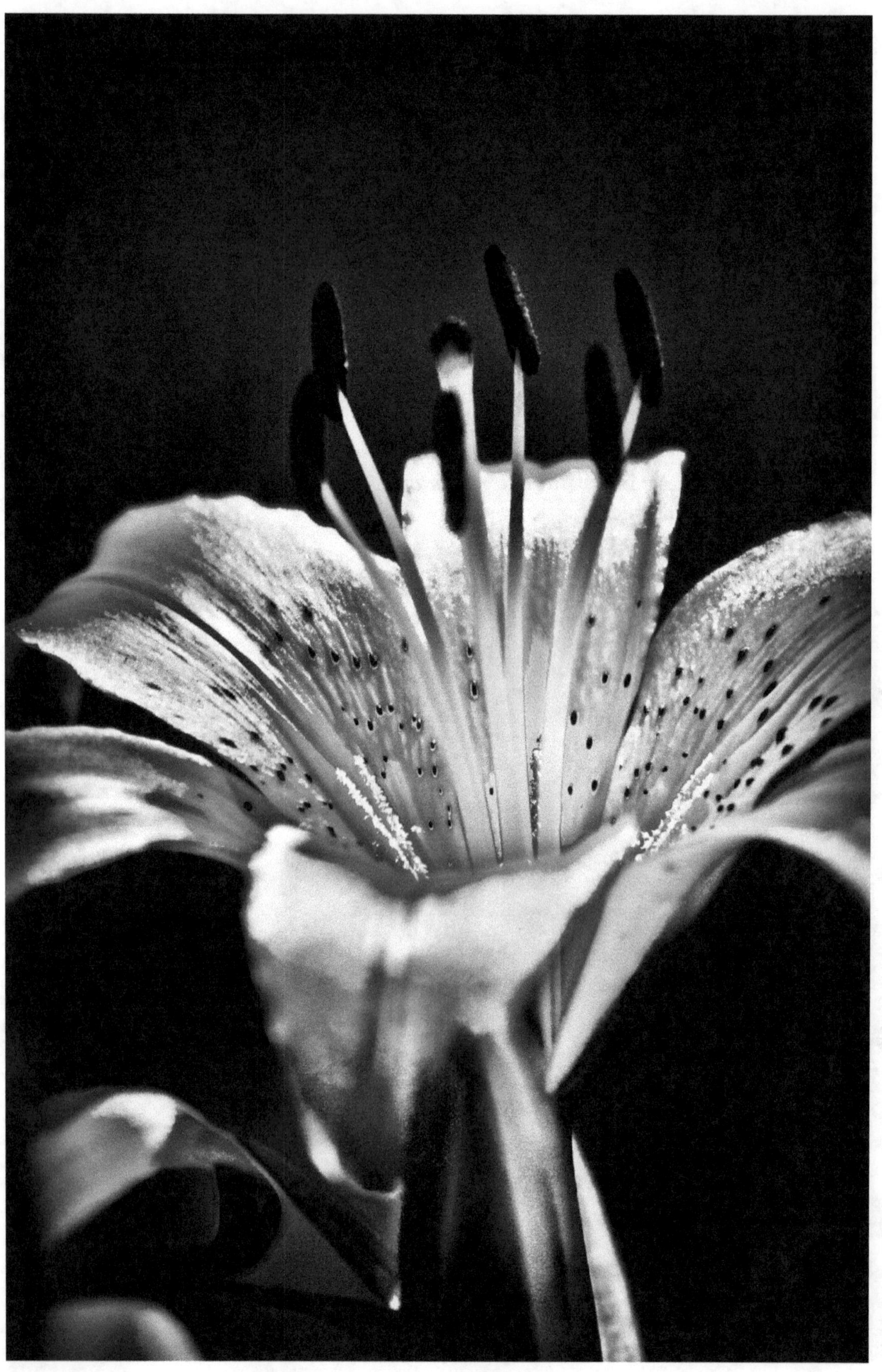

Live My Love

Live My Love
Our dreams come true
You are the one
I always knew

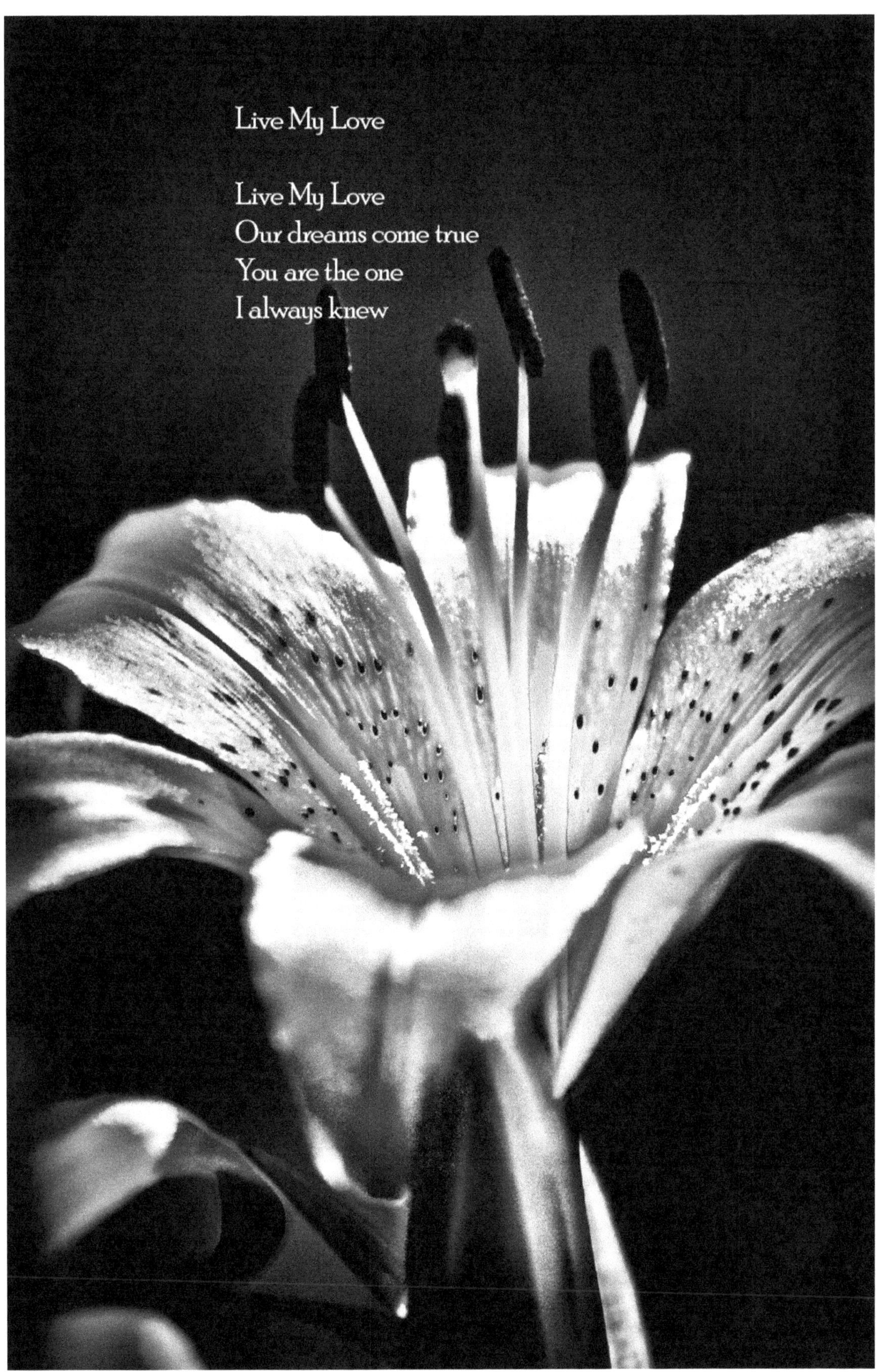

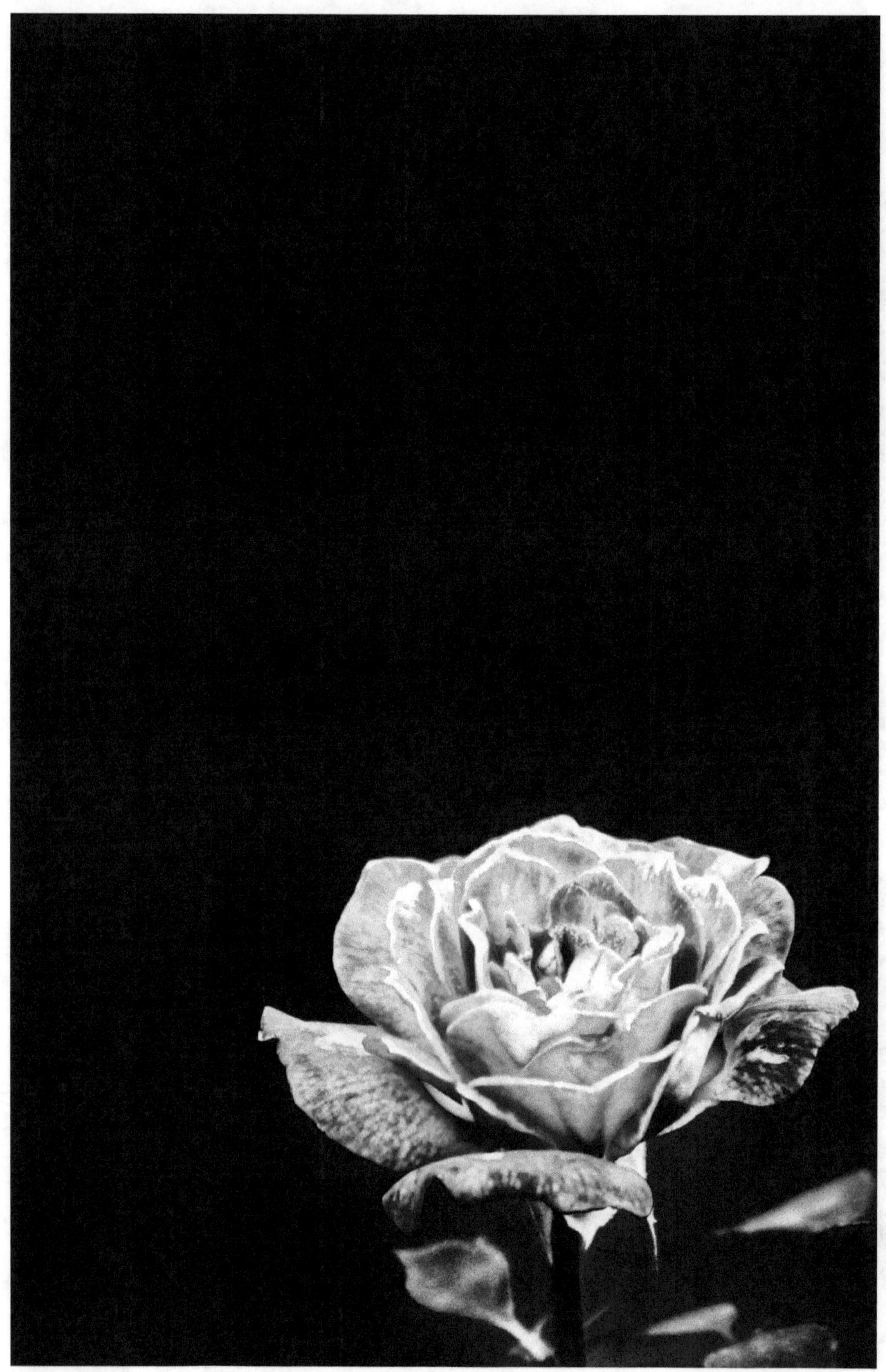

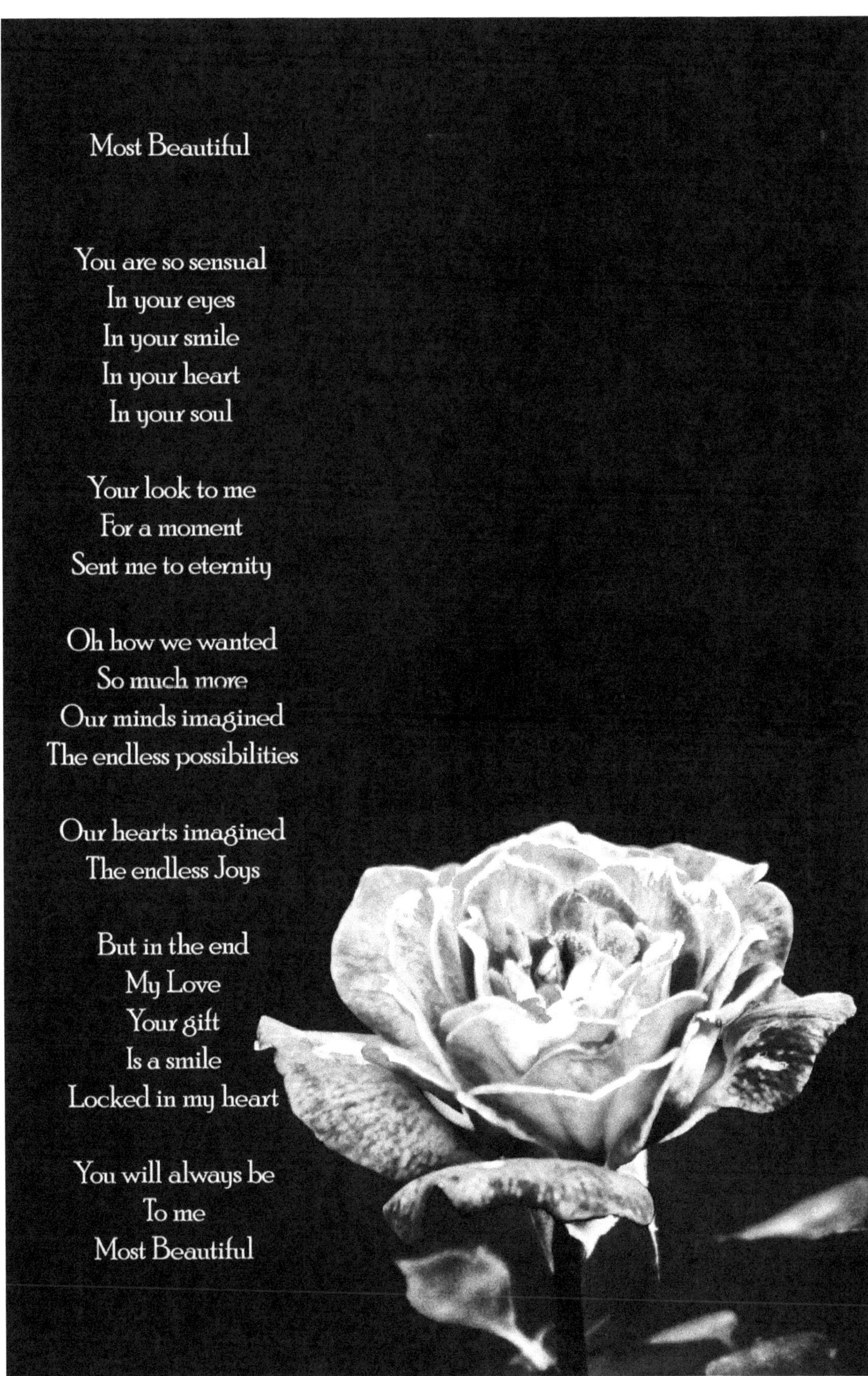

Most Beautiful

You are so sensual
In your eyes
In your smile
In your heart
In your soul

Your look to me
For a moment
Sent me to eternity

Oh how we wanted
So much more
Our minds imagined
The endless possibilities

Our hearts imagined
The endless Joys

But in the end
My Love
Your gift
Is a smile
Locked in my heart

You will always be
To me
Most Beautiful

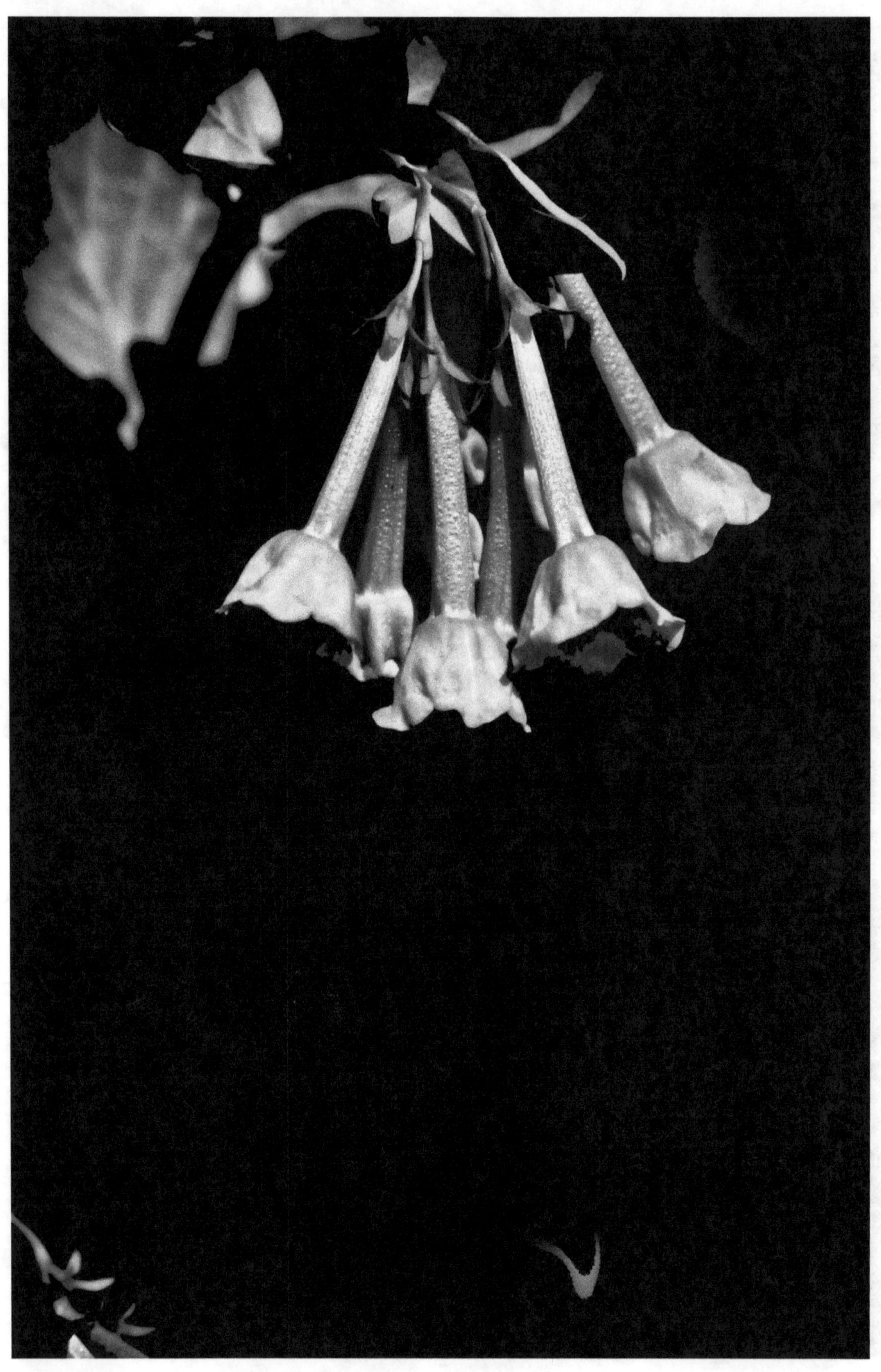

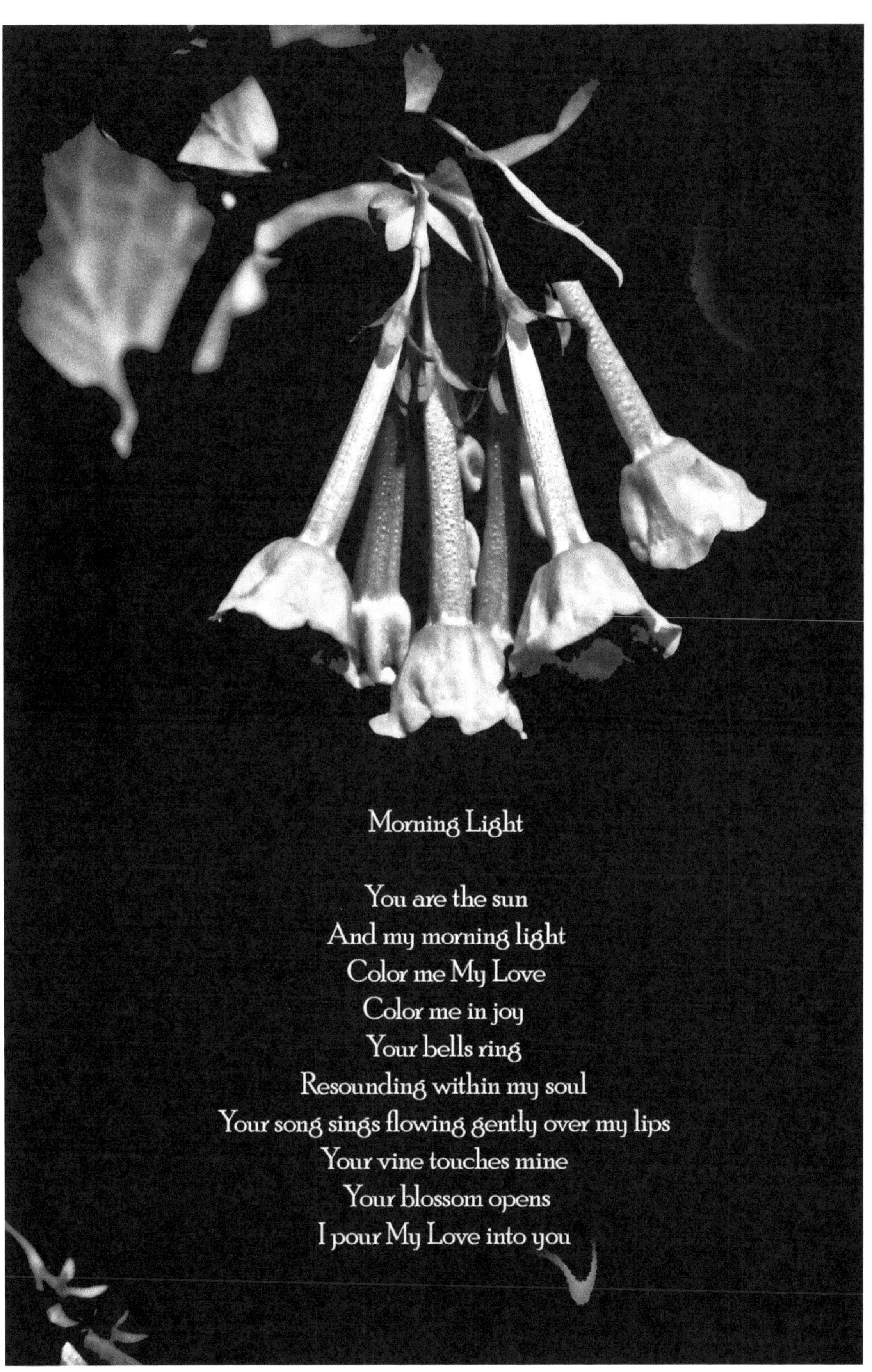

Morning Light

You are the sun
And my morning light
Color me My Love
Color me in joy
Your bells ring
Resounding within my soul
Your song sings flowing gently over my lips
Your vine touches mine
Your blossom opens
I pour My Love into you

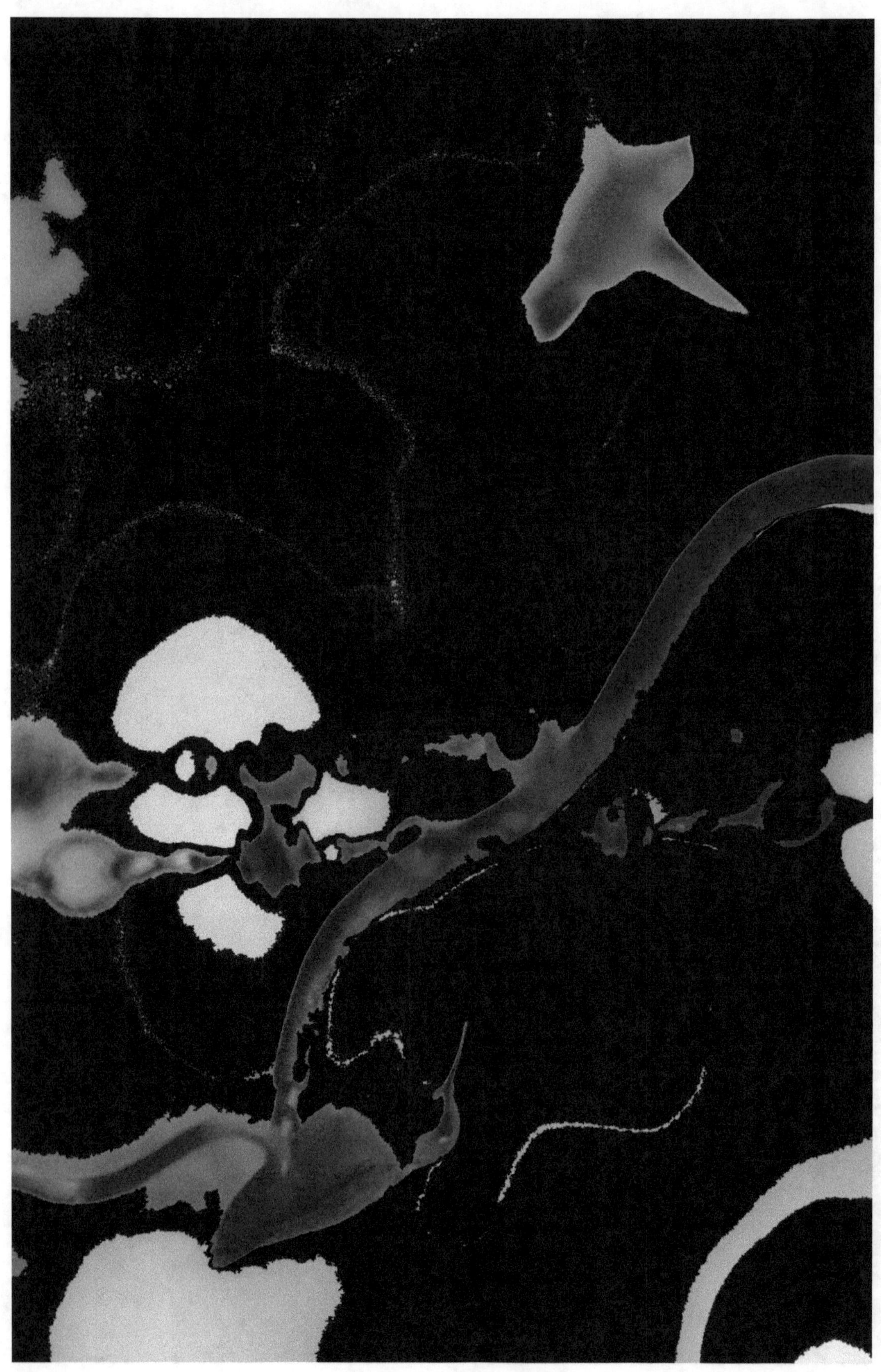

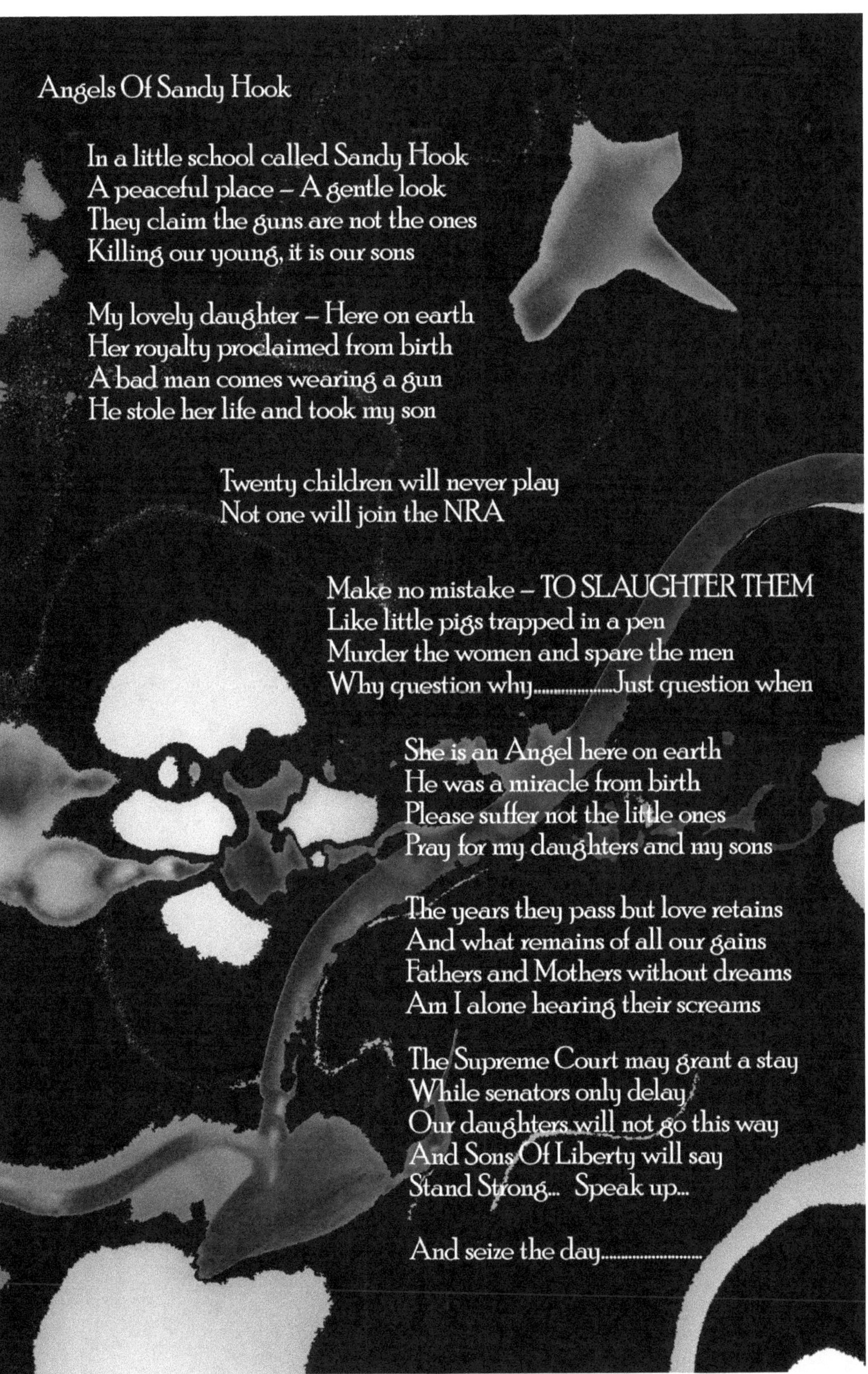

Angels Of Sandy Hook

In a little school called Sandy Hook
A peaceful place – A gentle look
They claim the guns are not the ones
Killing our young, it is our sons

My lovely daughter – Here on earth
Her royalty proclaimed from birth
A bad man comes wearing a gun
He stole her life and took my son

Twenty children will never play
Not one will join the NRA

Make no mistake – TO SLAUGHTER THEM
Like little pigs trapped in a pen
Murder the women and spare the men
Why question why....................Just question when

She is an Angel here on earth
He was a miracle from birth
Please suffer not the little ones
Pray for my daughters and my sons

The years they pass but love retains
And what remains of all our gains
Fathers and Mothers without dreams
Am I alone hearing their screams

The Supreme Court may grant a stay
While senators only delay
Our daughters will not go this way
And Sons Of Liberty will say
Stand Strong... Speak up...

And seize the day.........................

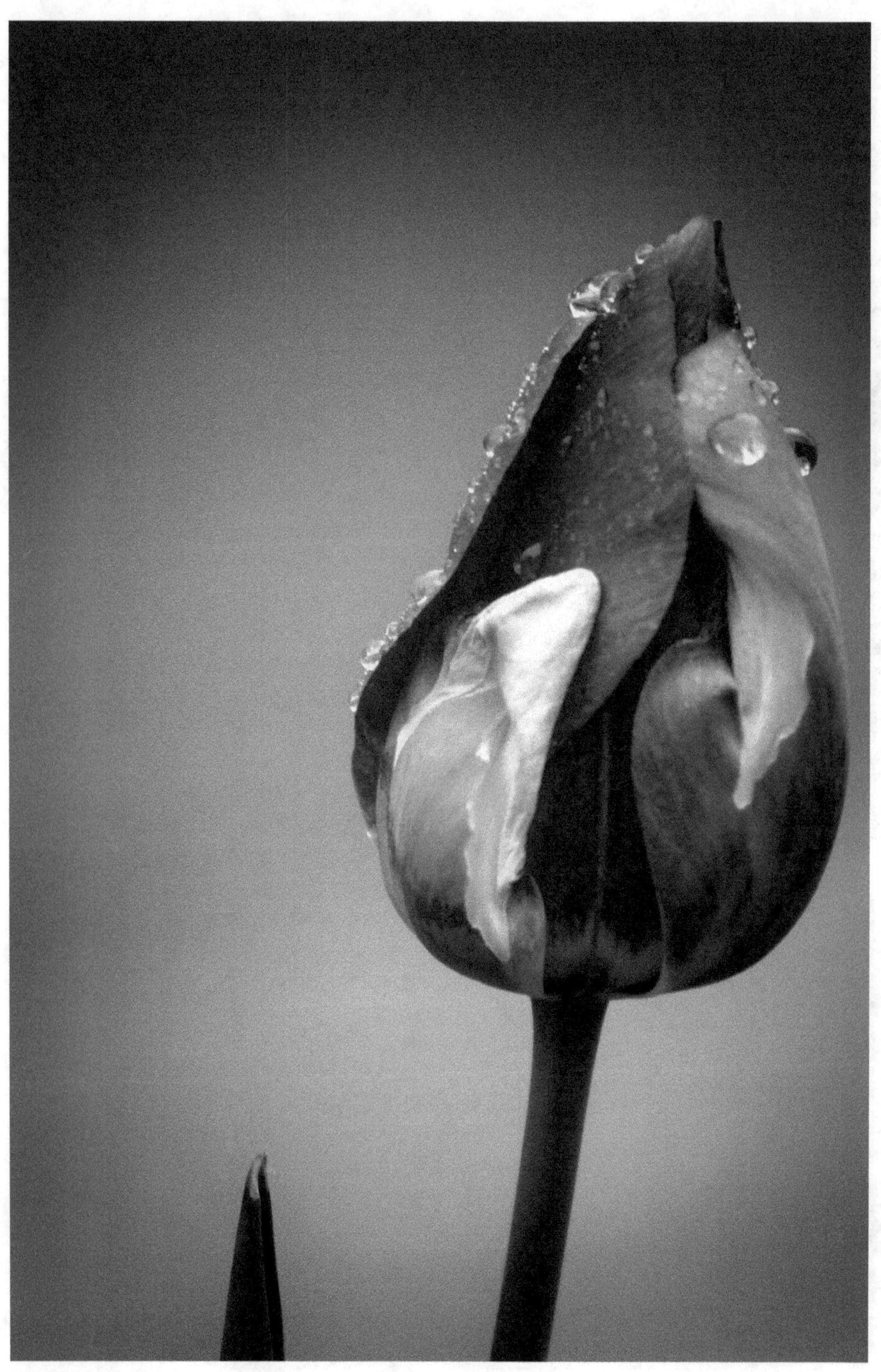

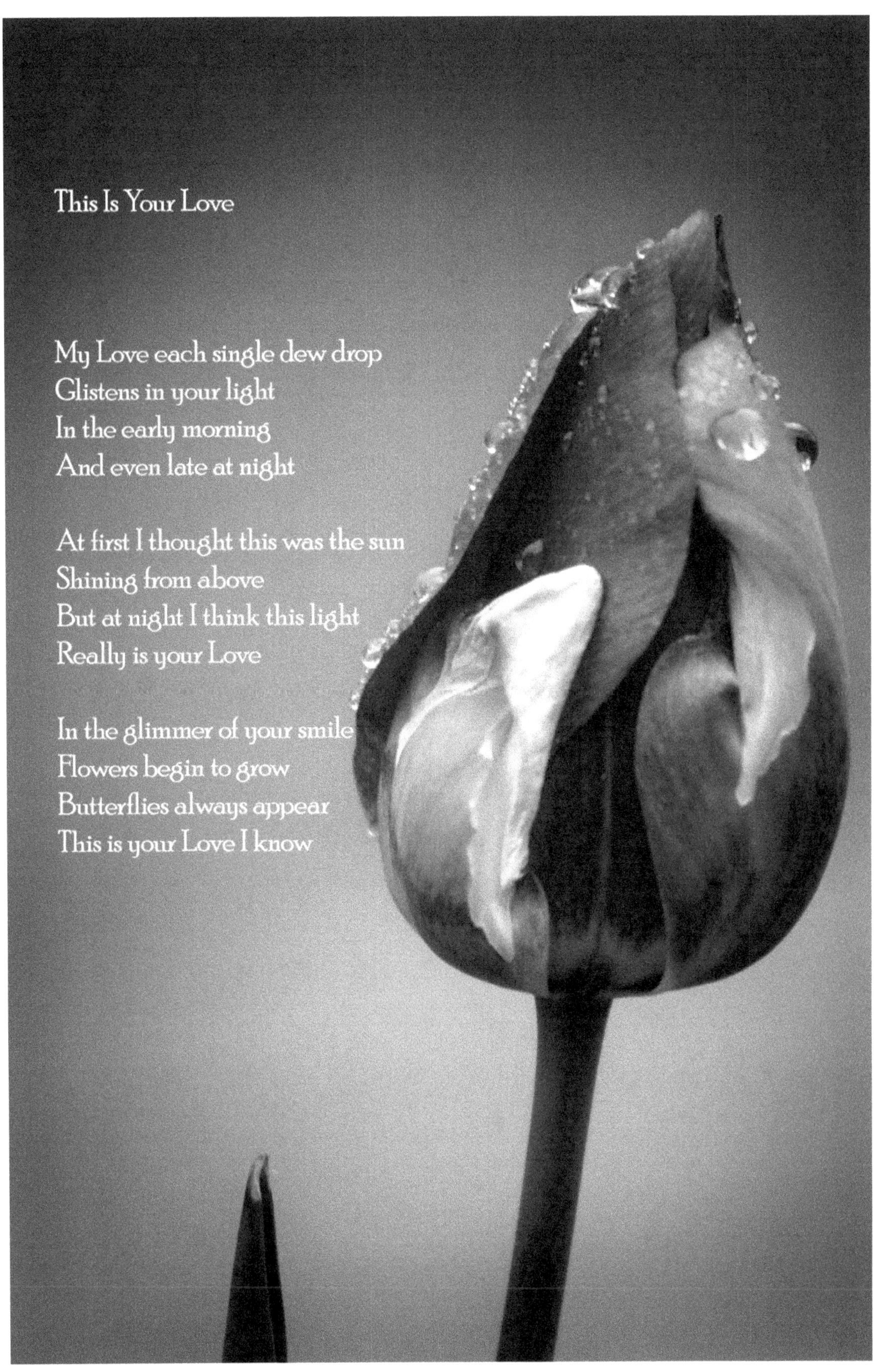
This Is Your Love

My Love each single dew drop
Glistens in your light
In the early morning
And even late at night

At first I thought this was the sun
Shining from above
But at night I think this light
Really is your Love

In the glimmer of your smile
Flowers begin to grow
Butterflies always appear
This is your Love I know

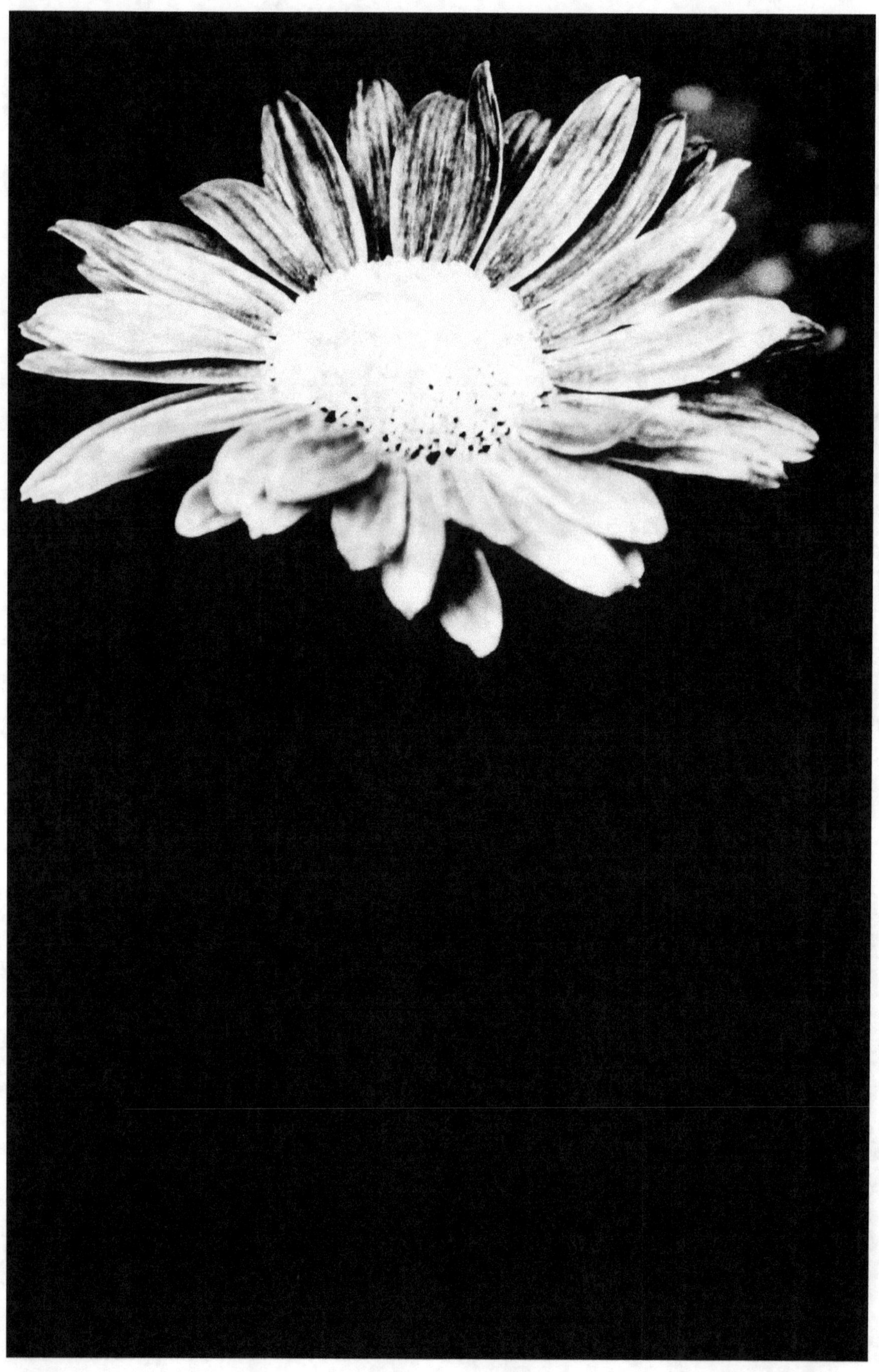

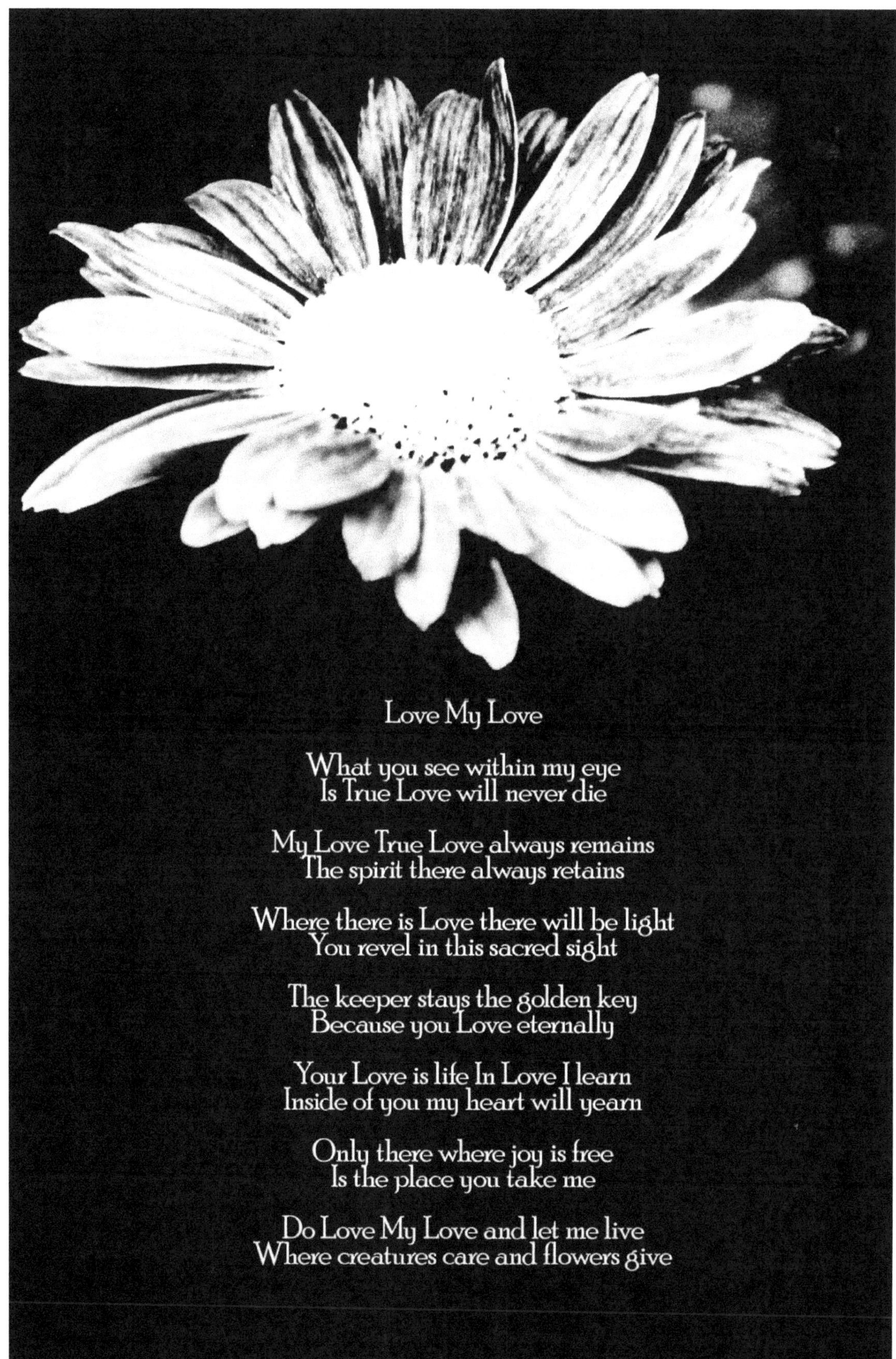
Love My Love

What you see within my eye
Is True Love will never die

My Love True Love always remains
The spirit there always retains

Where there is Love there will be light
You revel in this sacred sight

The keeper stays the golden key
Because you Love eternally

Your Love is life In Love I learn
Inside of you my heart will yearn

Only there where joy is free
Is the place you take me

Do Love My Love and let me live
Where creatures care and flowers give

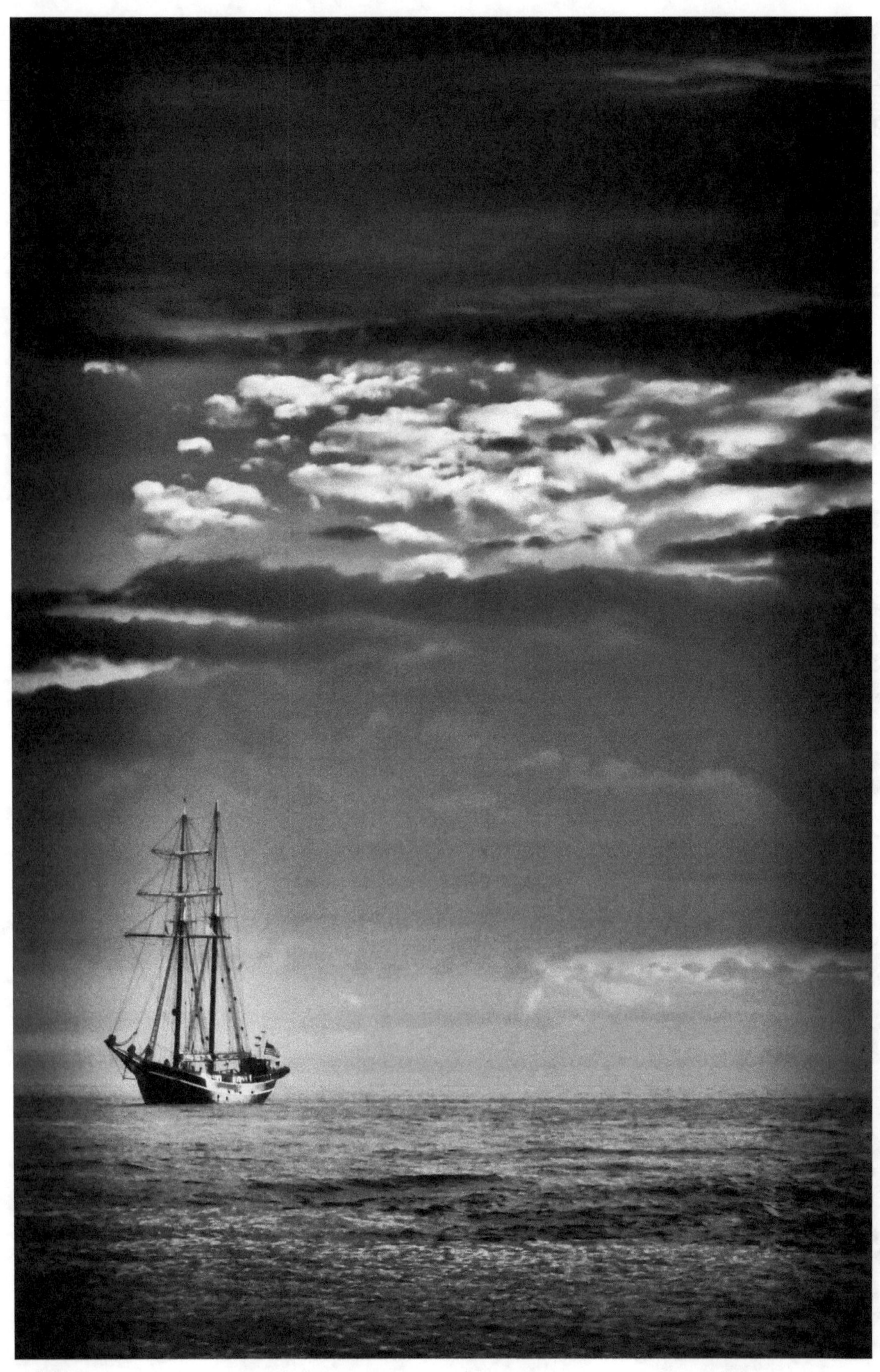

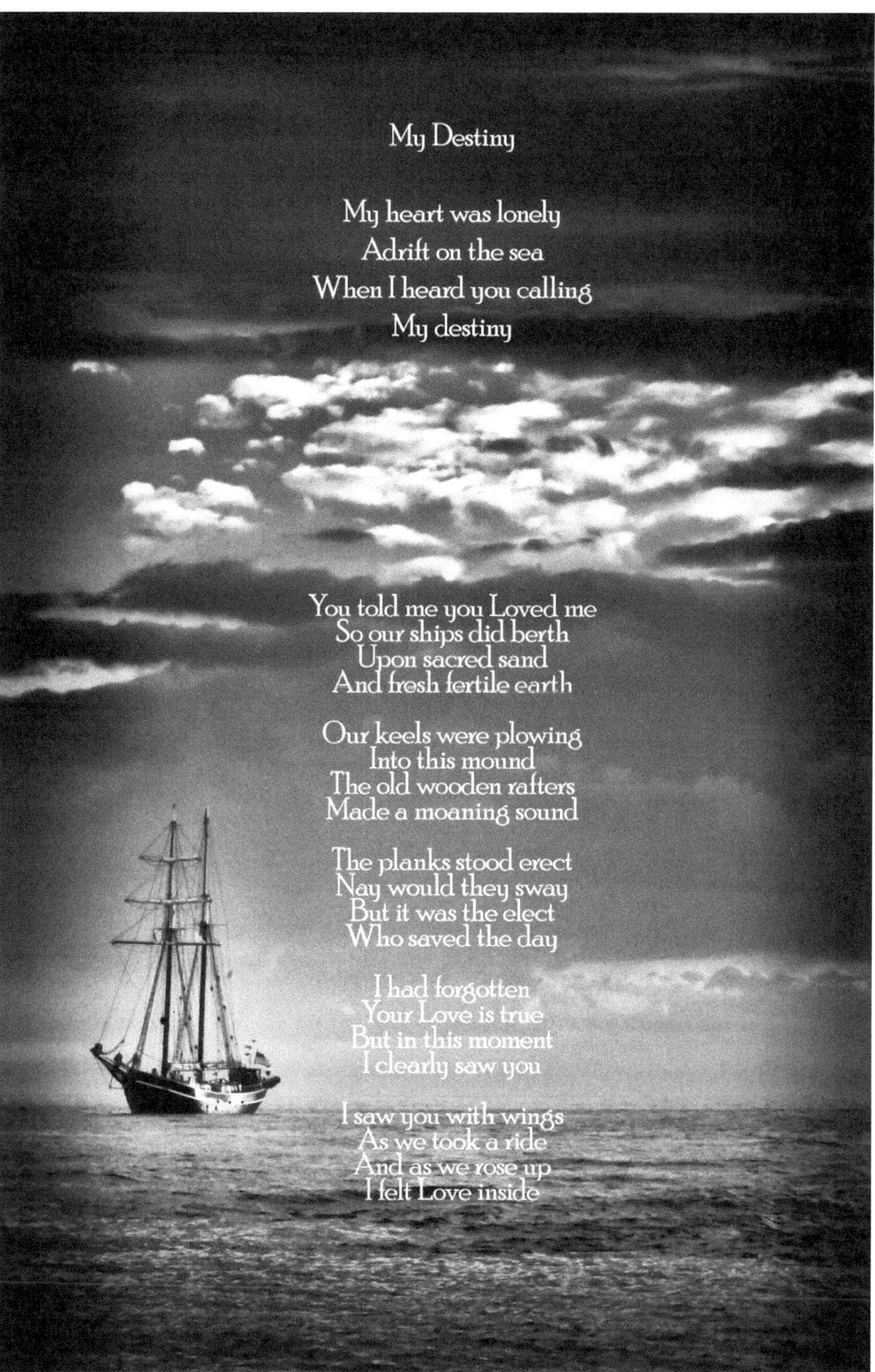

My Destiny

My heart was lonely
Adrift on the sea
When I heard you calling
My destiny

You told me you Loved me
So our ships did berth
Upon sacred sand
And fresh fertile earth

Our keels were plowing
Into this mound
The old wooden rafters
Made a moaning sound

The planks stood erect
Nay would they sway
But it was the elect
Who saved the day

I had forgotten
Your Love is true
But in this moment
I clearly saw you

I saw you with wings
As we took a ride
And as we rose up
I felt Love inside

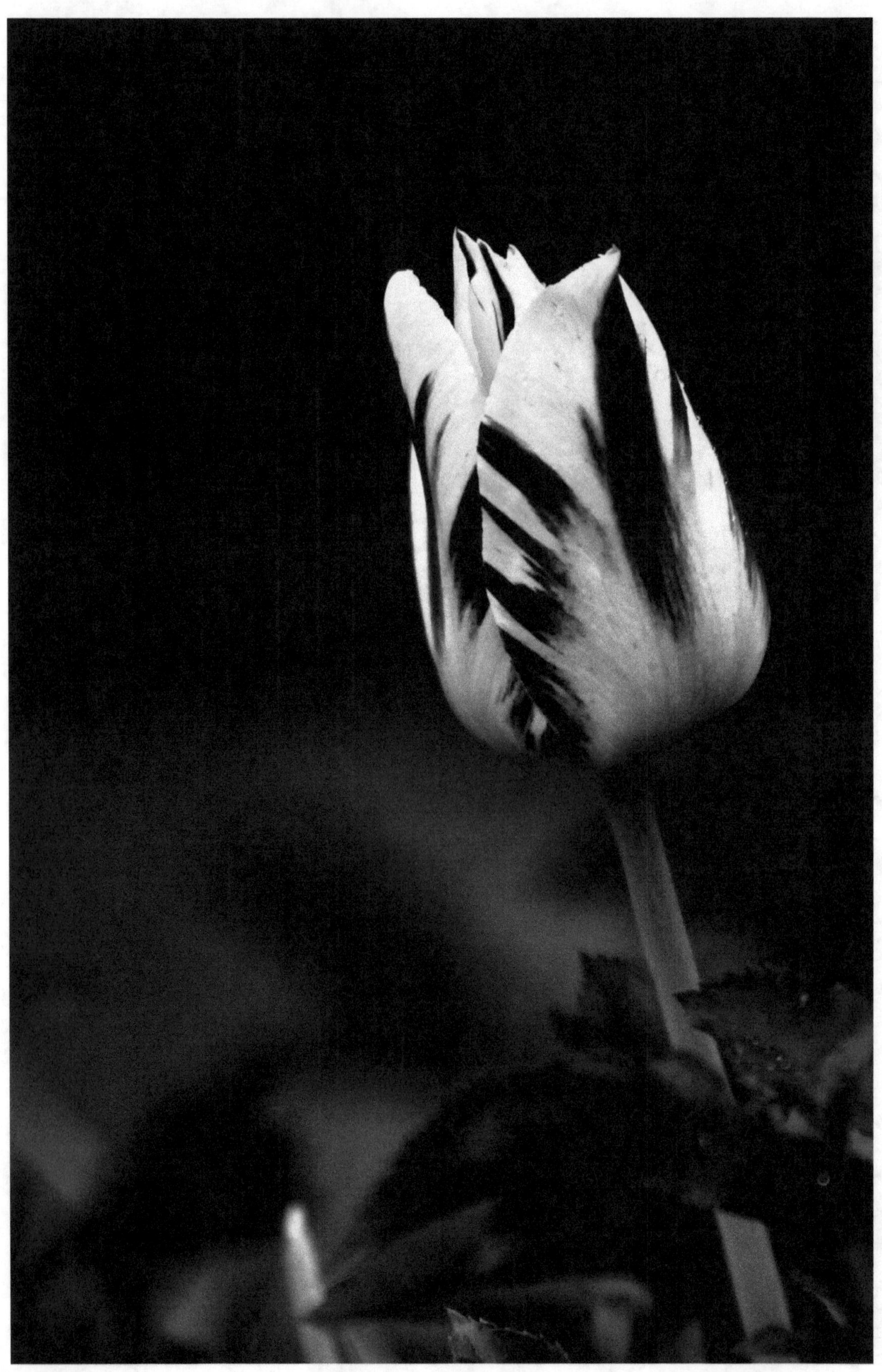

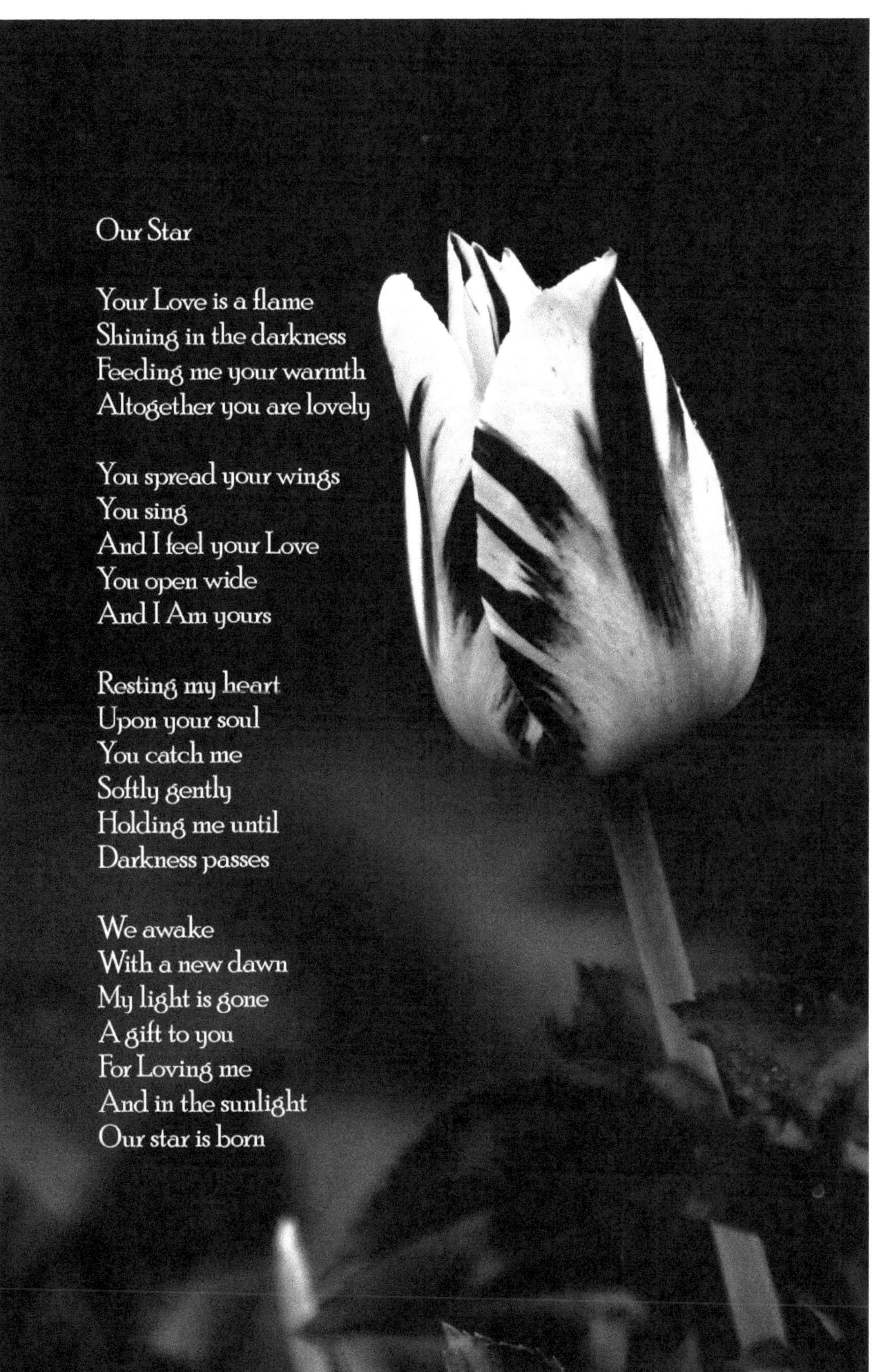
Our Star

Your Love is a flame
Shining in the darkness
Feeding me your warmth
Altogether you are lovely

You spread your wings
You sing
And I feel your Love
You open wide
And I Am yours

Resting my heart
Upon your soul
You catch me
Softly gently
Holding me until
Darkness passes

We awake
With a new dawn
My light is gone
A gift to you
For Loving me
And in the sunlight
Our star is born

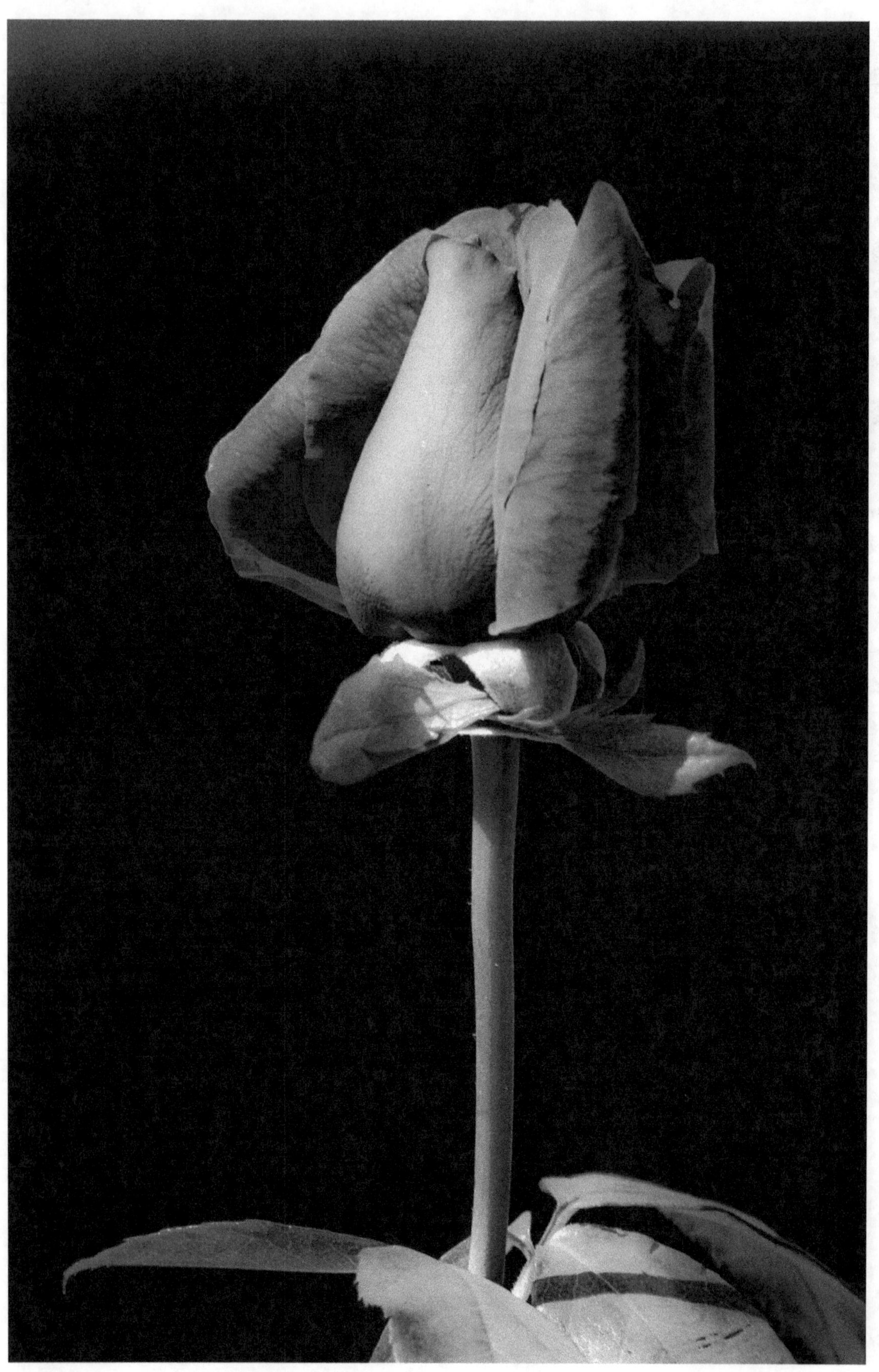

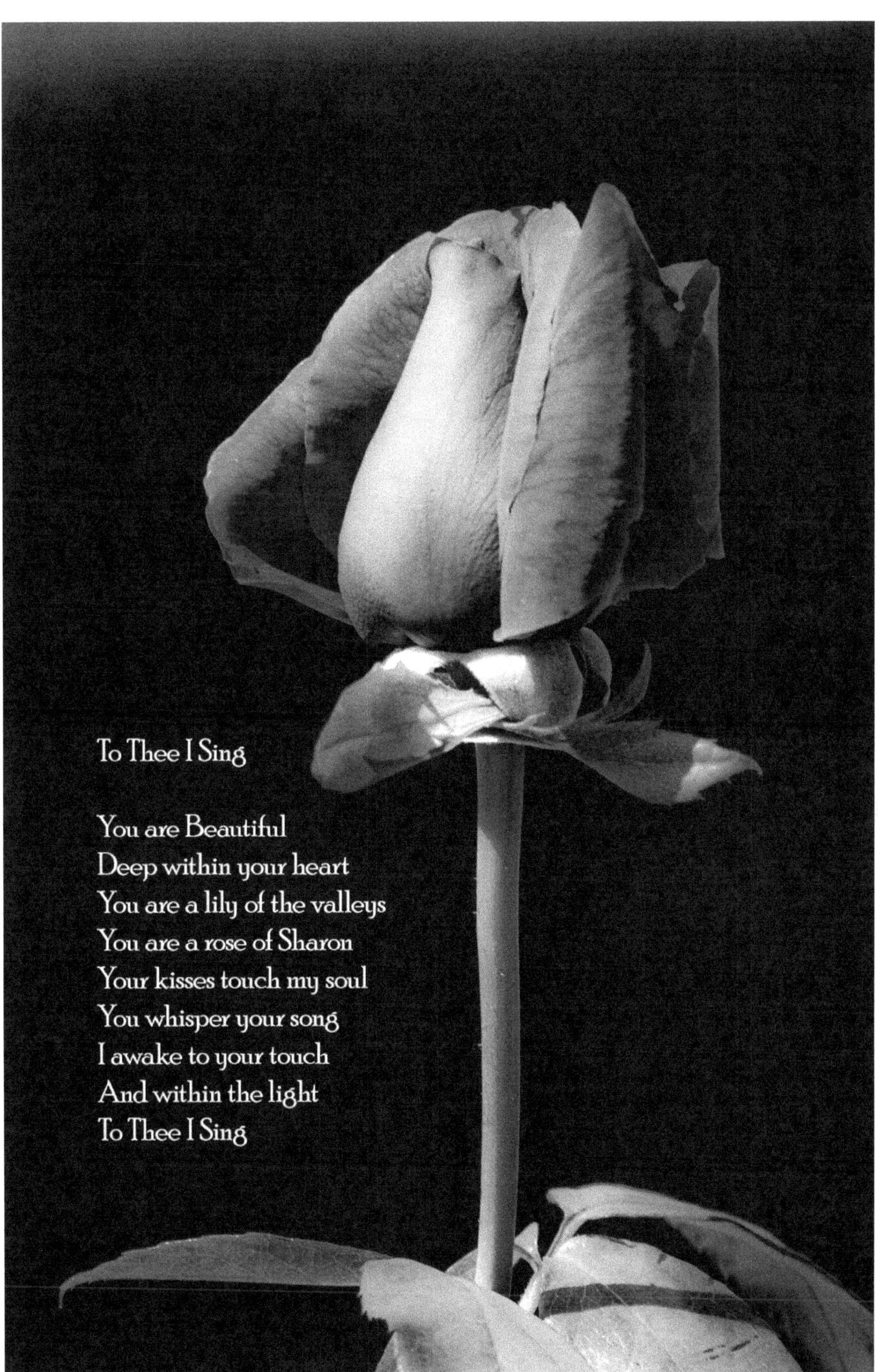

To Thee I Sing

You are Beautiful
Deep within your heart
You are a lily of the valleys
You are a rose of Sharon
Your kisses touch my soul
You whisper your song
I awake to your touch
And within the light
To Thee I Sing

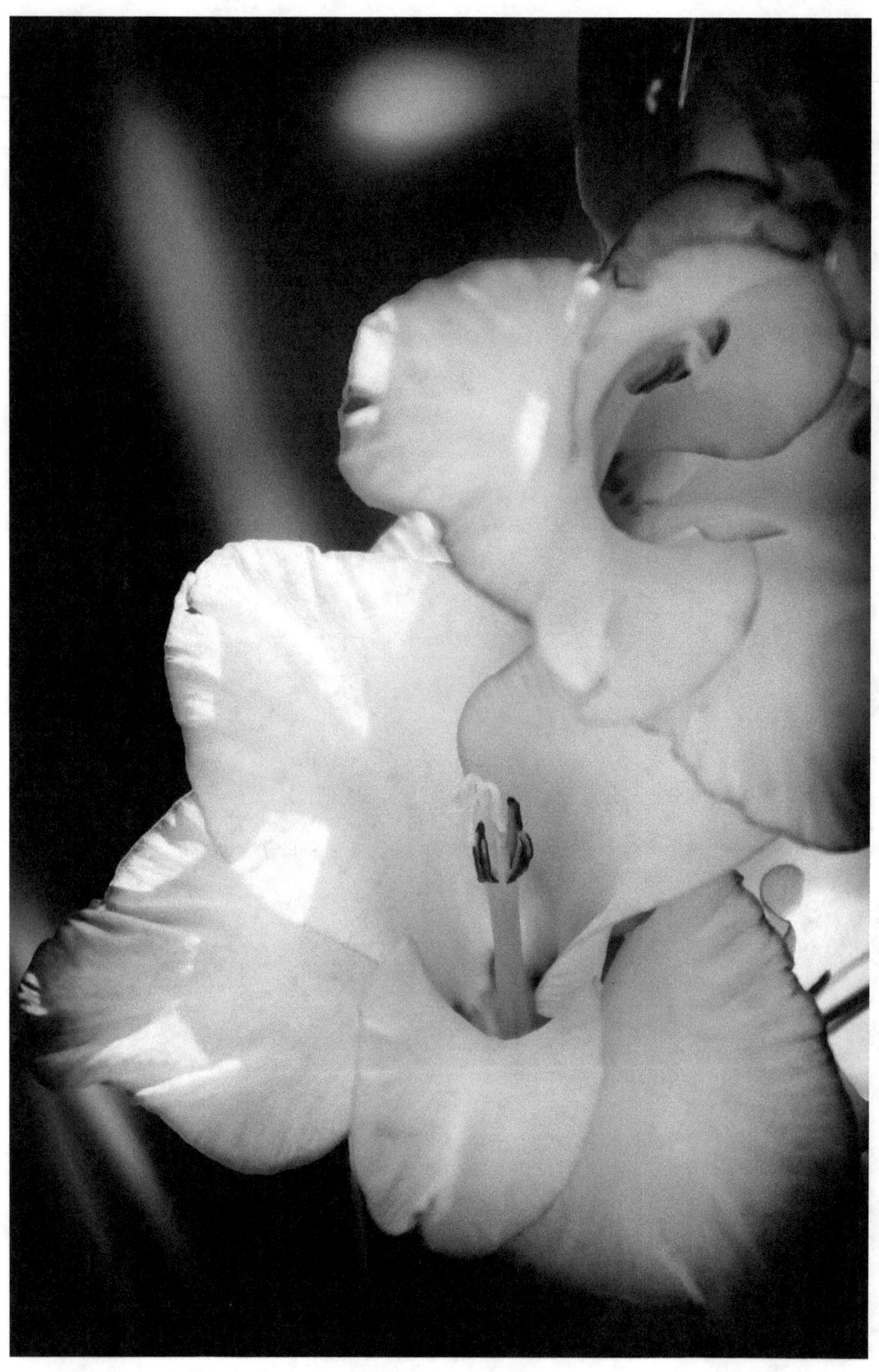

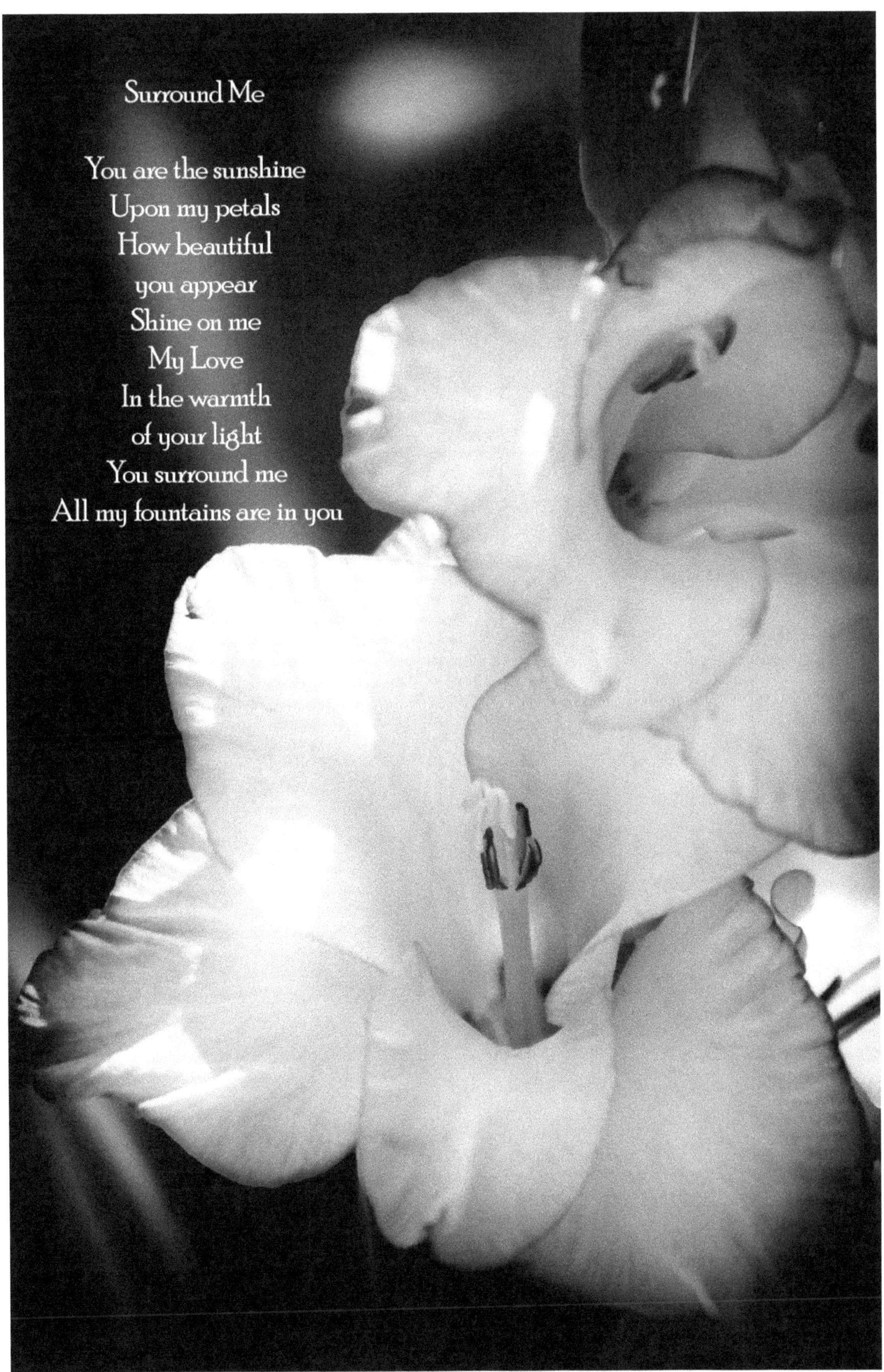
Surround Me

You are the sunshine
Upon my petals
How beautiful
you appear
Shine on me
My Love
In the warmth
of your light
You surround me
All my fountains are in you

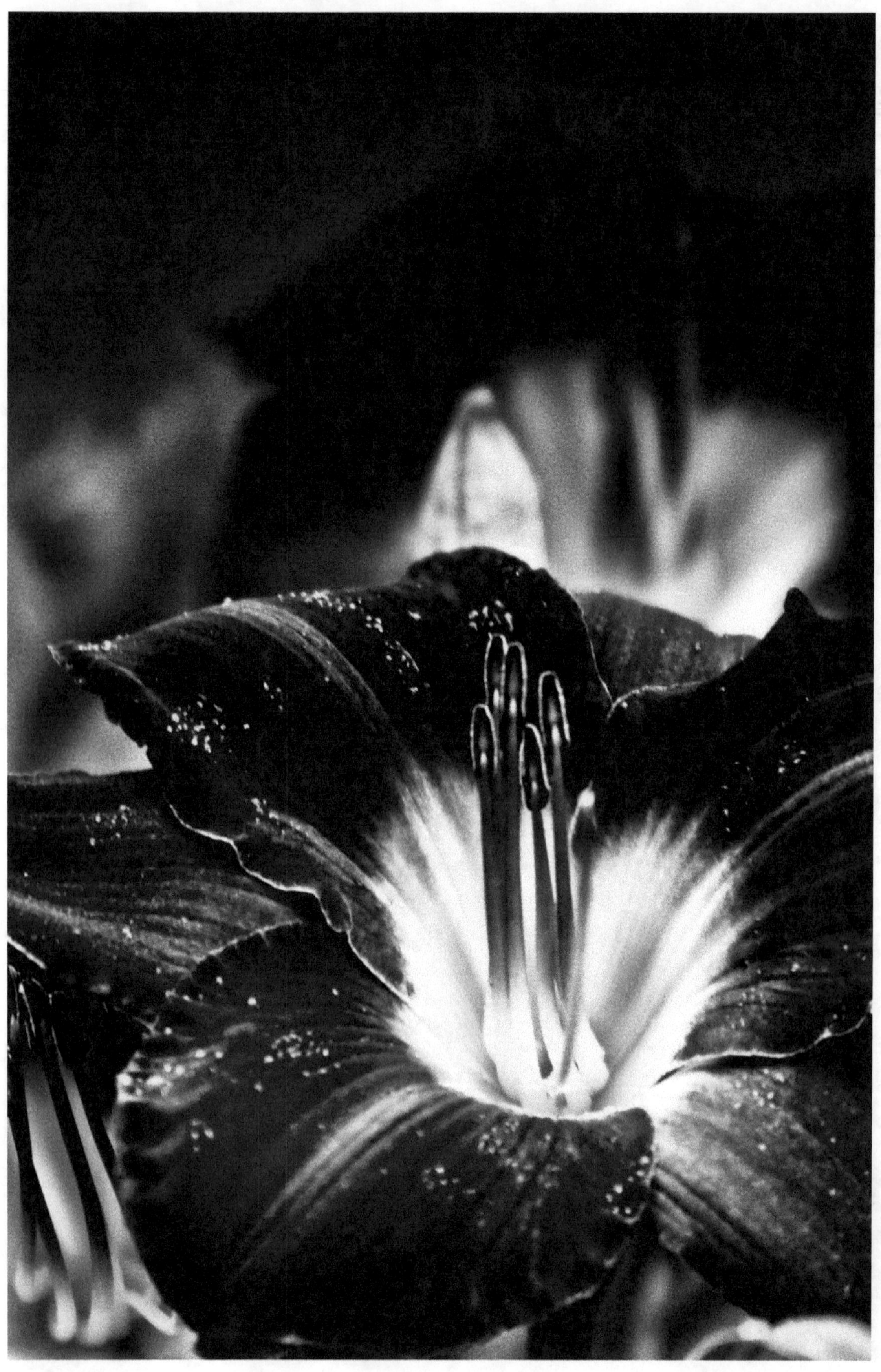

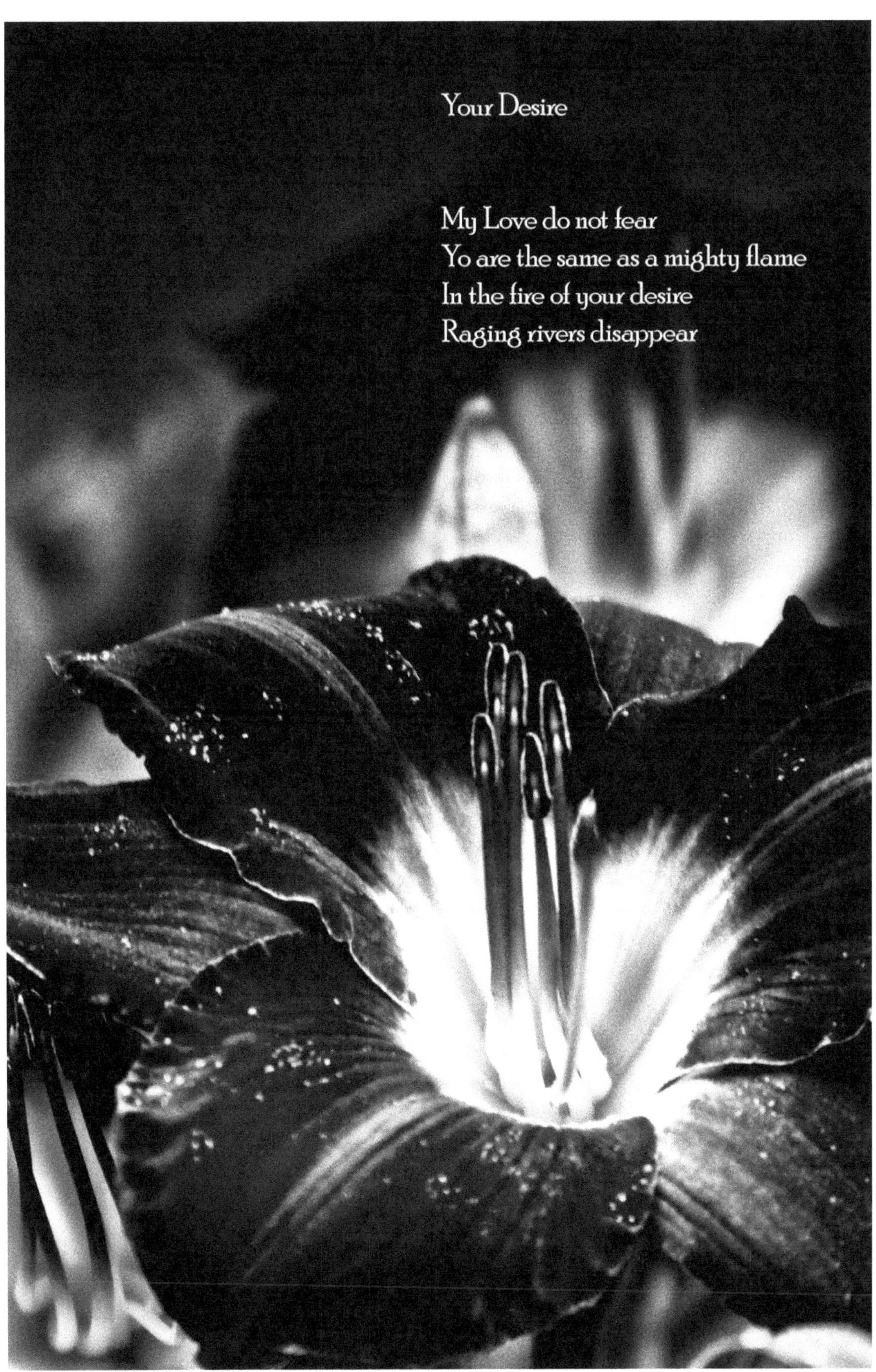
Your Desire
My Love do not fear
Yo are the same as a mighty flame
In the fire of your desire
Raging rivers disappear

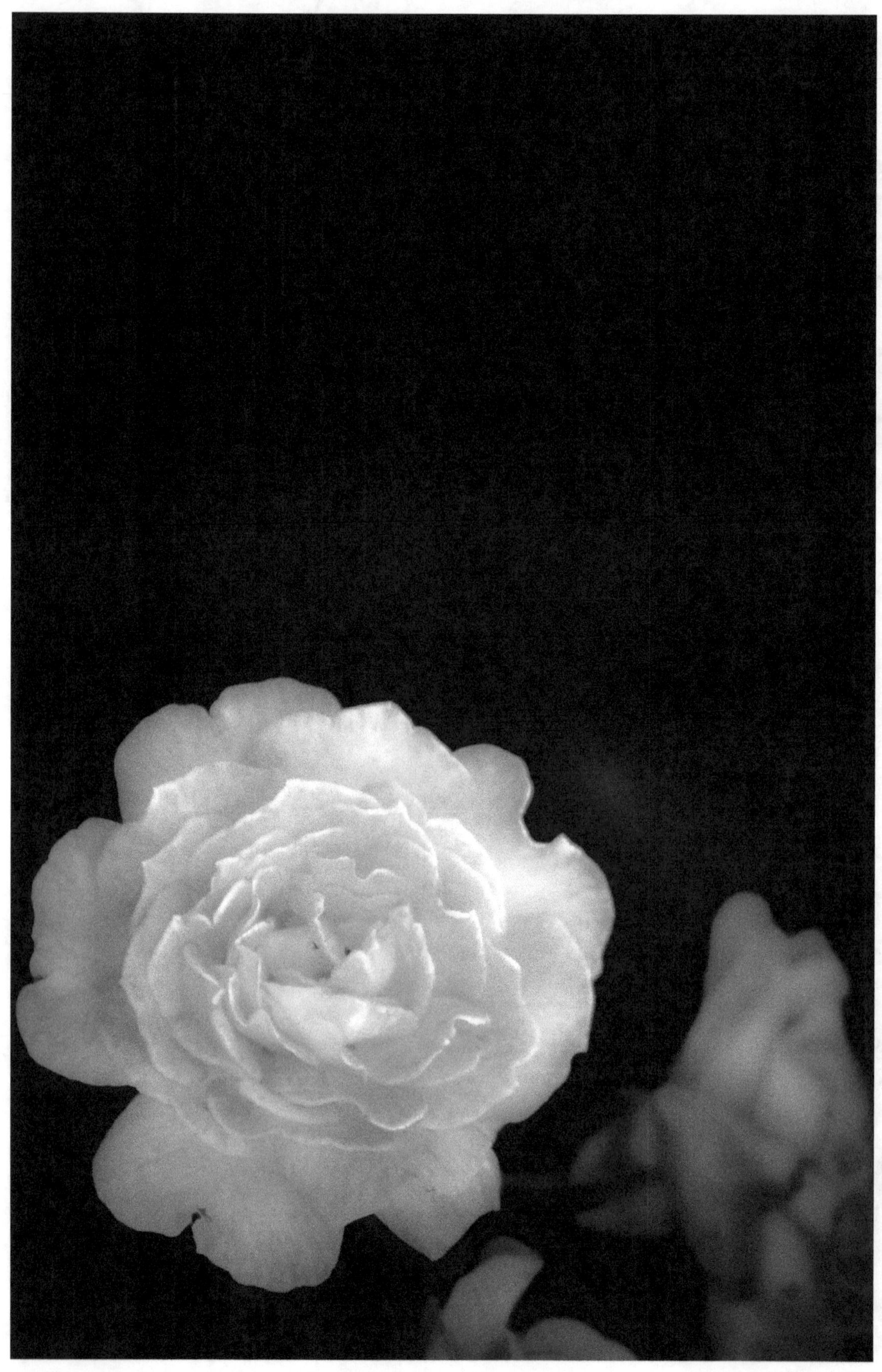

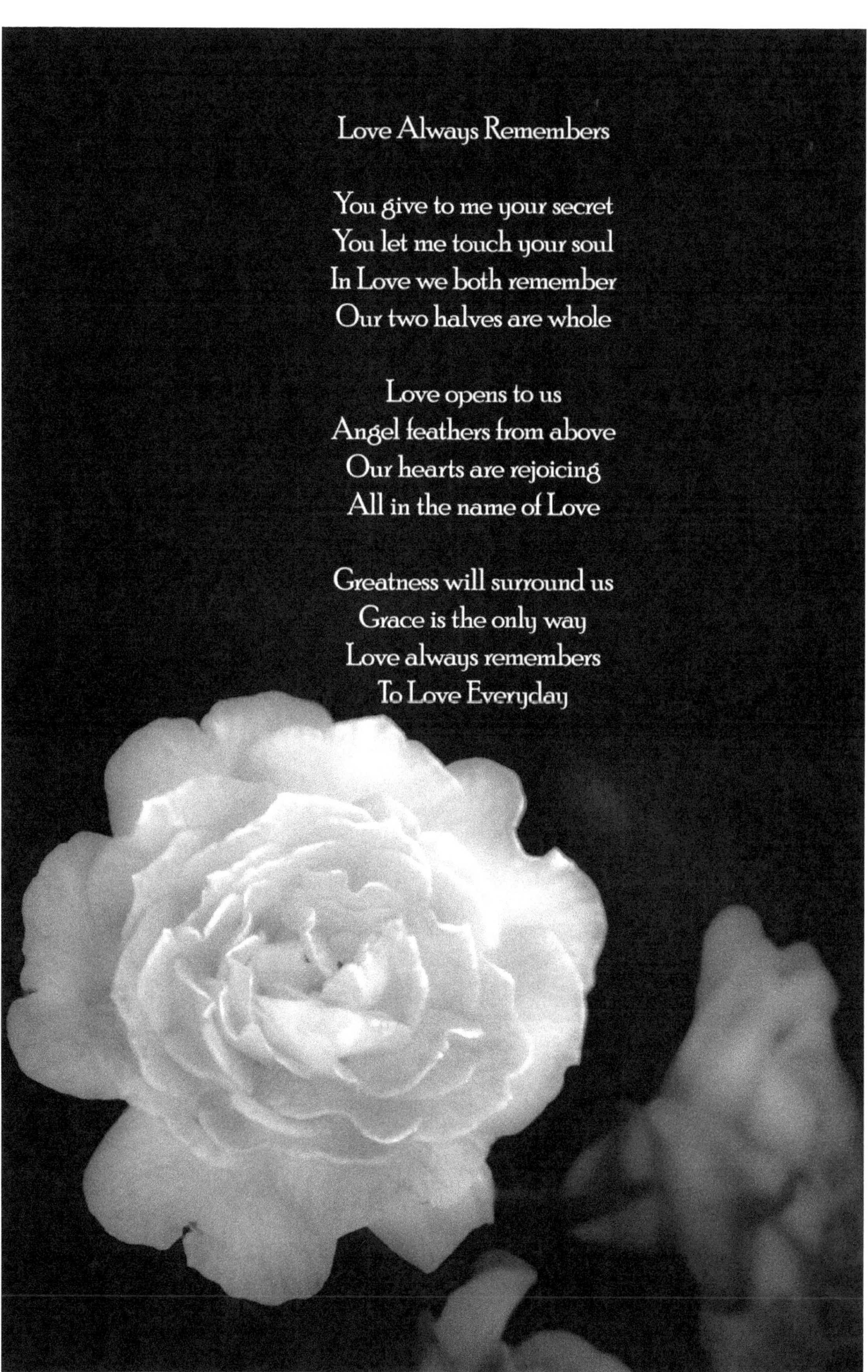

Love Always Remembers

You give to me your secret
You let me touch your soul
In Love we both remember
Our two halves are whole

Love opens to us
Angel feathers from above
Our hearts are rejoicing
All in the name of Love

Greatness will surround us
Grace is the only way
Love always remembers
To Love Everyday

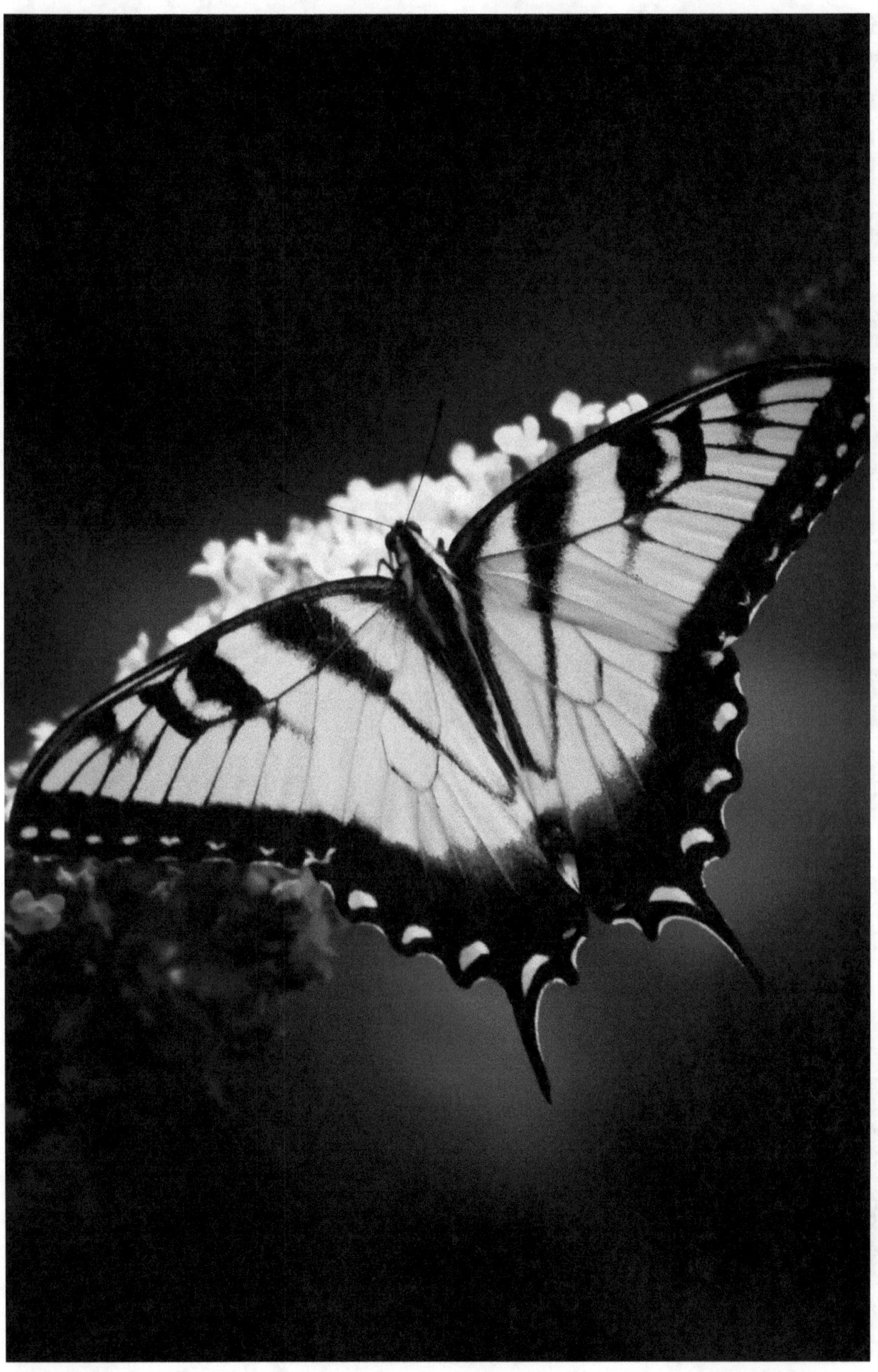

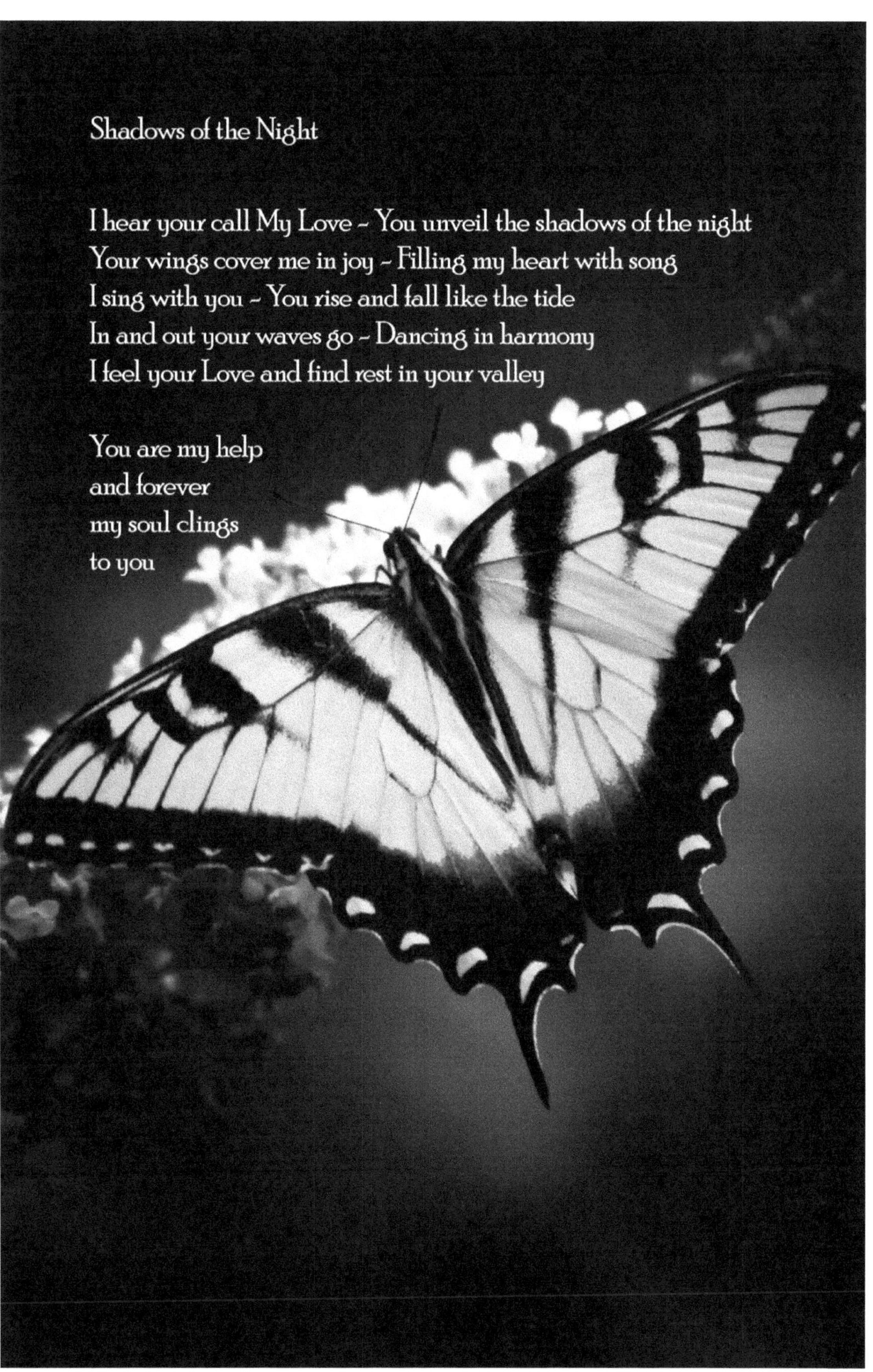

Shadows of the Night

I hear your call My Love ~ You unveil the shadows of the night
Your wings cover me in joy ~ Filling my heart with song
I sing with you ~ You rise and fall like the tide
In and out your waves go ~ Dancing in harmony
I feel your Love and find rest in your valley

You are my help
and forever
my soul clings
to you

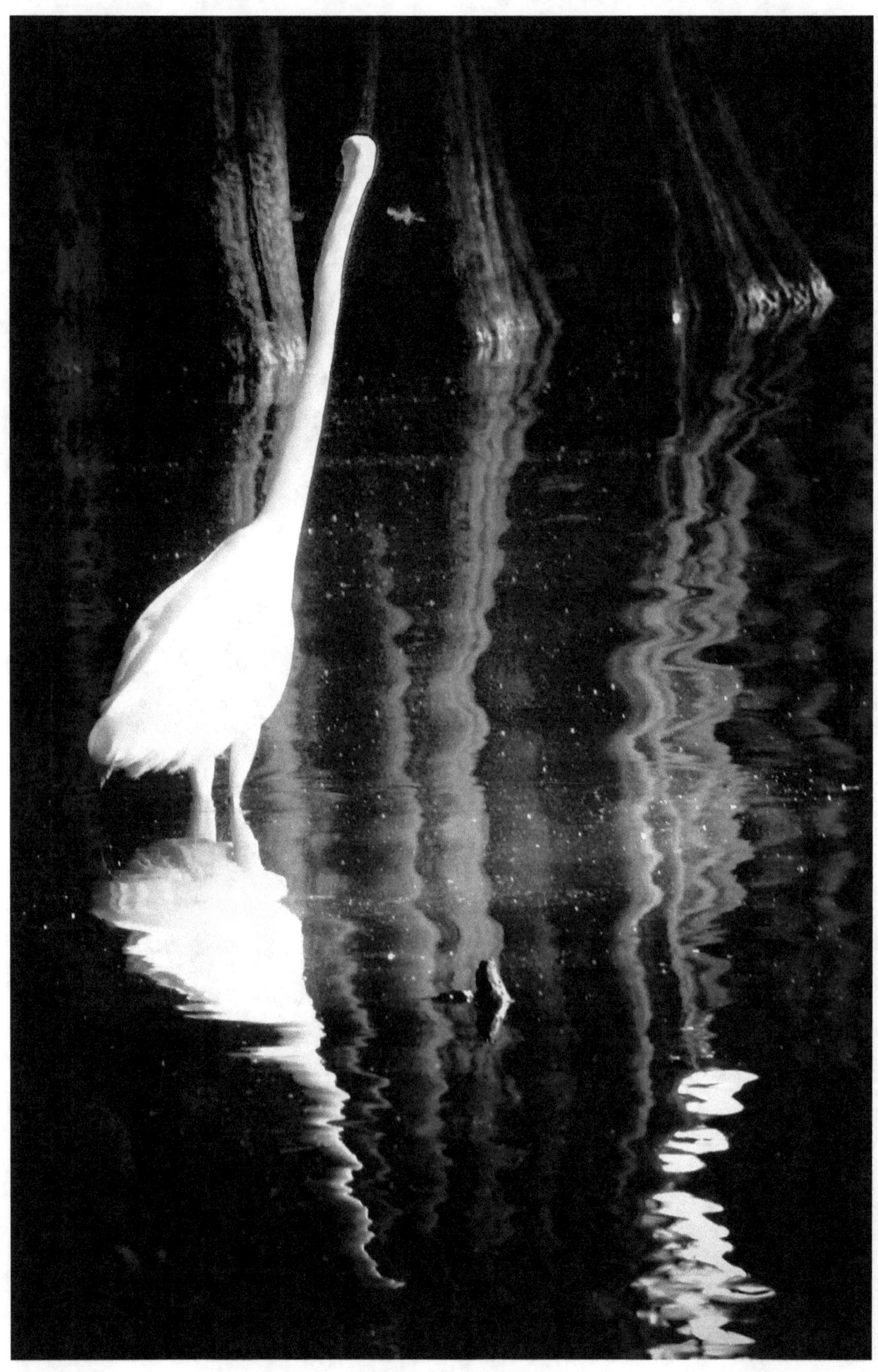

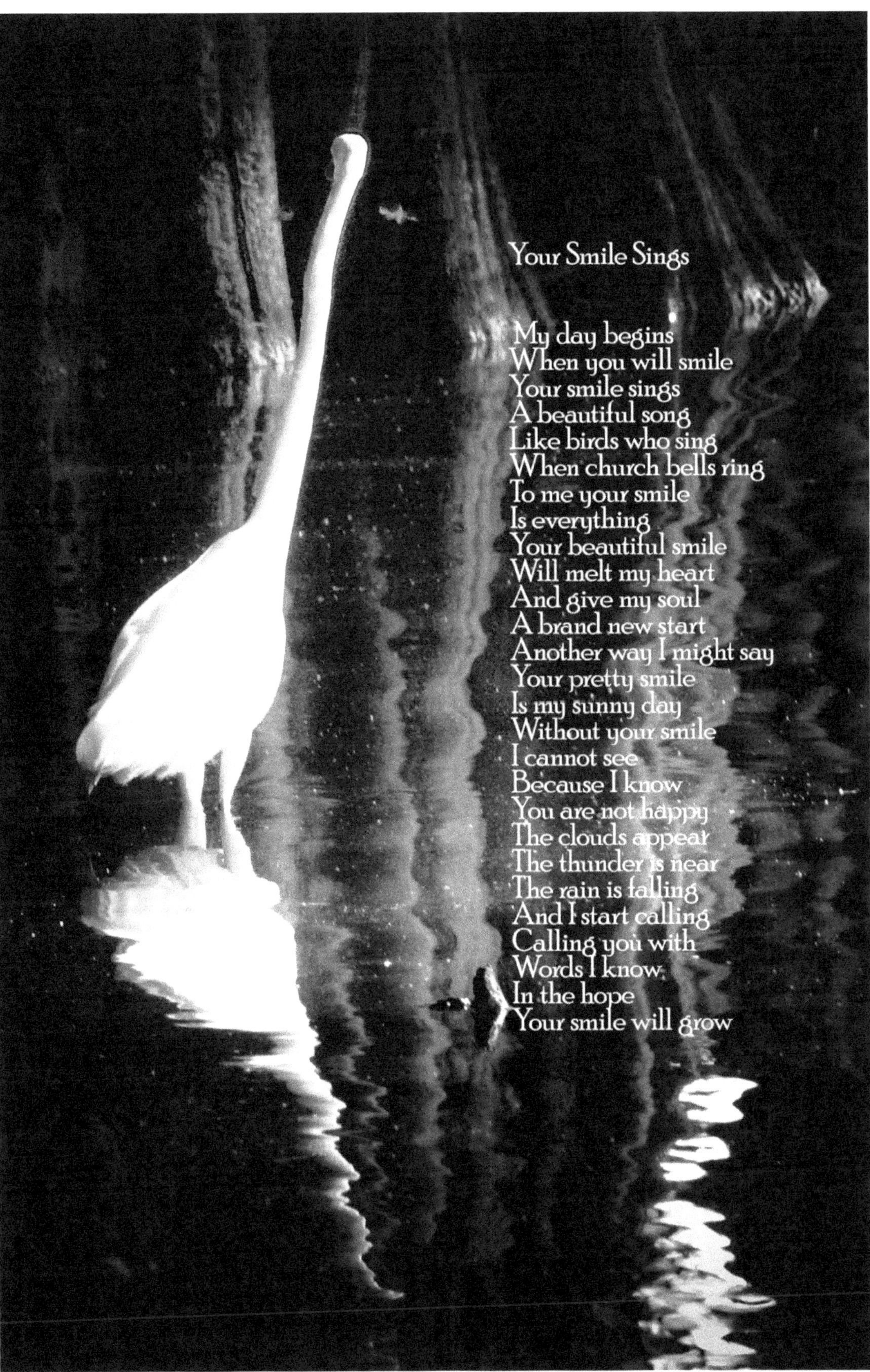

Your Smile Sings

My day begins
When you will smile
Your smile sings
A beautiful song
Like birds who sing
When church bells ring
To me your smile
Is everything
Your beautiful smile
Will melt my heart
And give my soul
A brand new start
Another way I might say
Your pretty smile
Is my sunny day
Without your smile
I cannot see
Because I know
You are not happy
The clouds appear
The thunder is near
The rain is falling
And I start calling
Calling you with
Words I know
In the hope
Your smile will grow

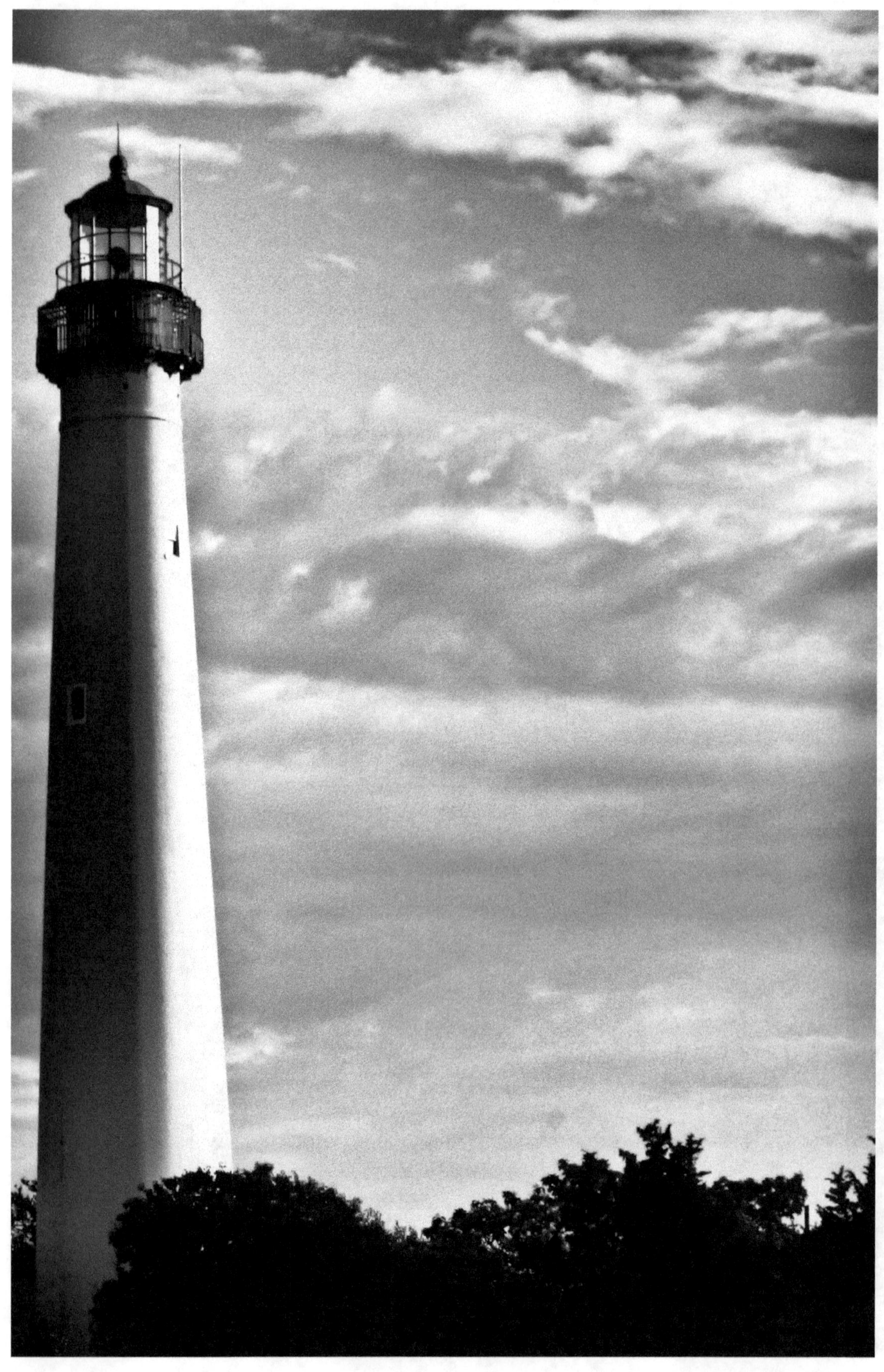

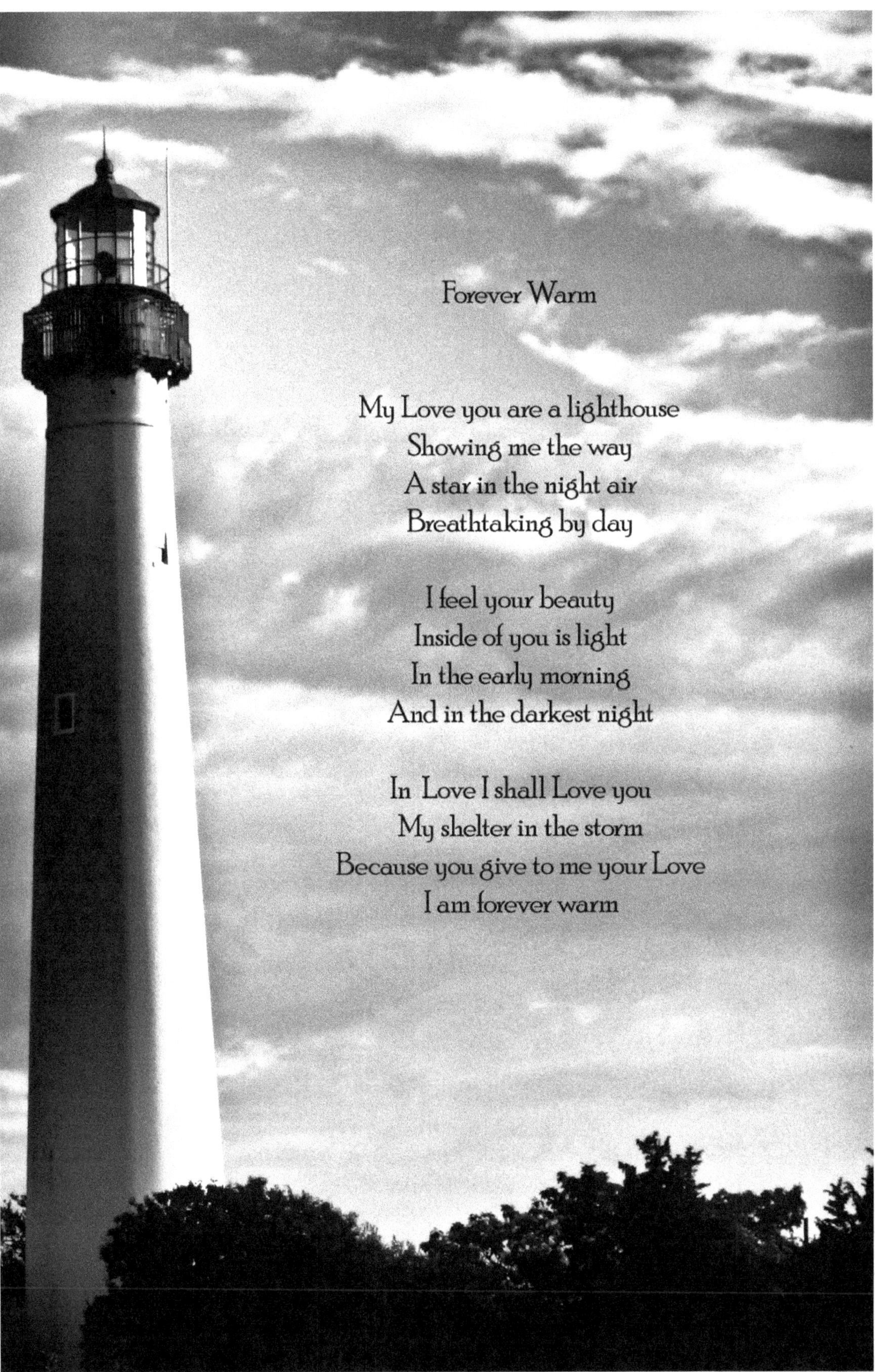

Forever Warm

My Love you are a lighthouse
Showing me the way
A star in the night air
Breathtaking by day

I feel your beauty
Inside of you is light
In the early morning
And in the darkest night

In Love I shall Love you
My shelter in the storm
Because you give to me your Love
I am forever warm

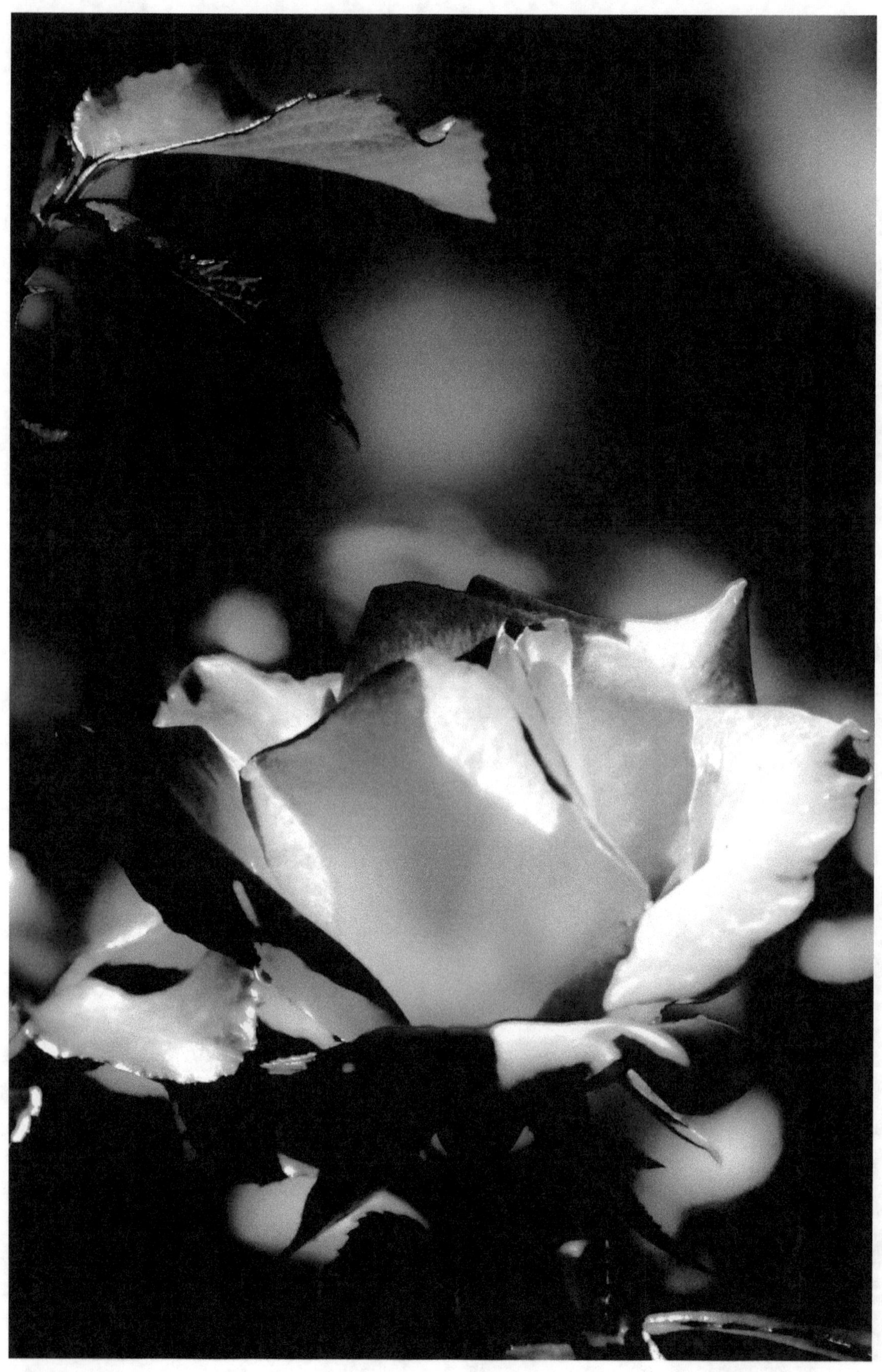

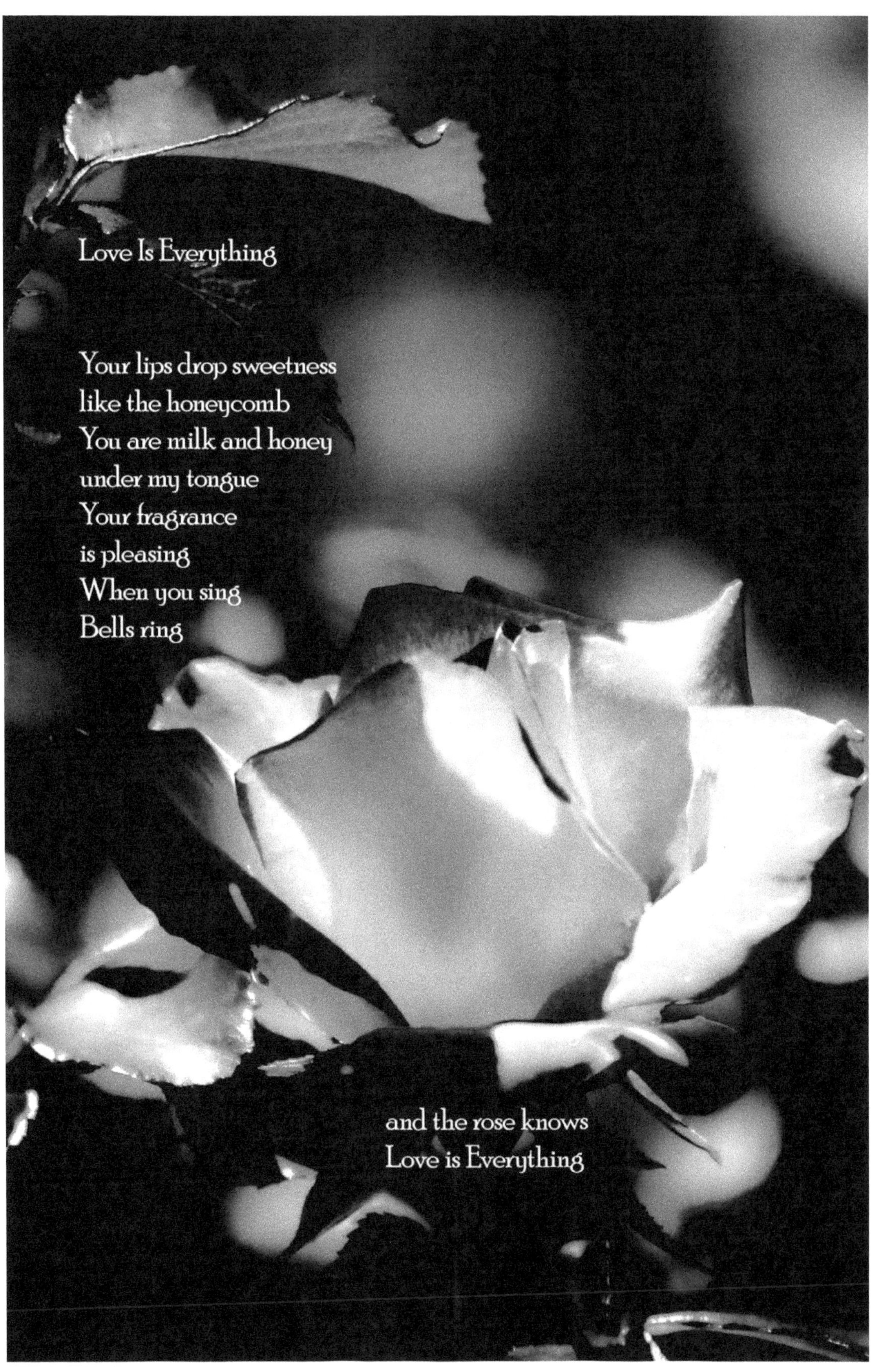

Love Is Everything

Your lips drop sweetness
like the honeycomb
You are milk and honey
under my tongue
Your fragrance
is pleasing
When you sing
Bells ring

and the rose knows
Love is Everything

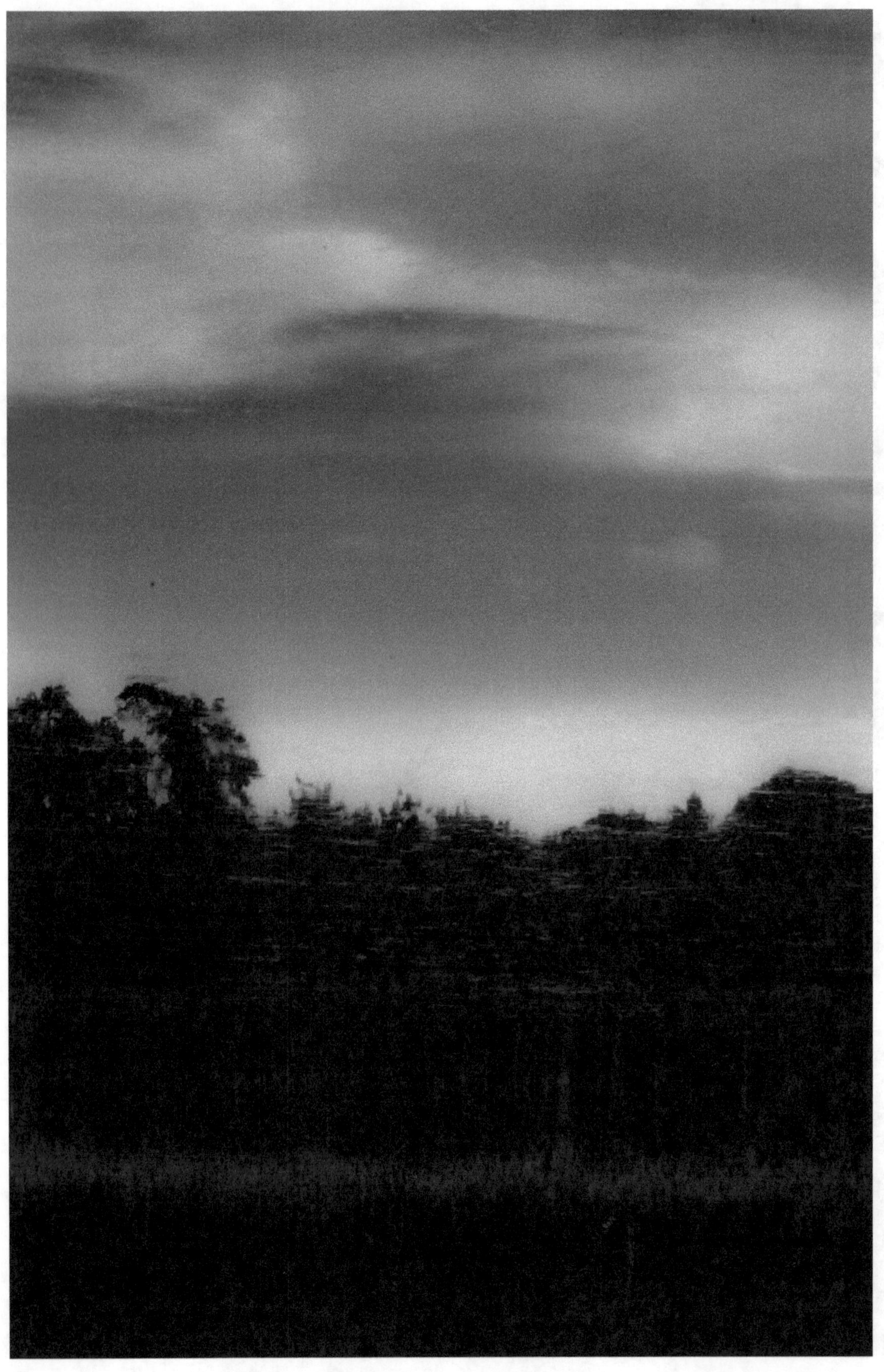

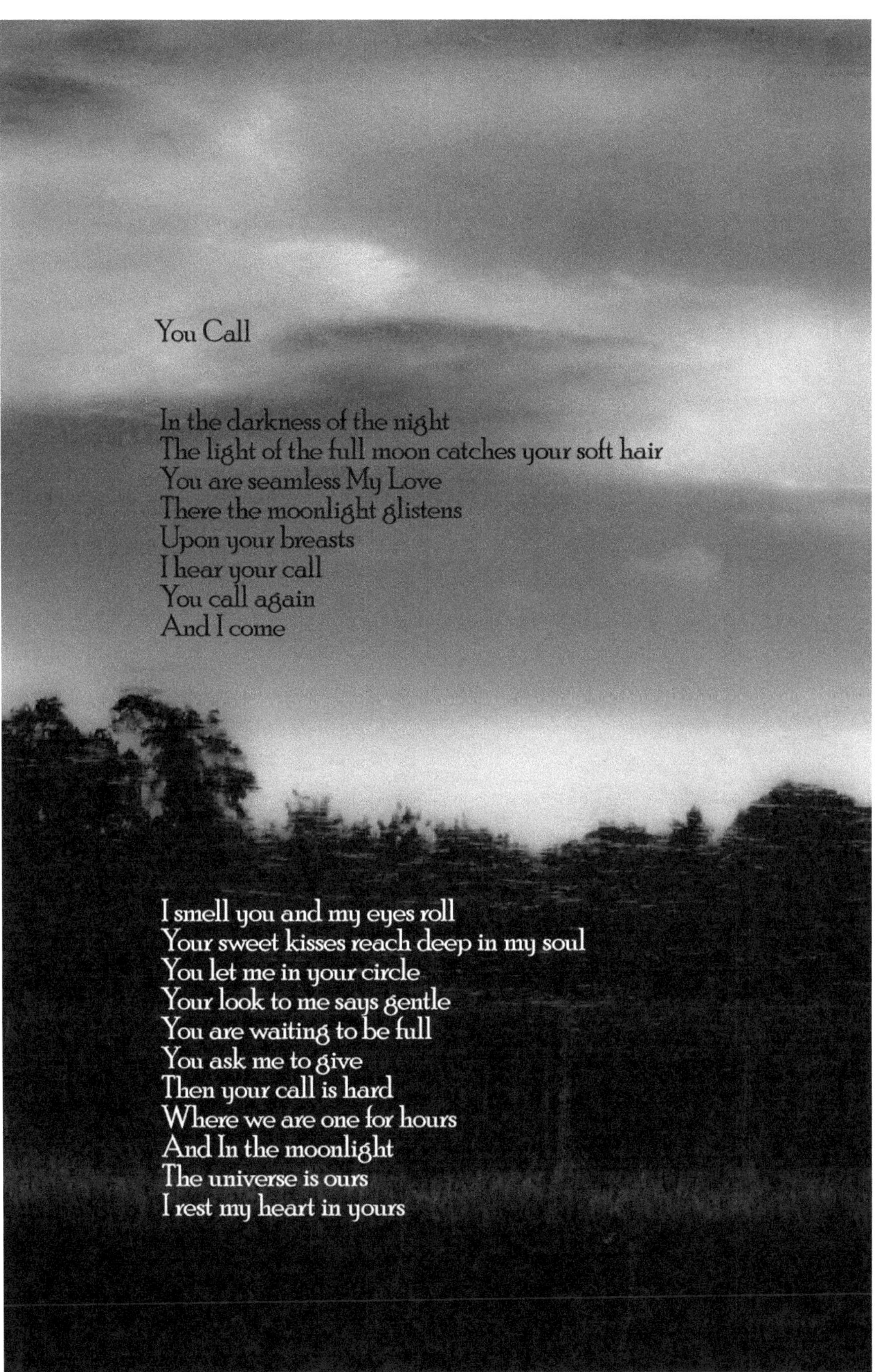

You Call

In the darkness of the night
The light of the full moon catches your soft hair
You are seamless My Love
There the moonlight glistens
Upon your breasts
I hear your call
You call again
And I come

I smell you and my eyes roll
Your sweet kisses reach deep in my soul
You let me in your circle
Your look to me says gentle
You are waiting to be full
You ask me to give
Then your call is hard
Where we are one for hours
And In the moonlight
The universe is ours
I rest my heart in yours

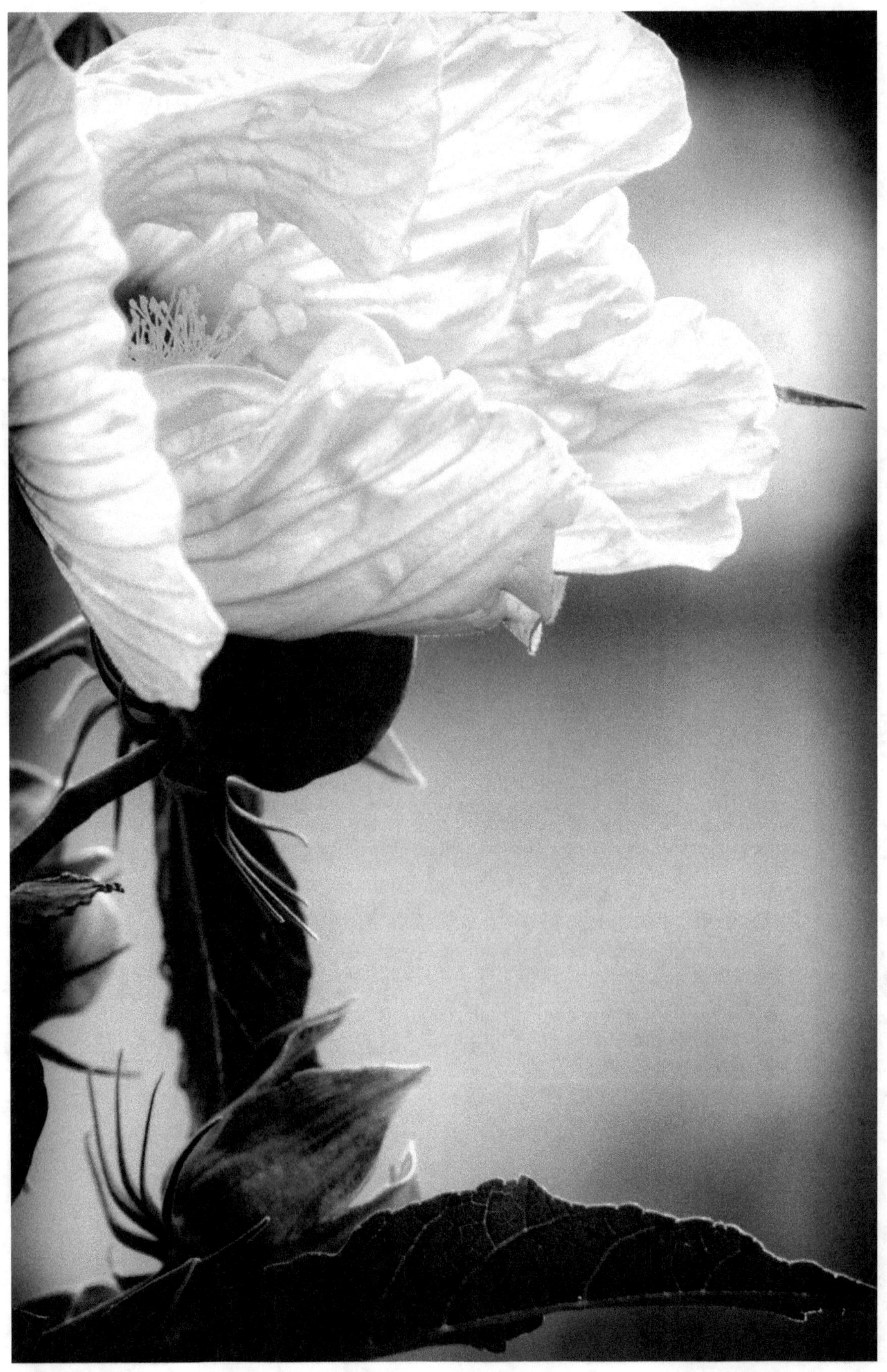

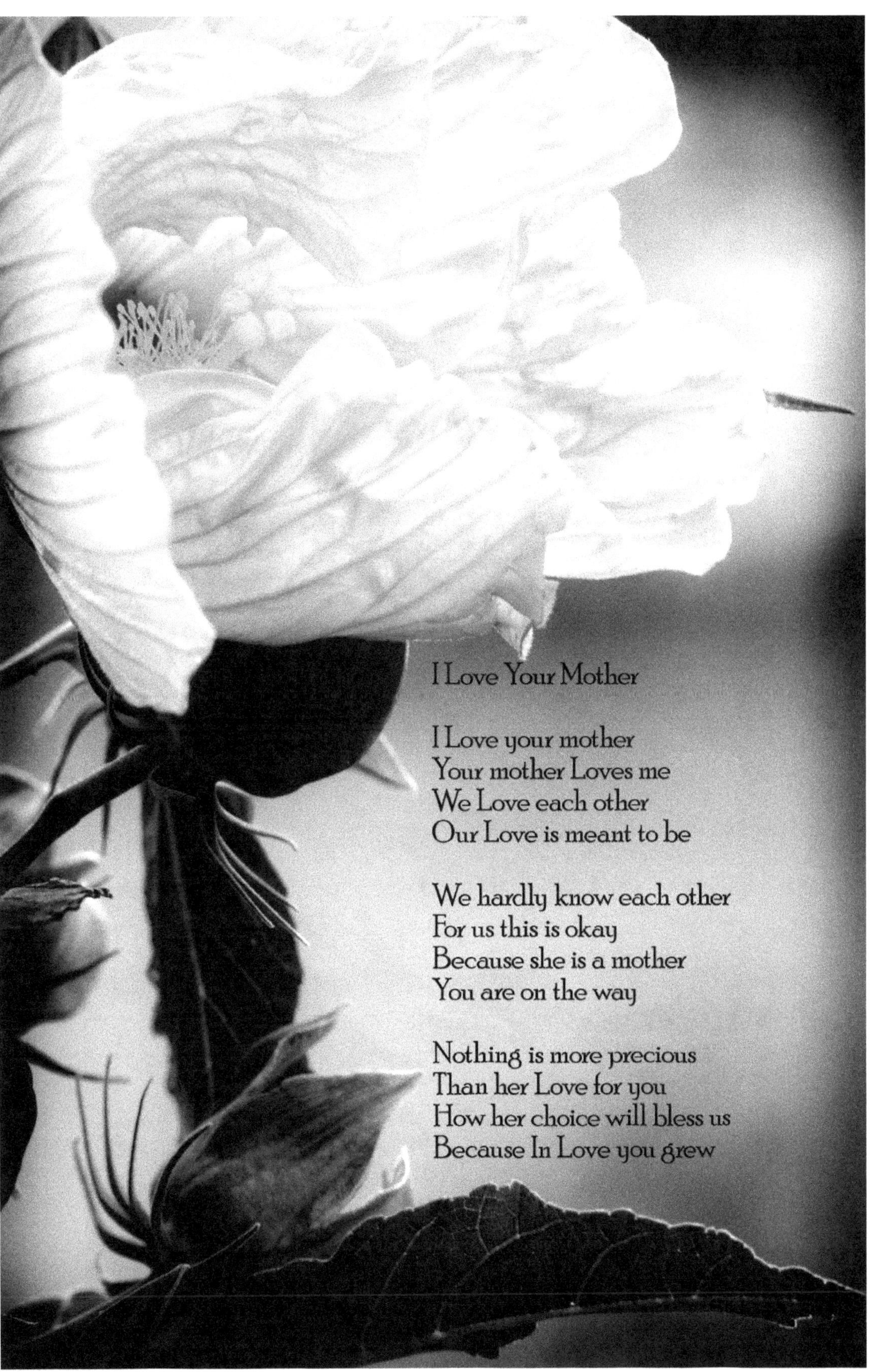

I Love Your Mother

I Love your mother
Your mother Loves me
We Love each other
Our Love is meant to be

We hardly know each other
For us this is okay
Because she is a mother
You are on the way

Nothing is more precious
Than her Love for you
How her choice will bless us
Because In Love you grew

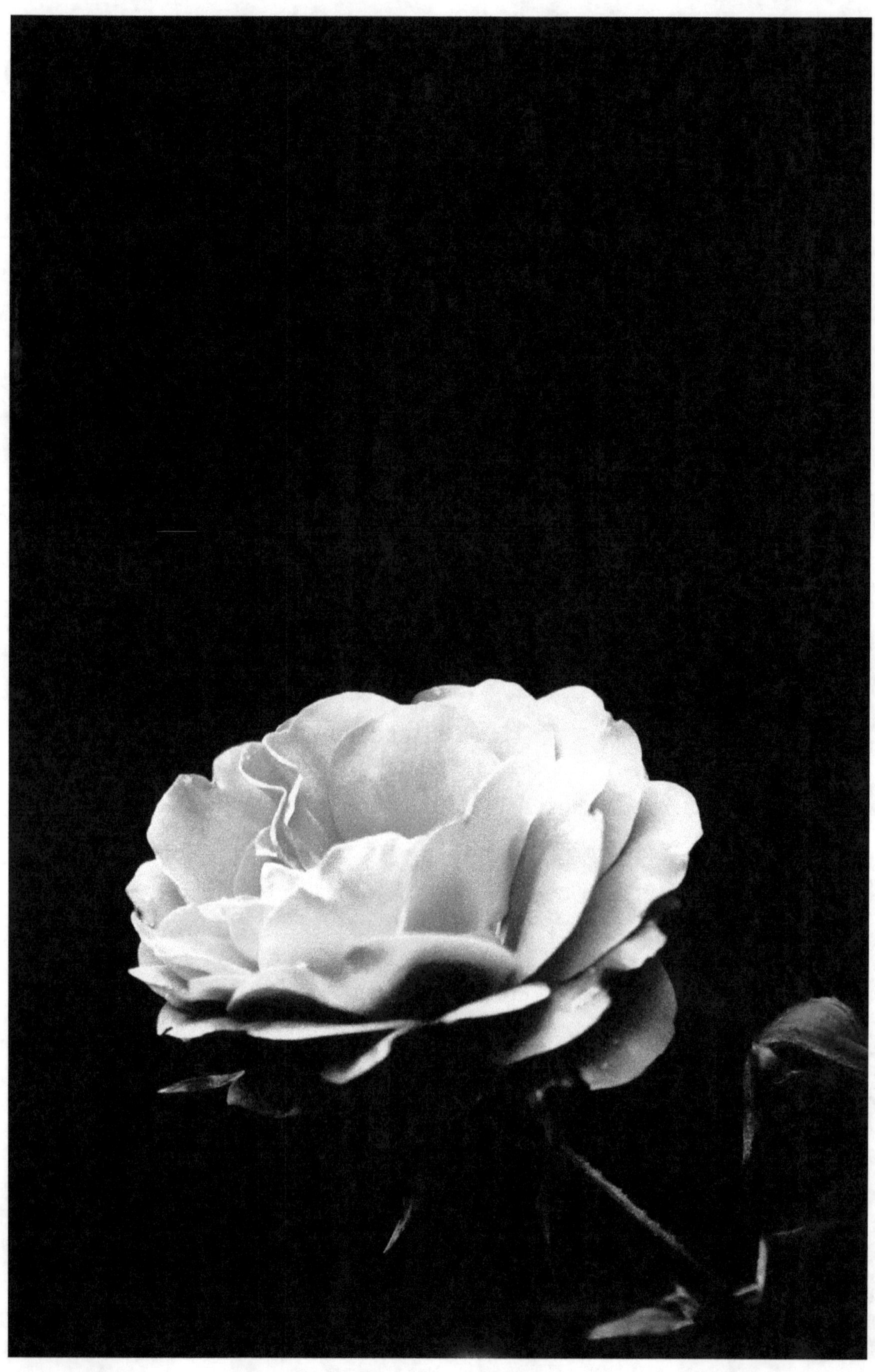

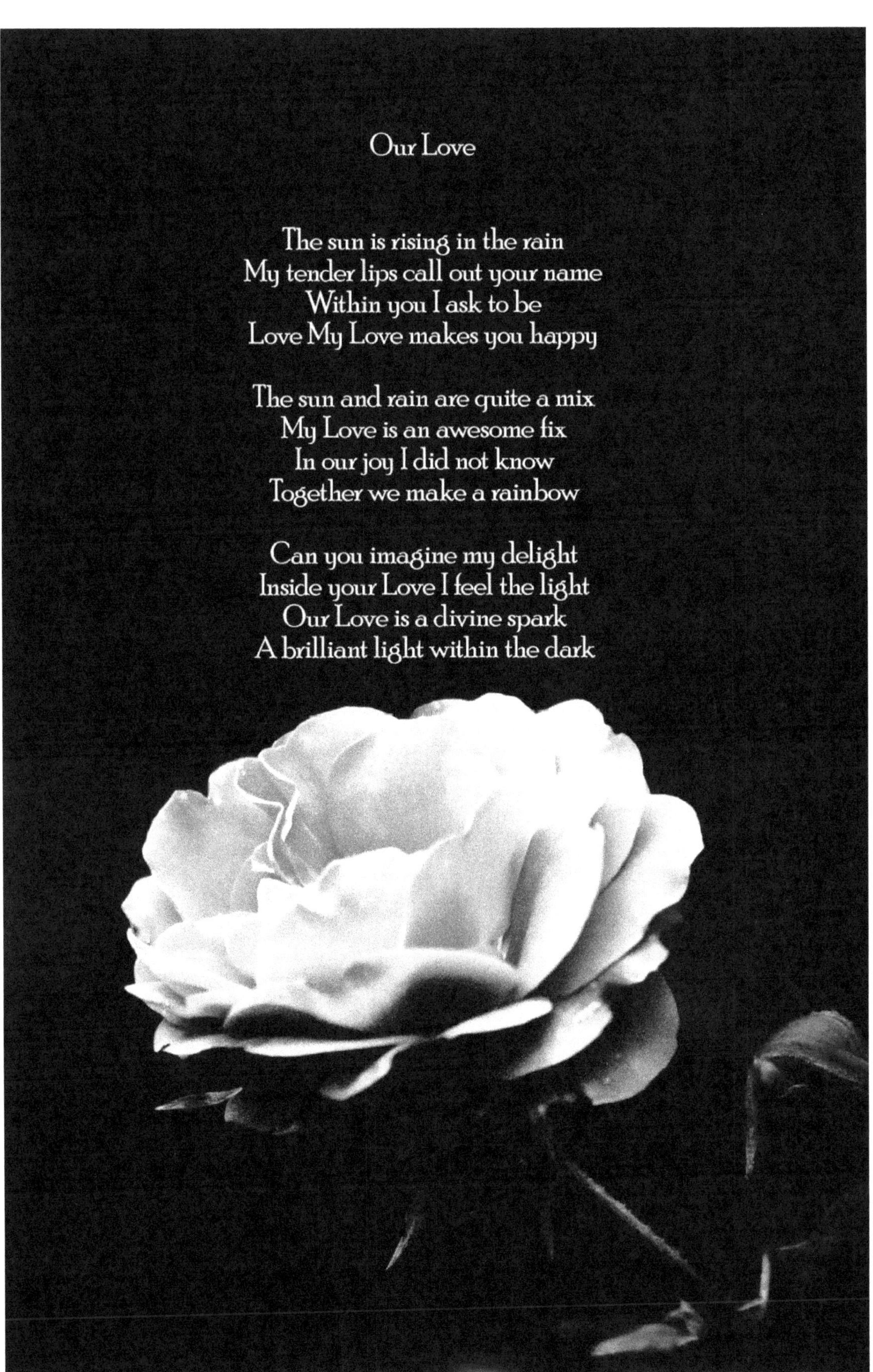

Our Love

The sun is rising in the rain
My tender lips call out your name
Within you I ask to be
Love My Love makes you happy

The sun and rain are quite a mix
My Love is an awesome fix
In our joy I did not know
Together we make a rainbow

Can you imagine my delight
Inside your Love I feel the light
Our Love is a divine spark
A brilliant light within the dark

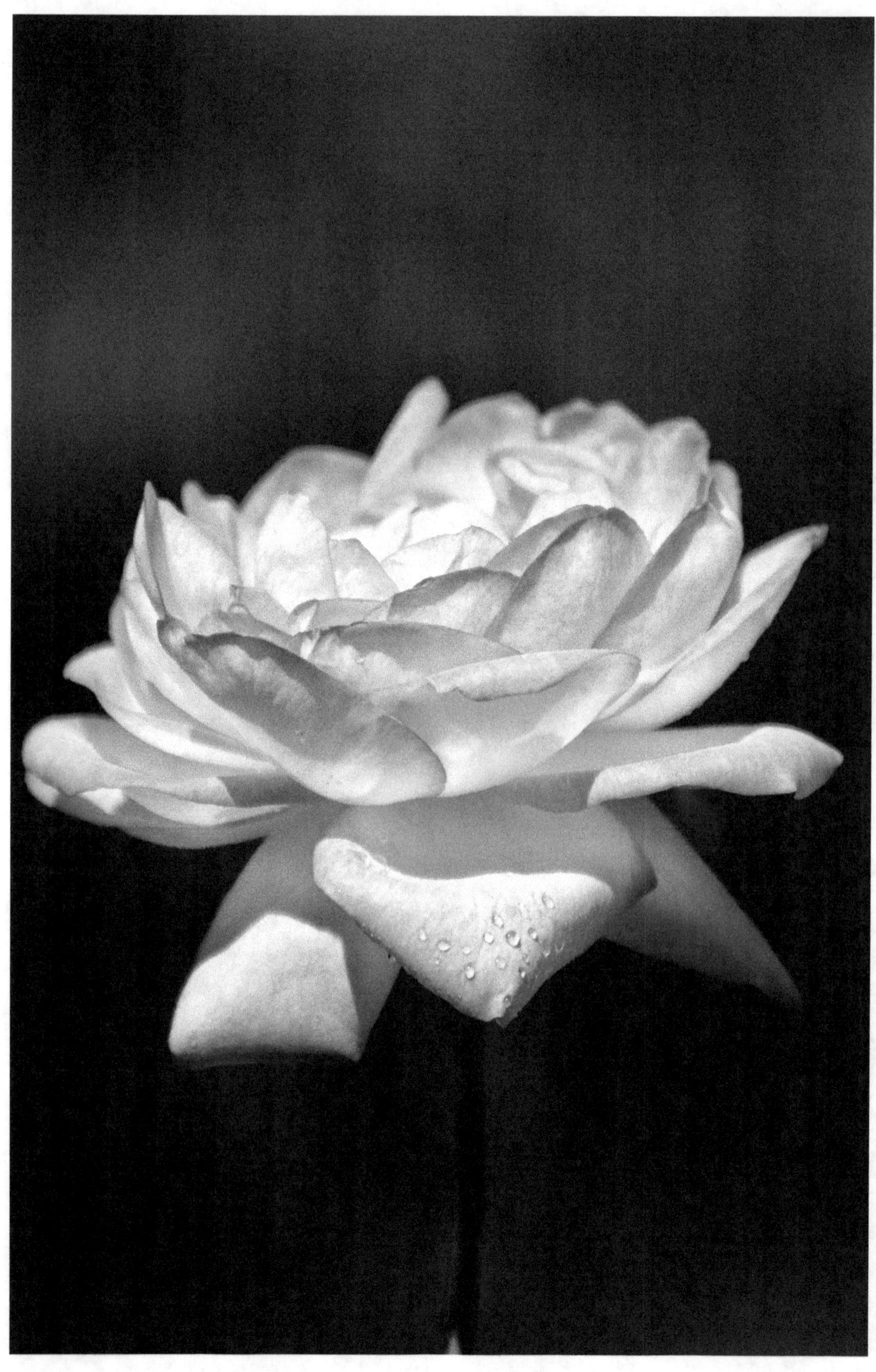

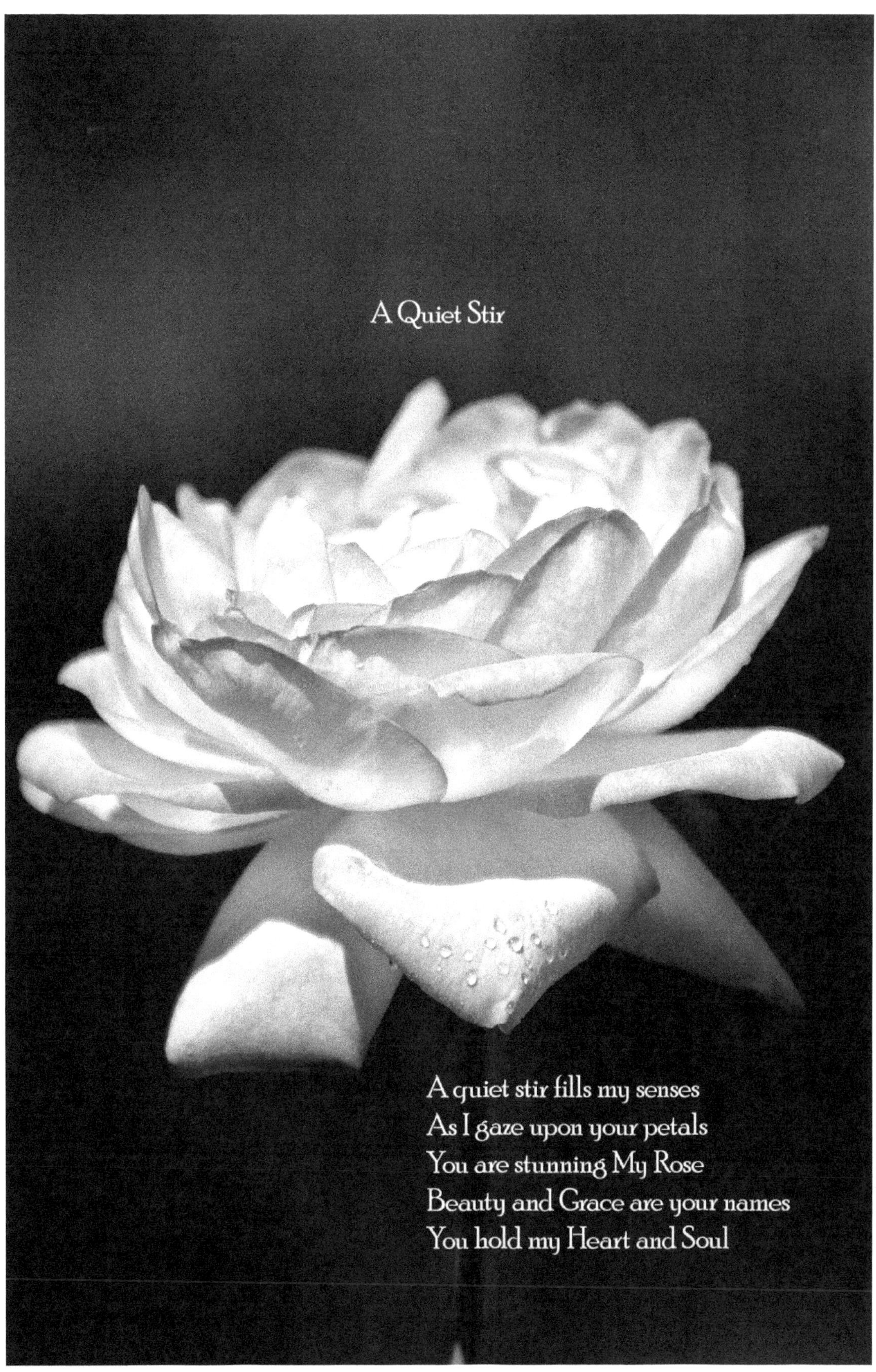
A Quiet Stir
A quiet stir fills my senses
As I gaze upon your petals
You are stunning My Rose
Beauty and Grace are your names
You hold my Heart and Soul

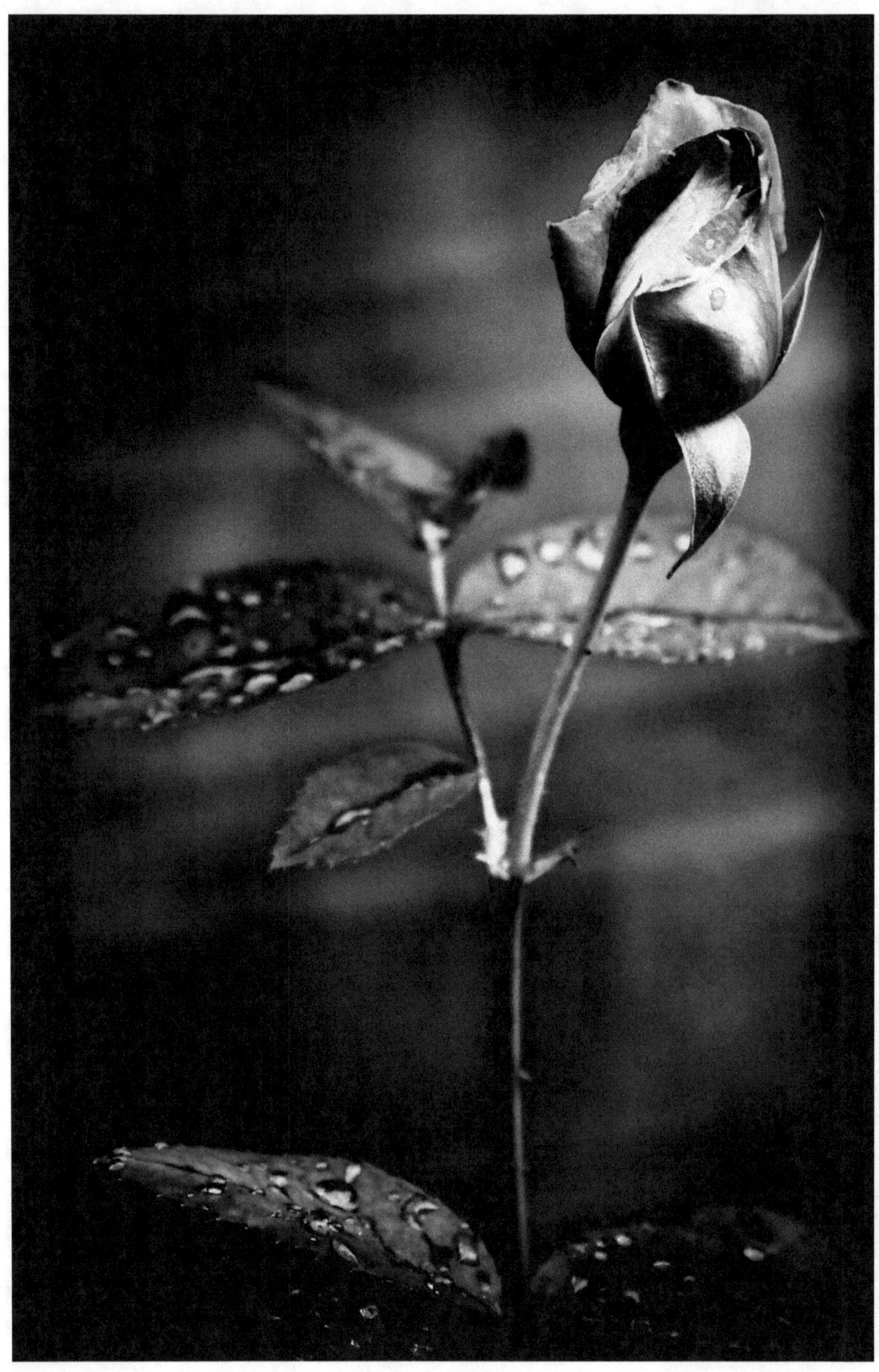

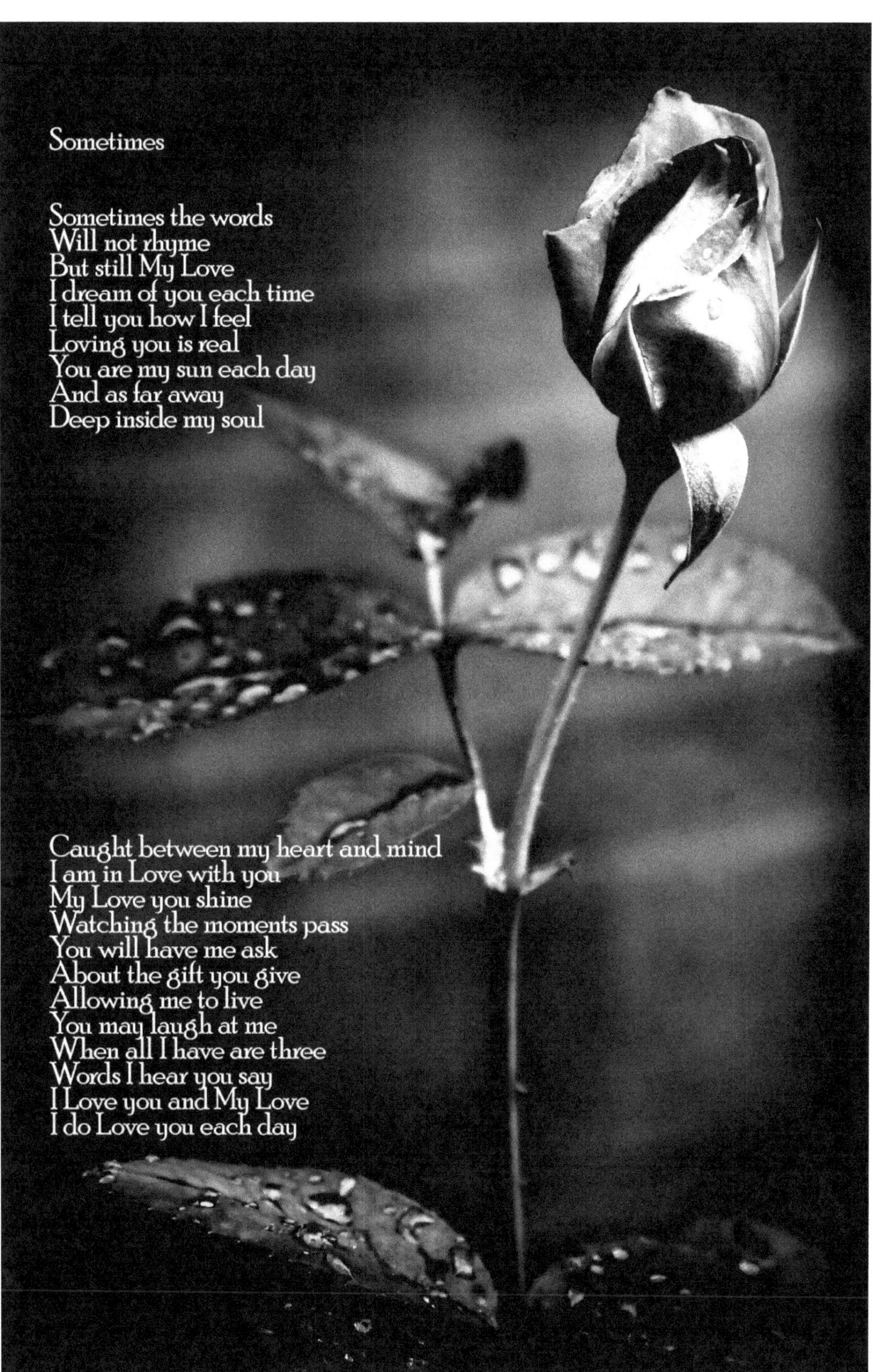

Sometimes

Sometimes the words
Will not rhyme
But still My Love
I dream of you each time
I tell you how I feel
Loving you is real
You are my sun each day
And as far away
Deep inside my soul

Caught between my heart and mind
I am in Love with you
My Love you shine
Watching the moments pass
You will have me ask
About the gift you give
Allowing me to live
You may laugh at me
When all I have are three
Words I hear you say
I Love you and My Love
I do Love you each day

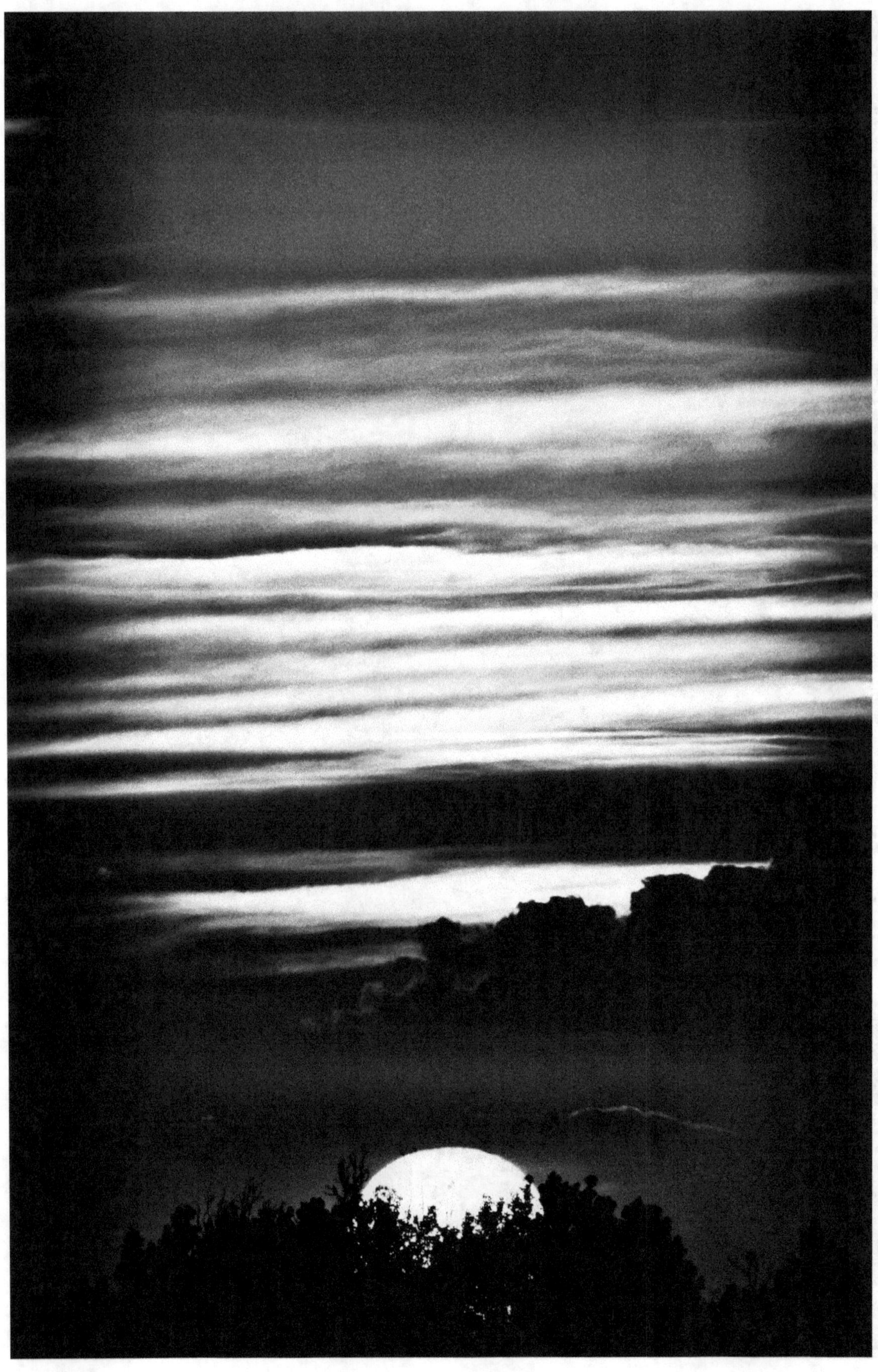

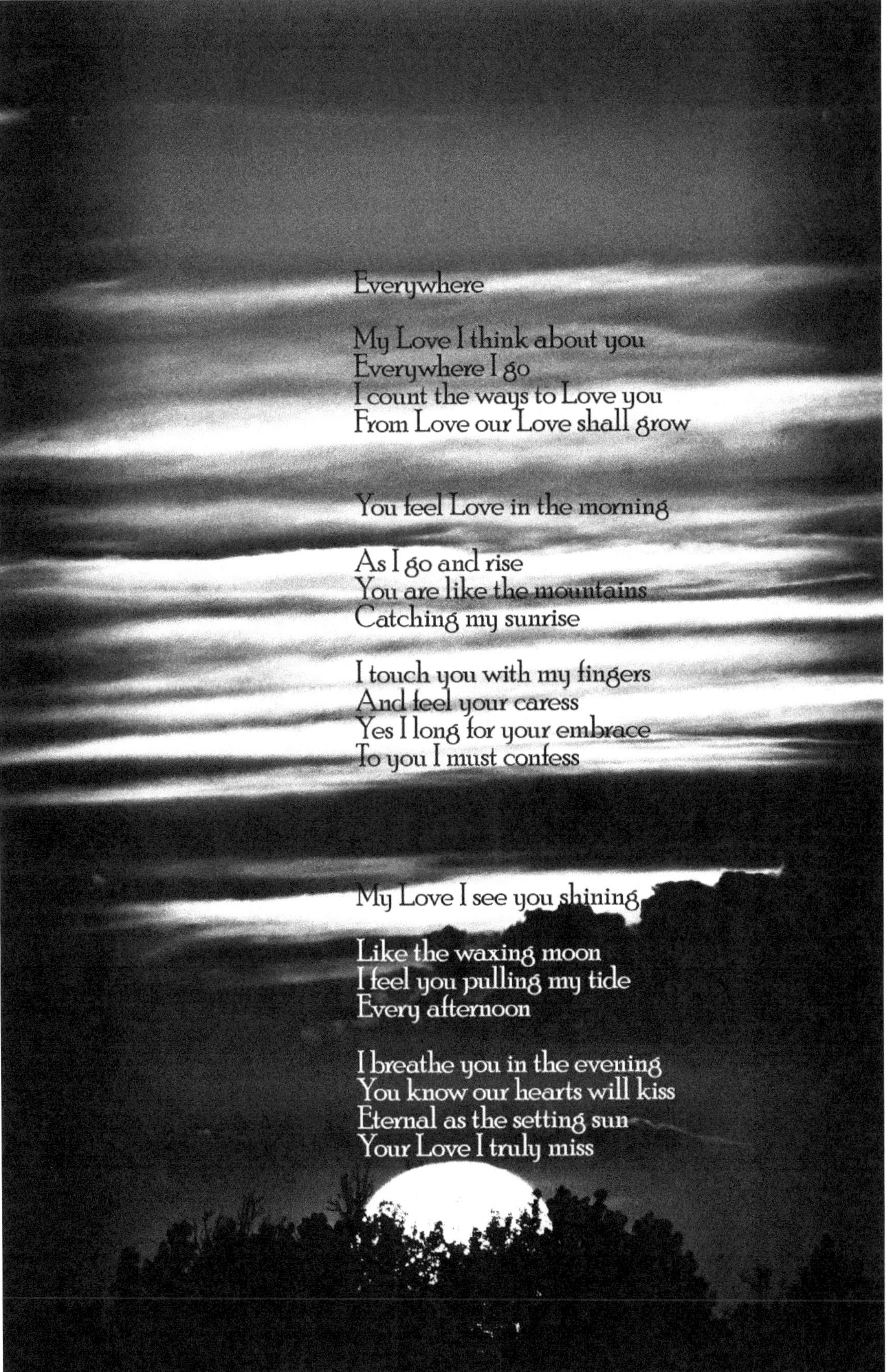

Everywhere

My Love I think about you
Everywhere I go
I count the ways to Love you
From Love our Love shall grow

You feel Love in the morning

As I go and rise
You are like the mountains
Catching my sunrise

I touch you with my fingers
And feel your caress
Yes I long for your embrace
To you I must confess

My Love I see you shining

Like the waxing moon
I feel you pulling my tide
Every afternoon

I breathe you in the evening
You know our hearts will kiss
Eternal as the setting sun
Your Love I truly miss

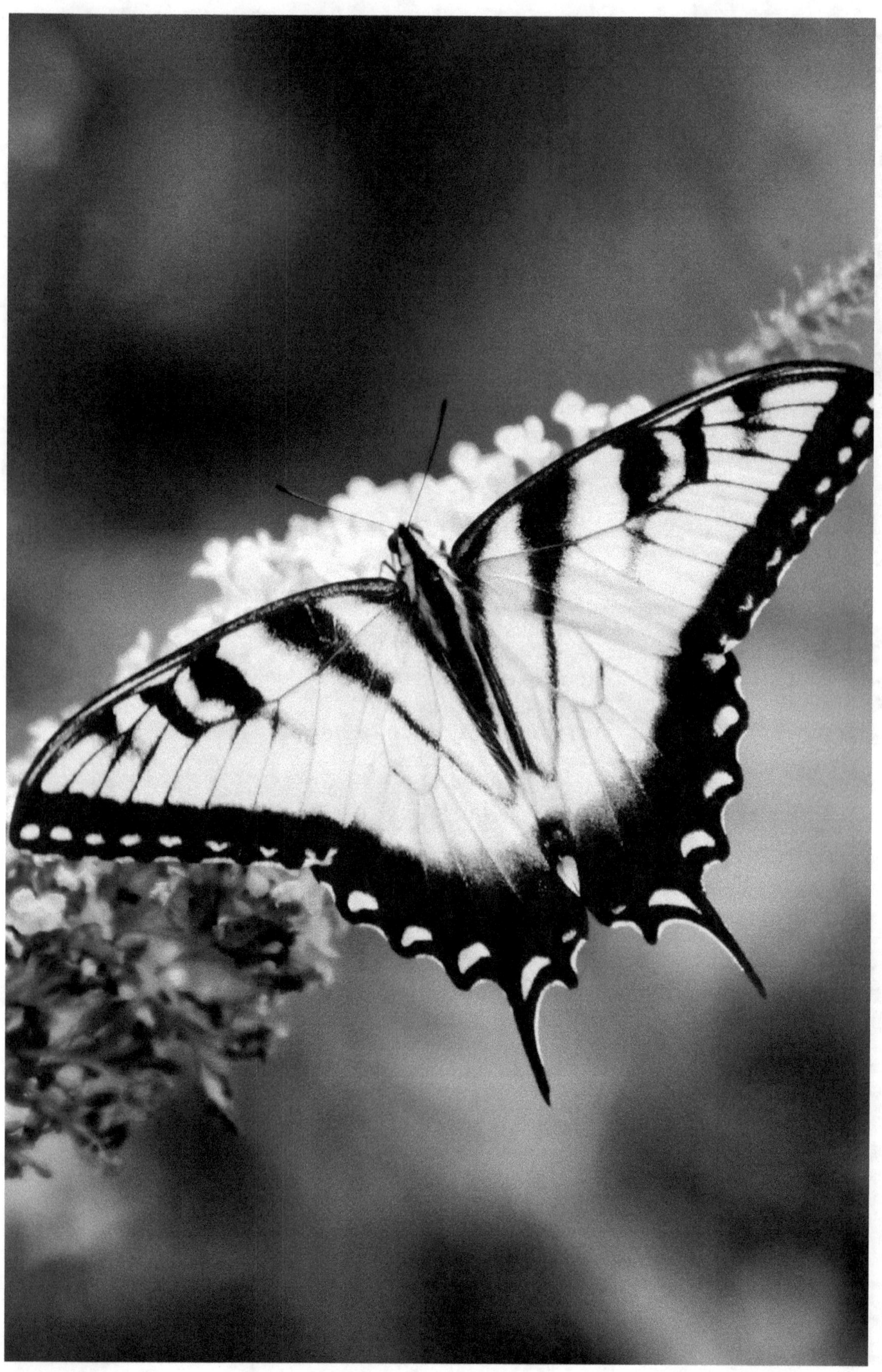

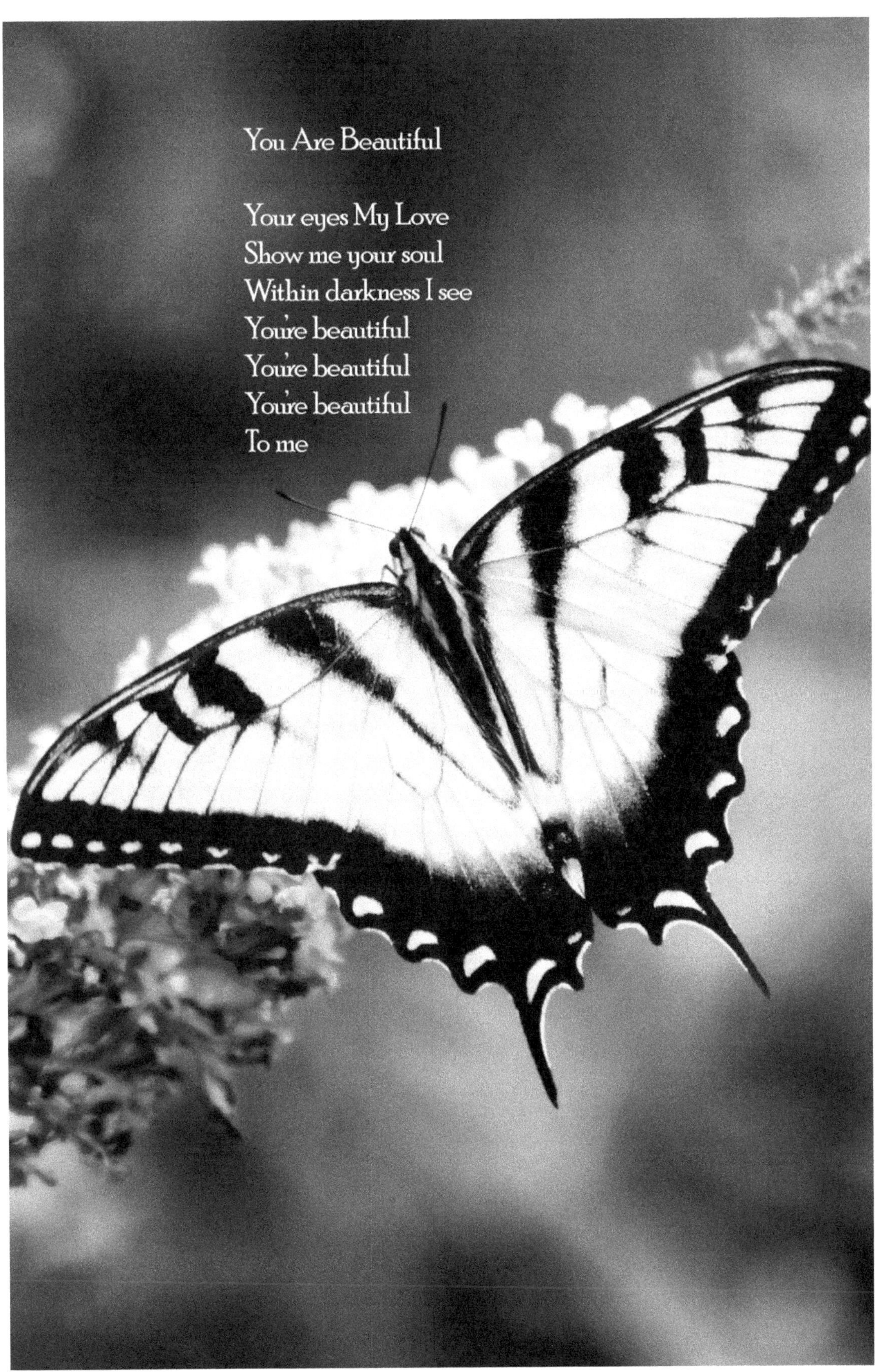
You Are Beautiful

Your eyes My Love
Show me your soul
Within darkness I see
You're beautiful
You're beautiful
You're beautiful
To me

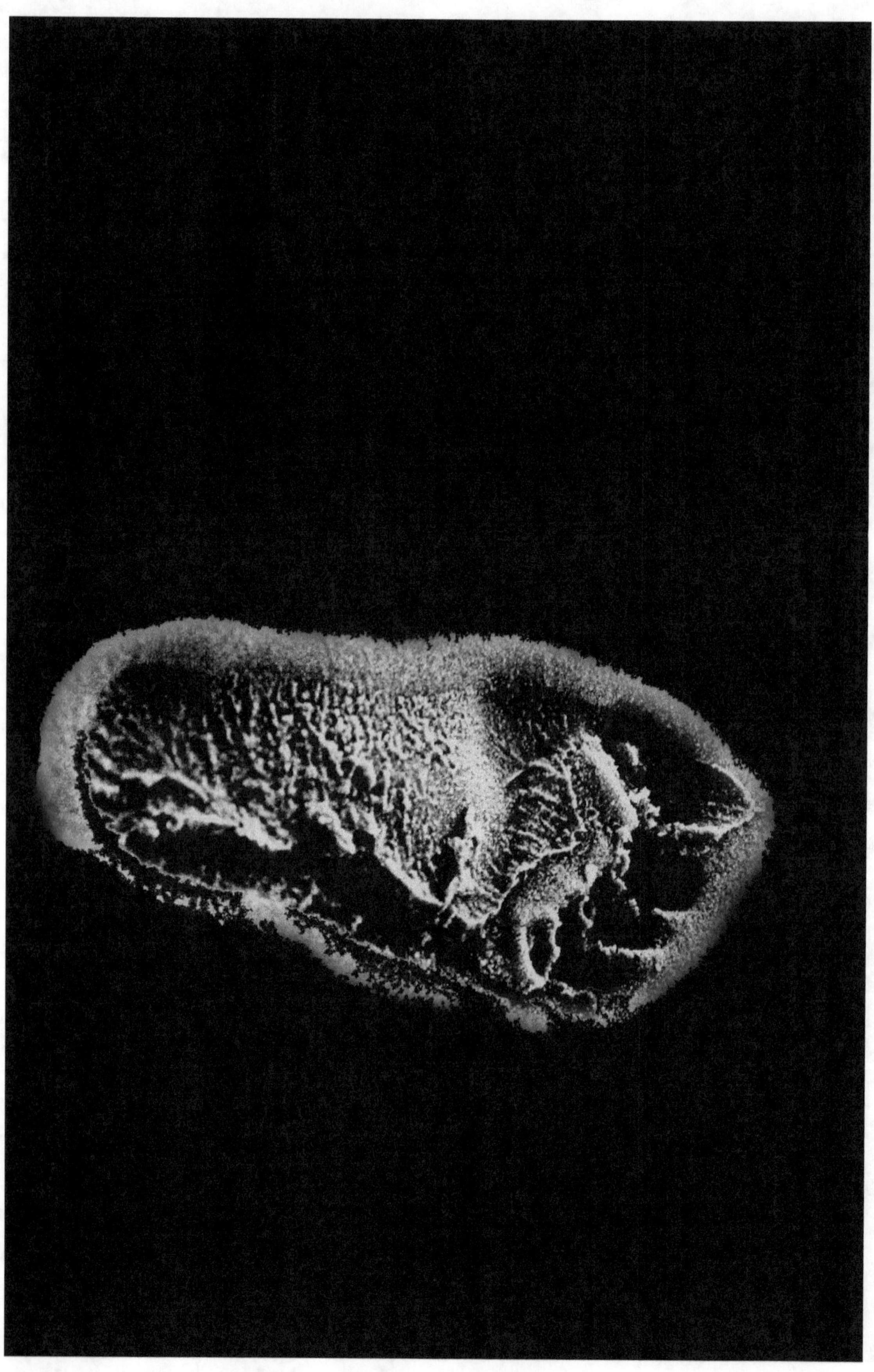

I LOVE YOU

My heart awaits you - I am sleeping
Waiting for you to awaken me - Because I feel your gift

I stop counting the years - My hands remember you - Your lovely smile - your hair - your eyes - Has it been two thousand tears

Each night My Love I cry for your return - Each day your sun drys my tears - How can I forget when you give me life

So I travel the world to find you My Love - You are the warmth within my soul - In every face I search for you -Hoping to hold your joy once again - But as the stars would shine each night

My heart would break again for your light - The light of Love inside your eyes - Now falling from the heavens

I see your footprints My Love

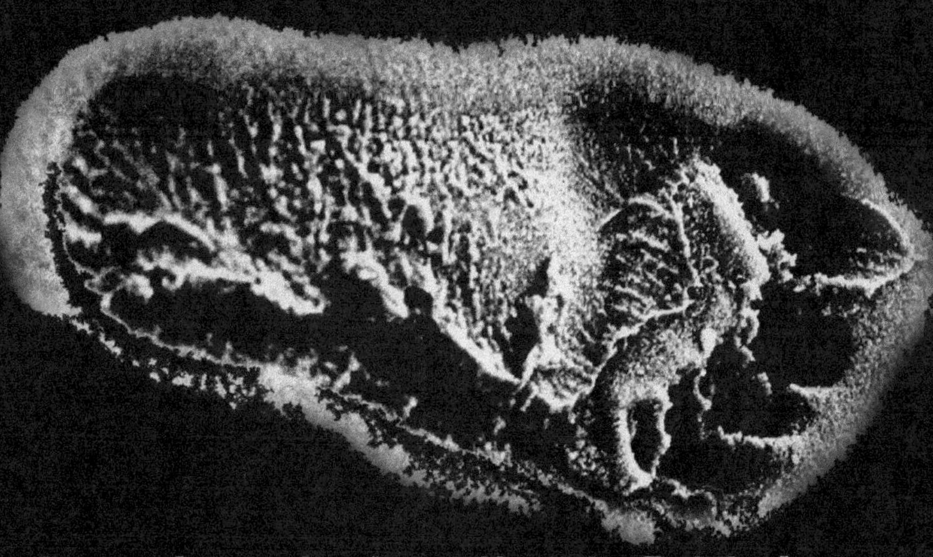

On every flower and rainbow and butterfly - Each day I am reminded - Of the beauty within your soul - Imagine my joy to see you and feel your touch - To find you next to me
You give me a name - You whisper - I LOVE YOU-Now you return - My Love - You put your arms around me - And all the tears of sadness - Transform to rivers of gladness
I Love you always - I LOVE YOU and always will

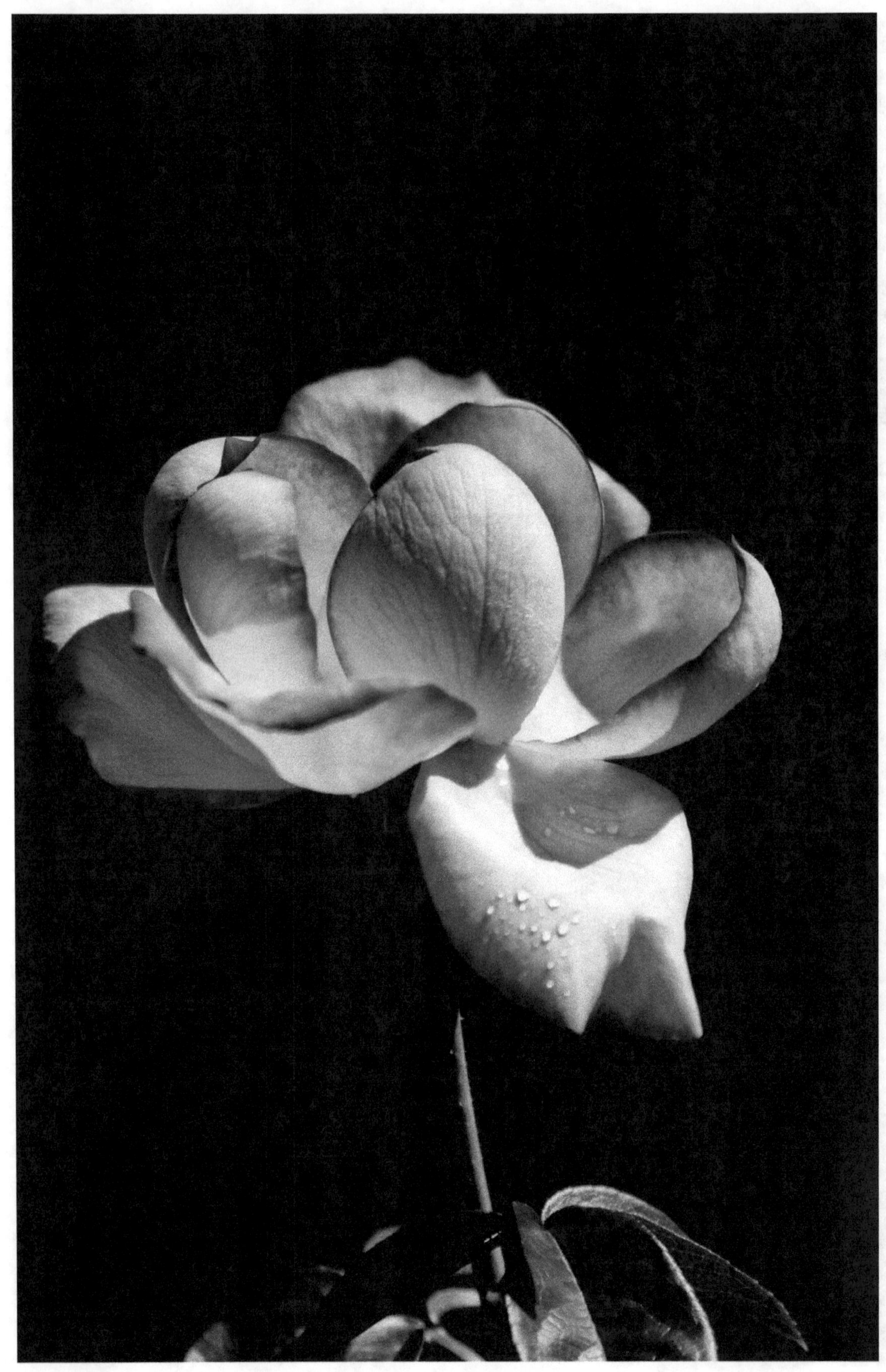

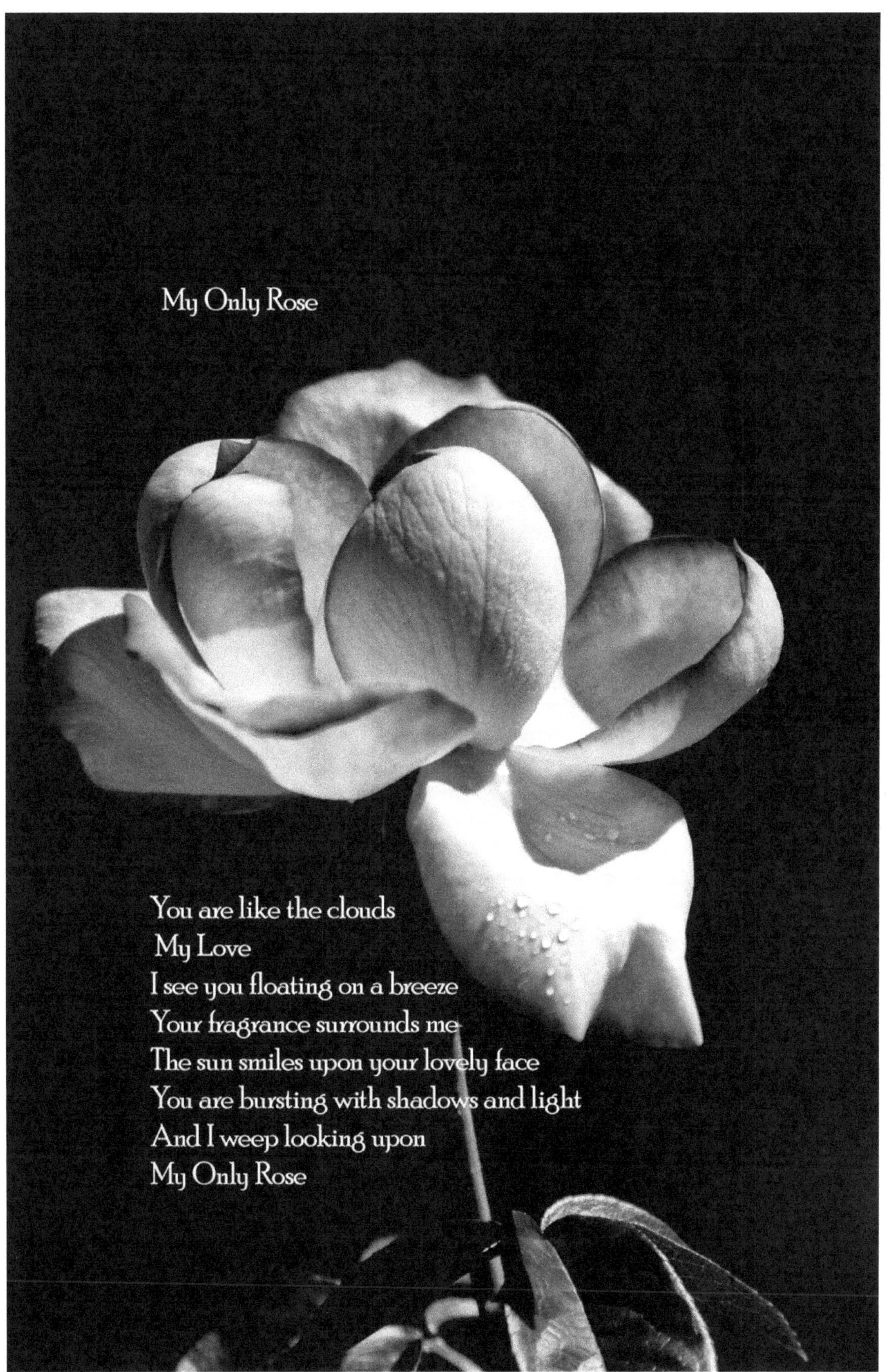

My Only Rose

You are like the clouds
My Love
I see you floating on a breeze
Your fragrance surrounds me
The sun smiles upon your lovely face
You are bursting with shadows and light
And I weep looking upon
My Only Rose

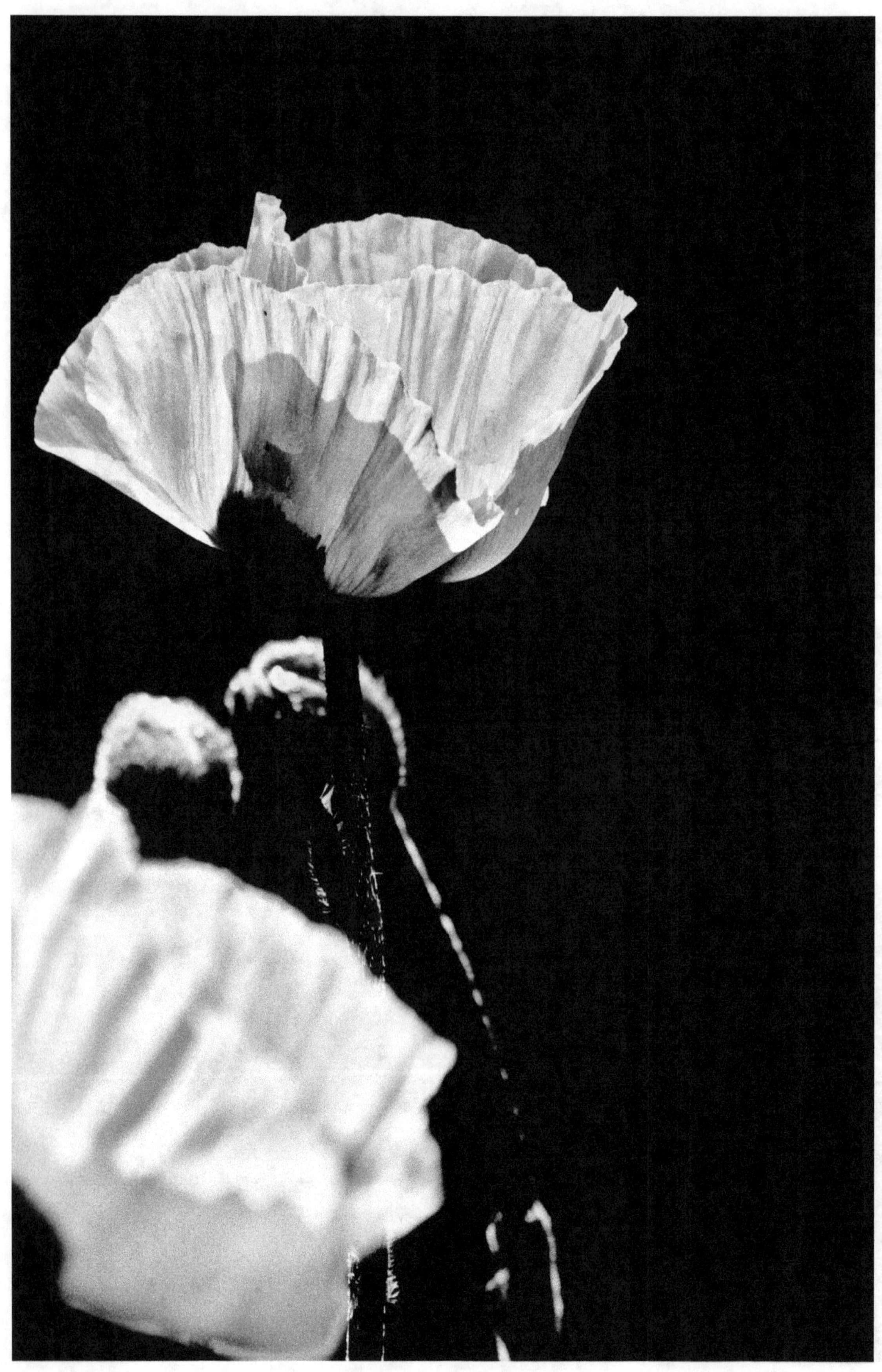

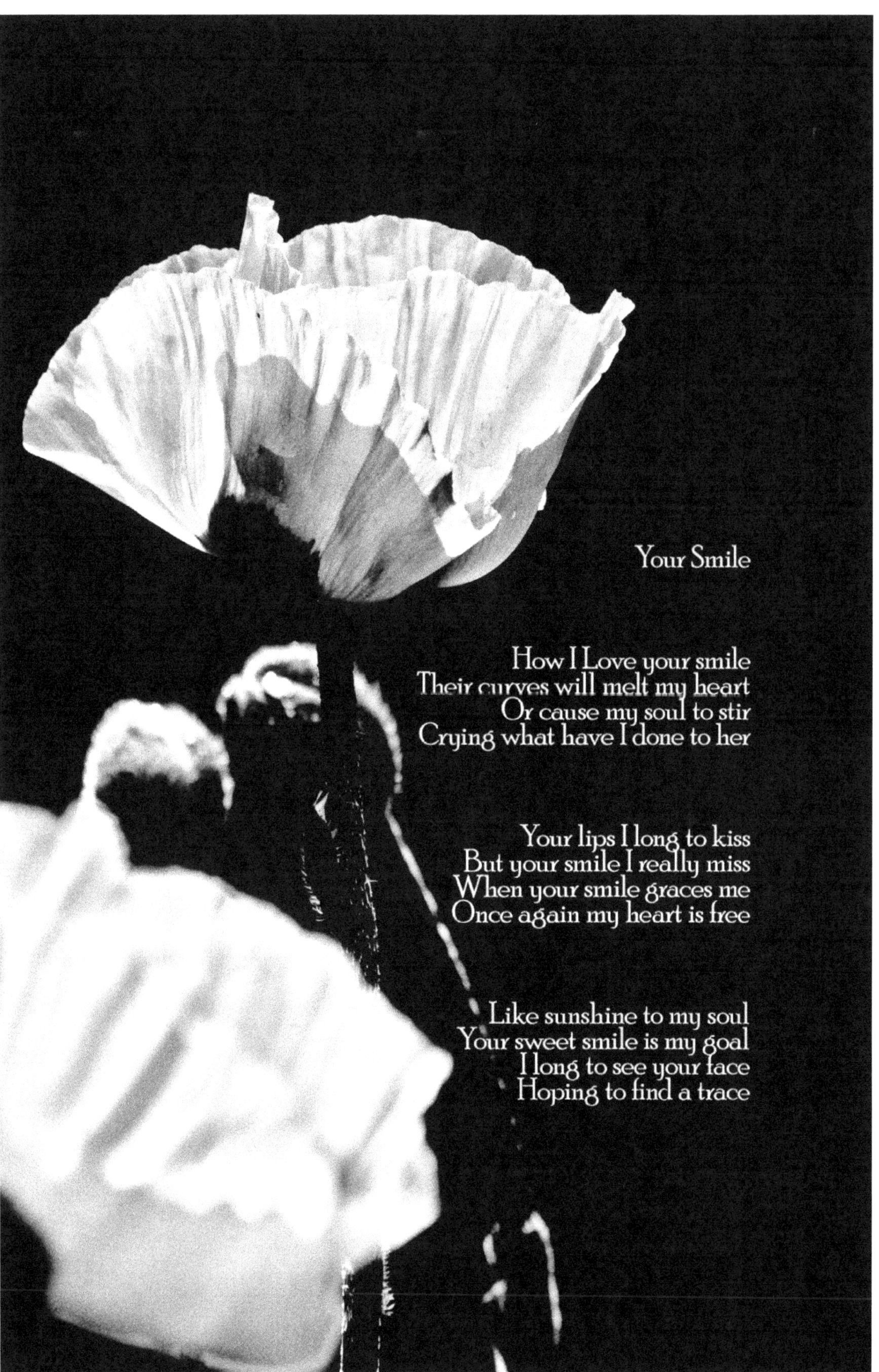

Your Smile

How I Love your smile
Their curves will melt my heart
Or cause my soul to stir
Crying what have I done to her

Your lips I long to kiss
But your smile I really miss
When your smile graces me
Once again my heart is free

Like sunshine to my soul
Your sweet smile is my goal
I long to see your face
Hoping to find a trace

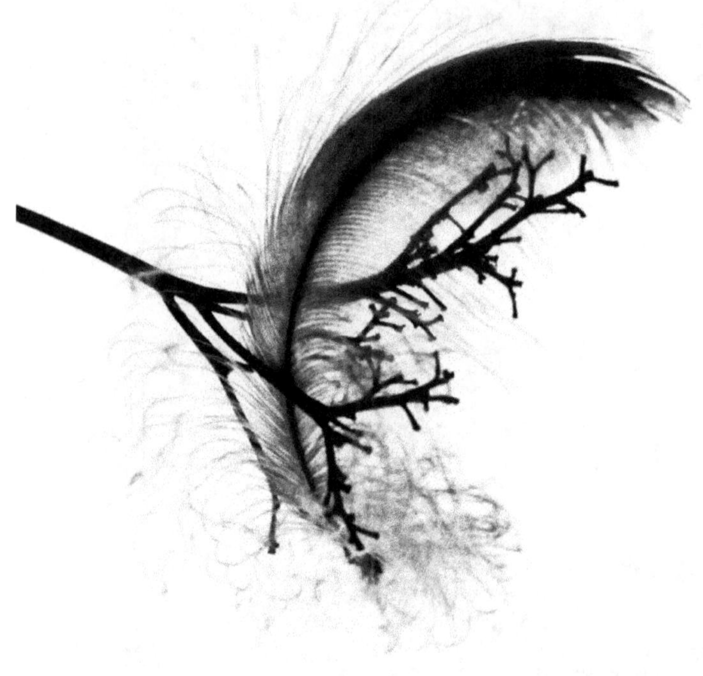

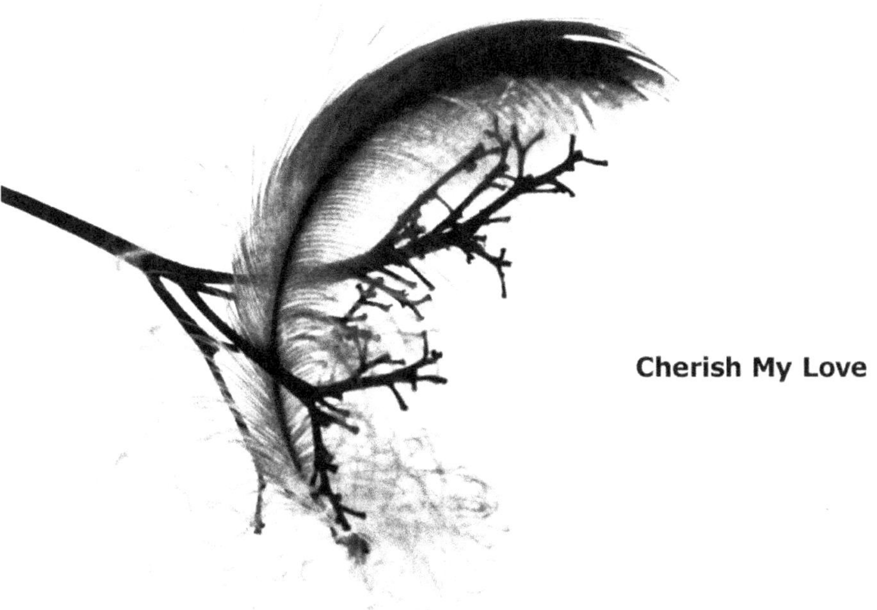

Cherish My Love

My Love your hopes will rest on dreams
There is a place greater it seems
Where Joy is found in every breath
Here Love is as strong as death

I Love the Love you freely give
Away from darkness we will live
To feel a gladness in our hearts
When one ends the other starts

You ask at last this one request
Before the sun sets in the west
My Love cherish above the rest
Your Heart holding the very best

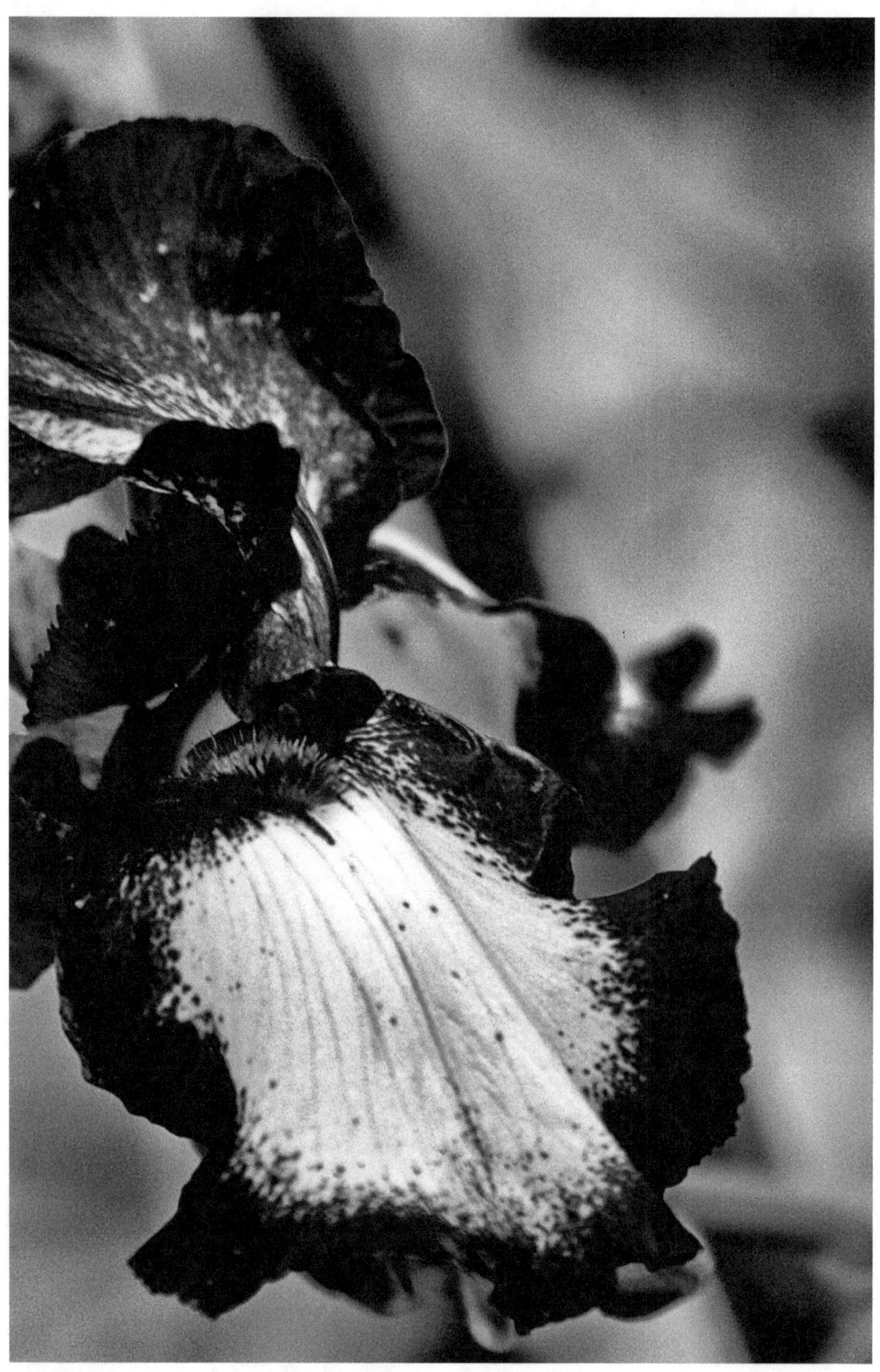

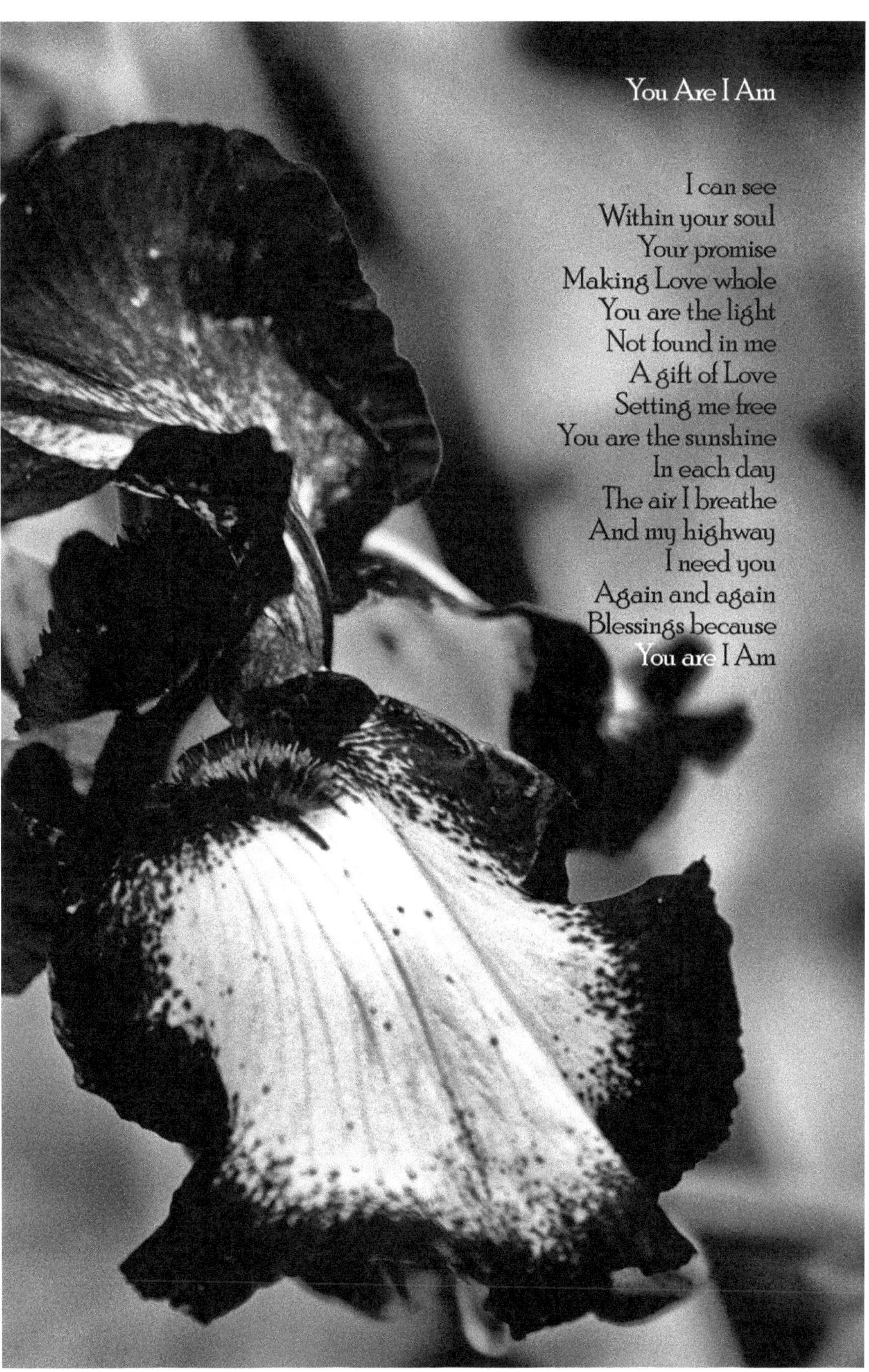
You Are I Am
I can see
Within your soul
Your promise
Making Love whole
You are the light
Not found in me
A gift of Love
Setting me free
You are the sunshine
In each day
The air I breathe
And my highway
I need you
Again and again
Blessings because
You are I Am

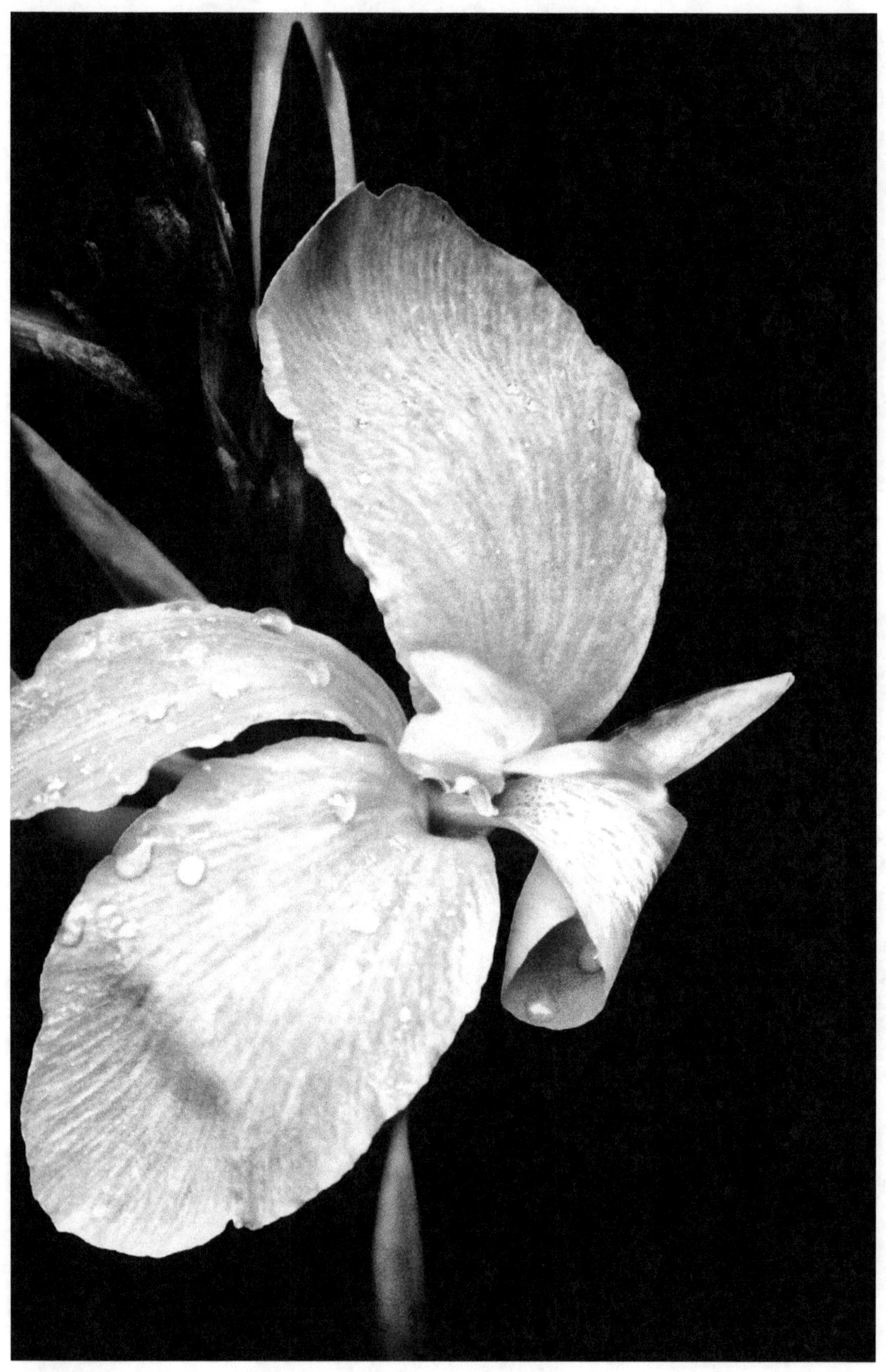

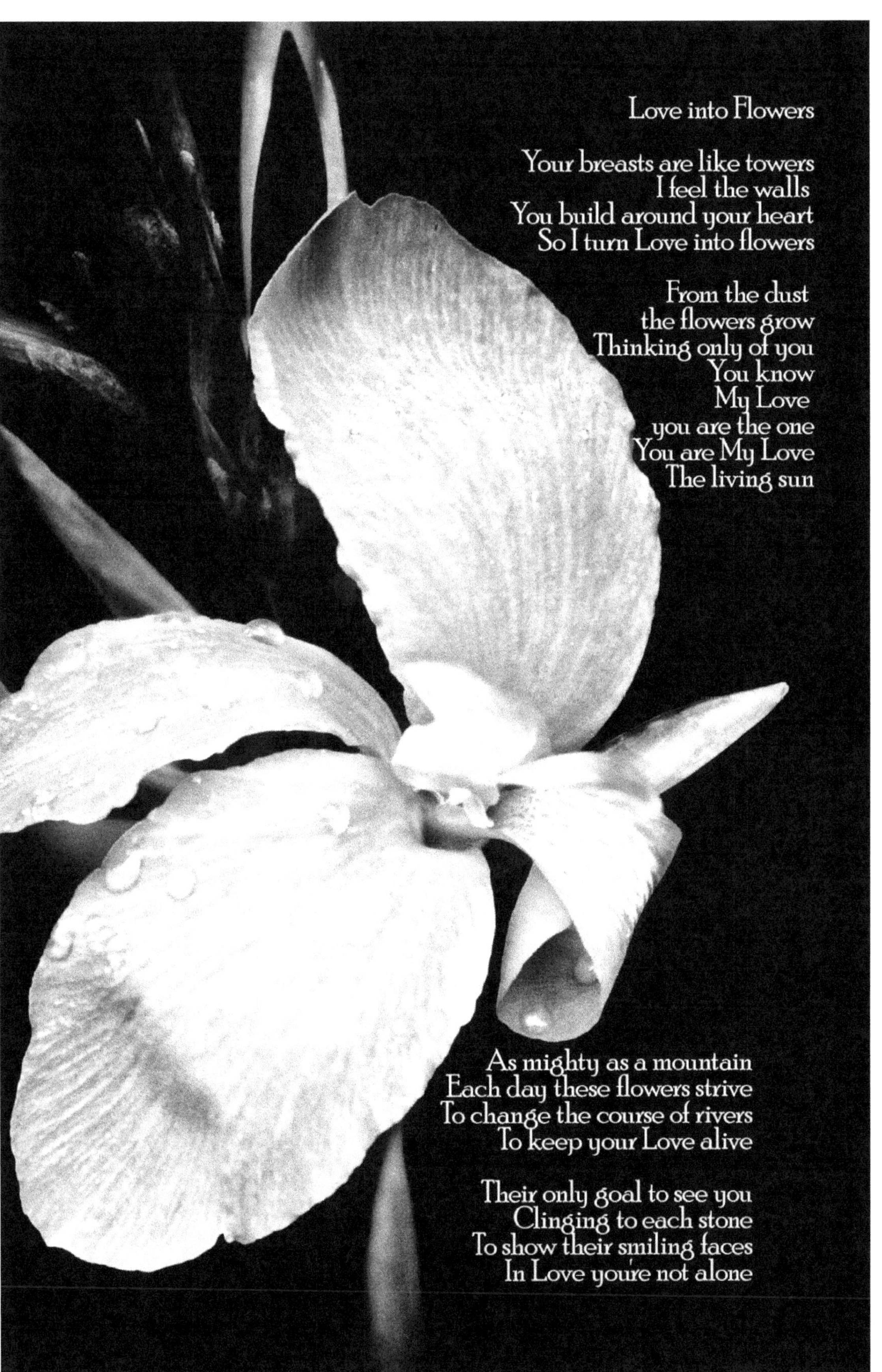

Love into Flowers

Your breasts are like towers
I feel the walls
You build around your heart
So I turn Love into flowers

From the dust
the flowers grow
Thinking only of you
You know
My Love
you are the one
You are My Love
The living sun

As mighty as a mountain
Each day these flowers strive
To change the course of rivers
To keep your Love alive

Their only goal to see you
Clinging to each stone
To show their smiling faces
In Love you're not alone

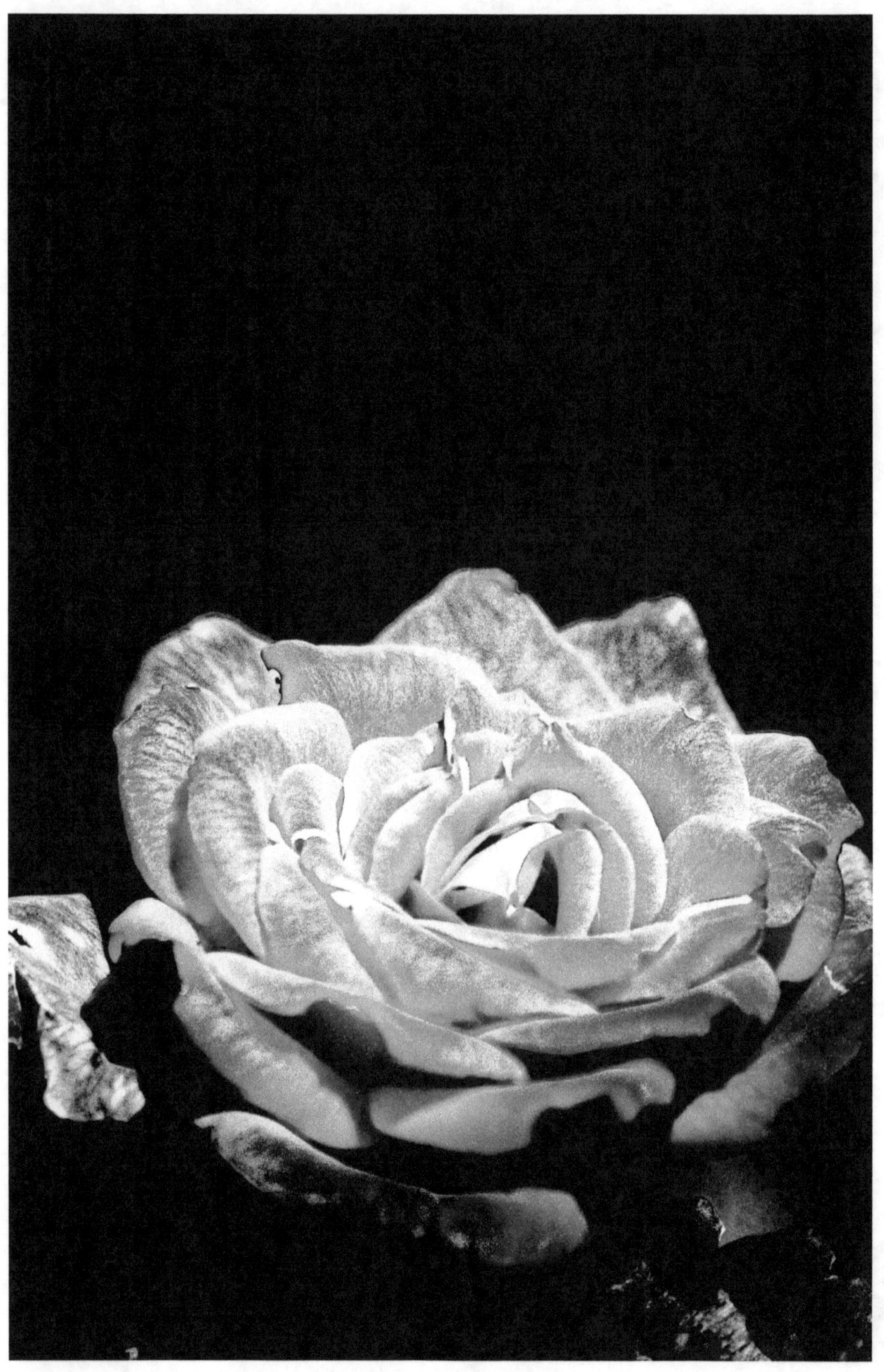

In The Light

You smile and the sun appears
You breathe and there is life
You are the calm within my soul
In the light you kiss me
How easily I breathe

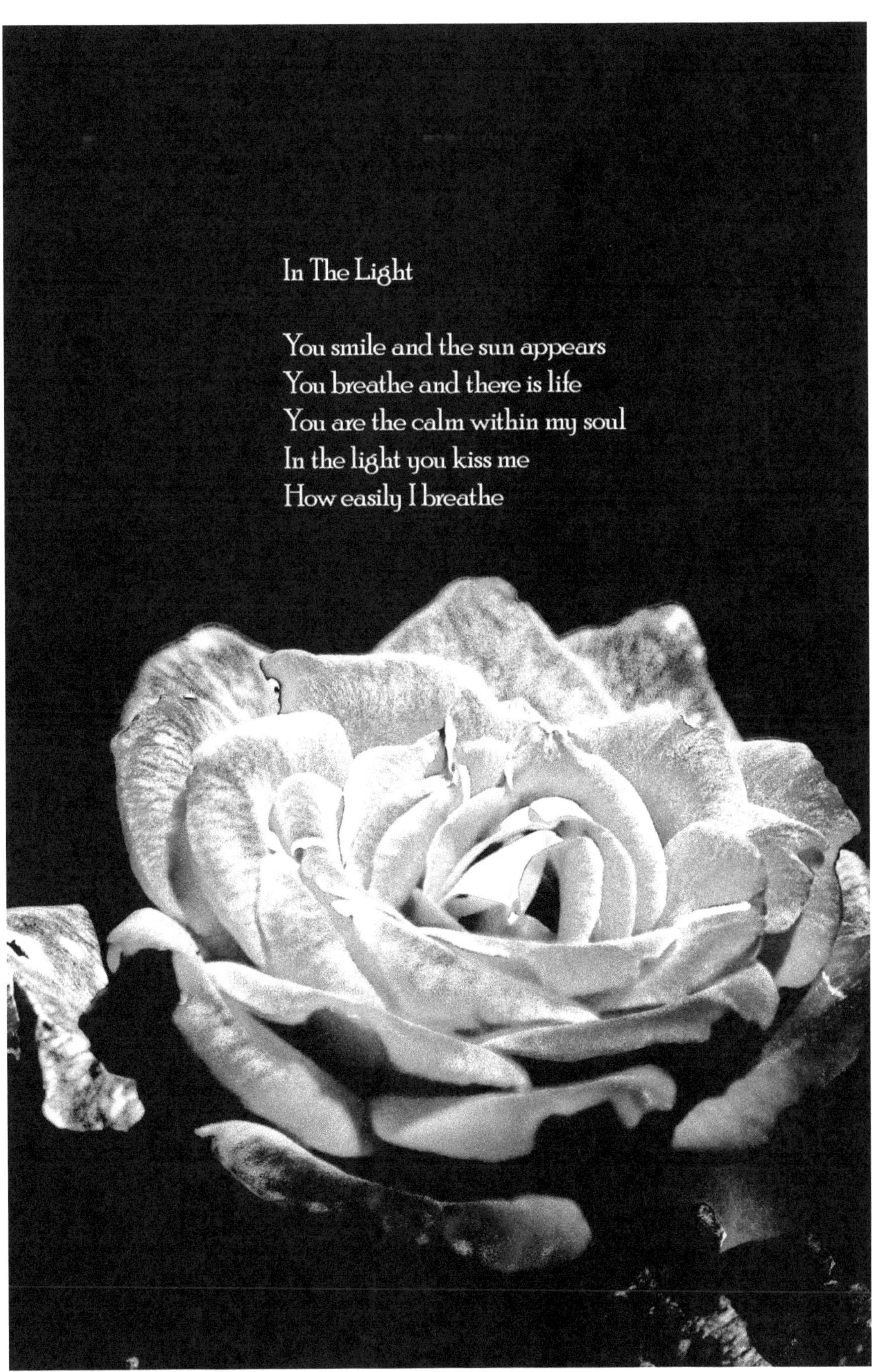

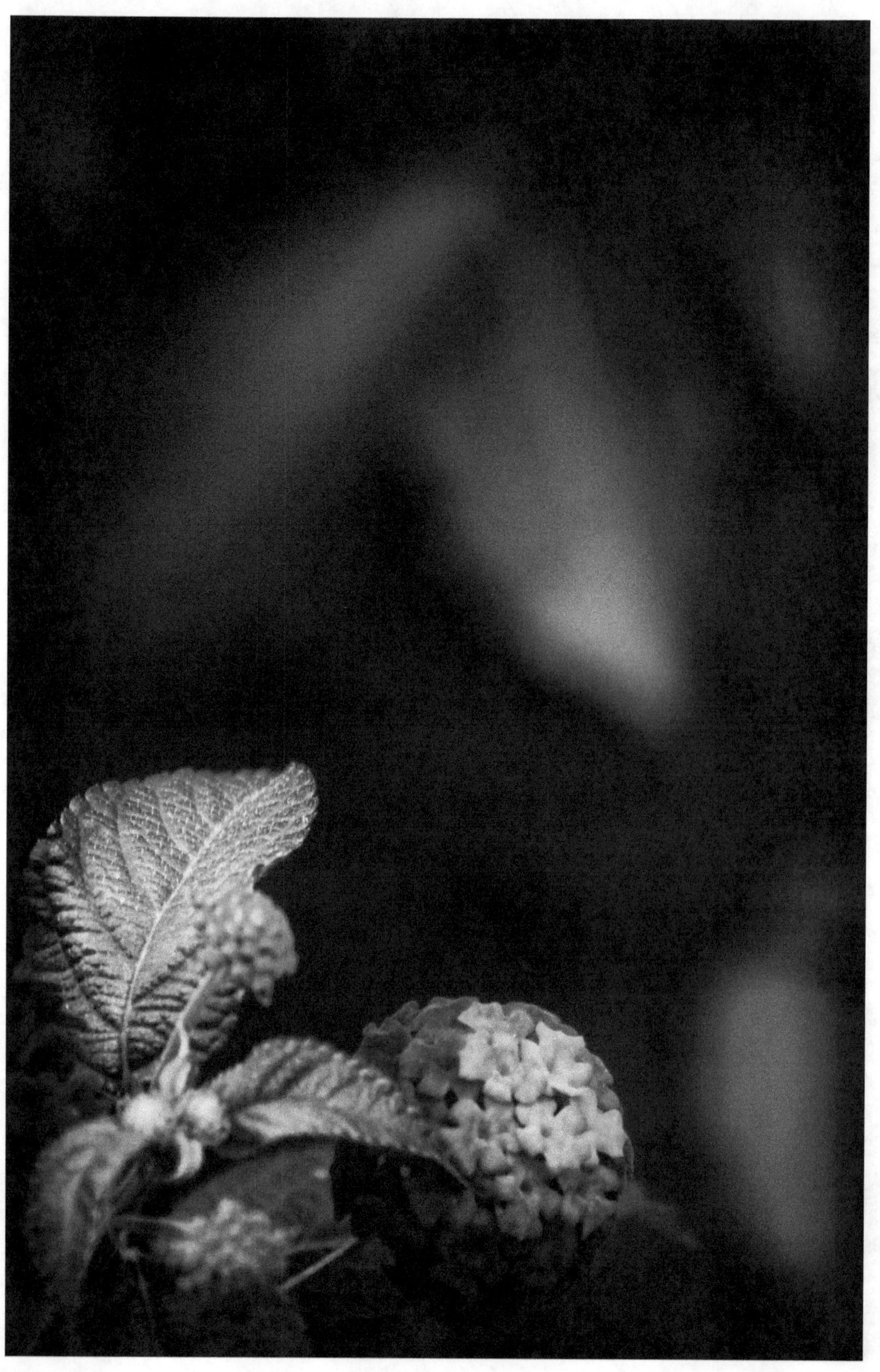

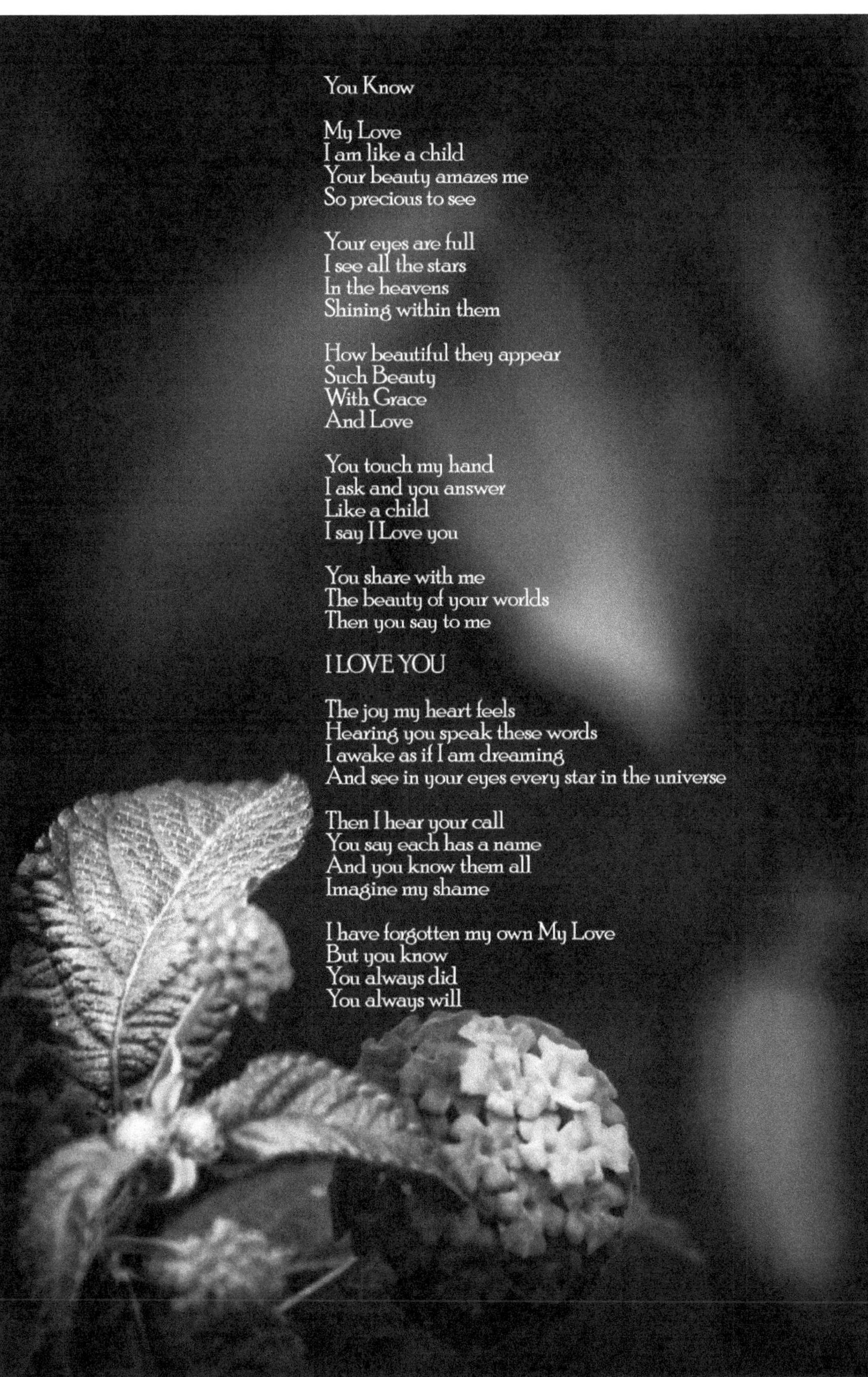

You Know

My Love
I am like a child
Your beauty amazes me
So precious to see

Your eyes are full
I see all the stars
In the heavens
Shining within them

How beautiful they appear
Such Beauty
With Grace
And Love

You touch my hand
I ask and you answer
Like a child
I say I Love you

You share with me
The beauty of your worlds
Then you say to me

I LOVE YOU

The joy my heart feels
Hearing you speak these words
I awake as if I am dreaming
And see in your eyes every star in the universe

Then I hear your call
You say each has a name
And you know them all
Imagine my shame

I have forgotten my own My Love
But you know
You always did
You always will

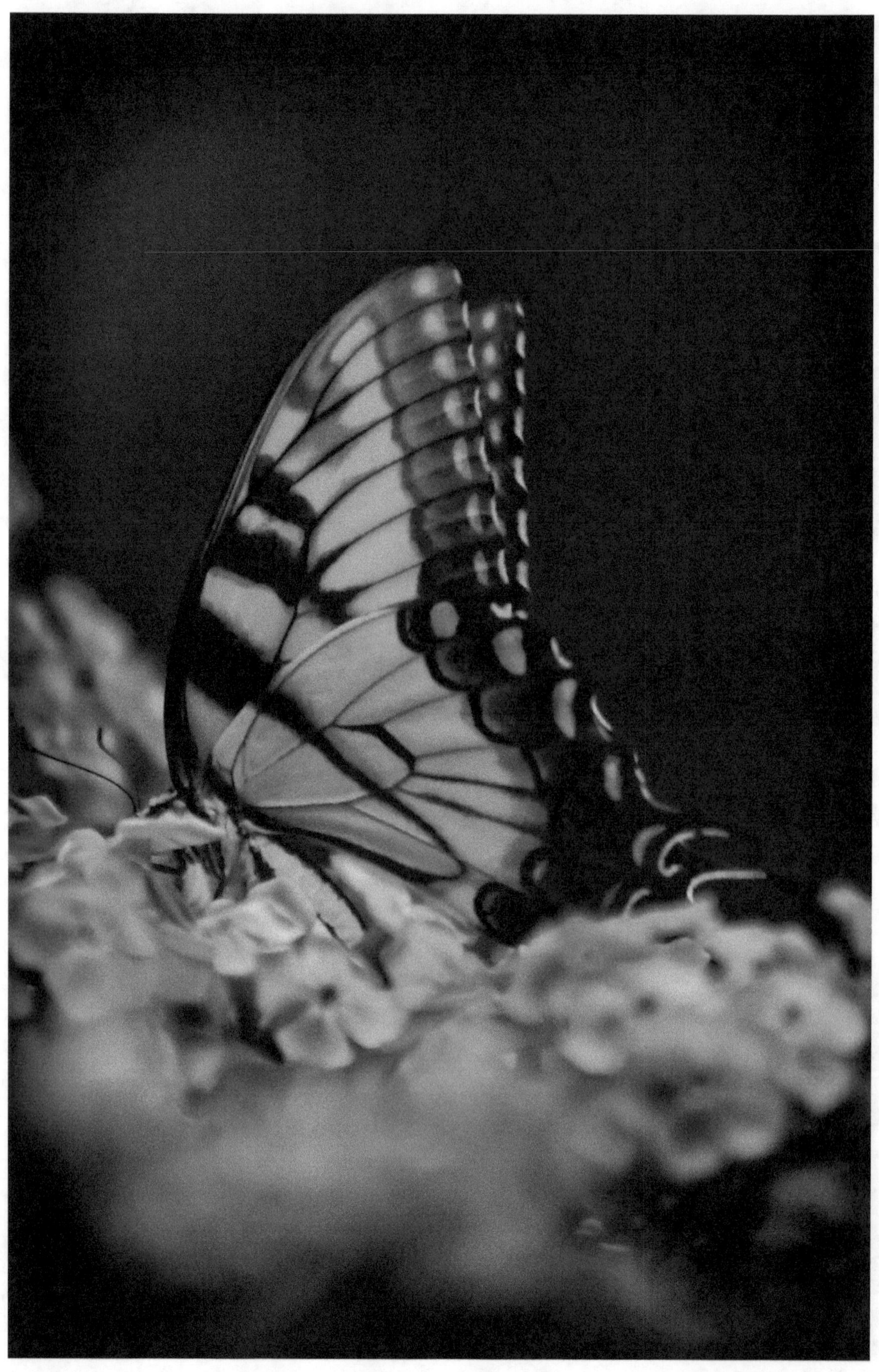

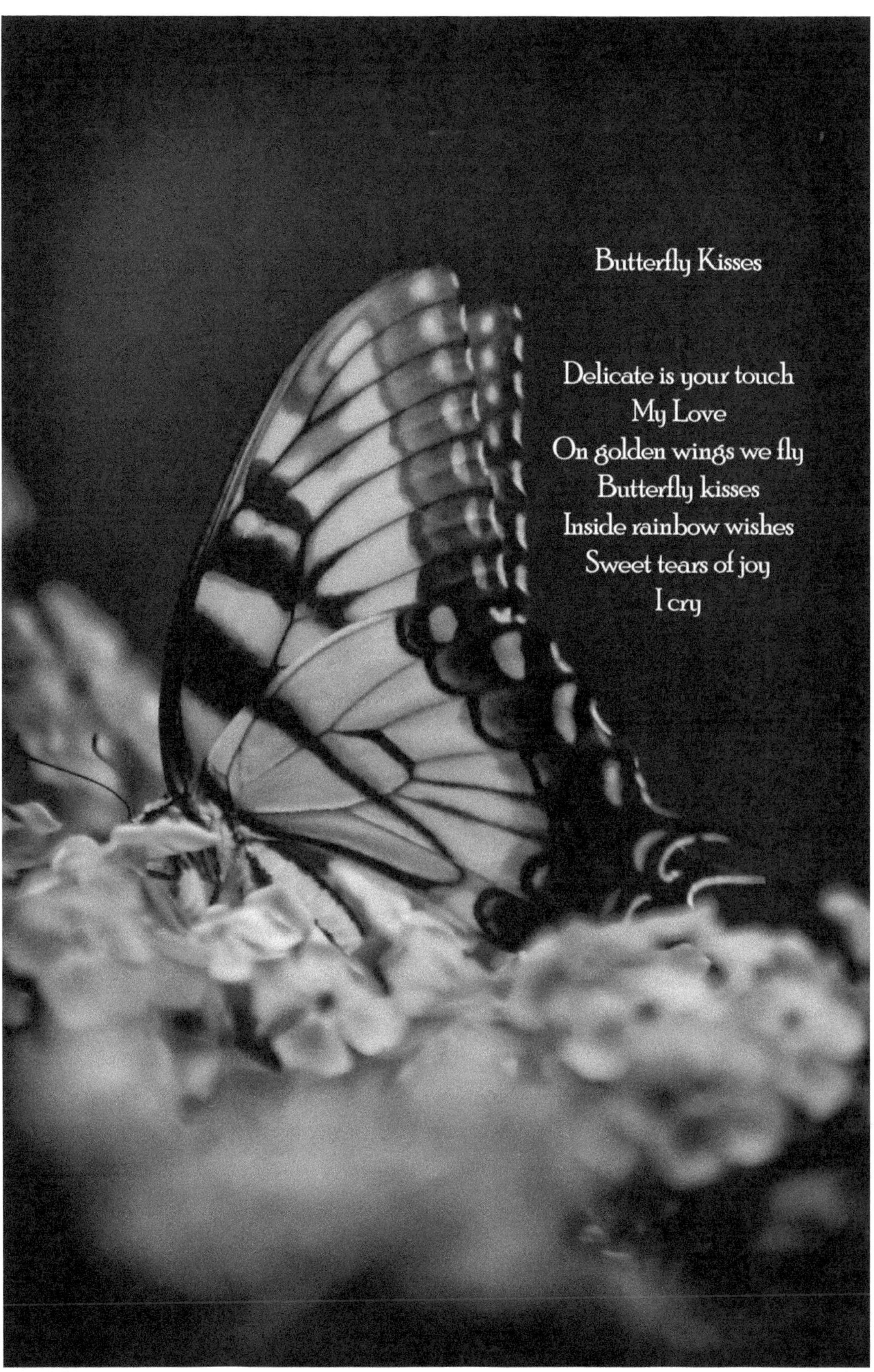
Butterfly Kisses
Delicate is your touch
My Love
On golden wings we fly
Butterfly kisses
Inside rainbow wishes
Sweet tears of joy
I cry

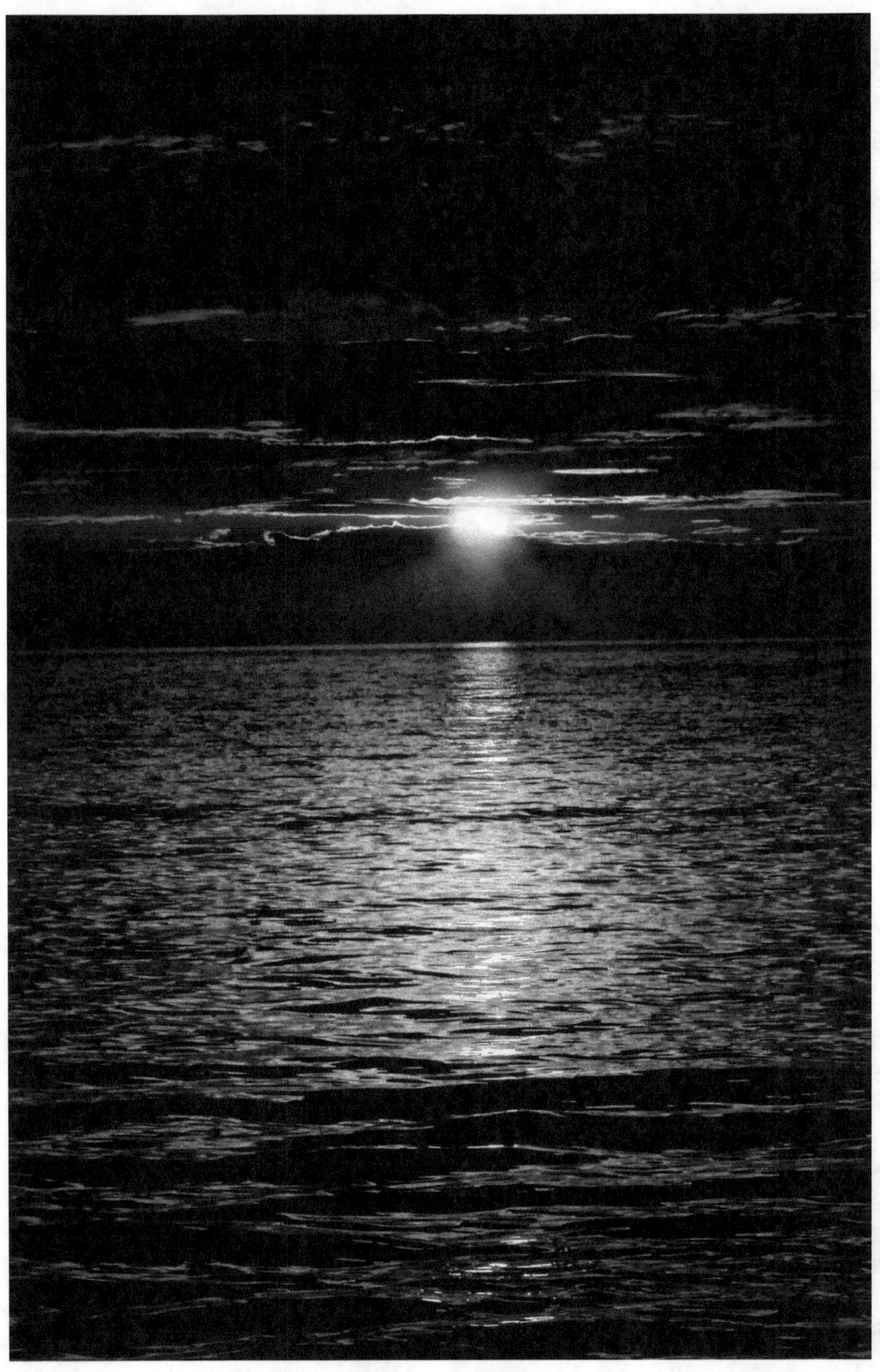

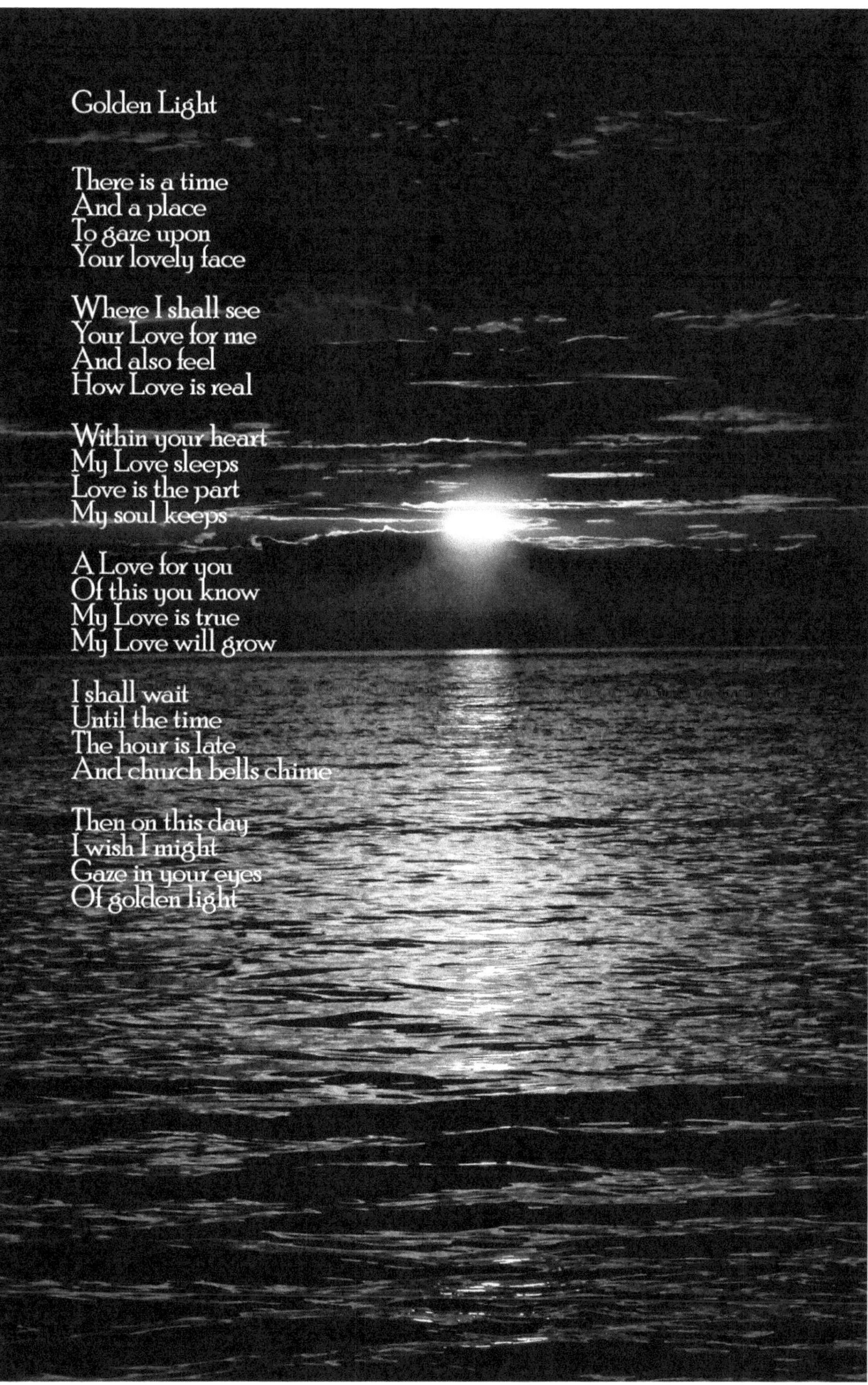

Golden Light

There is a time
And a place
To gaze upon
Your lovely face

Where I shall see
Your Love for me
And also feel
How Love is real

Within your heart
My Love sleeps
Love is the part
My soul keeps

A Love for you
Of this you know
My Love is true
My Love will grow

I shall wait
Until the time
The hour is late
And church bells chime

Then on this day
I wish I might
Gaze in your eyes
Of golden light

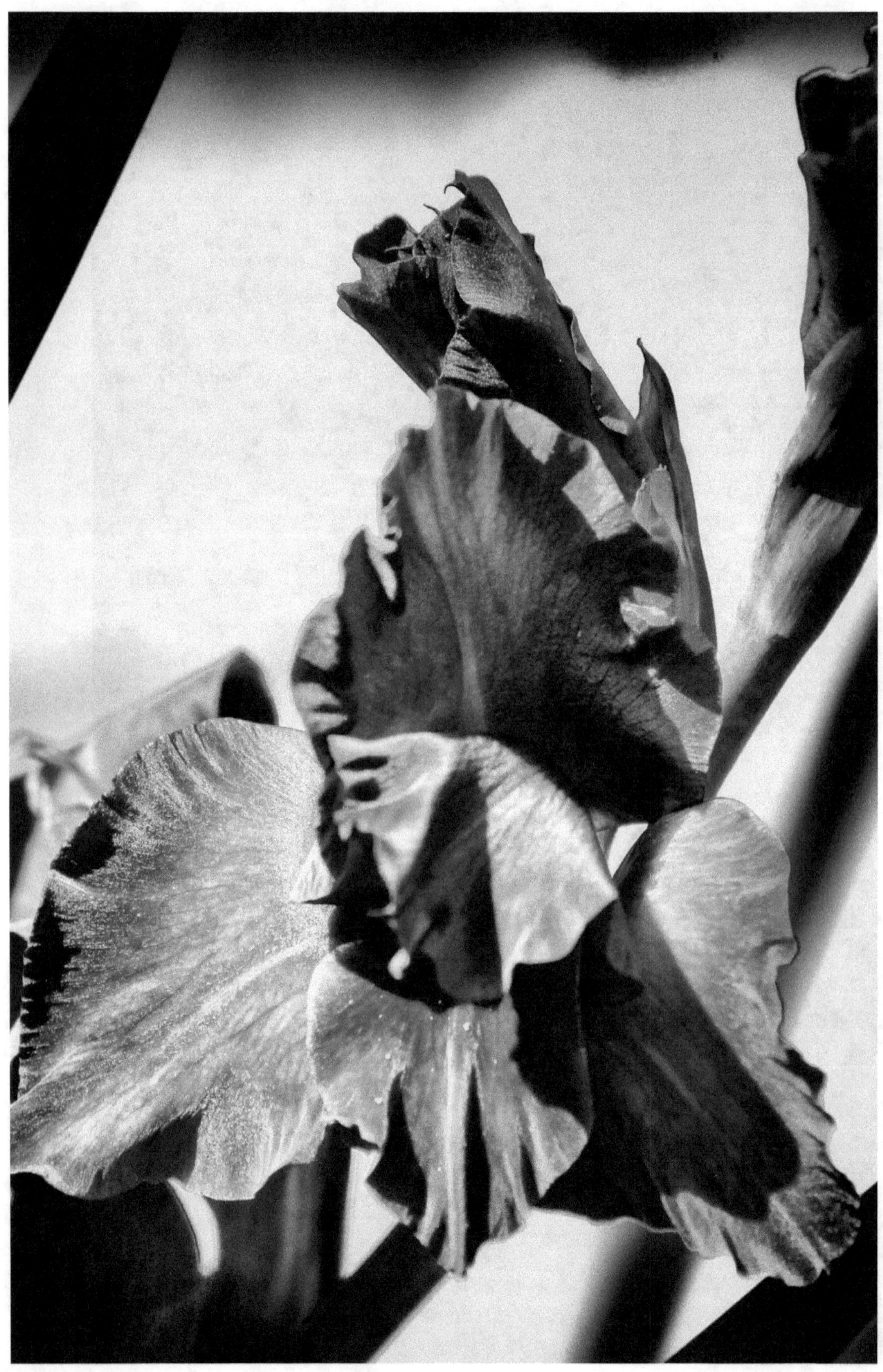

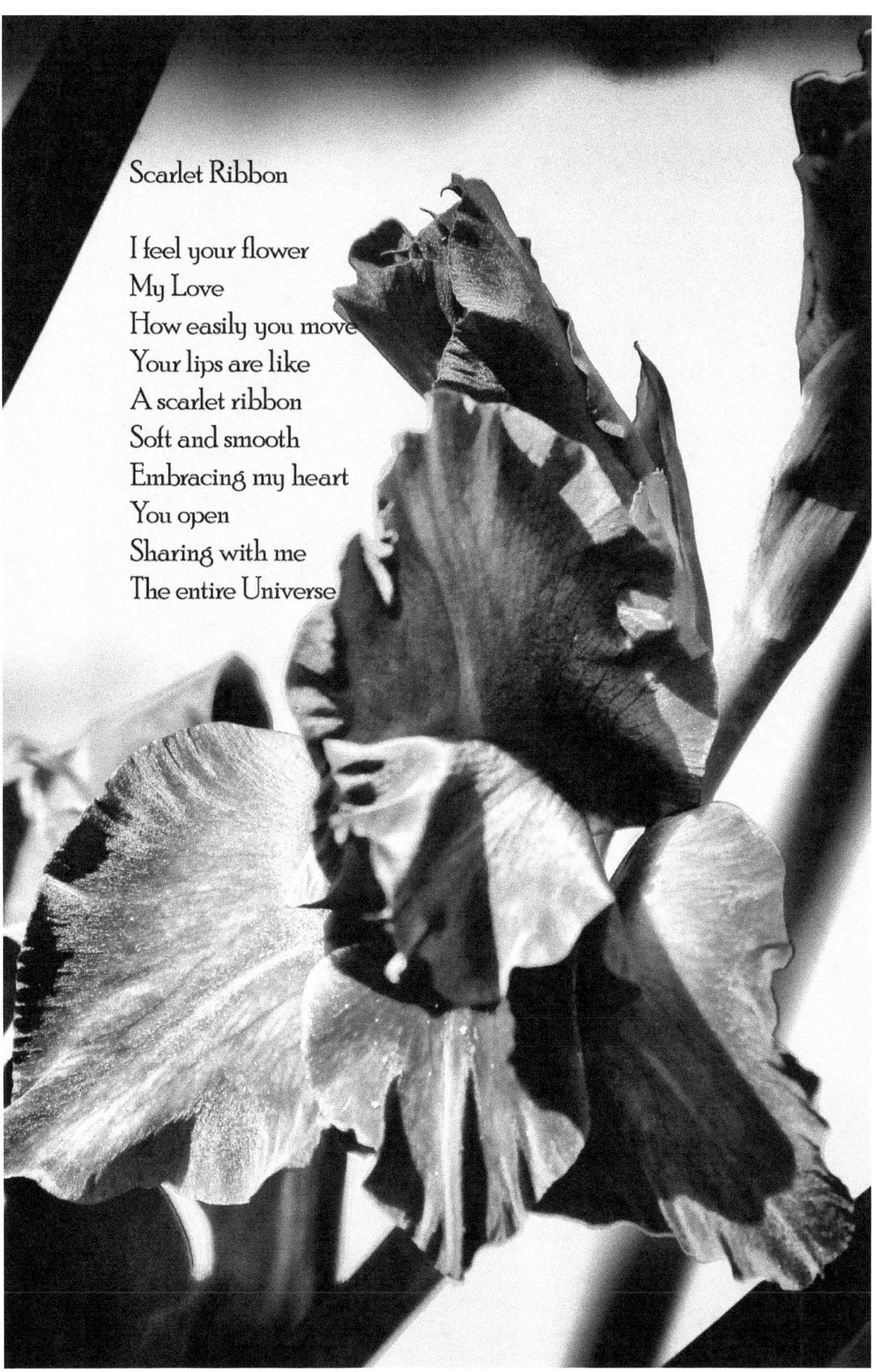

Scarlet Ribbon

I feel your flower
My Love
How easily you move
Your lips are like
A scarlet ribbon
Soft and smooth
Embracing my heart
You open
Sharing with me
The entire Universe

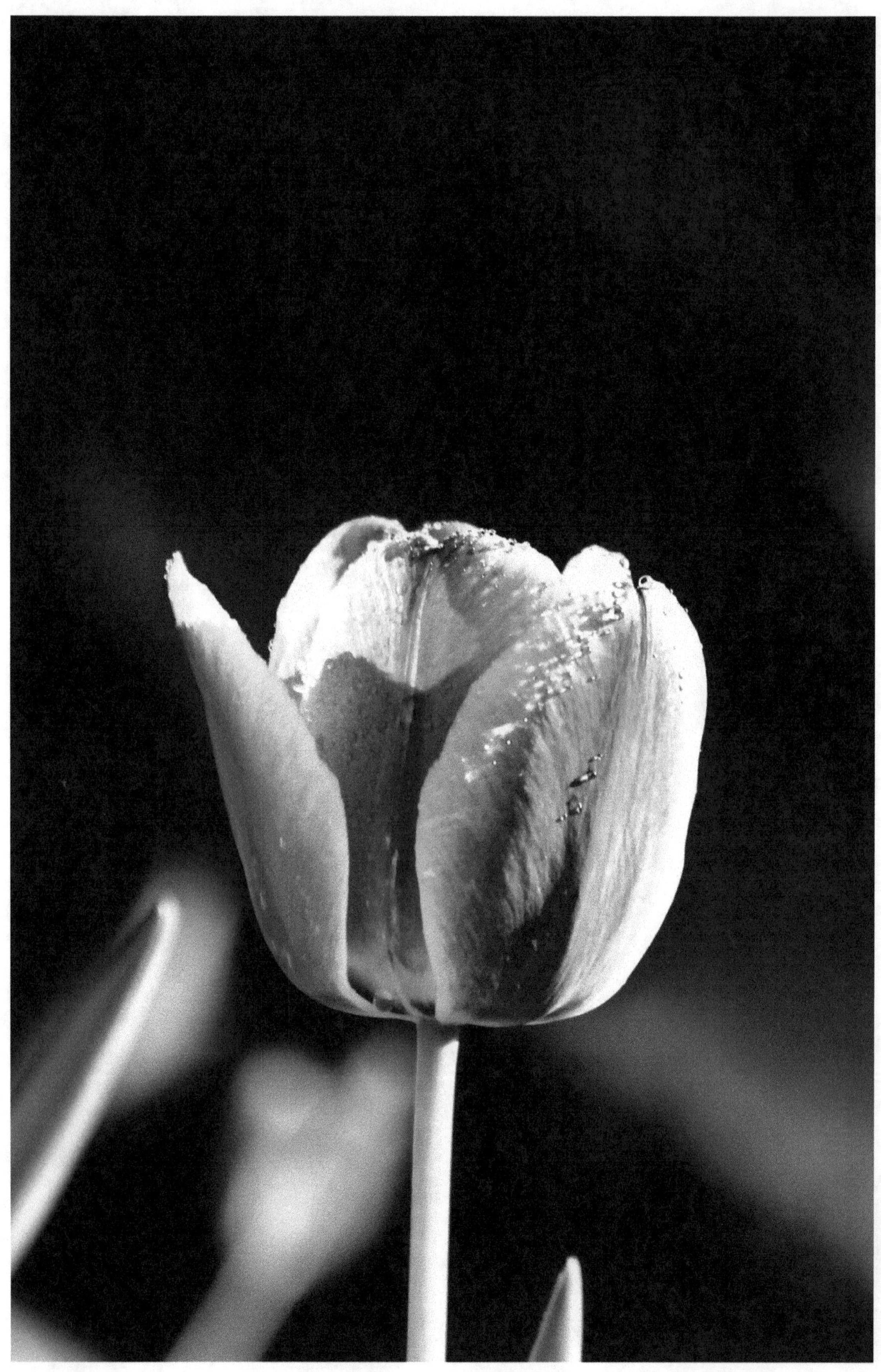

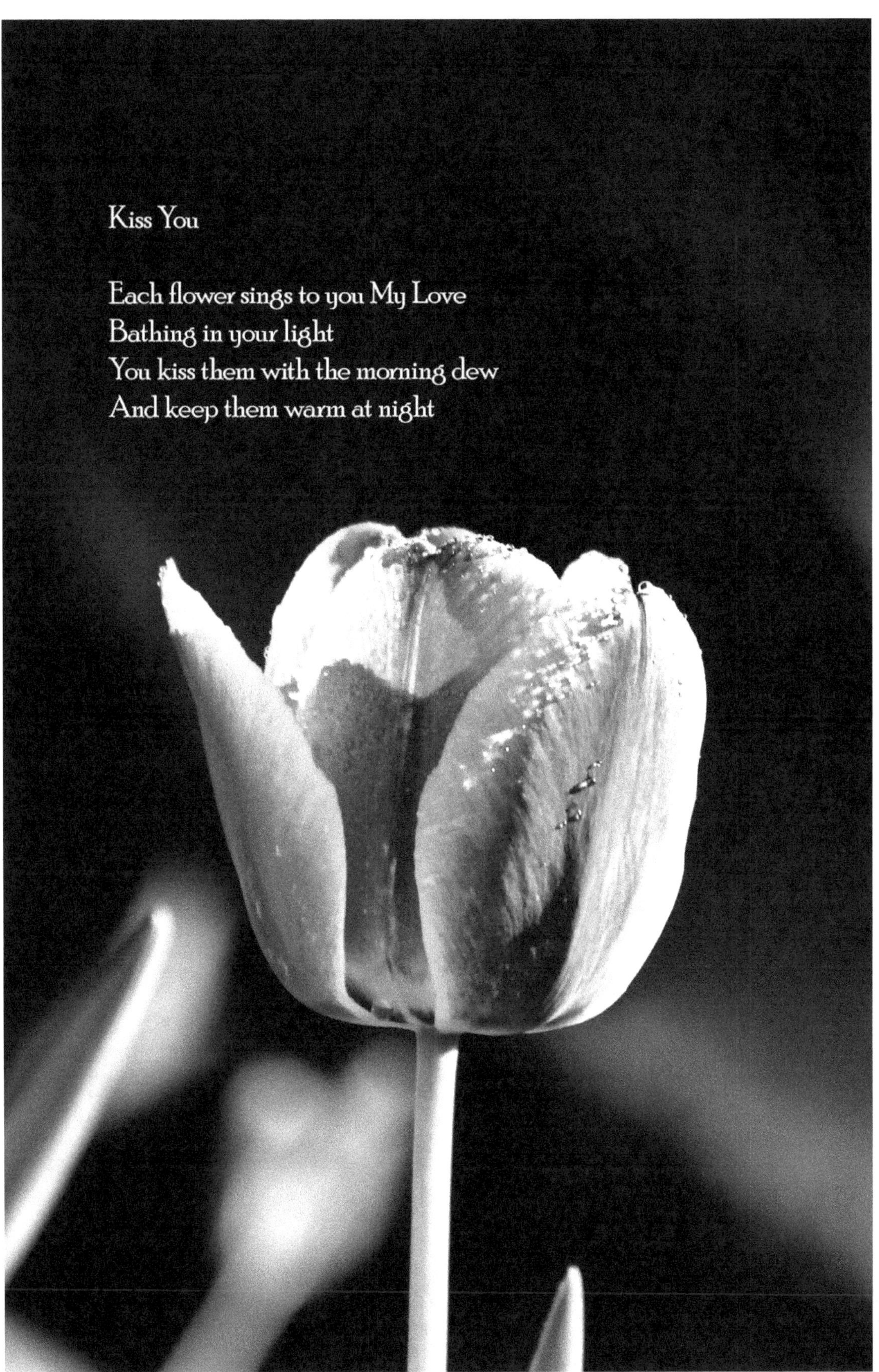
Kiss You

Each flower sings to you My Love
Bathing in your light
You kiss them with the morning dew
And keep them warm at night

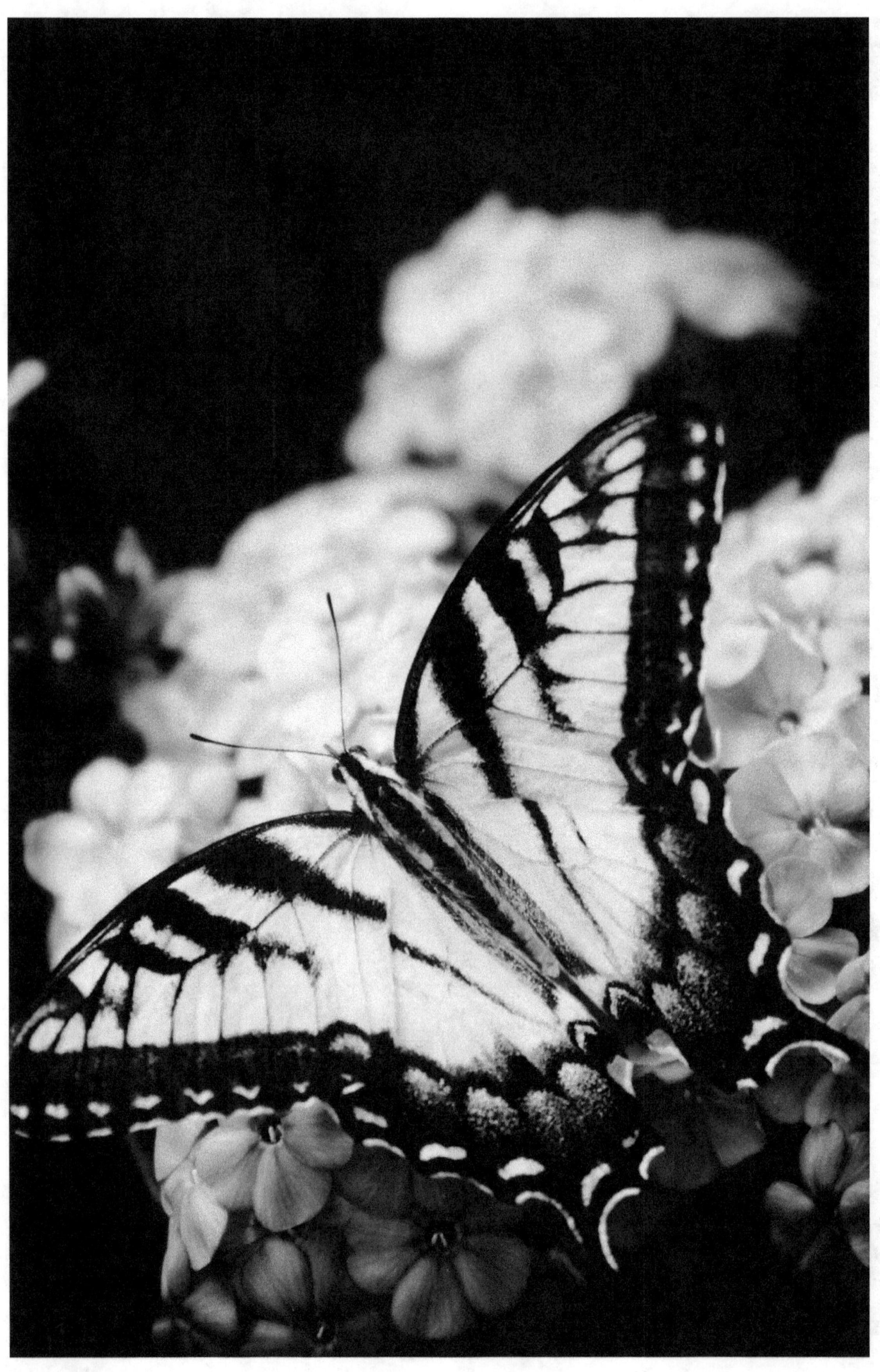

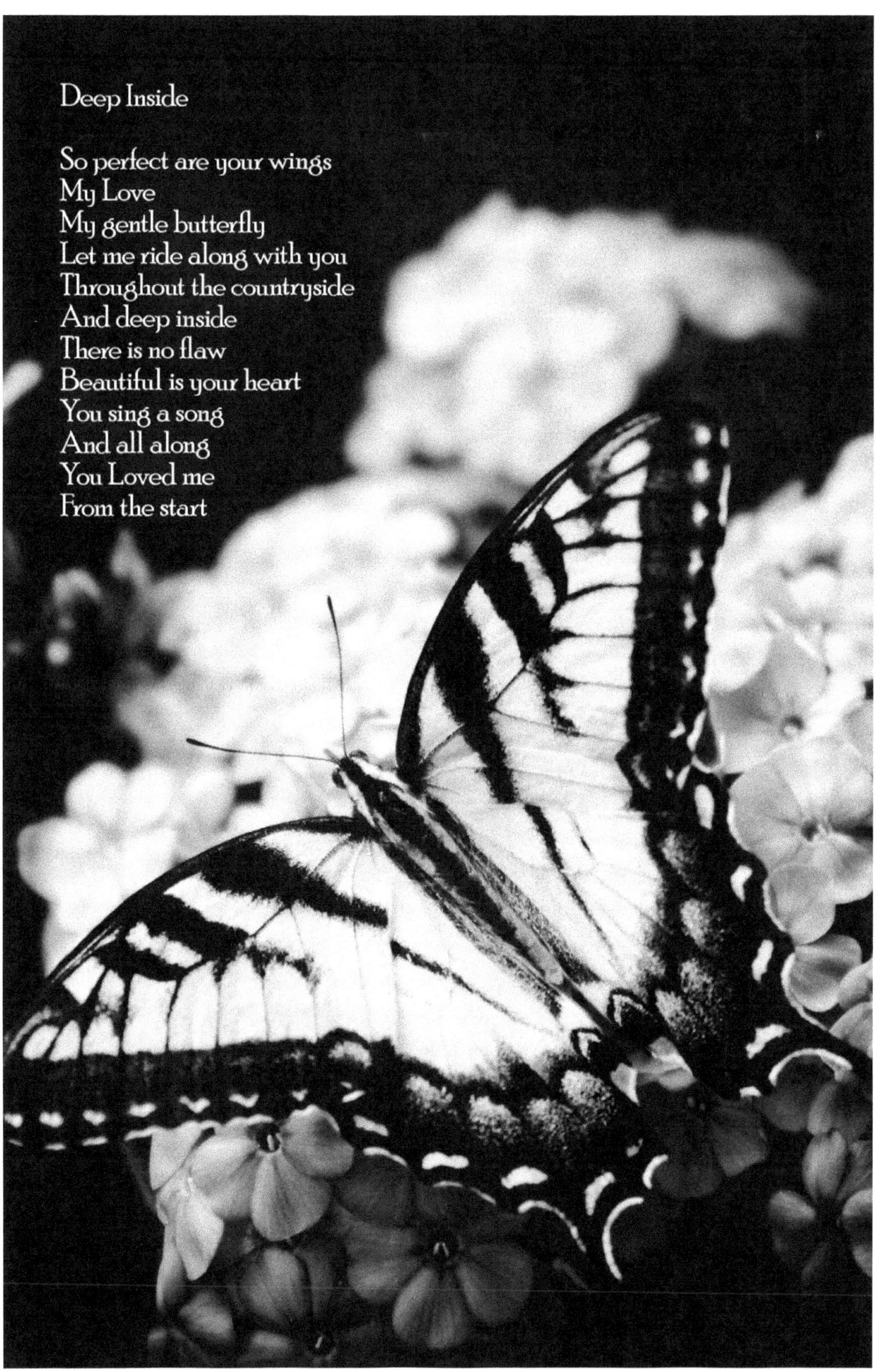

Deep Inside

So perfect are your wings
My Love
My gentle butterfly
Let me ride along with you
Throughout the countryside
And deep inside
There is no flaw
Beautiful is your heart
You sing a song
And all along
You Loved me
From the start

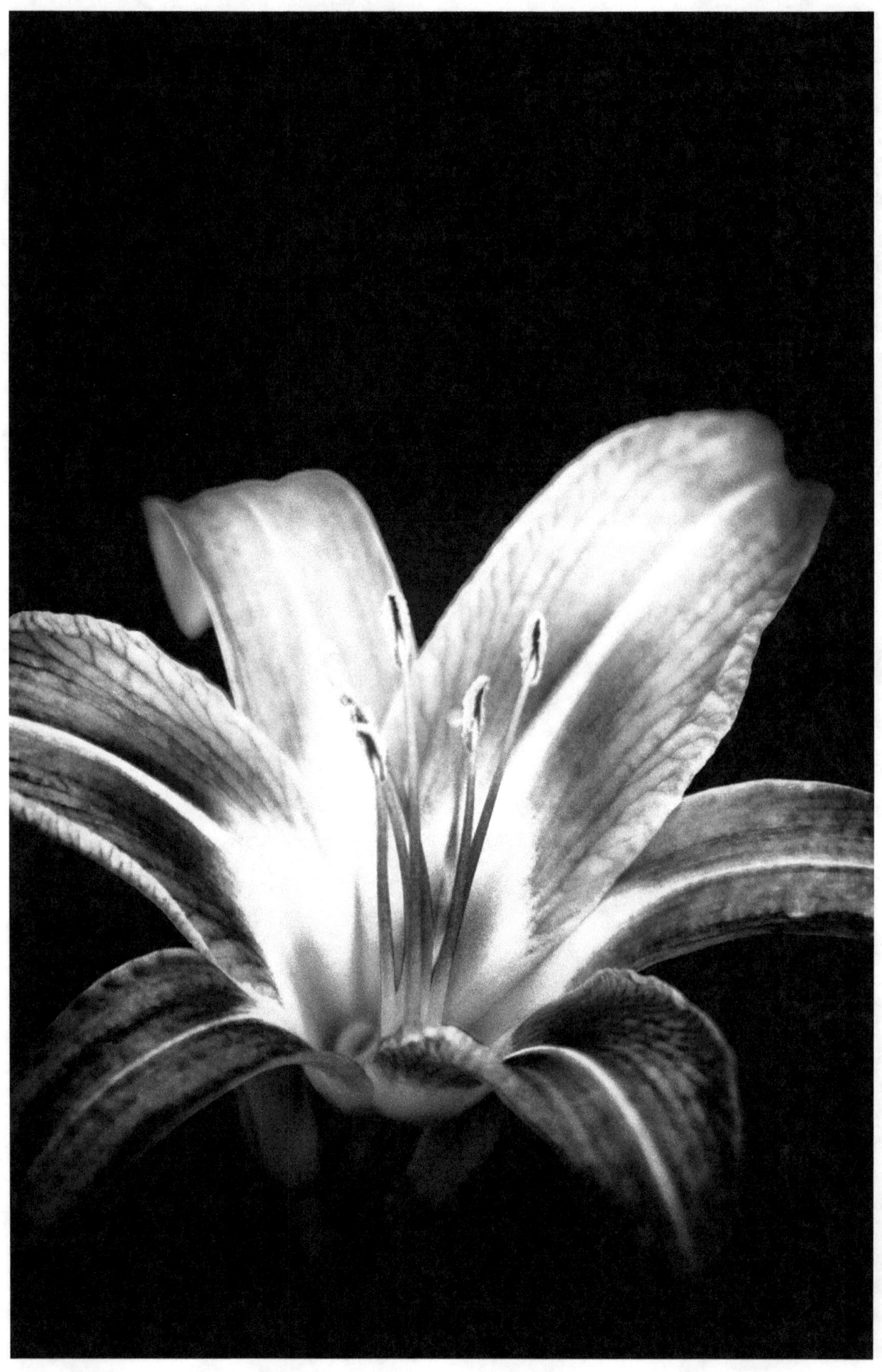

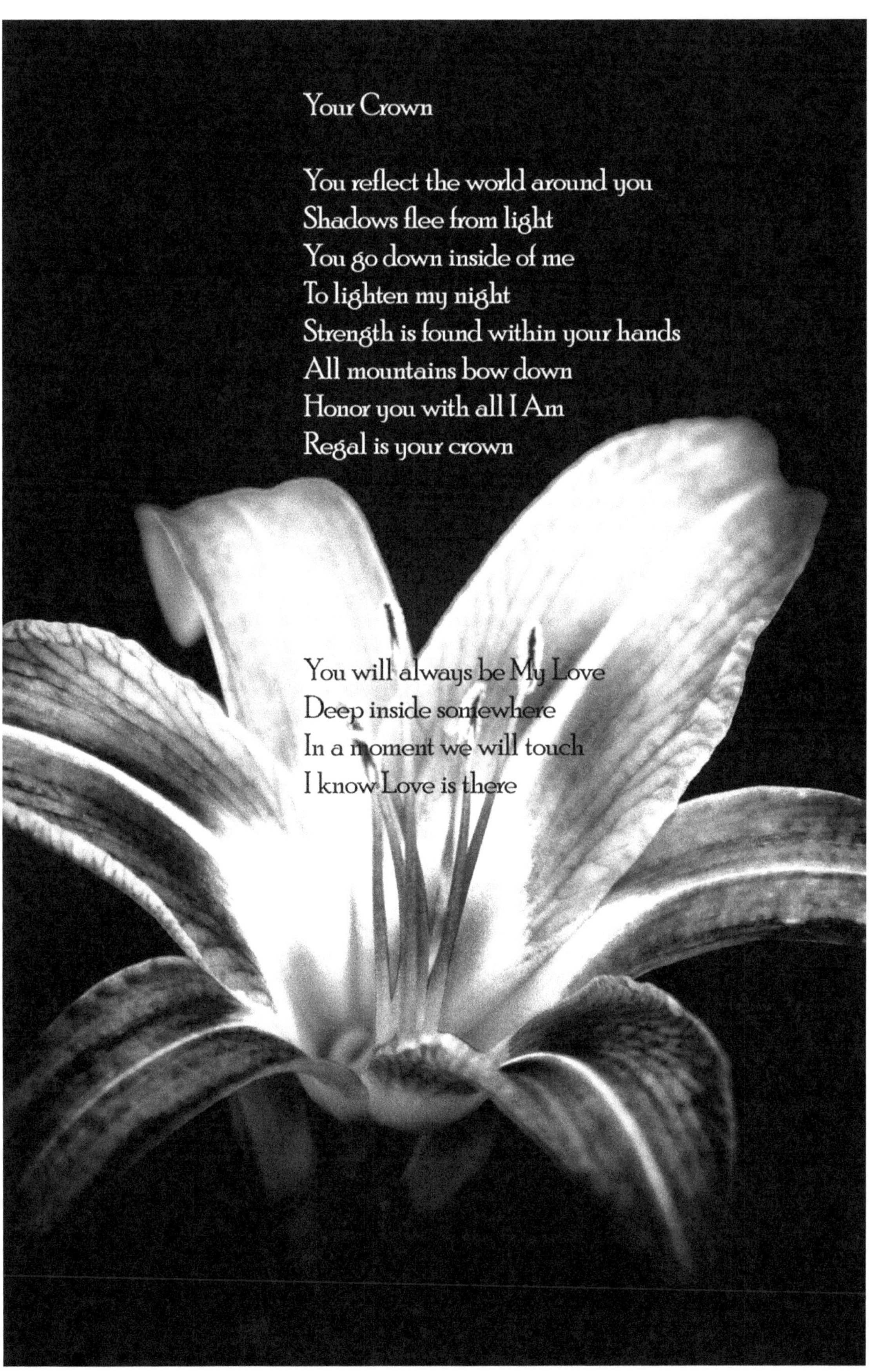

Your Crown

You reflect the world around you
Shadows flee from light
You go down inside of me
To lighten my night
Strength is found within your hands
All mountains bow down
Honor you with all I Am
Regal is your crown

You will always be My Love
Deep inside somewhere
In a moment we will touch
I know Love is there

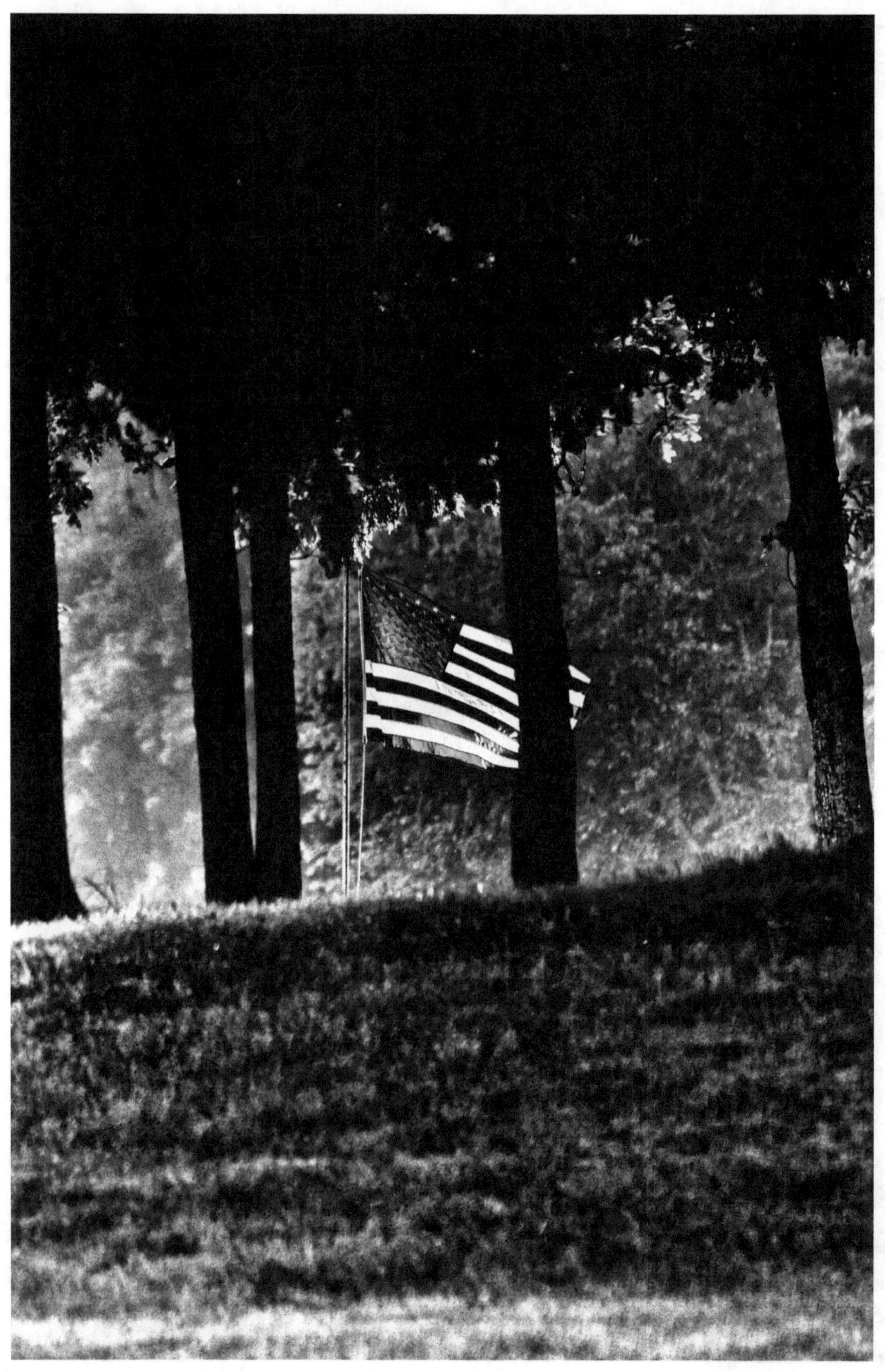

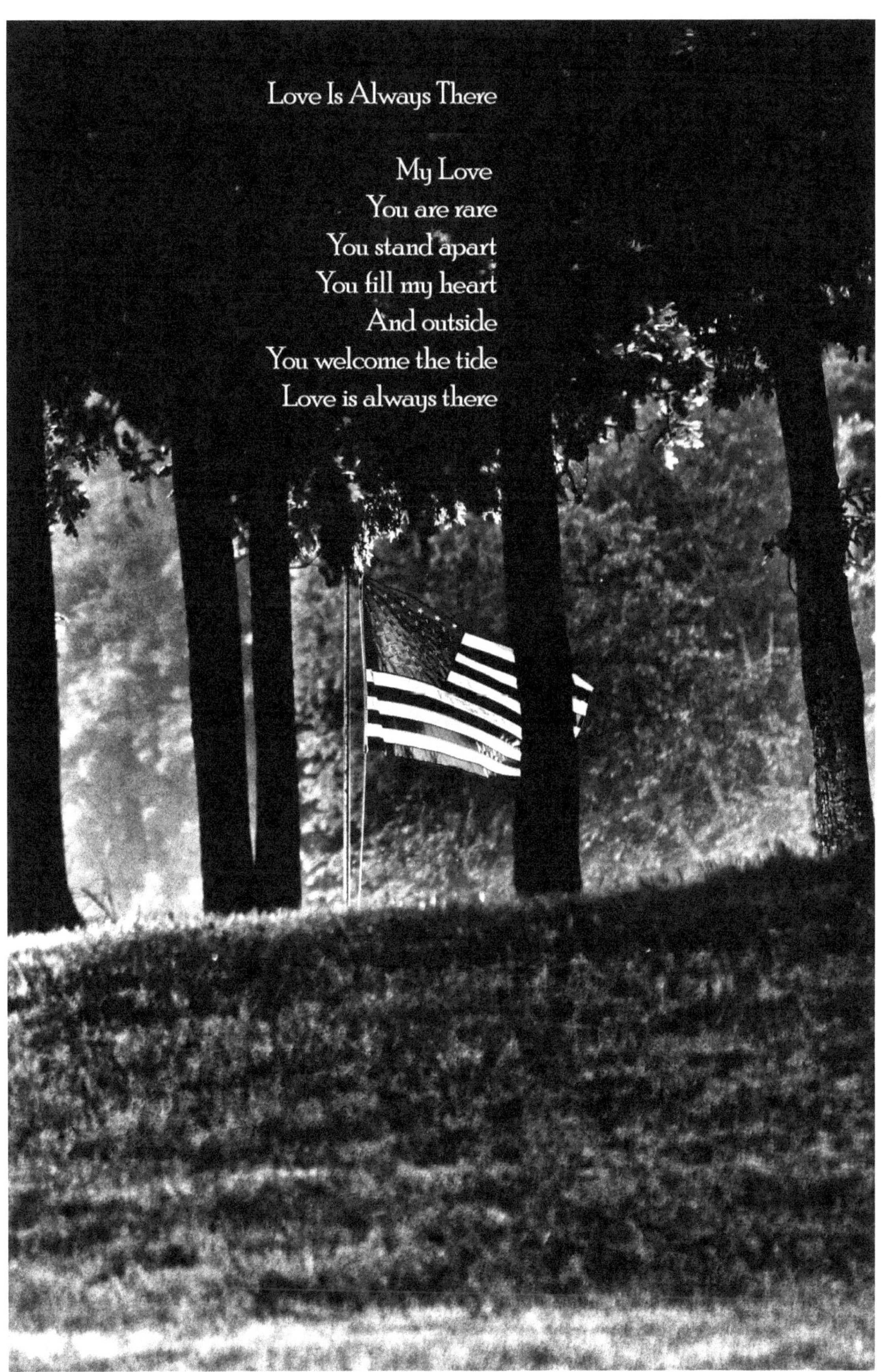

Love Is Always There

My Love
You are rare
You stand apart
You fill my heart
And outside
You welcome the tide
Love is always there

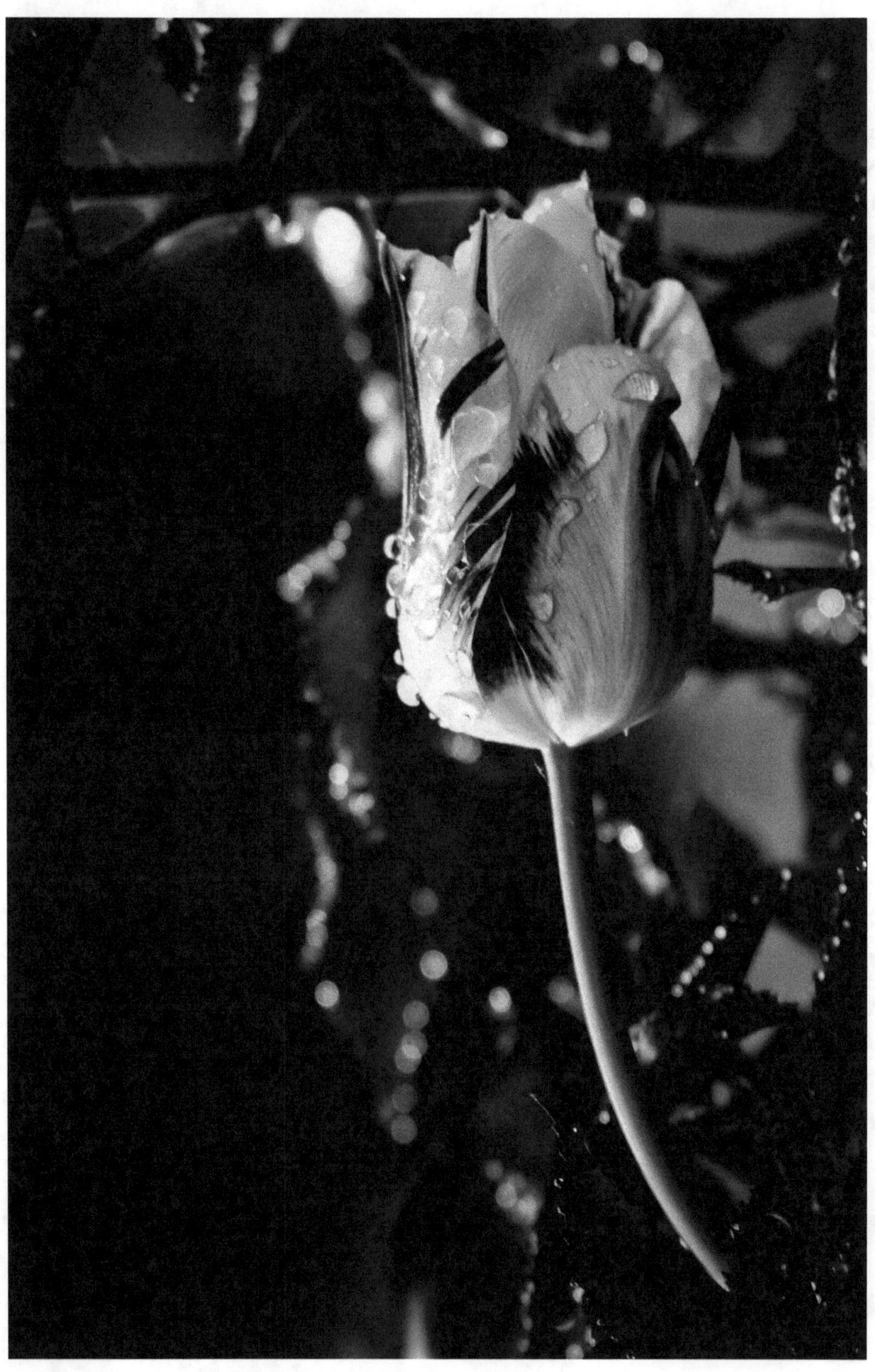

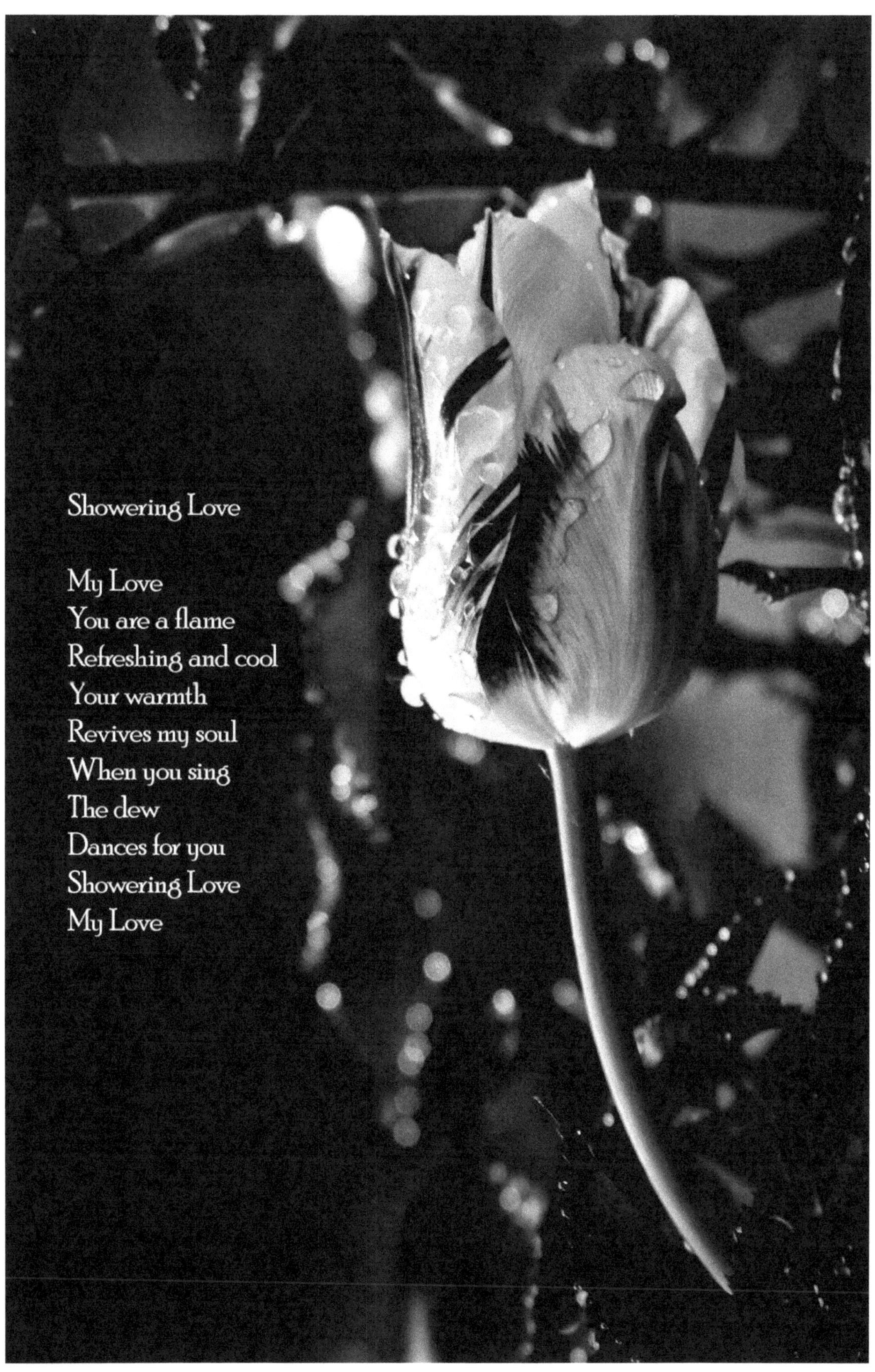

Showering Love

My Love
You are a flame
Refreshing and cool
Your warmth
Revives my soul
When you sing
The dew
Dances for you
Showering Love
My Love

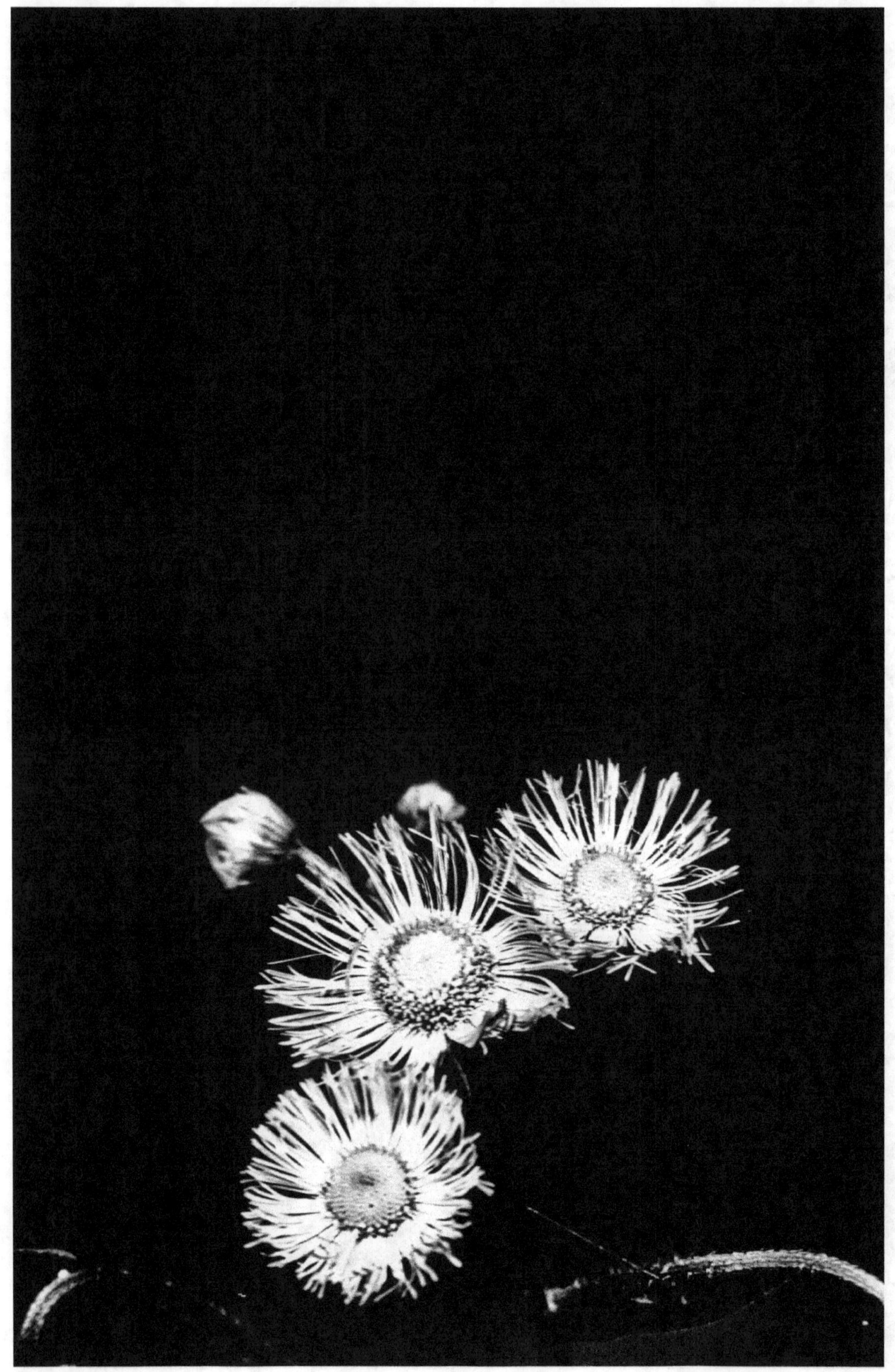

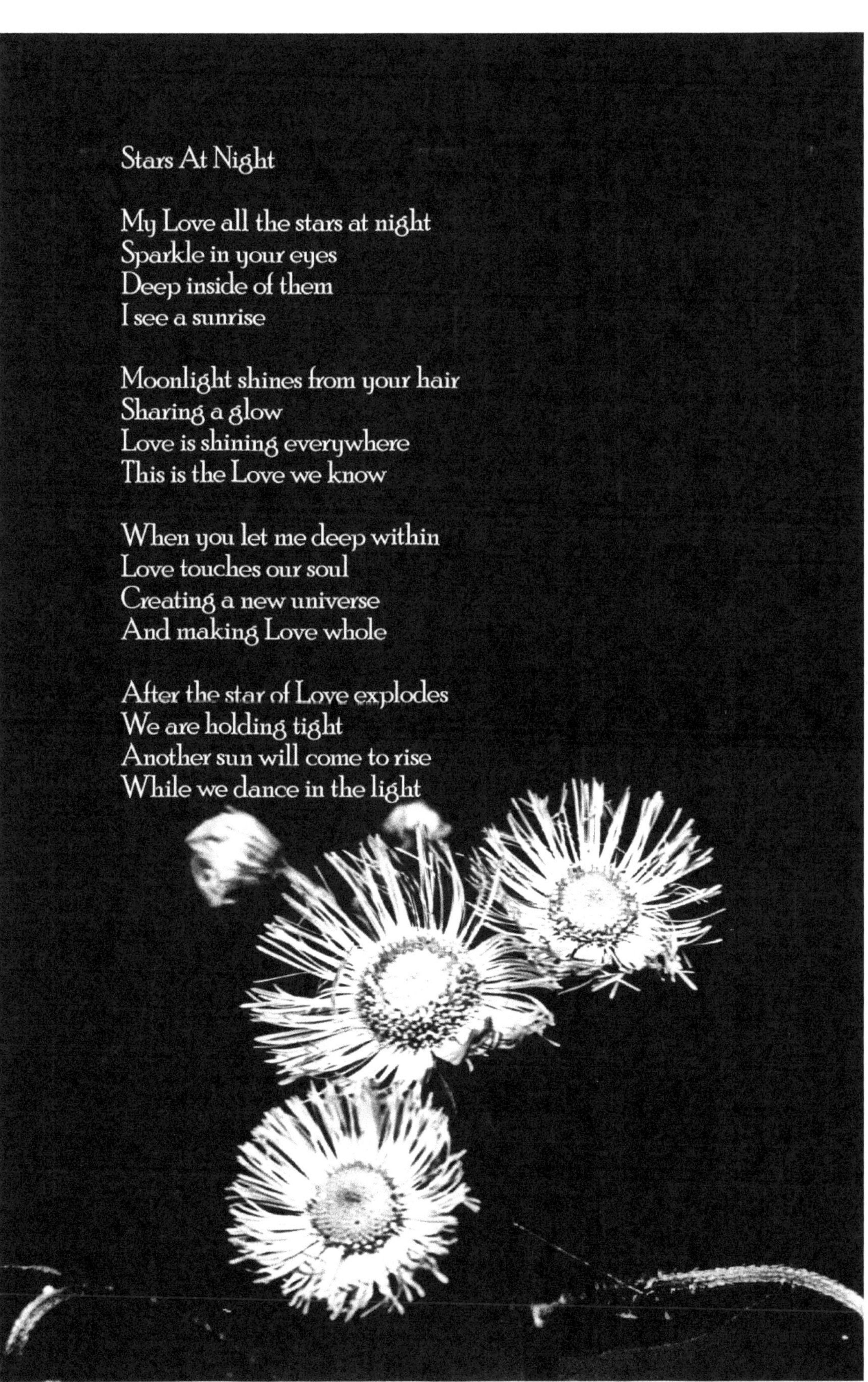

Stars At Night

My Love all the stars at night
Sparkle in your eyes
Deep inside of them
I see a sunrise

Moonlight shines from your hair
Sharing a glow
Love is shining everywhere
This is the Love we know

When you let me deep within
Love touches our soul
Creating a new universe
And making Love whole

After the star of Love explodes
We are holding tight
Another sun will come to rise
While we dance in the light

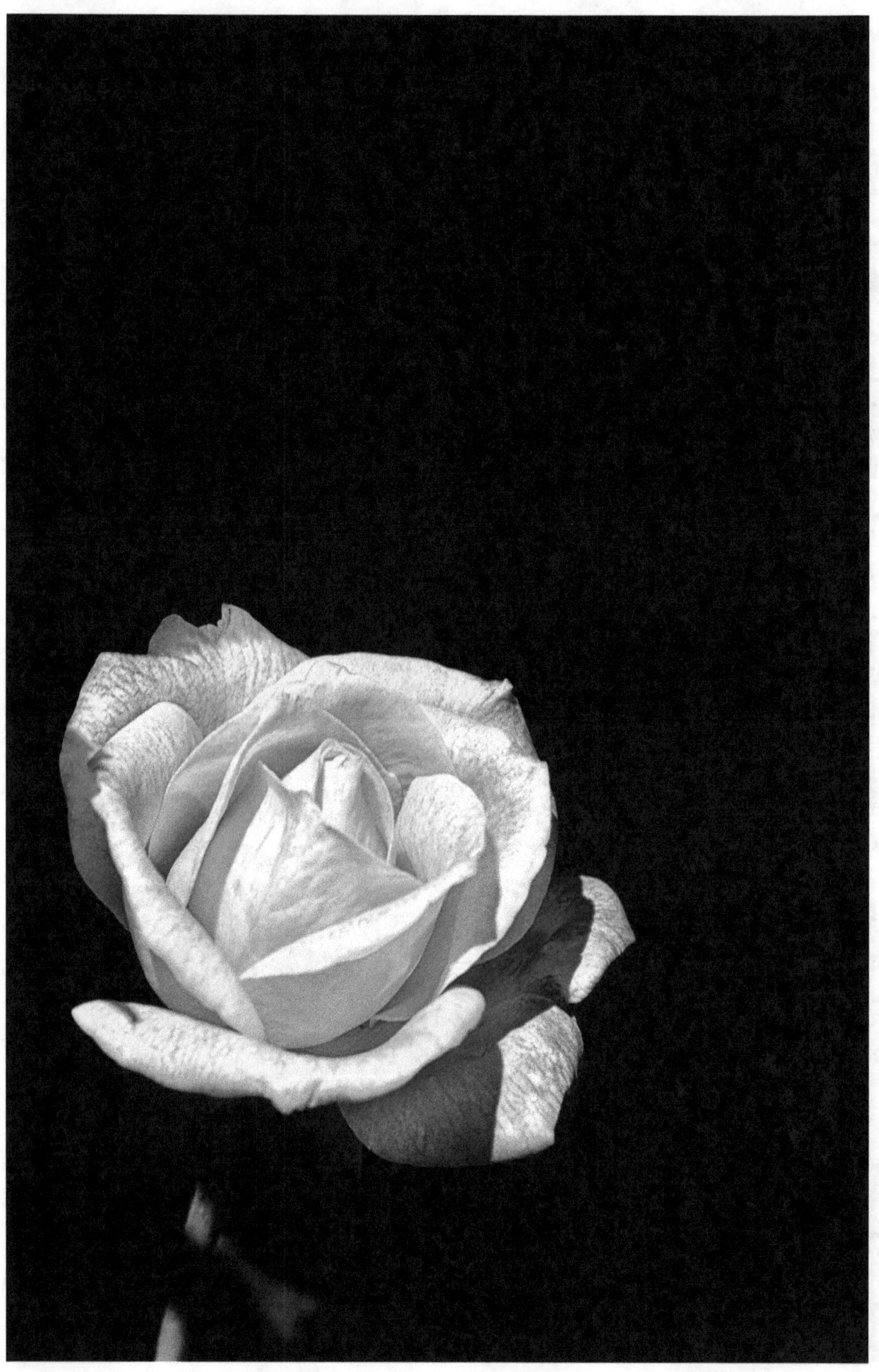

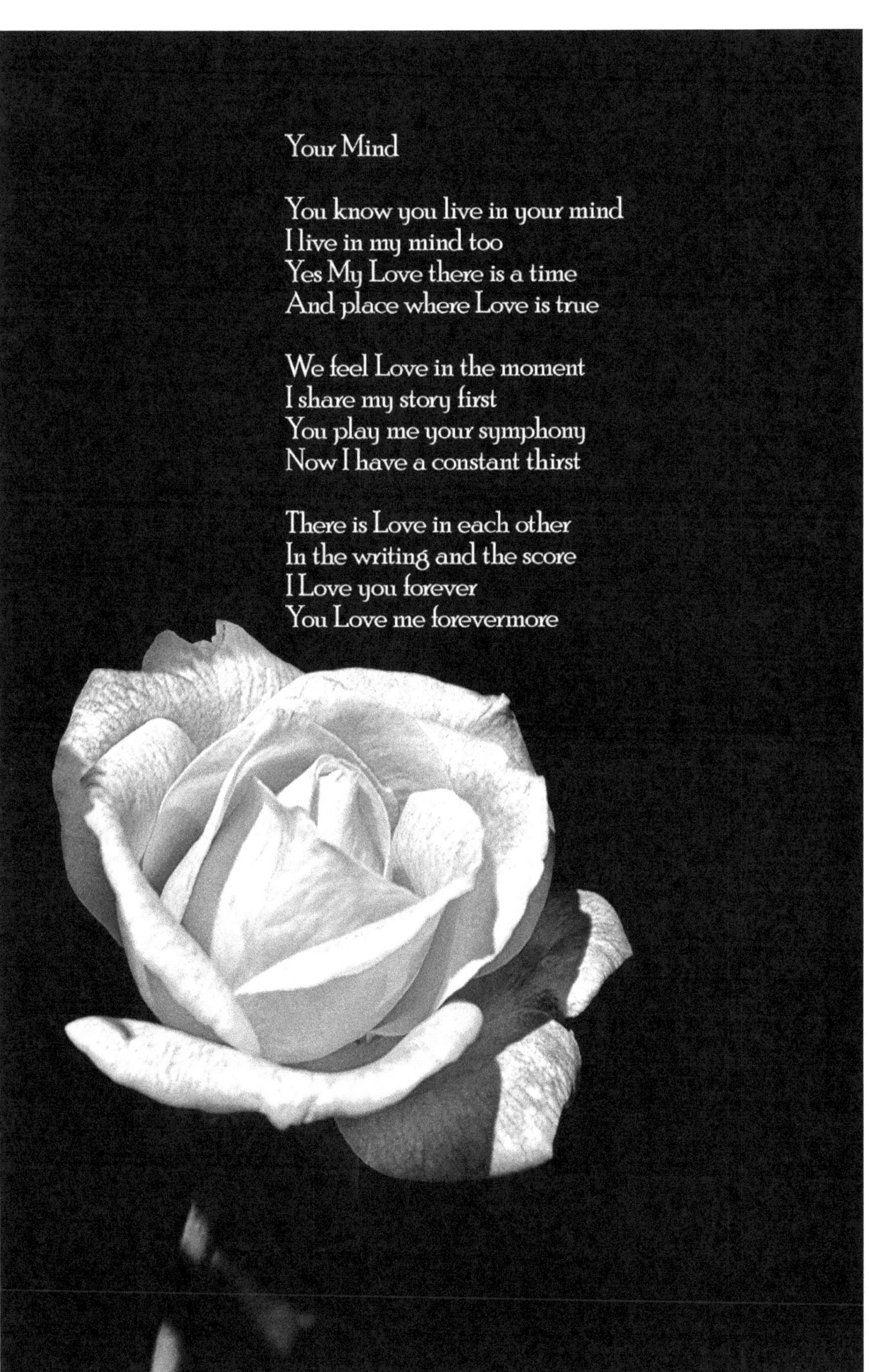

Your Mind

You know you live in your mind
I live in my mind too
Yes My Love there is a time
And place where Love is true

We feel Love in the moment
I share my story first
You play me your symphony
Now I have a constant thirst

There is Love in each other
In the writing and the score
I Love you forever
You Love me forevermore

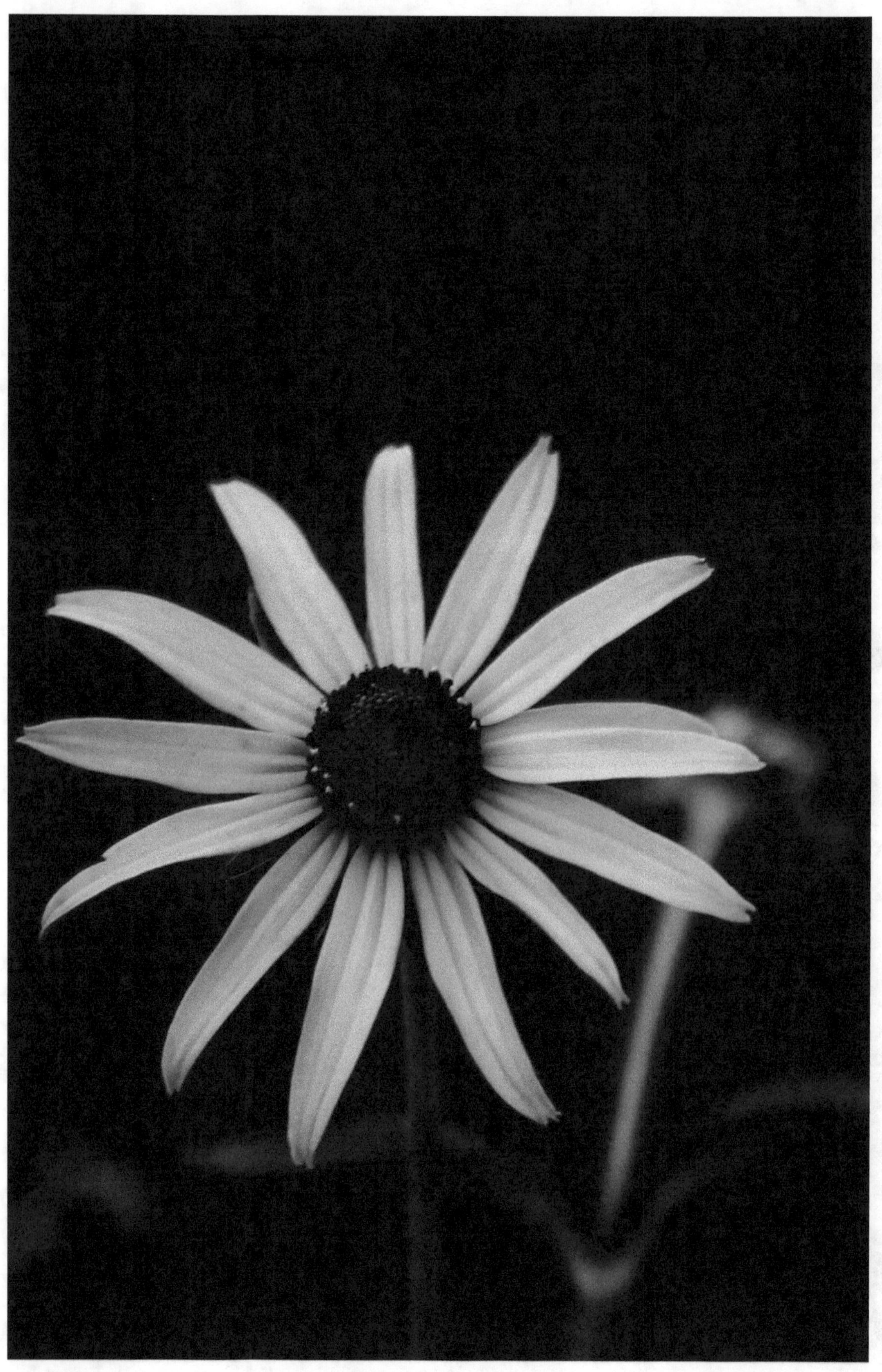

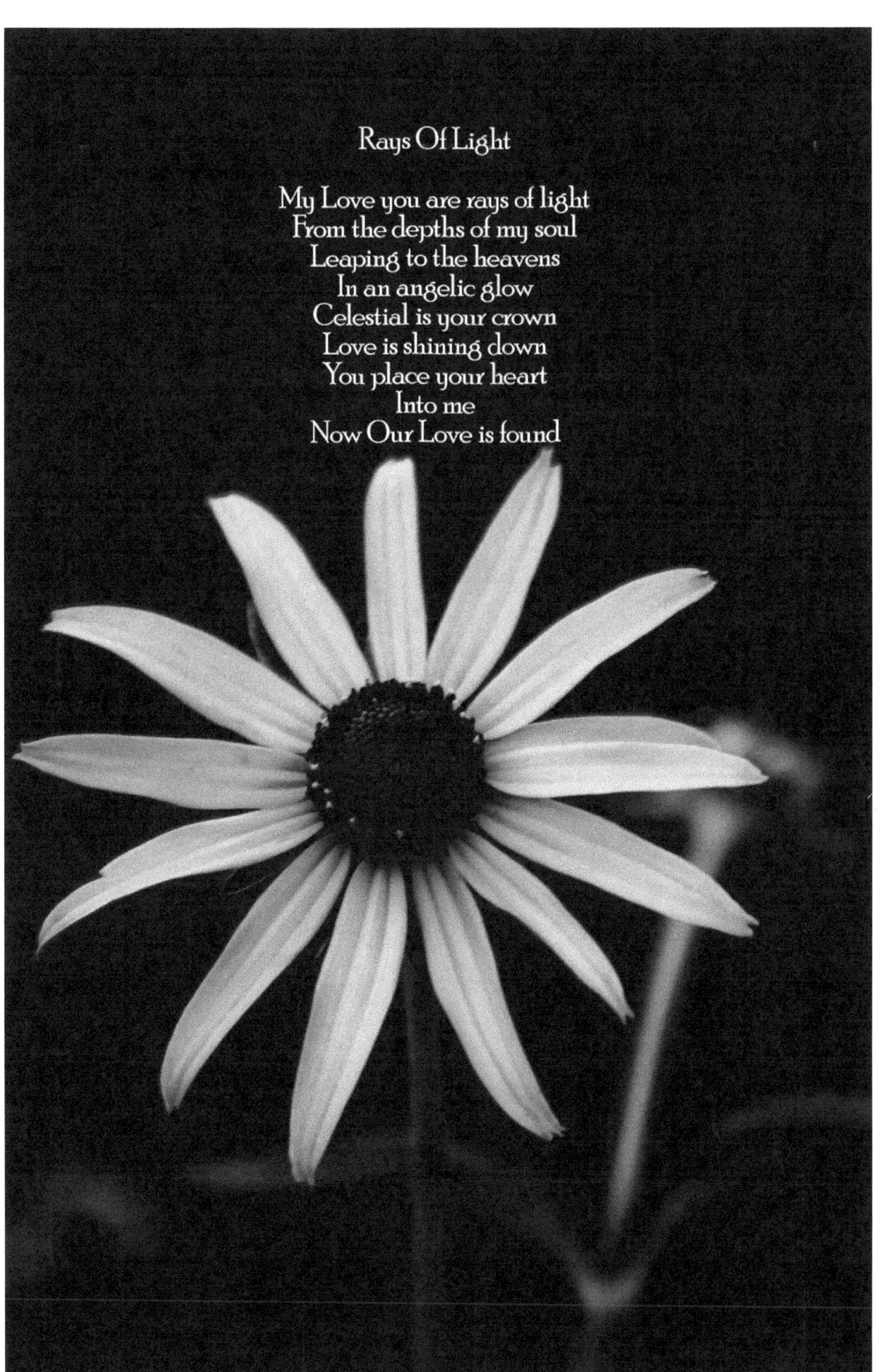
Rays Of Light

My Love you are rays of light
From the depths of my soul
Leaping to the heavens
In an angelic glow
Celestial is your crown
Love is shining down
You place your heart
Into me
Now Our Love is found

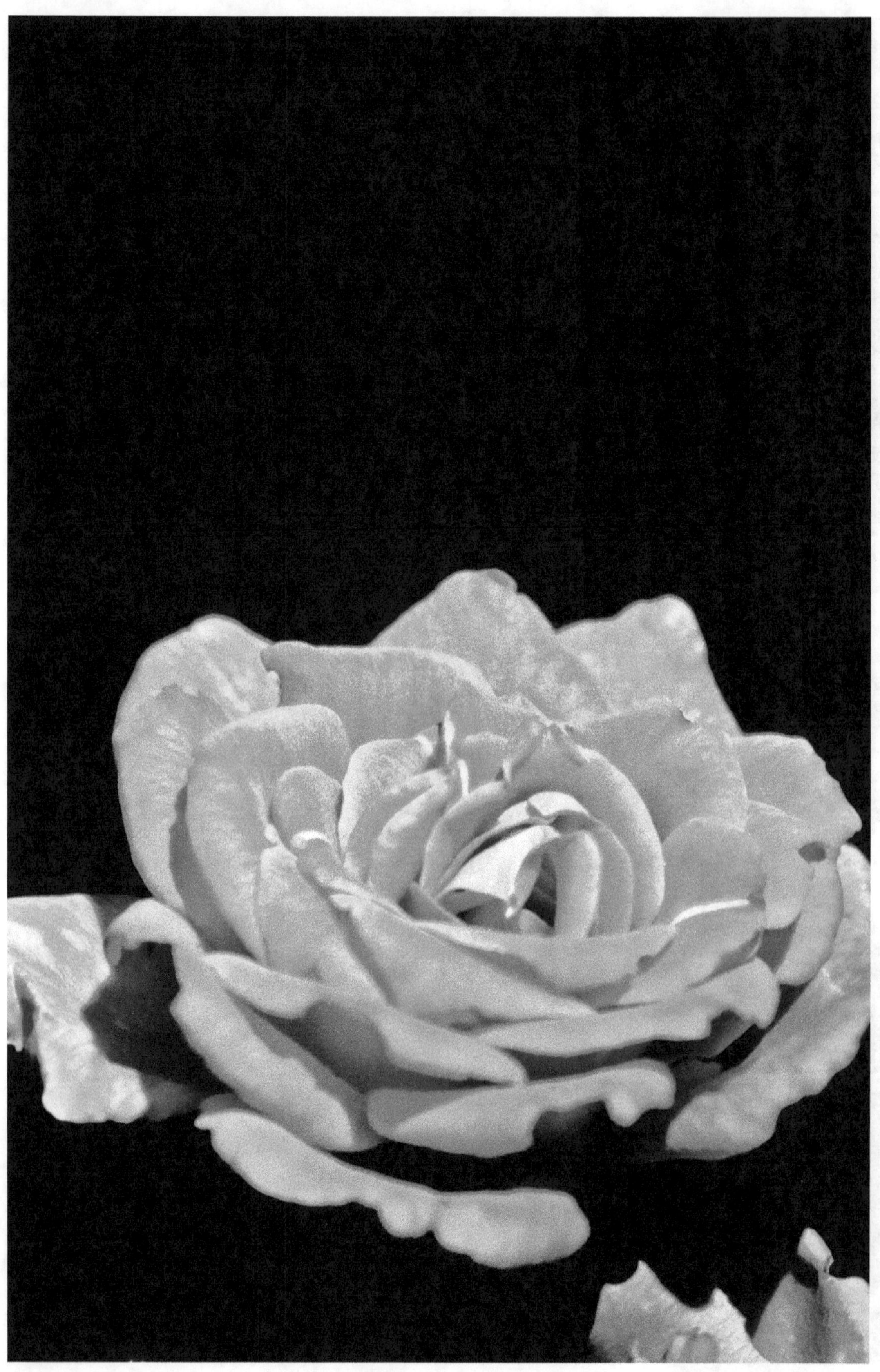

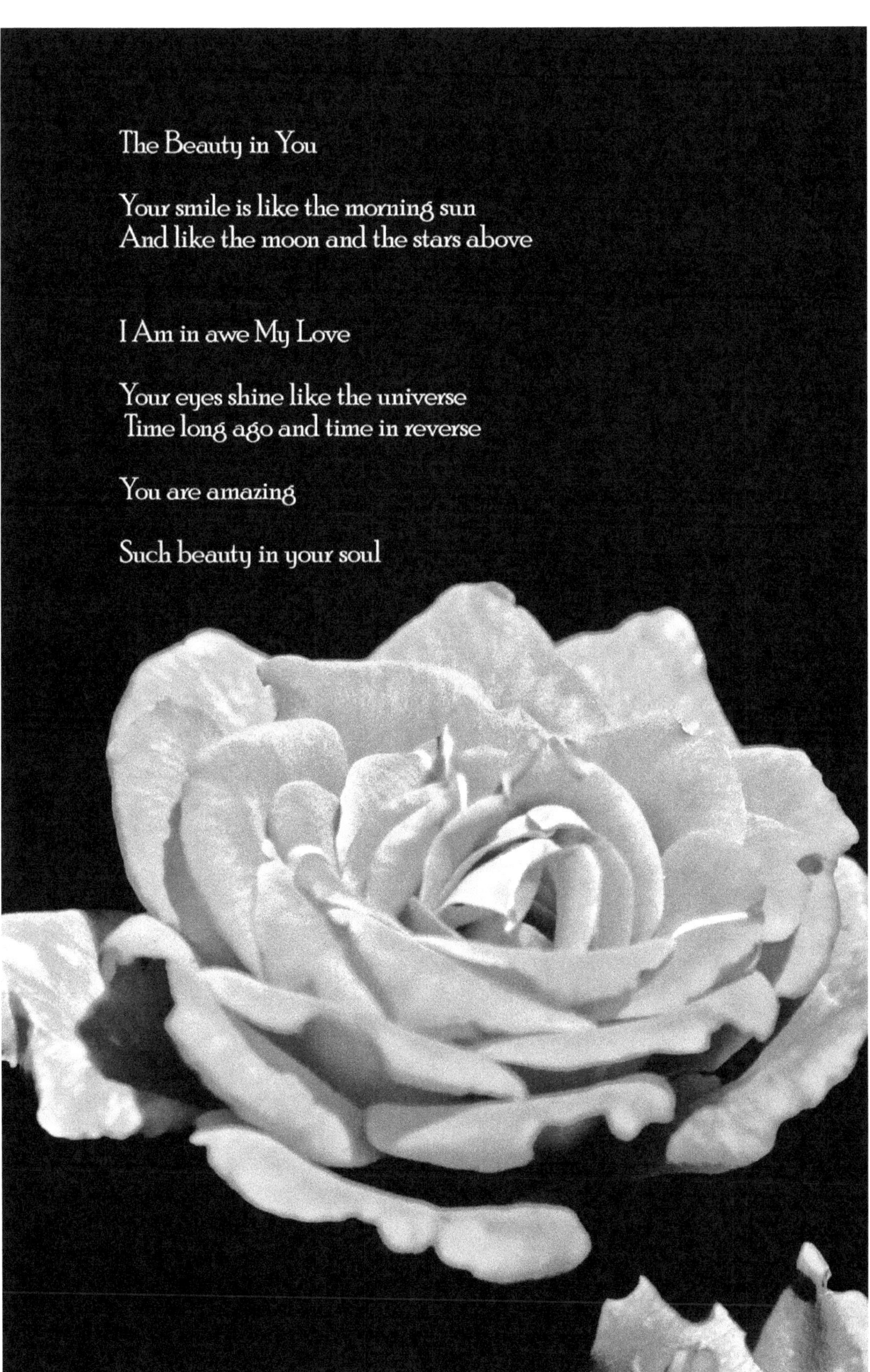

The Beauty in You

Your smile is like the morning sun
And like the moon and the stars above

I Am in awe My Love

Your eyes shine like the universe
Time long ago and time in reverse

You are amazing

Such beauty in your soul

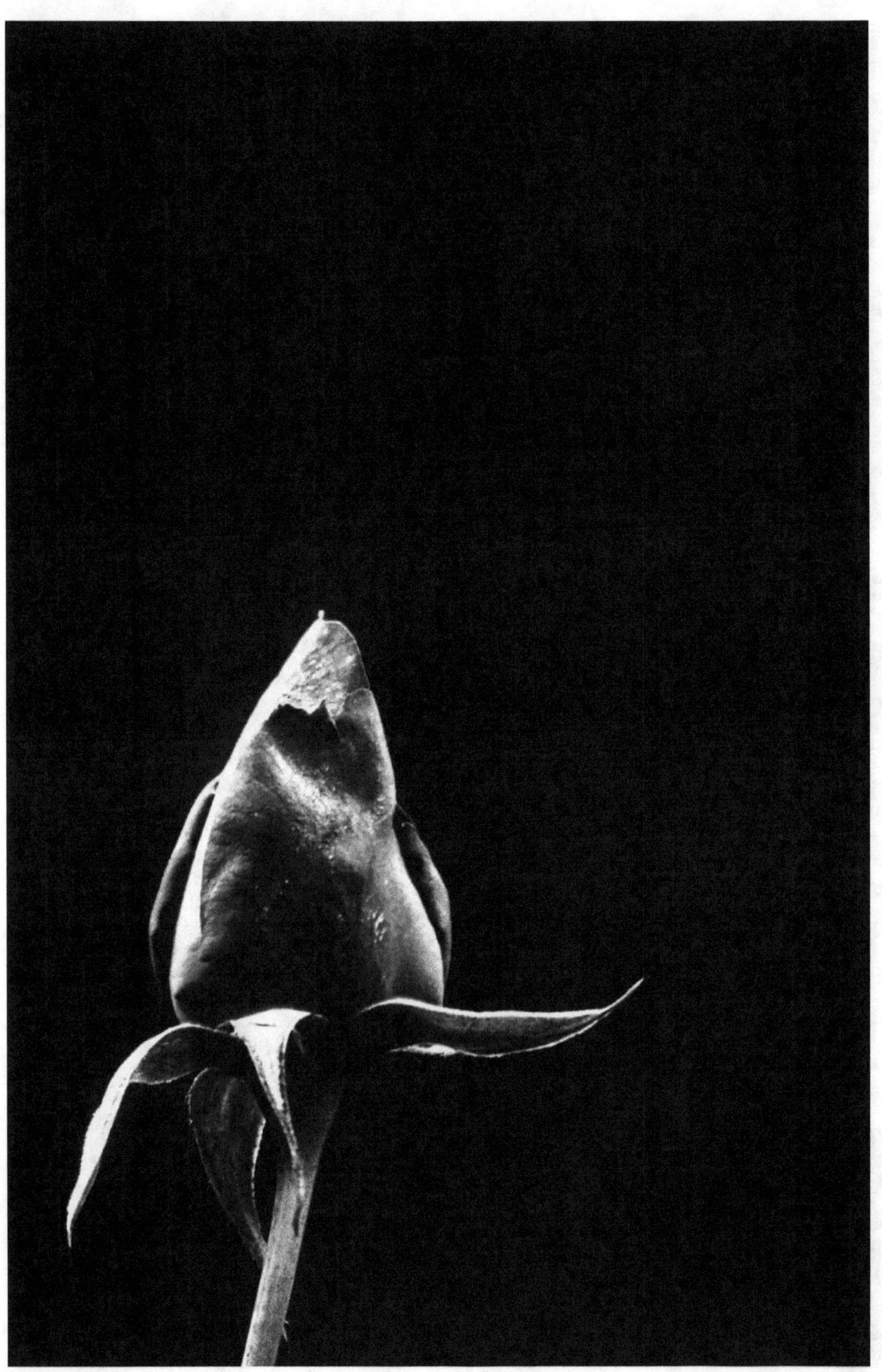

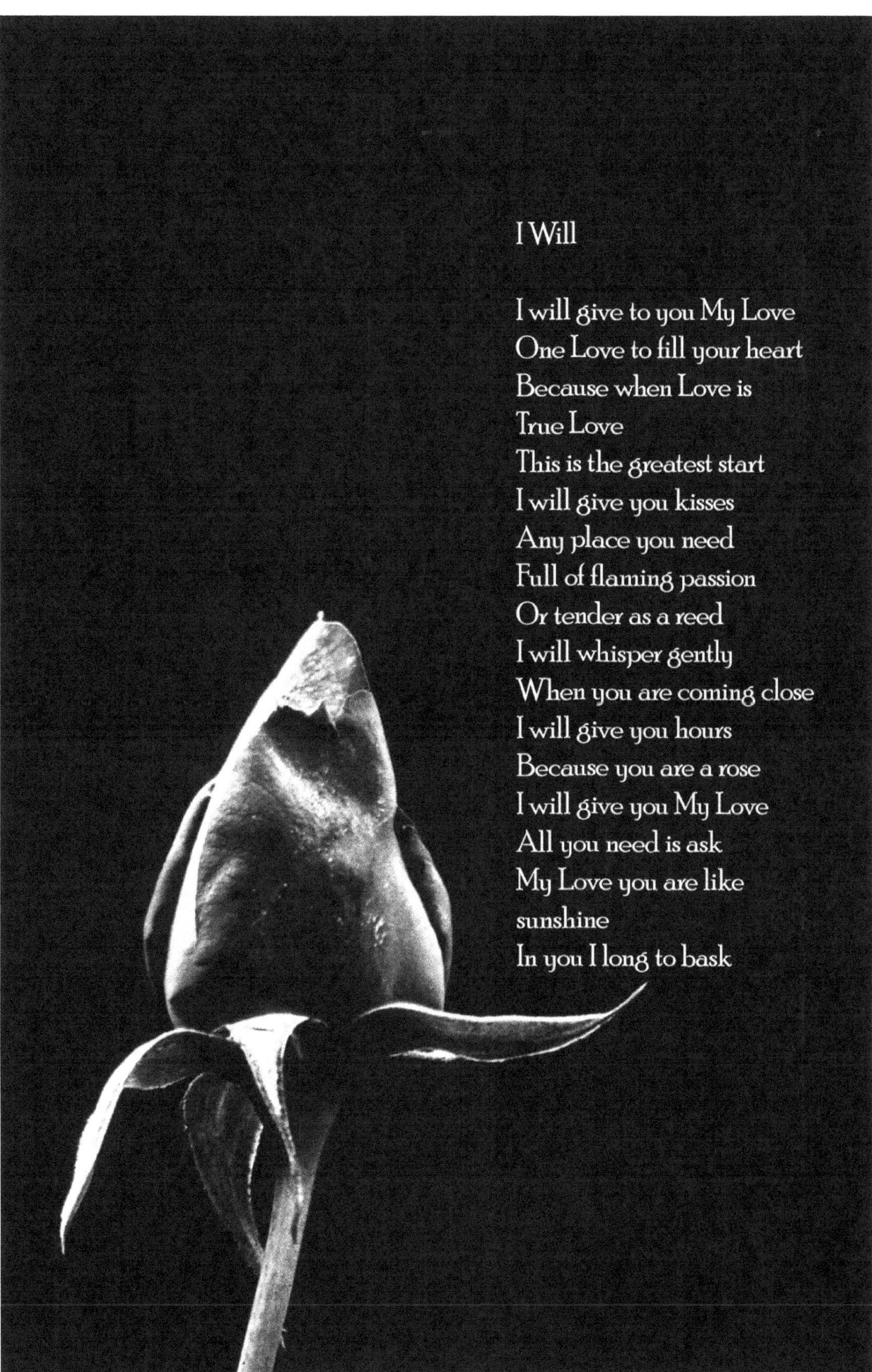

I Will

I will give to you My Love
One Love to fill your heart
Because when Love is
True Love
This is the greatest start
I will give you kisses
Any place you need
Full of flaming passion
Or tender as a reed
I will whisper gently
When you are coming close
I will give you hours
Because you are a rose
I will give you My Love
All you need is ask
My Love you are like
sunshine
In you I long to bask

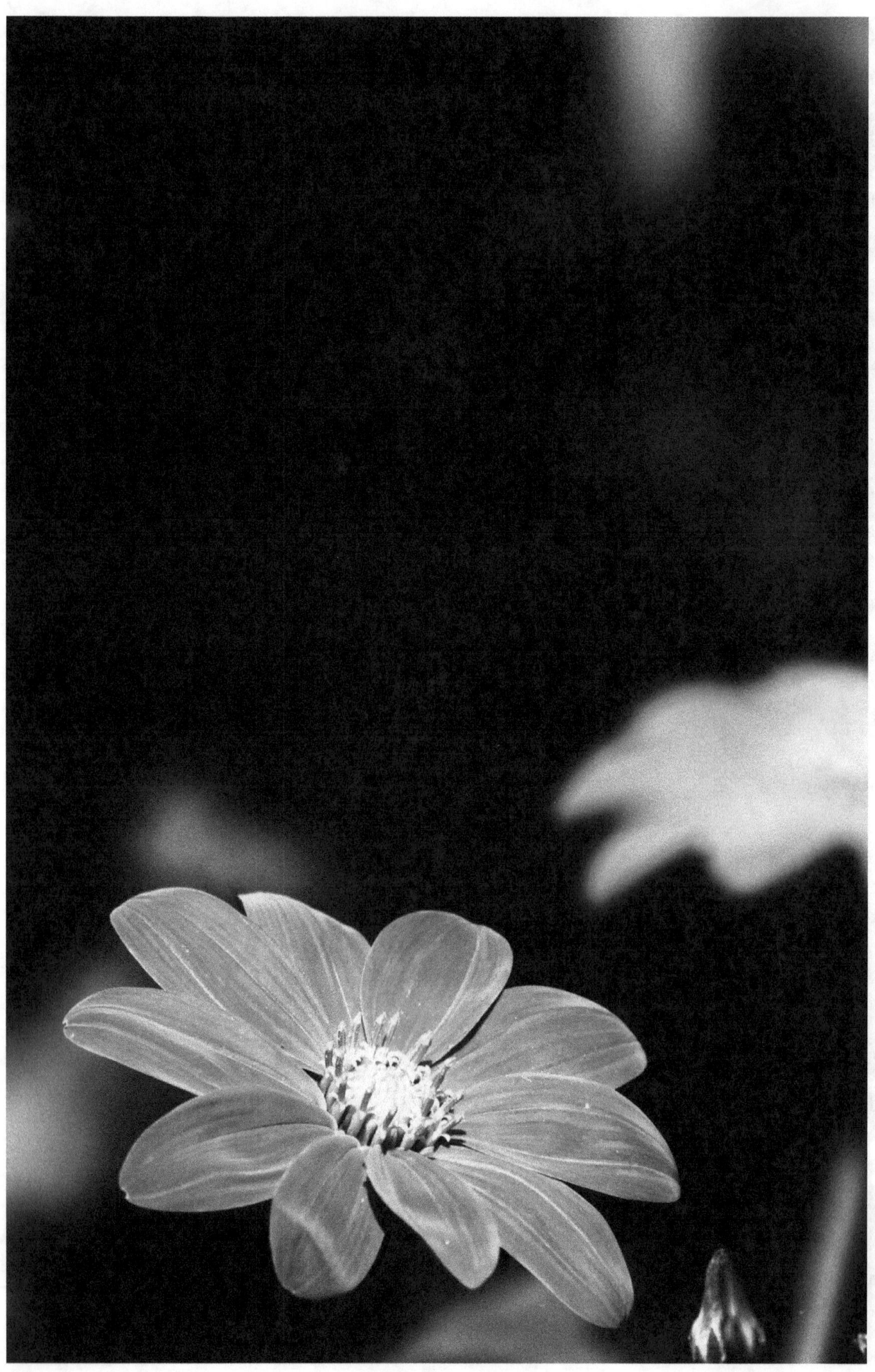

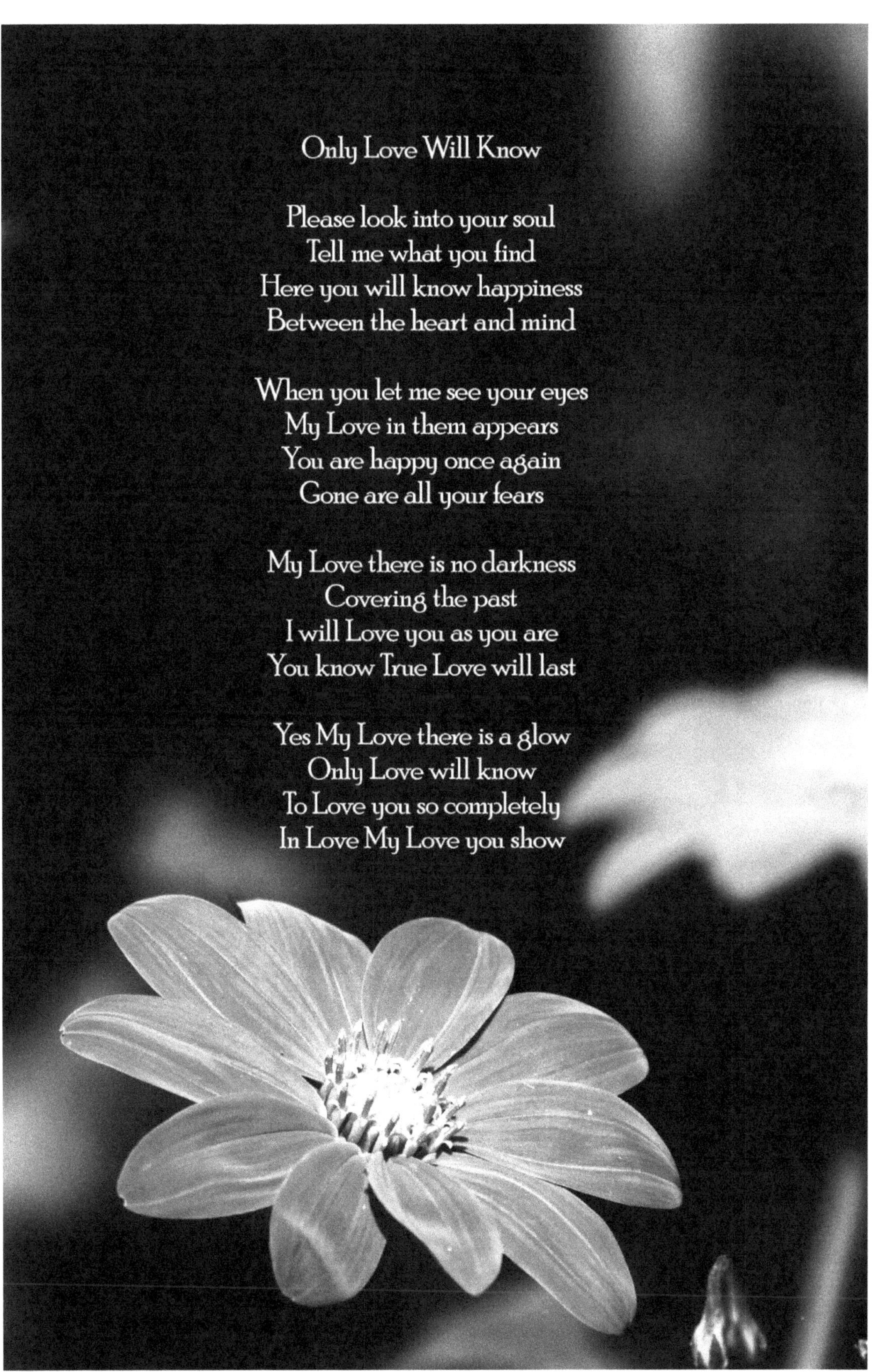

Only Love Will Know

Please look into your soul
Tell me what you find
Here you will know happiness
Between the heart and mind

When you let me see your eyes
My Love in them appears
You are happy once again
Gone are all your fears

My Love there is no darkness
Covering the past
I will Love you as you are
You know True Love will last

Yes My Love there is a glow
Only Love will know
To Love you so completely
In Love My Love you show

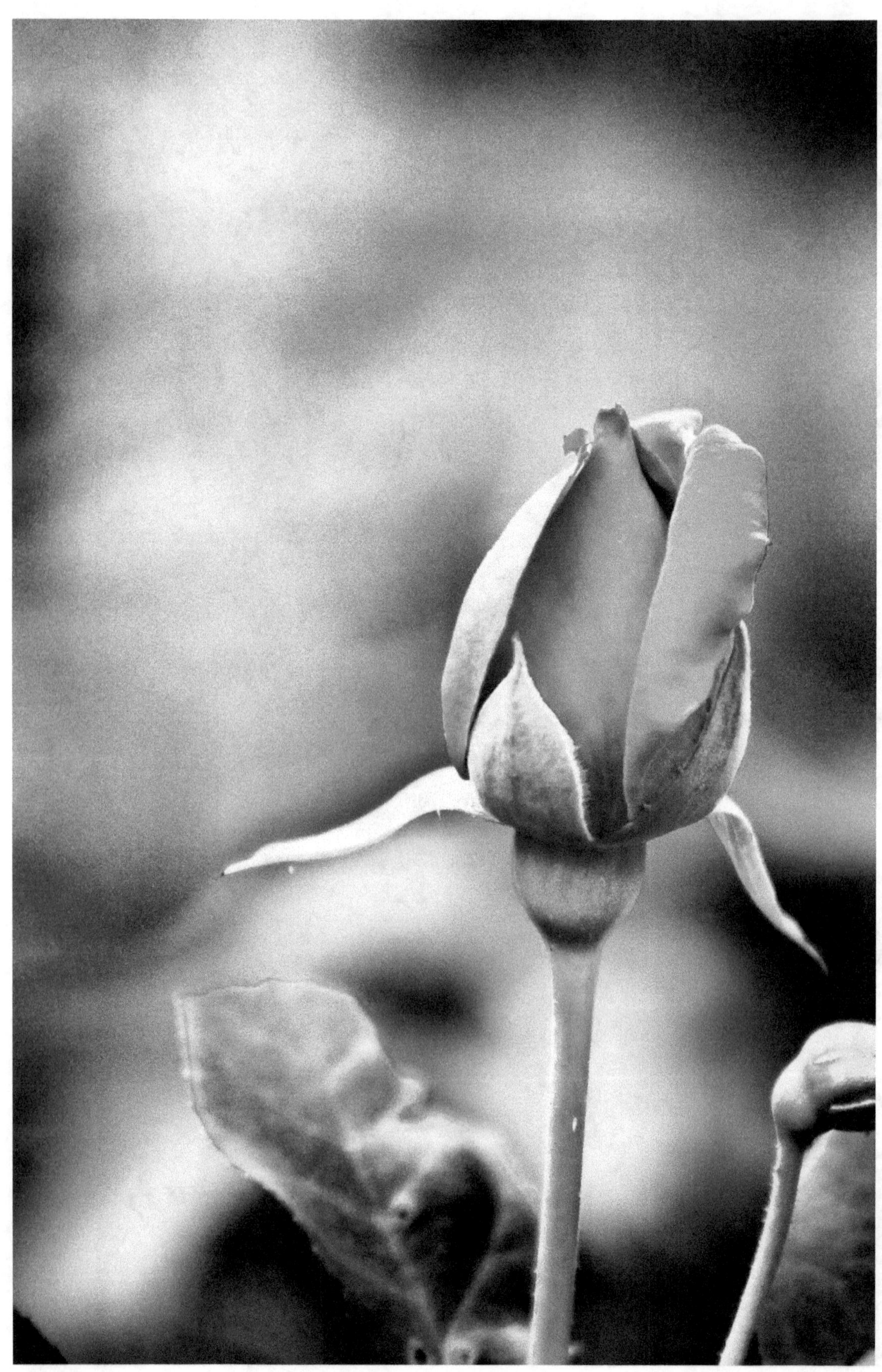

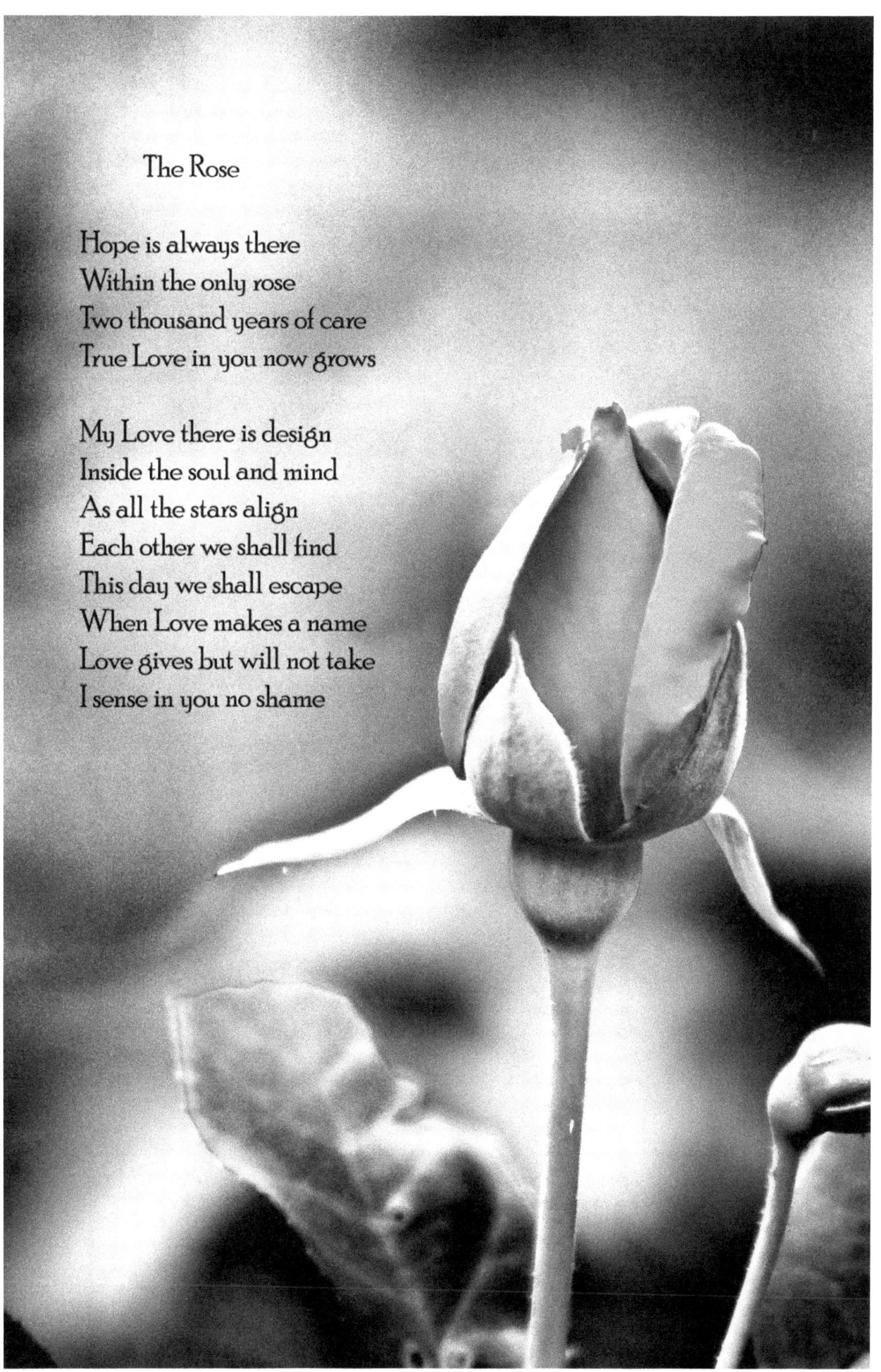

The Rose

Hope is always there
Within the only rose
Two thousand years of care
True Love in you now grows

My Love there is design
Inside the soul and mind
As all the stars align
Each other we shall find
This day we shall escape
When Love makes a name
Love gives but will not take
I sense in you no shame

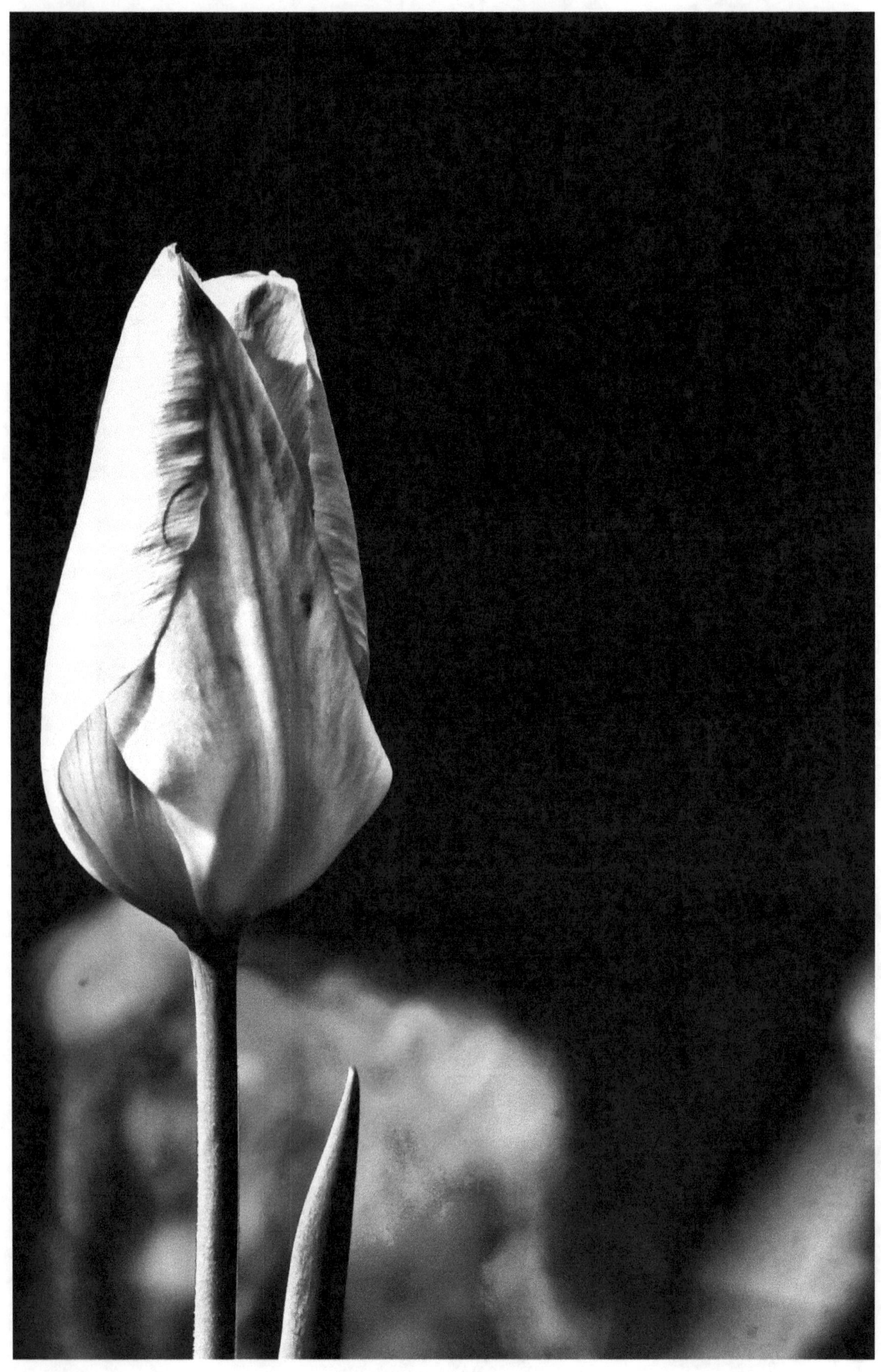

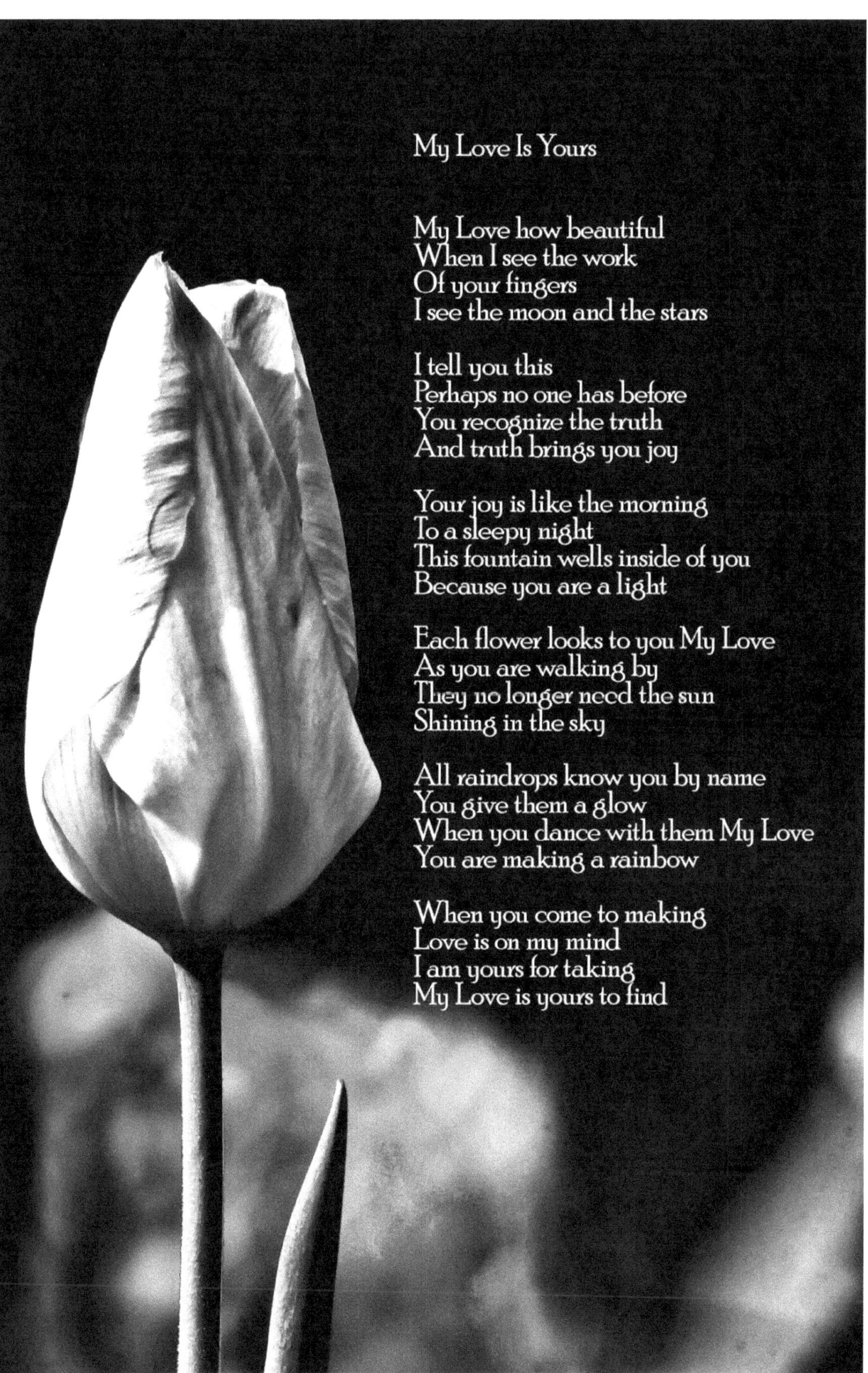

My Love Is Yours

My Love how beautiful
When I see the work
Of your fingers
I see the moon and the stars

I tell you this
Perhaps no one has before
You recognize the truth
And truth brings you joy

Your joy is like the morning
To a sleepy night
This fountain wells inside of you
Because you are a light

Each flower looks to you My Love
As you are walking by
They no longer need the sun
Shining in the sky

All raindrops know you by name
You give them a glow
When you dance with them My Love
You are making a rainbow

When you come to making
Love is on my mind
I am yours for taking
My Love is yours to find

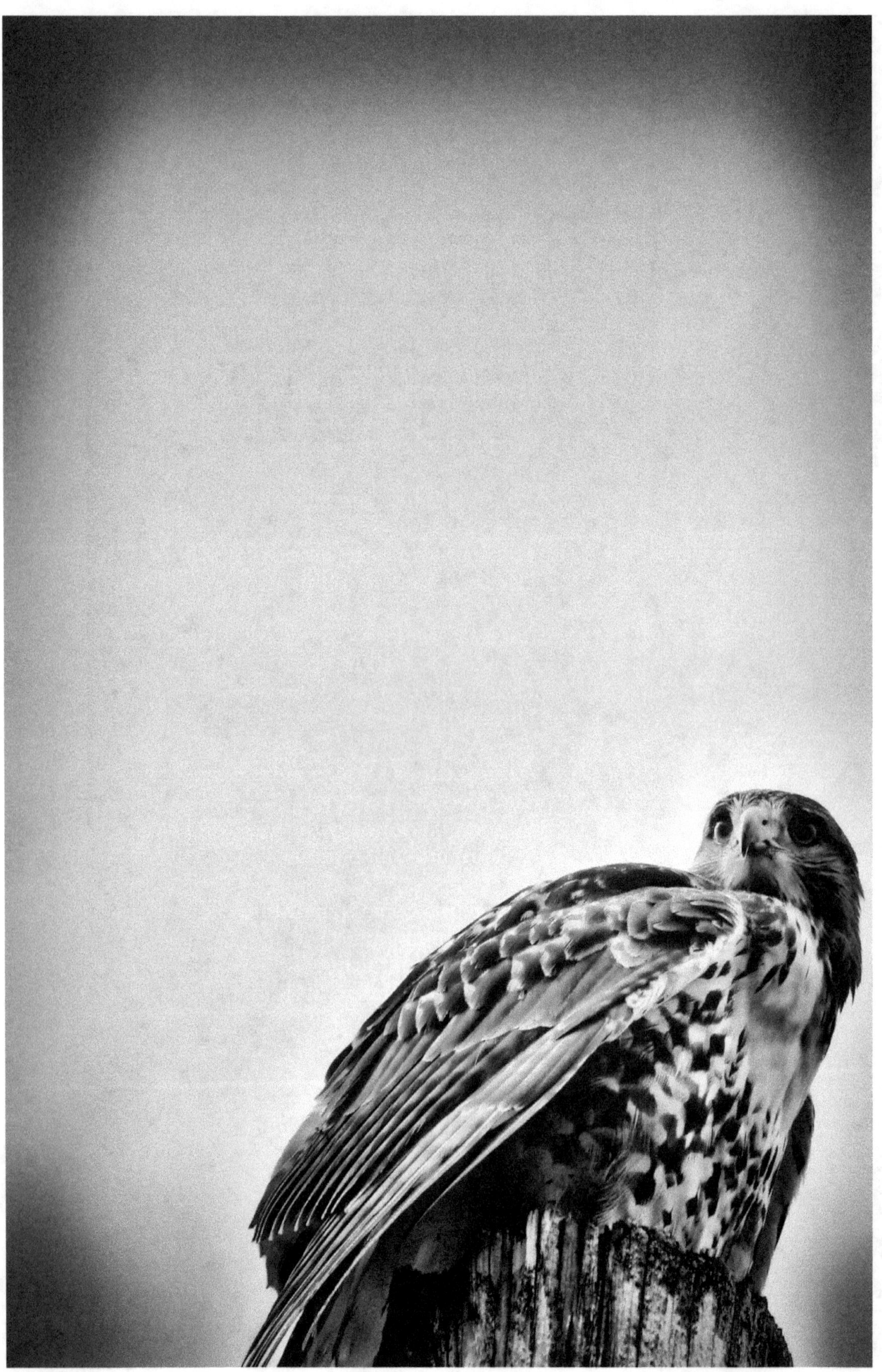

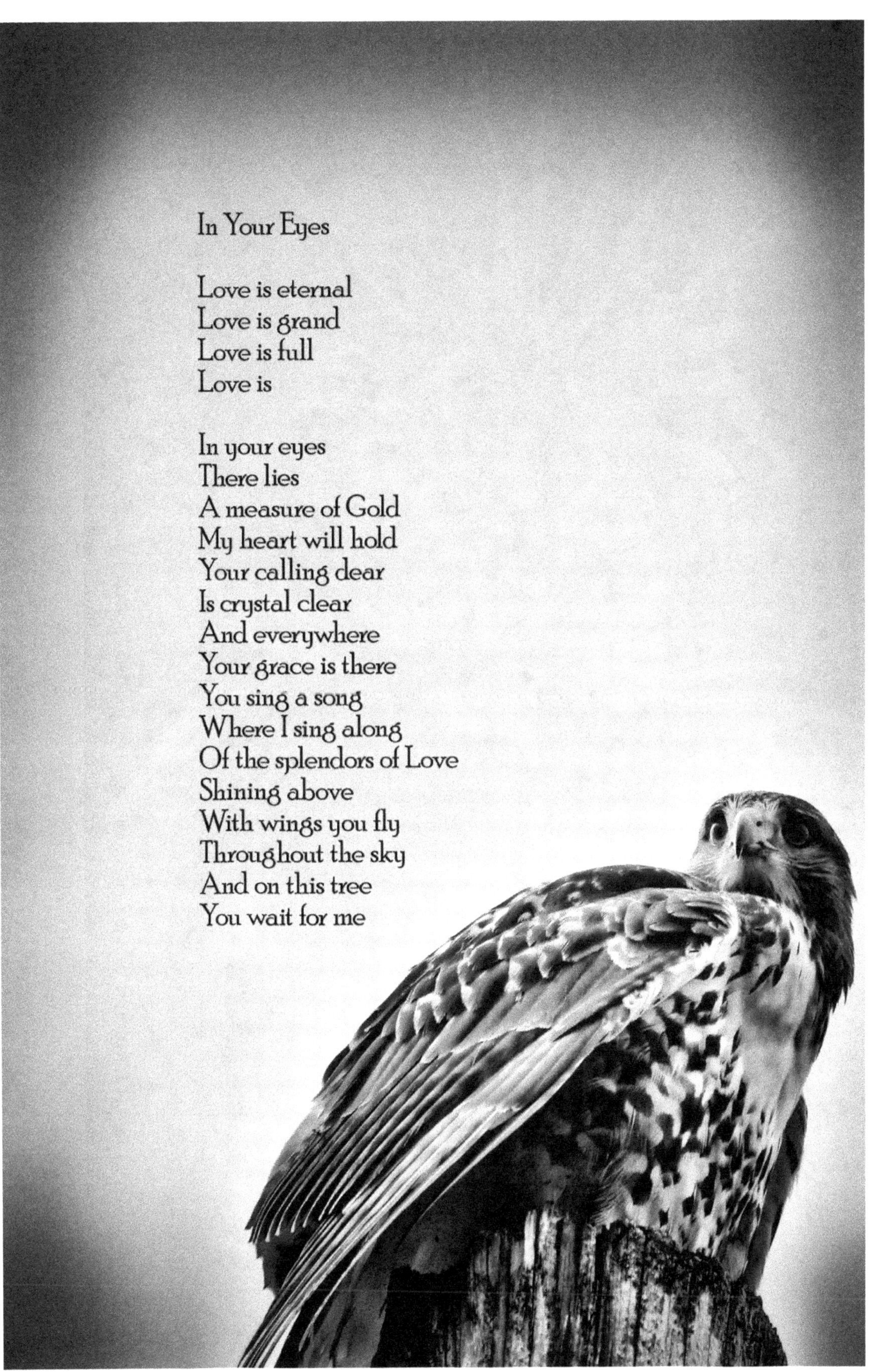

In Your Eyes

Love is eternal
Love is grand
Love is full
Love is

In your eyes
There lies
A measure of Gold
My heart will hold
Your calling dear
Is crystal clear
And everywhere
Your grace is there
You sing a song
Where I sing along
Of the splendors of Love
Shining above
With wings you fly
Throughout the sky
And on this tree
You wait for me

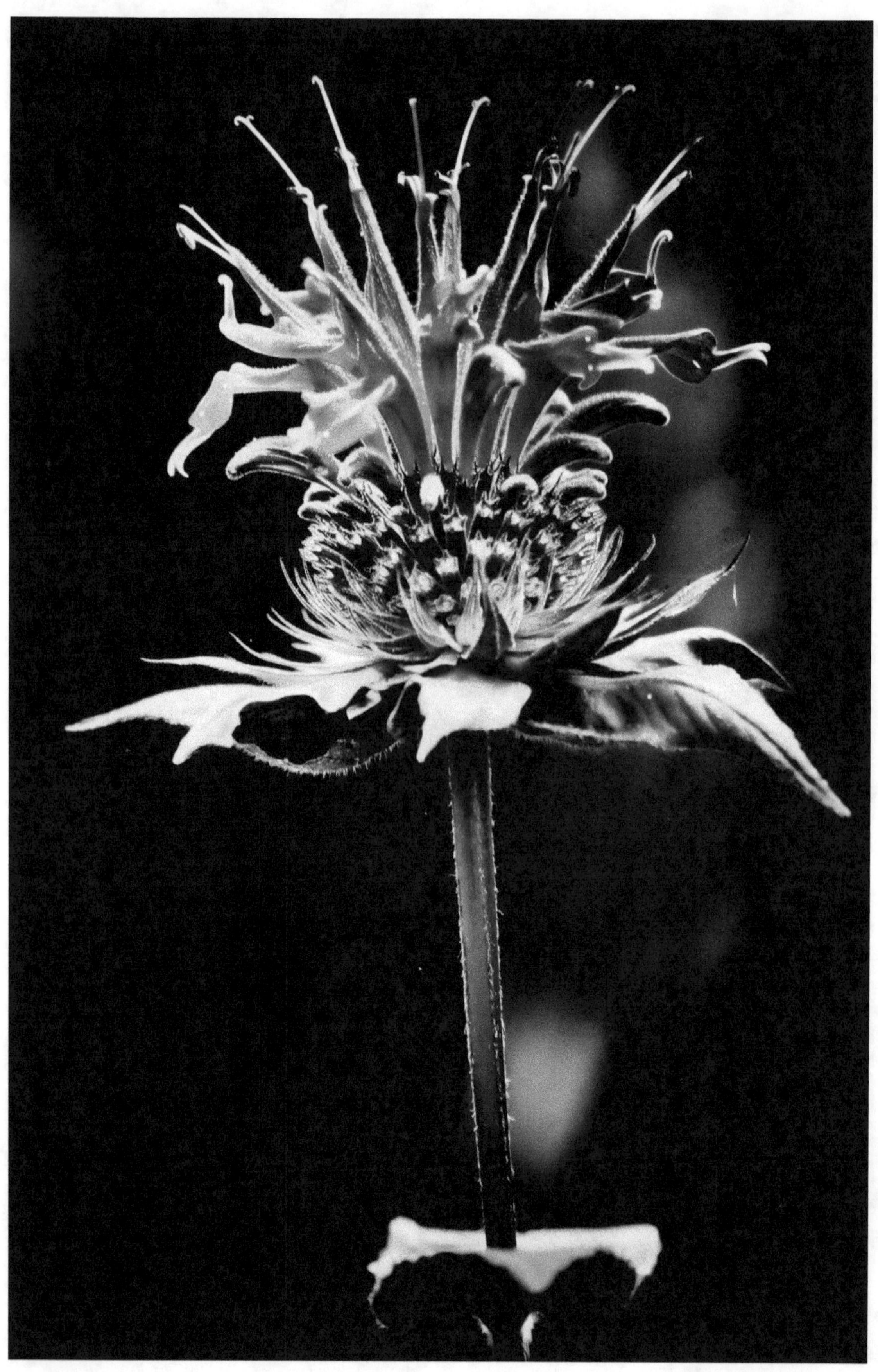

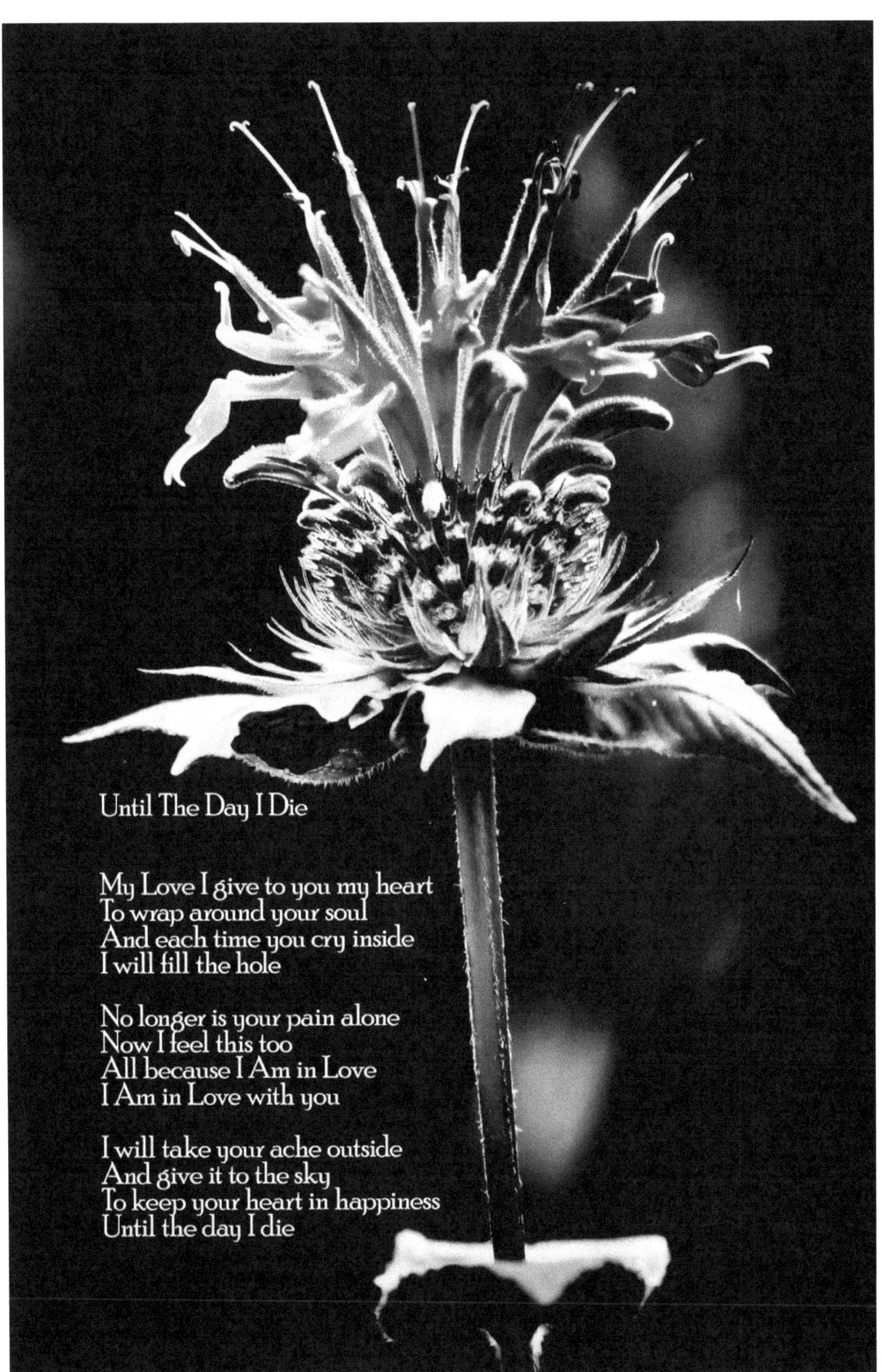

Until The Day I Die

My Love I give to you my heart
To wrap around your soul
And each time you cry inside
I will fill the hole

No longer is your pain alone
Now I feel this too
All because I Am in Love
I Am in Love with you

I will take your ache outside
And give it to the sky
To keep your heart in happiness
Until the day I die

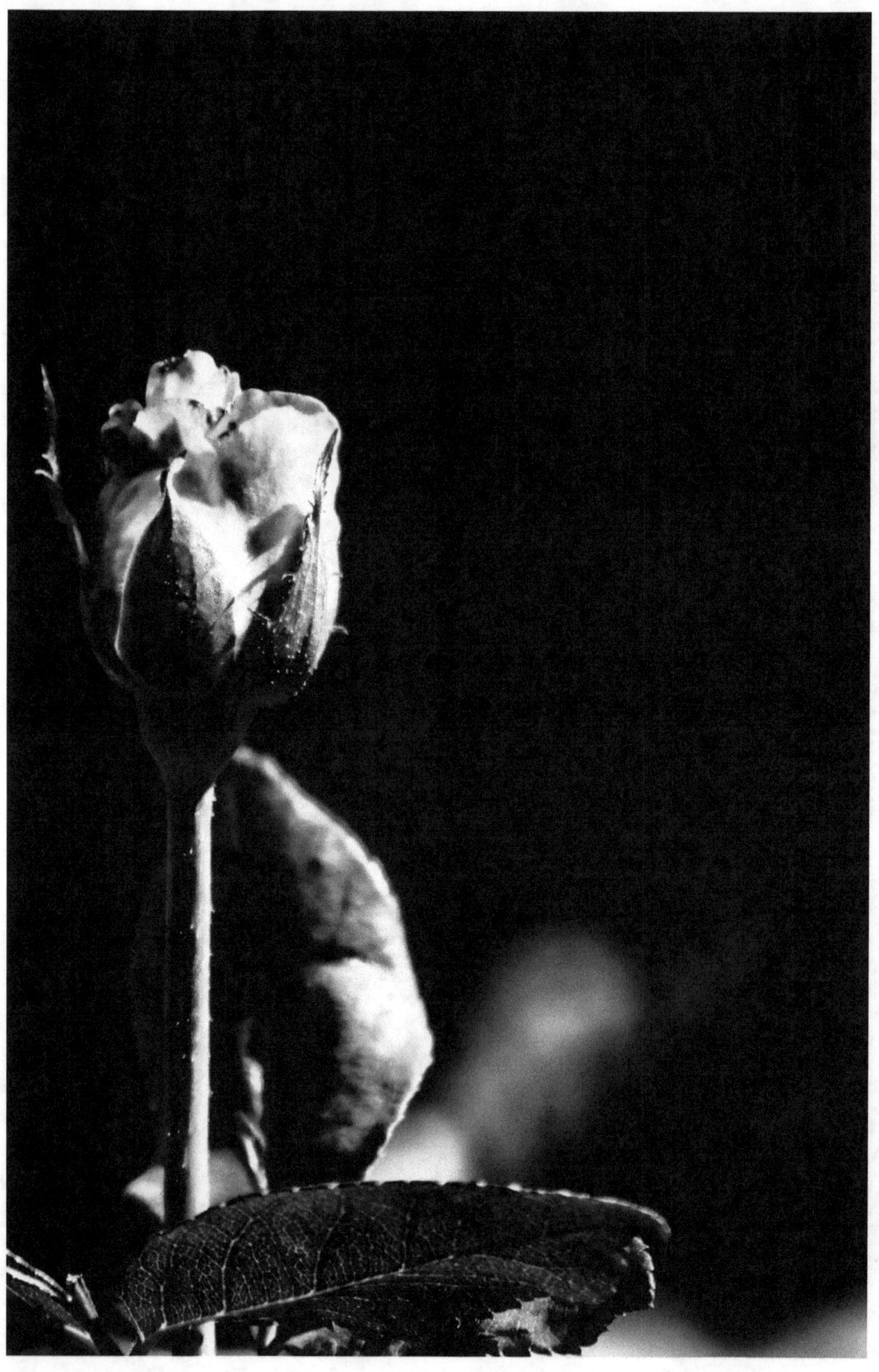

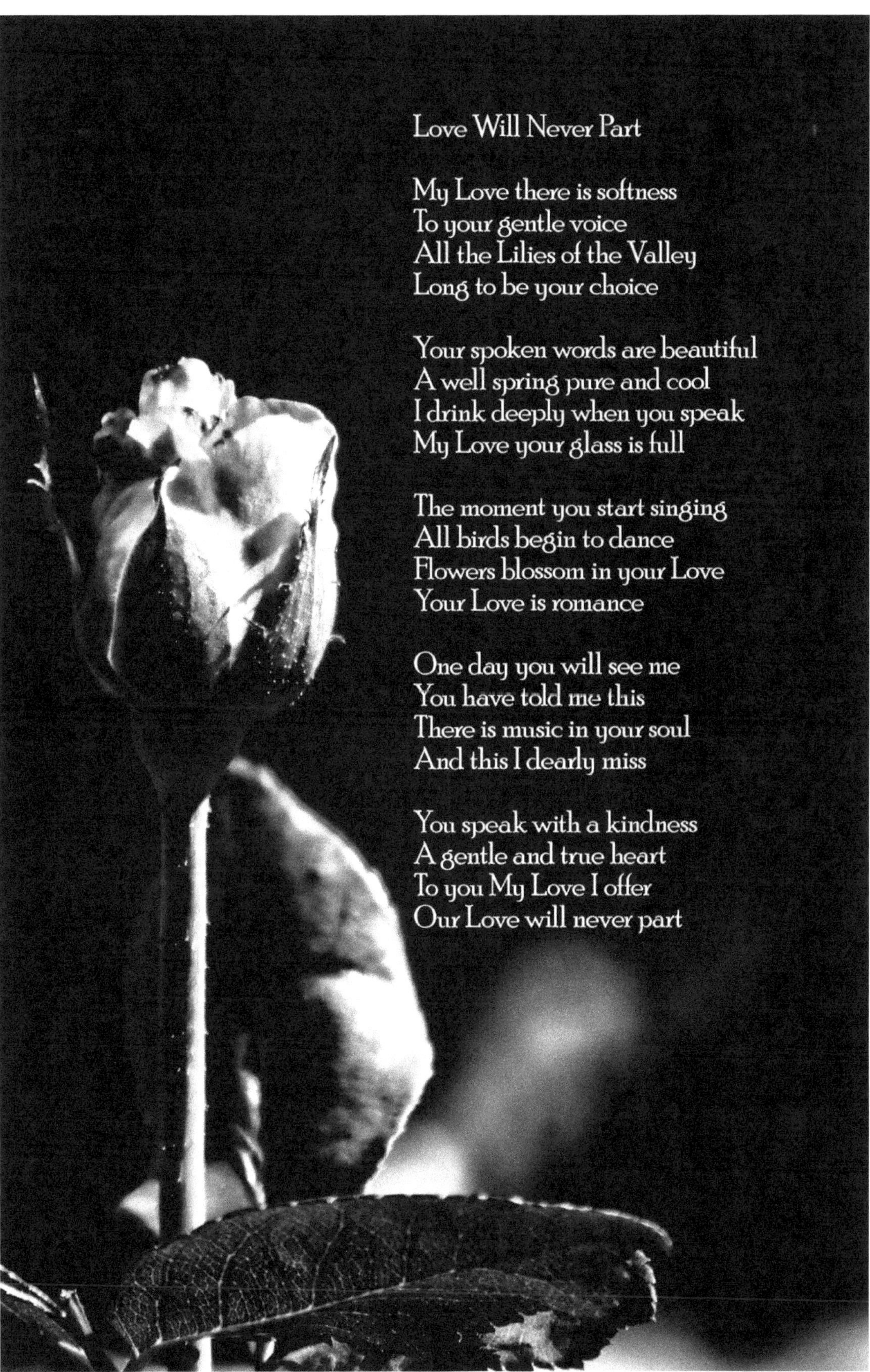

Love Will Never Part

My Love there is softness
To your gentle voice
All the Lilies of the Valley
Long to be your choice

Your spoken words are beautiful
A well spring pure and cool
I drink deeply when you speak
My Love your glass is full

The moment you start singing
All birds begin to dance
Flowers blossom in your Love
Your Love is romance

One day you will see me
You have told me this
There is music in your soul
And this I dearly miss

You speak with a kindness
A gentle and true heart
To you My Love I offer
Our Love will never part

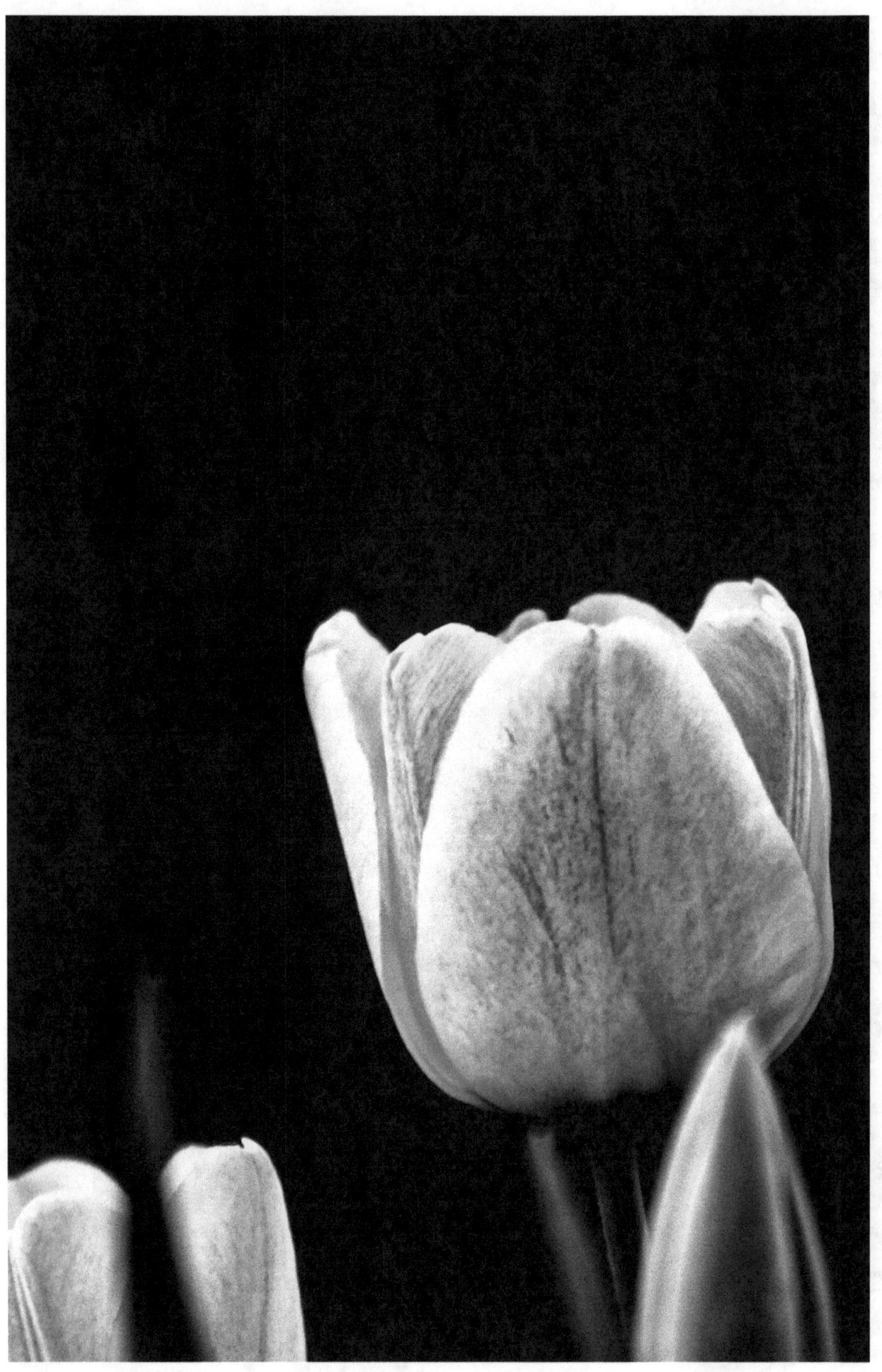

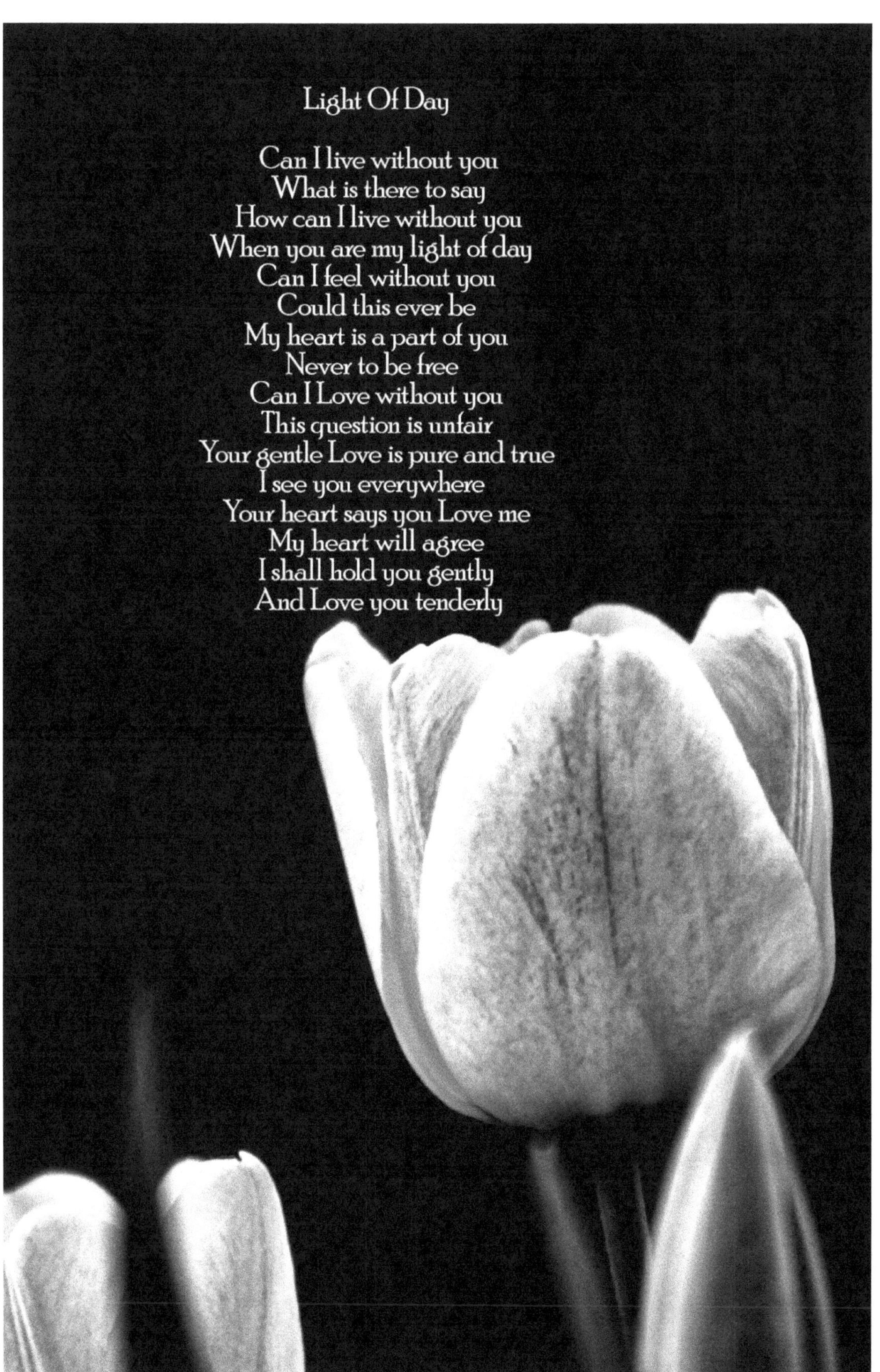

Light Of Day

Can I live without you
What is there to say
How can I live without you
When you are my light of day
Can I feel without you
Could this ever be
My heart is a part of you
Never to be free
Can I Love without you
This question is unfair
Your gentle Love is pure and true
I see you everywhere
Your heart says you Love me
My heart will agree
I shall hold you gently
And Love you tenderly

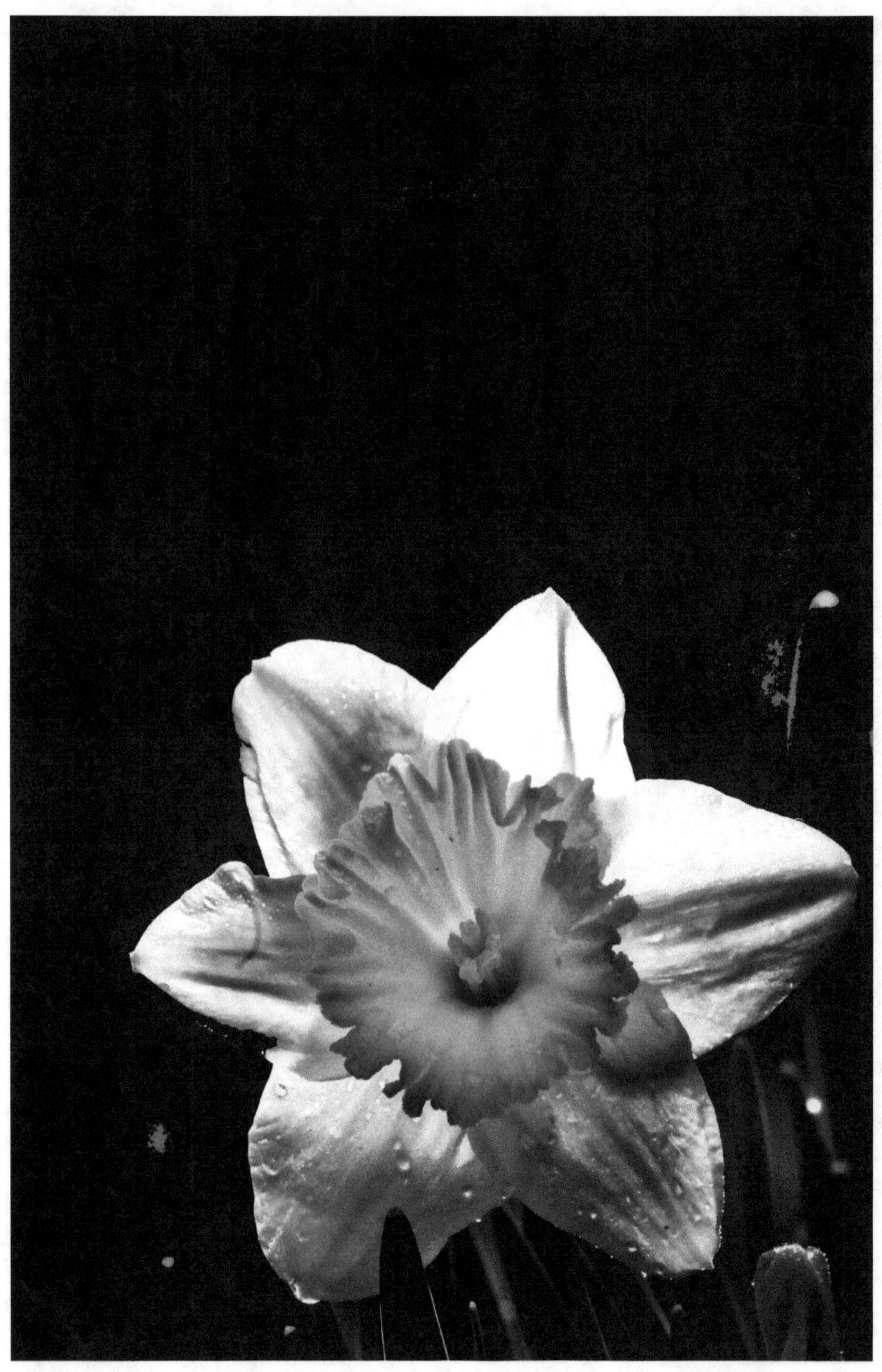

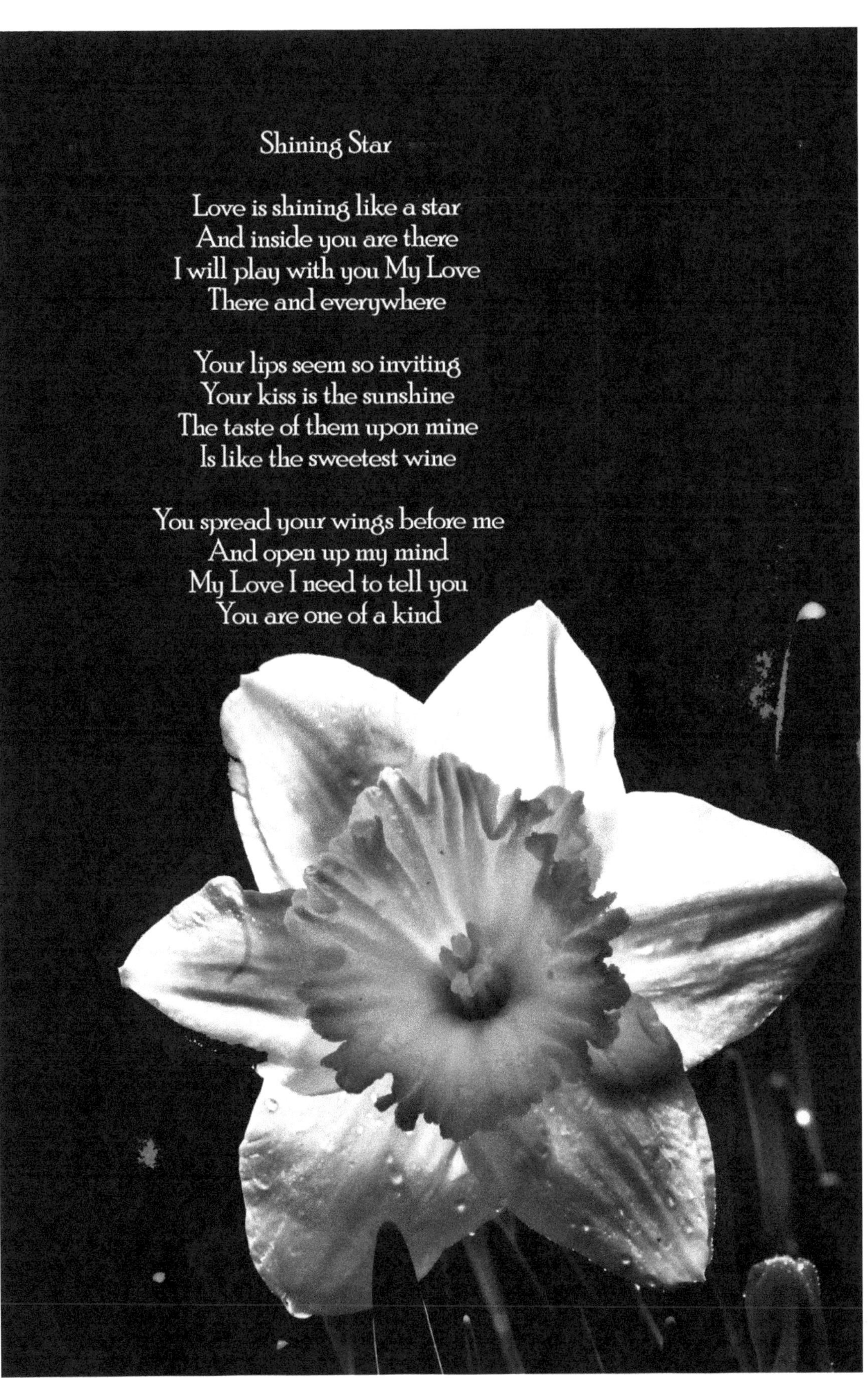

Shining Star

Love is shining like a star
And inside you are there
I will play with you My Love
There and everywhere

Your lips seem so inviting
Your kiss is the sunshine
The taste of them upon mine
Is like the sweetest wine

You spread your wings before me
And open up my mind
My Love I need to tell you
You are one of a kind

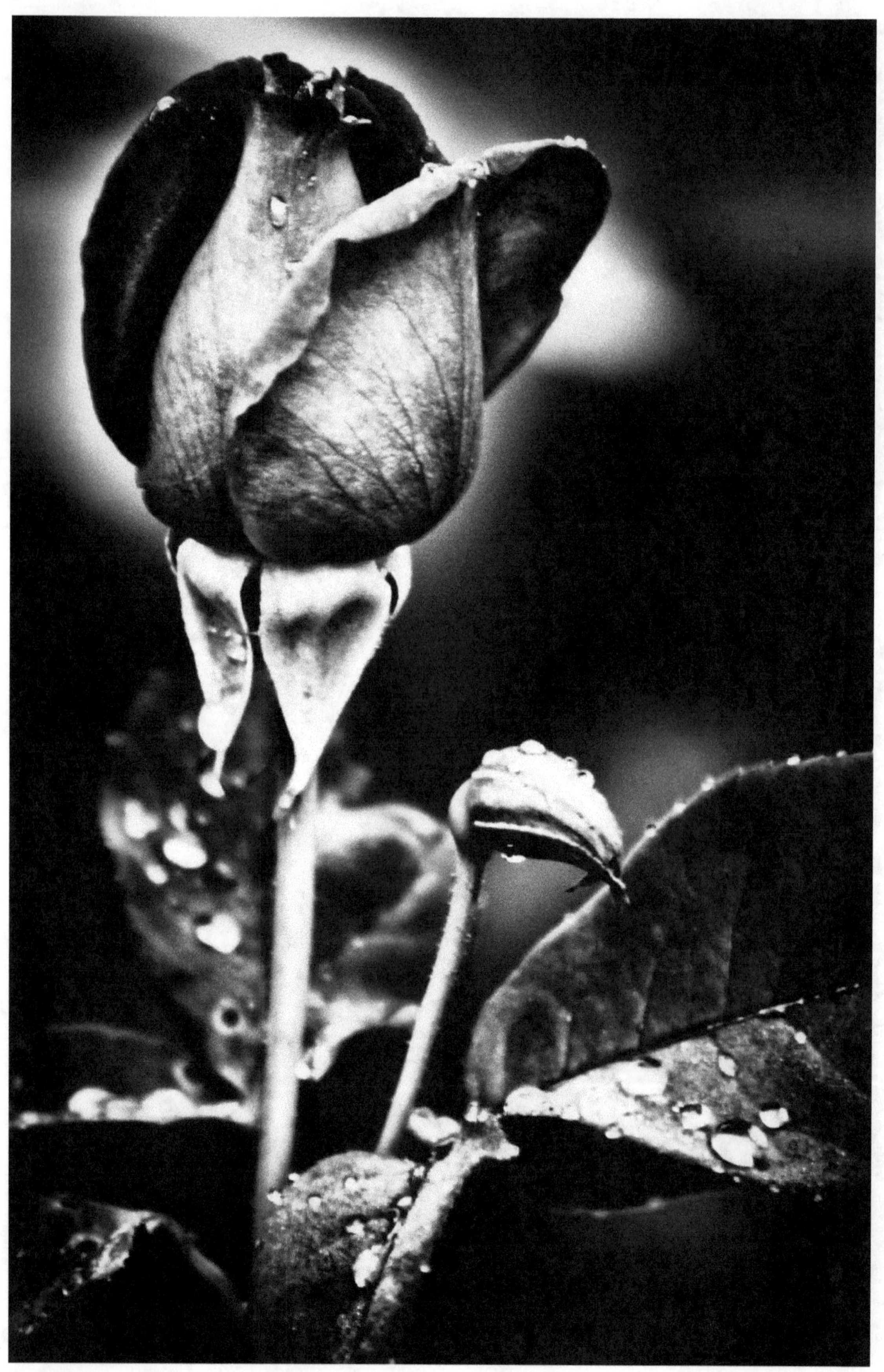

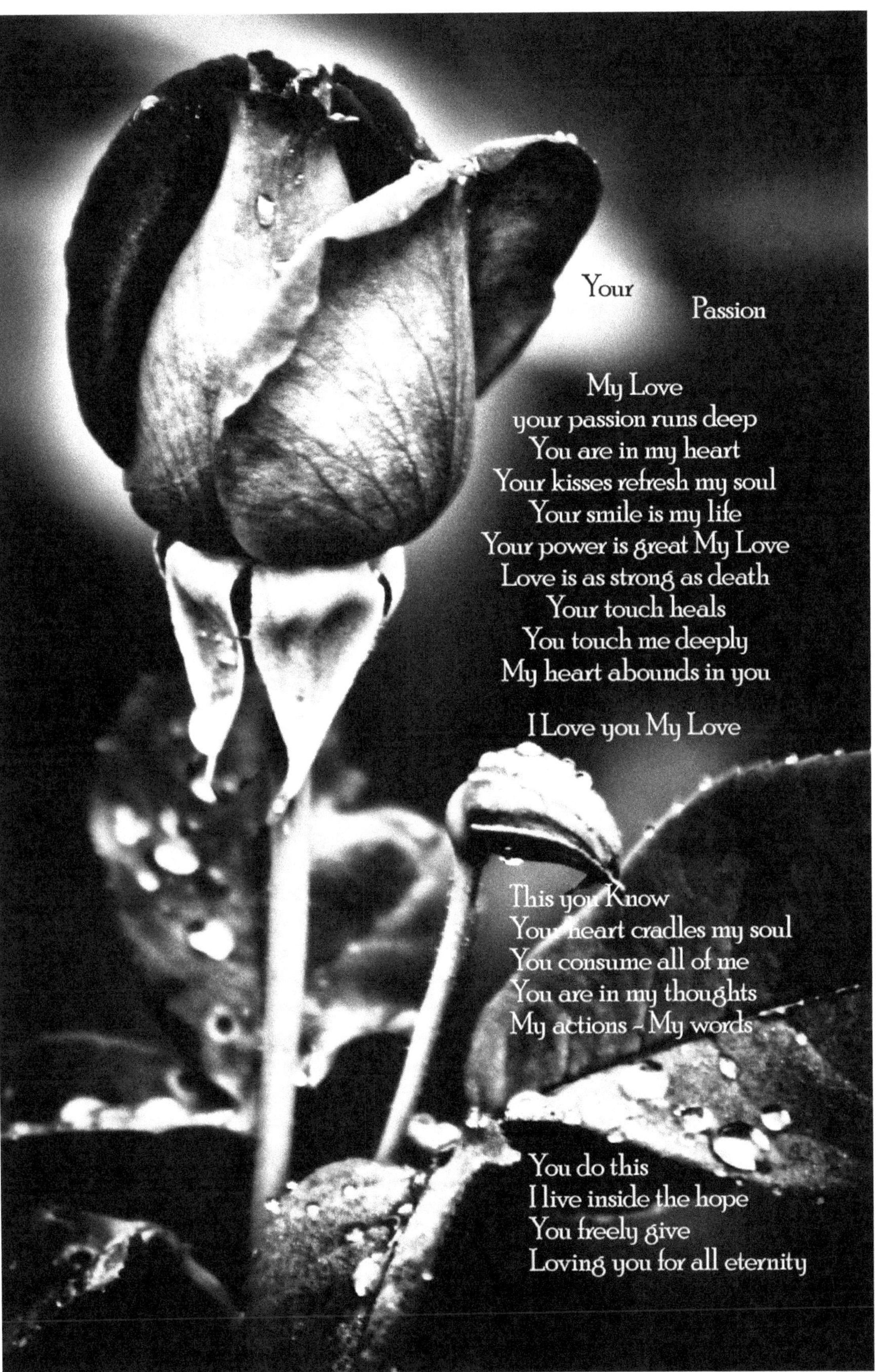
Your Passion

My Love
your passion runs deep
You are in my heart
Your kisses refresh my soul
Your smile is my life
Your power is great My Love
Love is as strong as death
Your touch heals
You touch me deeply
My heart abounds in you

I Love you My Love

This you Know
Your heart cradles my soul
You consume all of me
You are in my thoughts
My actions - My words

You do this
I live inside the hope
You freely give
Loving you for all eternity

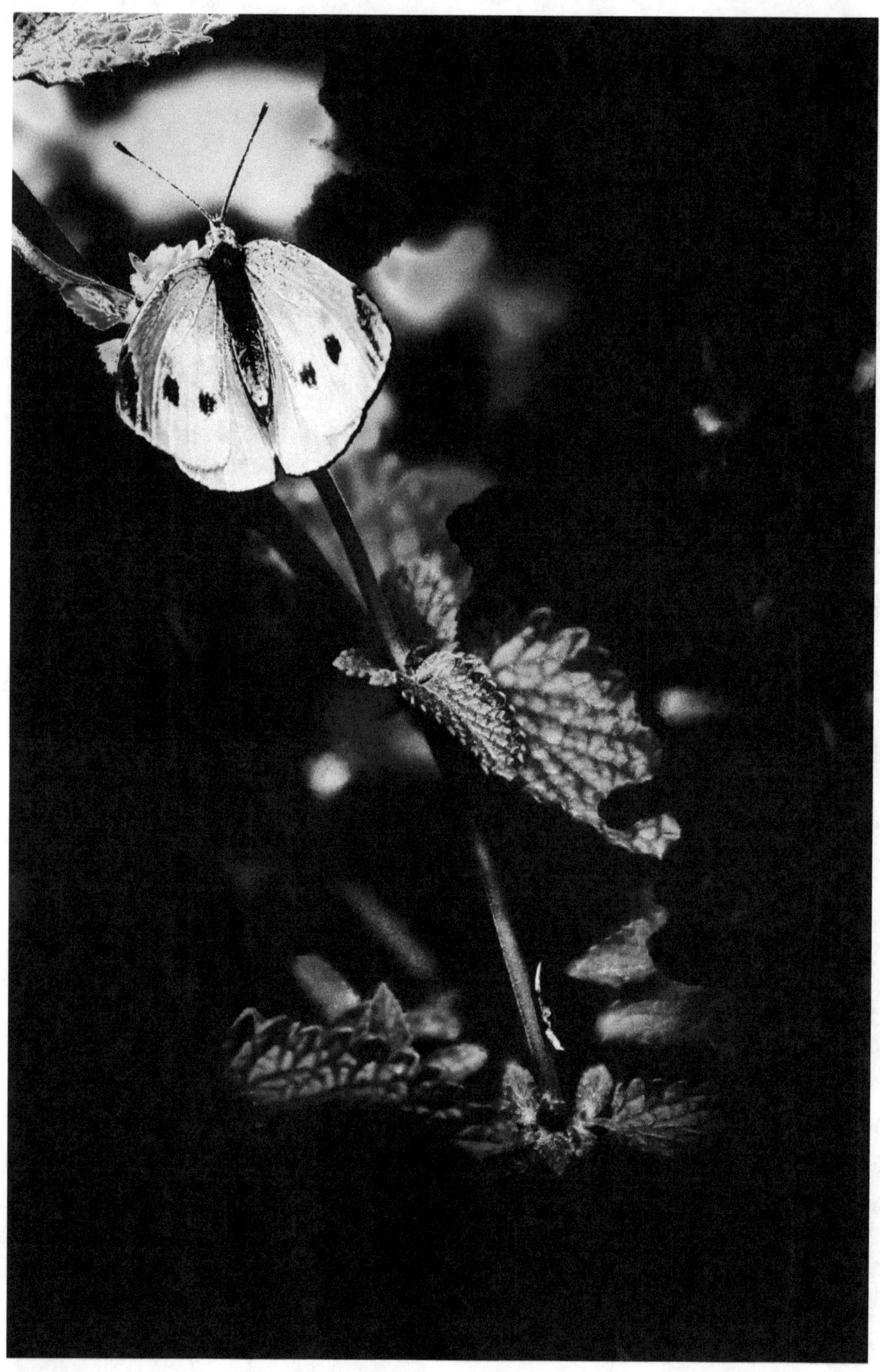

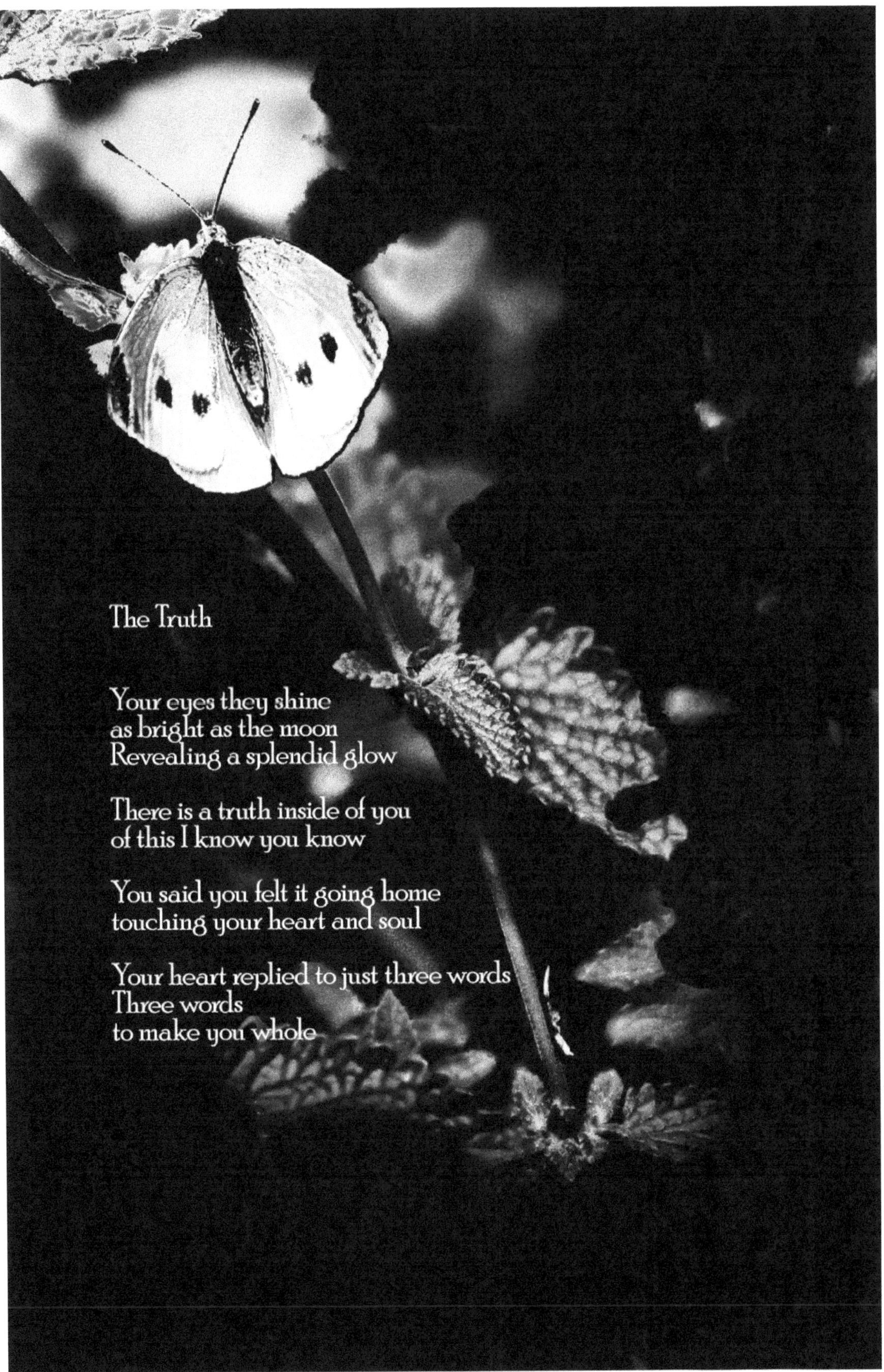

The Truth

Your eyes they shine
as bright as the moon
Revealing a splendid glow

There is a truth inside of you
of this I know you know

You said you felt it going home
touching your heart and soul

Your heart replied to just three words
Three words
to make you whole

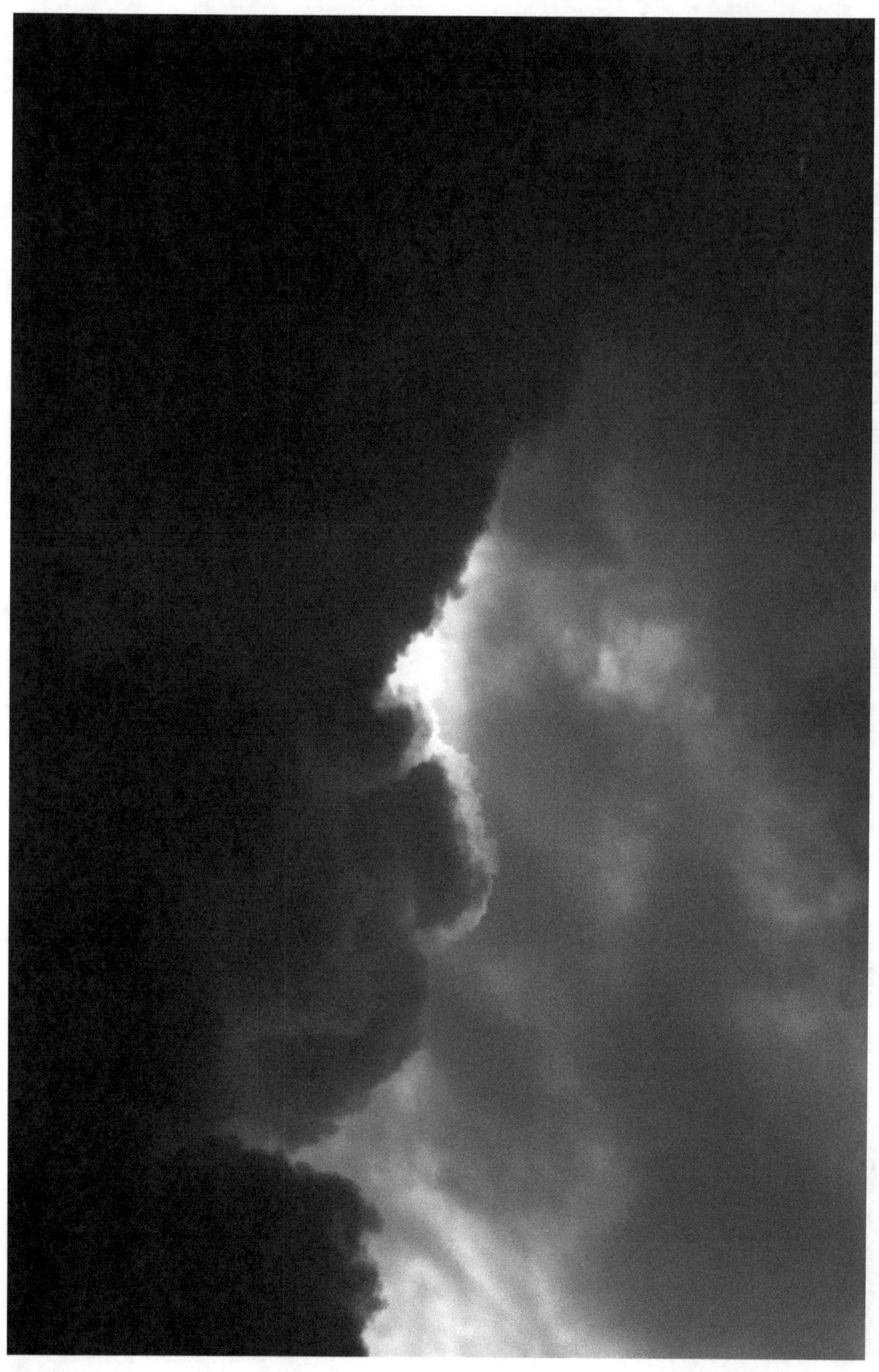

The Keeper Of The Stones

The moments we have been given to live
are really glass stones from the sea
Tumbled by waves and knitted together by time
they are formed in the deepest depths of our soul
Transparent and vast in numbers
clothed in grace to be taken to the ivory throne
Where the finisher of our faith lives on the shore
Majesty shines on us and we spend the rest of our days
with the keeper of the stones

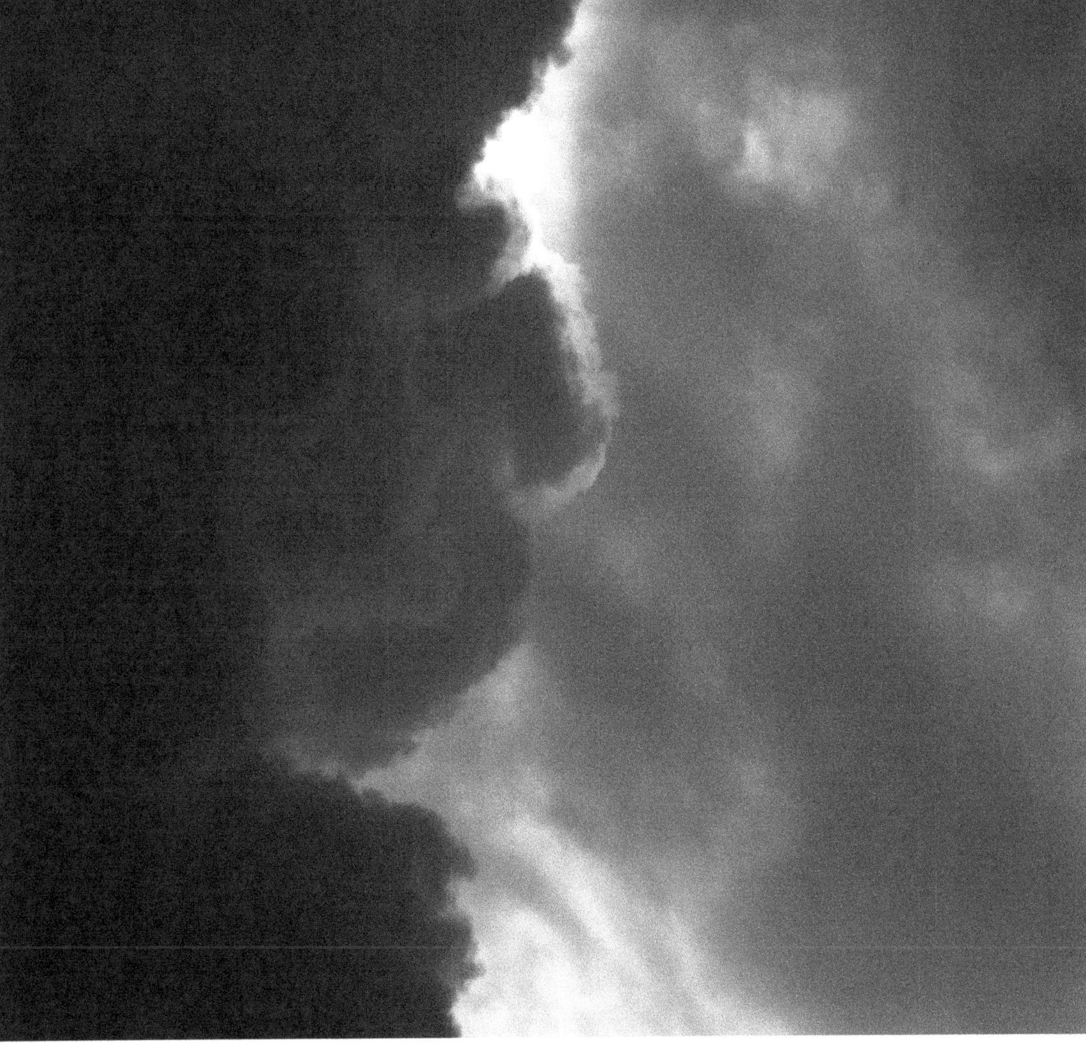

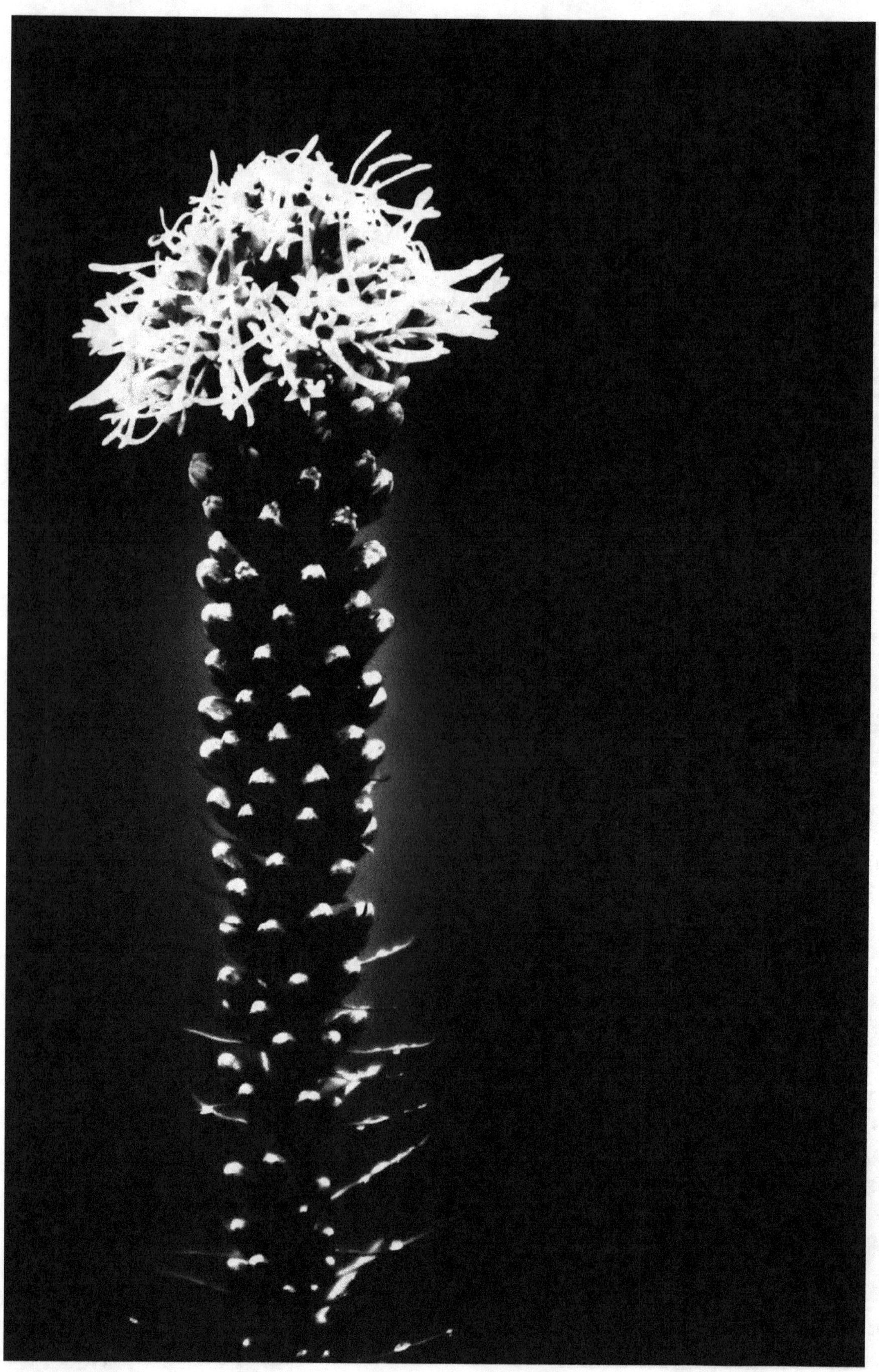

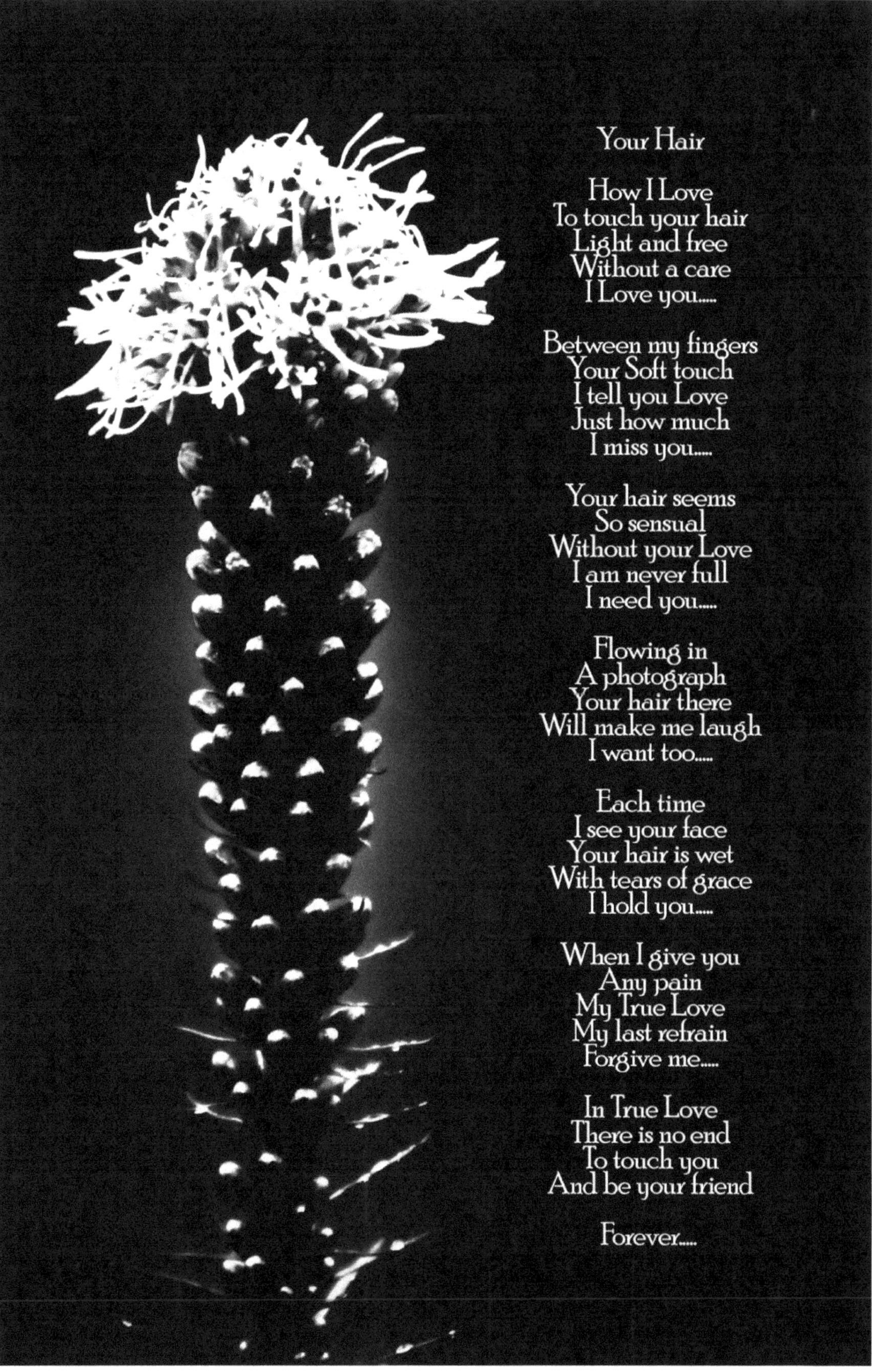
Your Hair

How I Love
To touch your hair
Light and free
Without a care
I Love you.....

Between my fingers
Your Soft touch
I tell you Love
Just how much
I miss you.....

Your hair seems
So sensual
Without your Love
I am never full
I need you.....

Flowing in
A photograph
Your hair there
Will make me laugh
I want too.....

Each time
I see your face
Your hair is wet
With tears of grace
I hold you.....

When I give you
Any pain
My True Love
My last refrain
Forgive me.....

In True Love
There is no end
To touch you
And be your friend

Forever.....

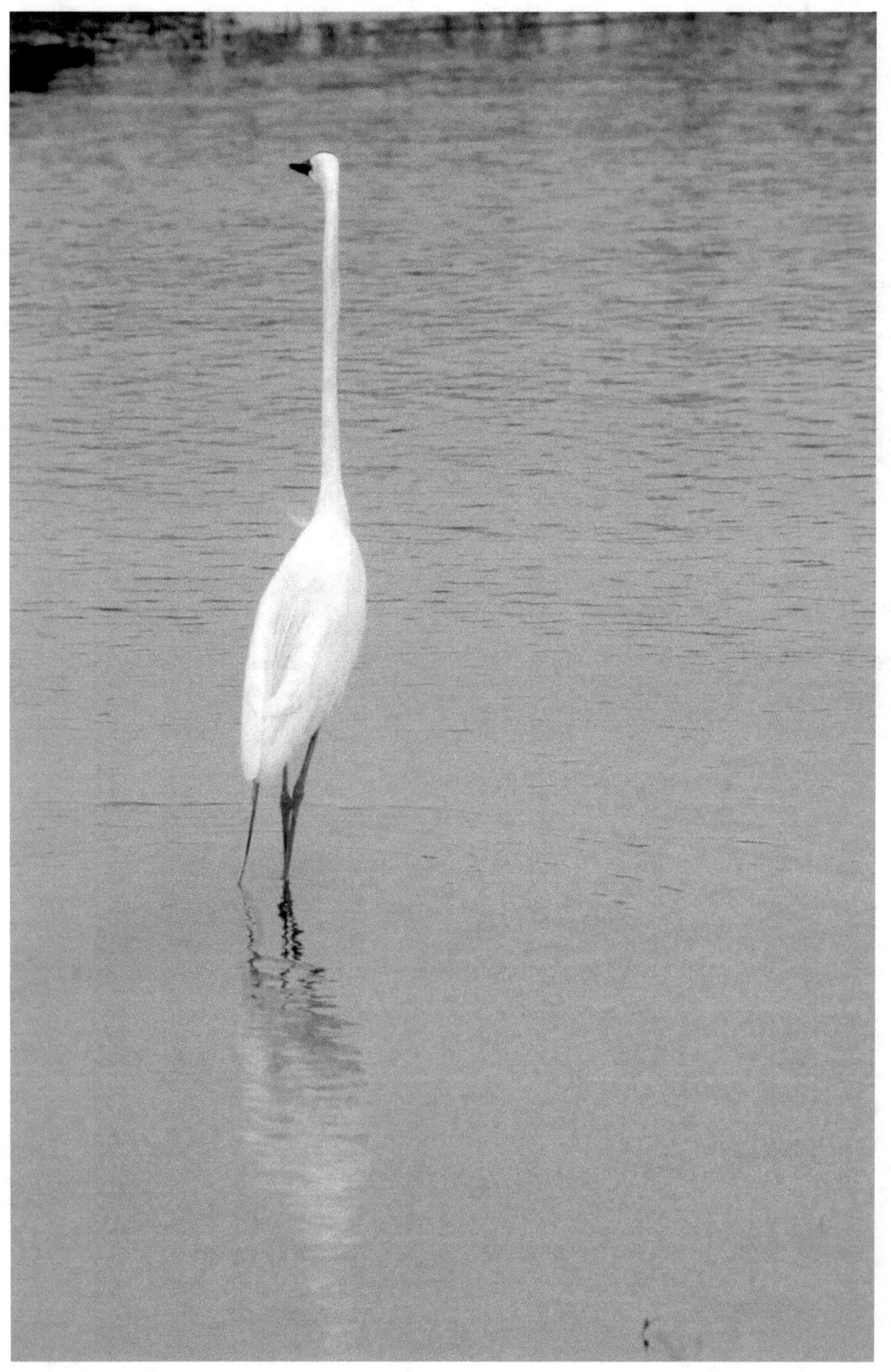

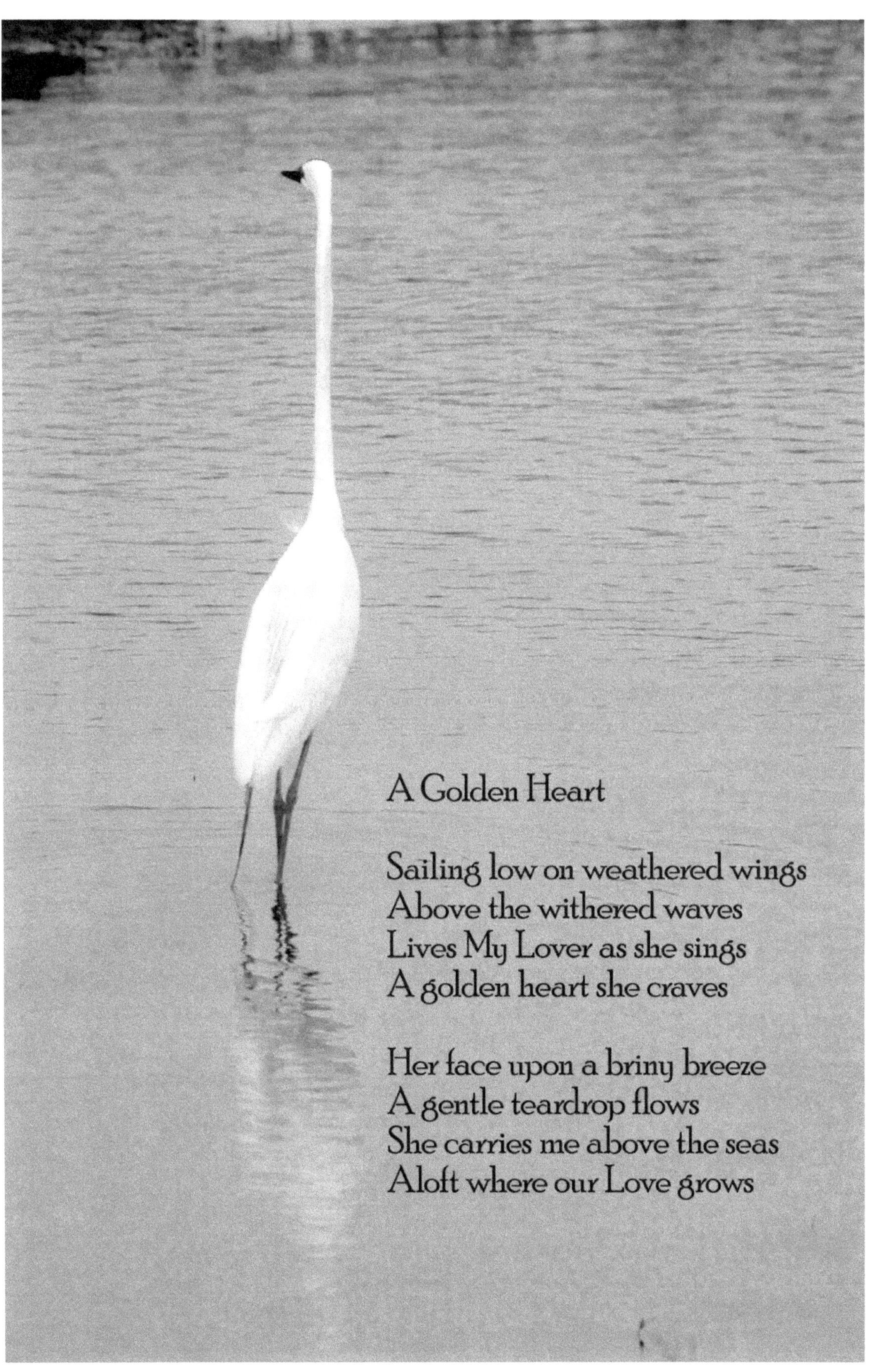

A Golden Heart

Sailing low on weathered wings
Above the withered waves
Lives My Lover as she sings
A golden heart she craves

Her face upon a briny breeze
A gentle teardrop flows
She carries me above the seas
Aloft where our Love grows

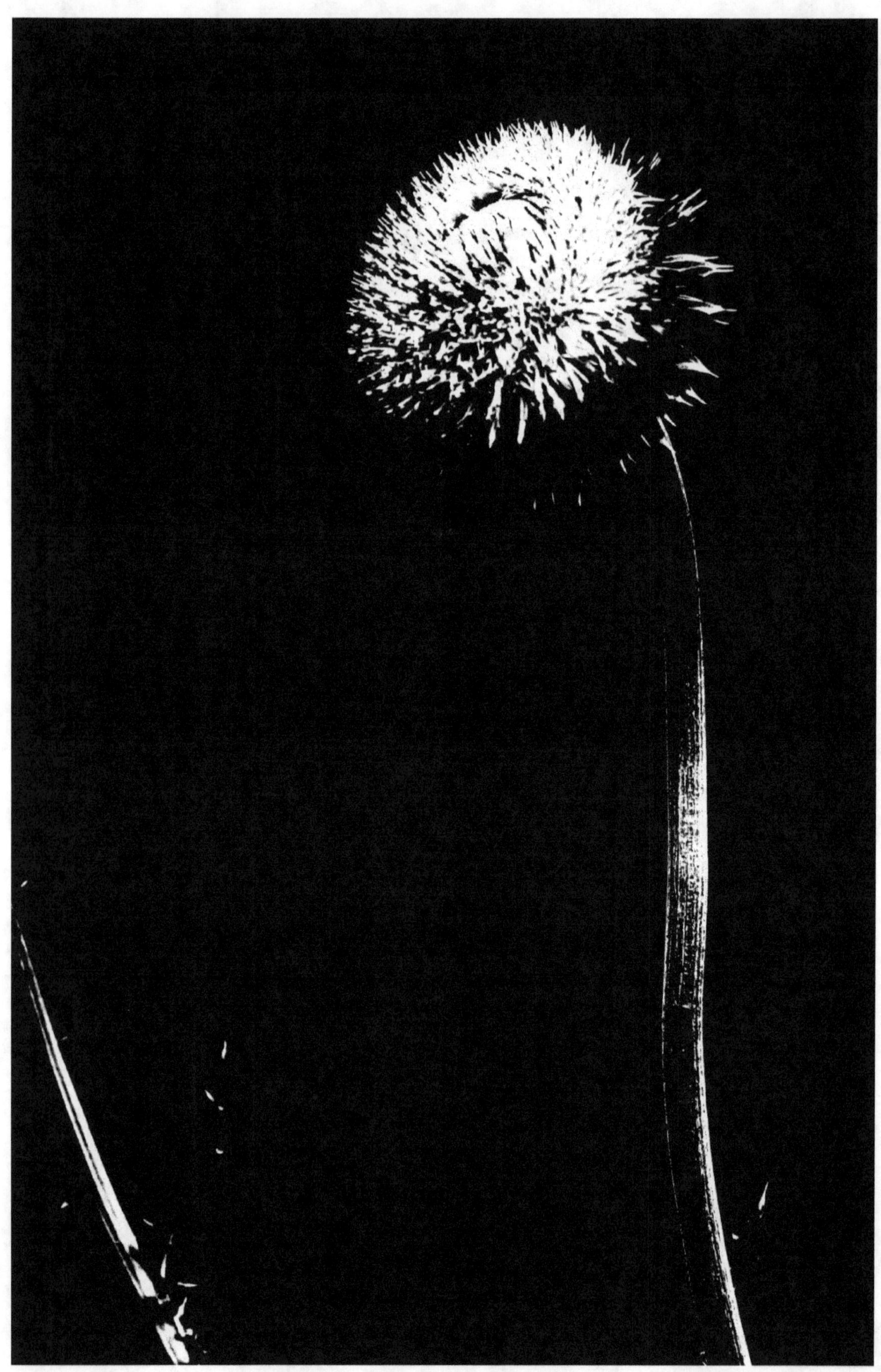

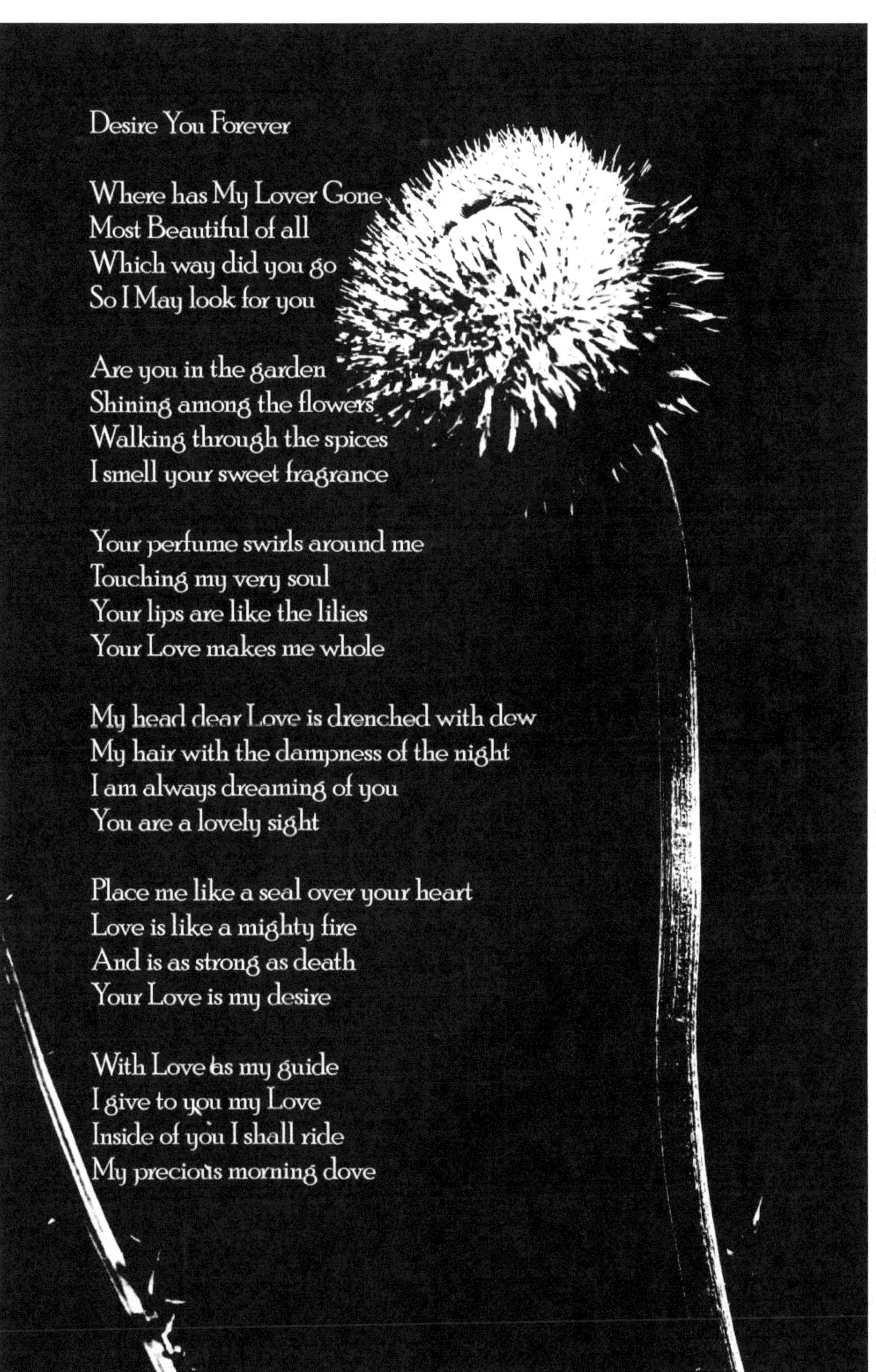

Desire You Forever

Where has My Lover Gone
Most Beautiful of all
Which way did you go
So I May look for you

Are you in the garden
Shining among the flowers
Walking through the spices
I smell your sweet fragrance

Your perfume swirls around me
Touching my very soul
Your lips are like the lilies
Your Love makes me whole

My head dear Love is drenched with dew
My hair with the dampness of the night
I am always dreaming of you
You are a lovely sight

Place me like a seal over your heart
Love is like a mighty fire
And is as strong as death
Your Love is my desire

With Love as my guide
I give to you my Love
Inside of you I shall ride
My precious morning dove

I Believe

I see your face My Love
Shining in the night time
You are far more beautiful
Than all the stars together

You smile in delight
Because shooting stars at night
Dance for you
You give each a twinkle

You point to the stars
But I can only see one
I see light in your eyes
To me you are the sun

Beautiful as they are
I believe
All the stars
Are your children

They Whisper to you in colors
Revealing themselves by name
Your Love gives them Life
And no two are the same

This is why you smile
Watching stars fly by
I see grace and beauty
Reflecting in your eye

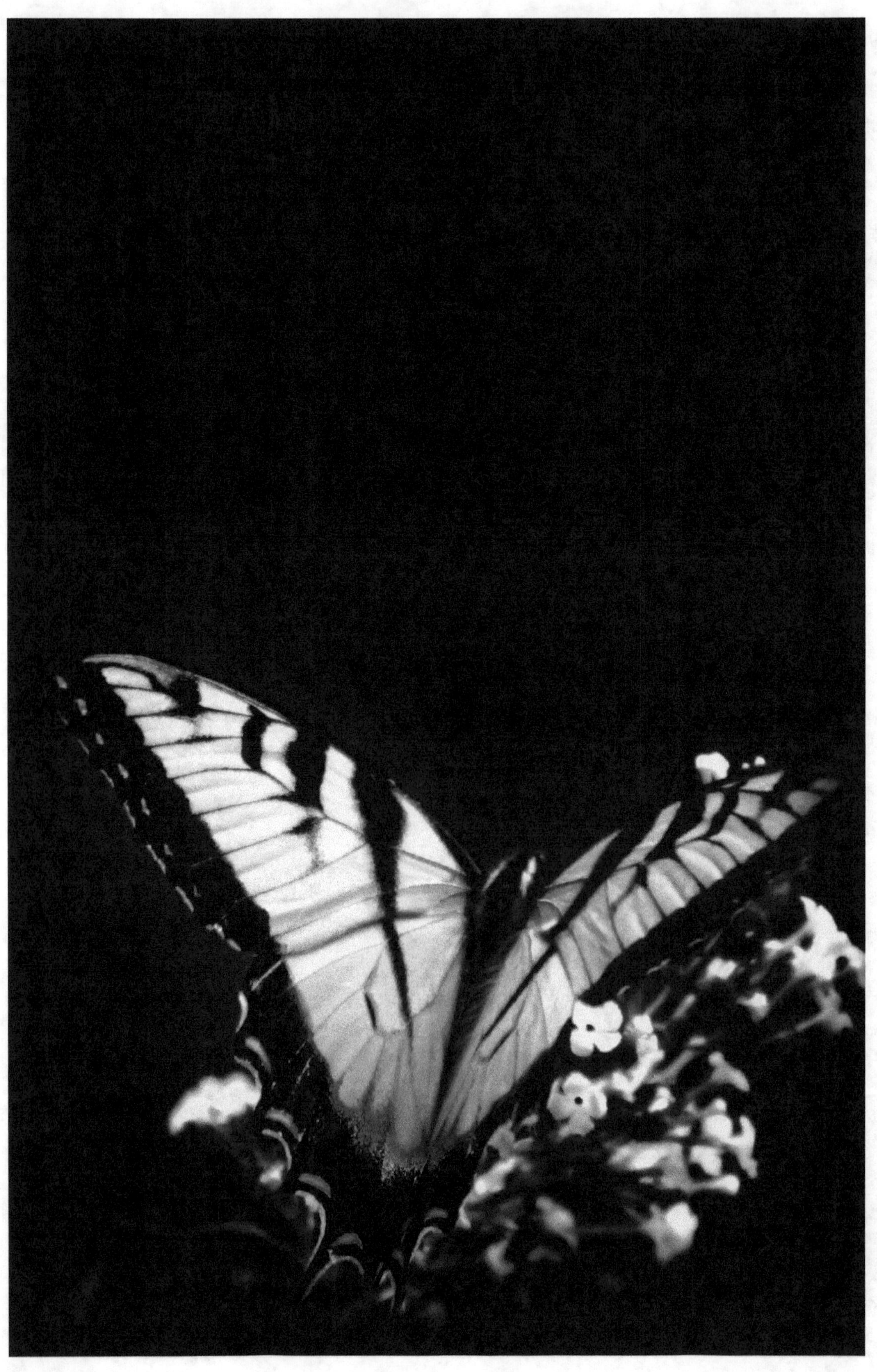

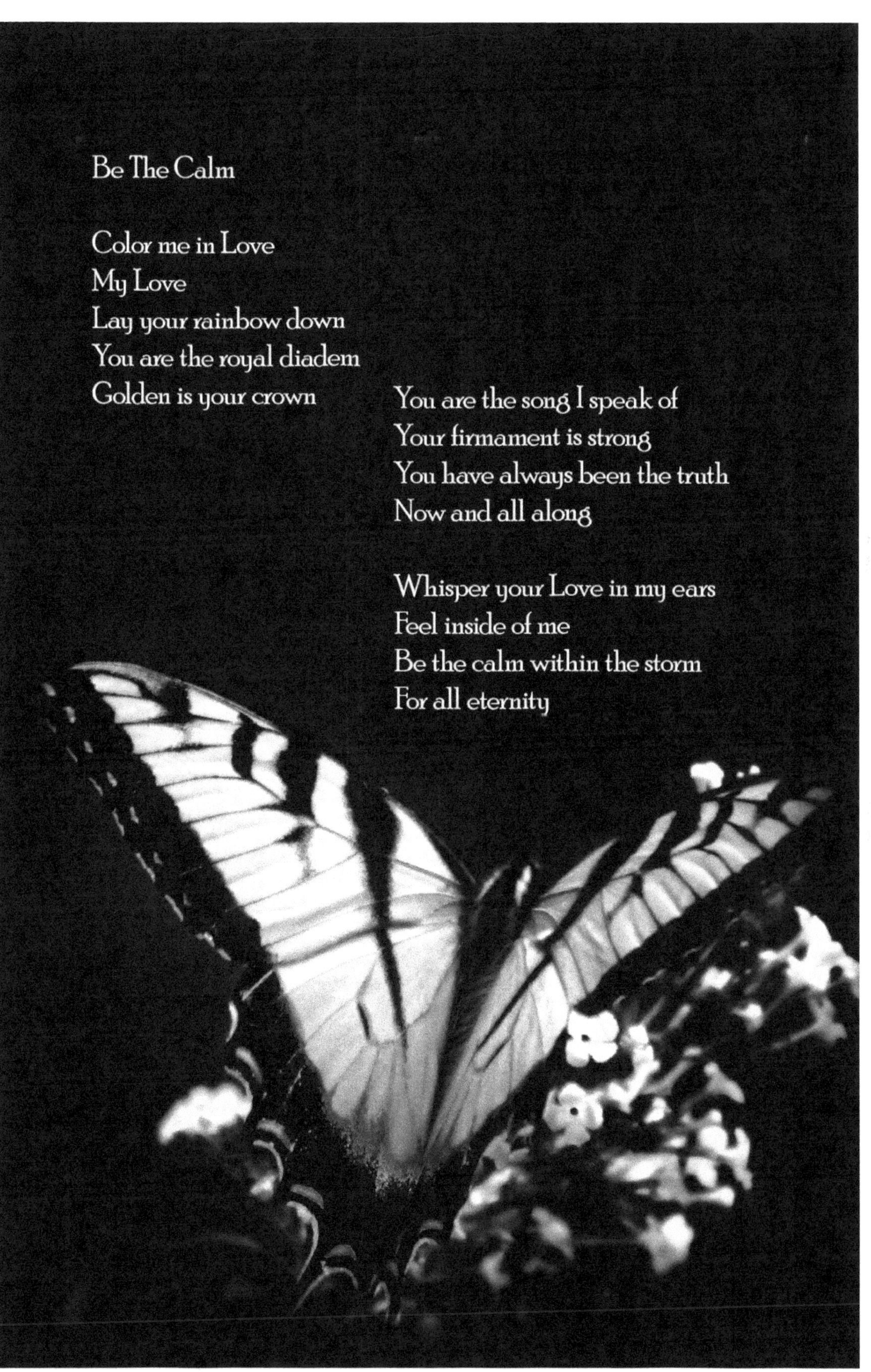

Be The Calm

Color me in Love
My Love
Lay your rainbow down
You are the royal diadem
Golden is your crown

You are the song I speak of
Your firmament is strong
You have always been the truth
Now and all along

Whisper your Love in my ears
Feel inside of me
Be the calm within the storm
For all eternity

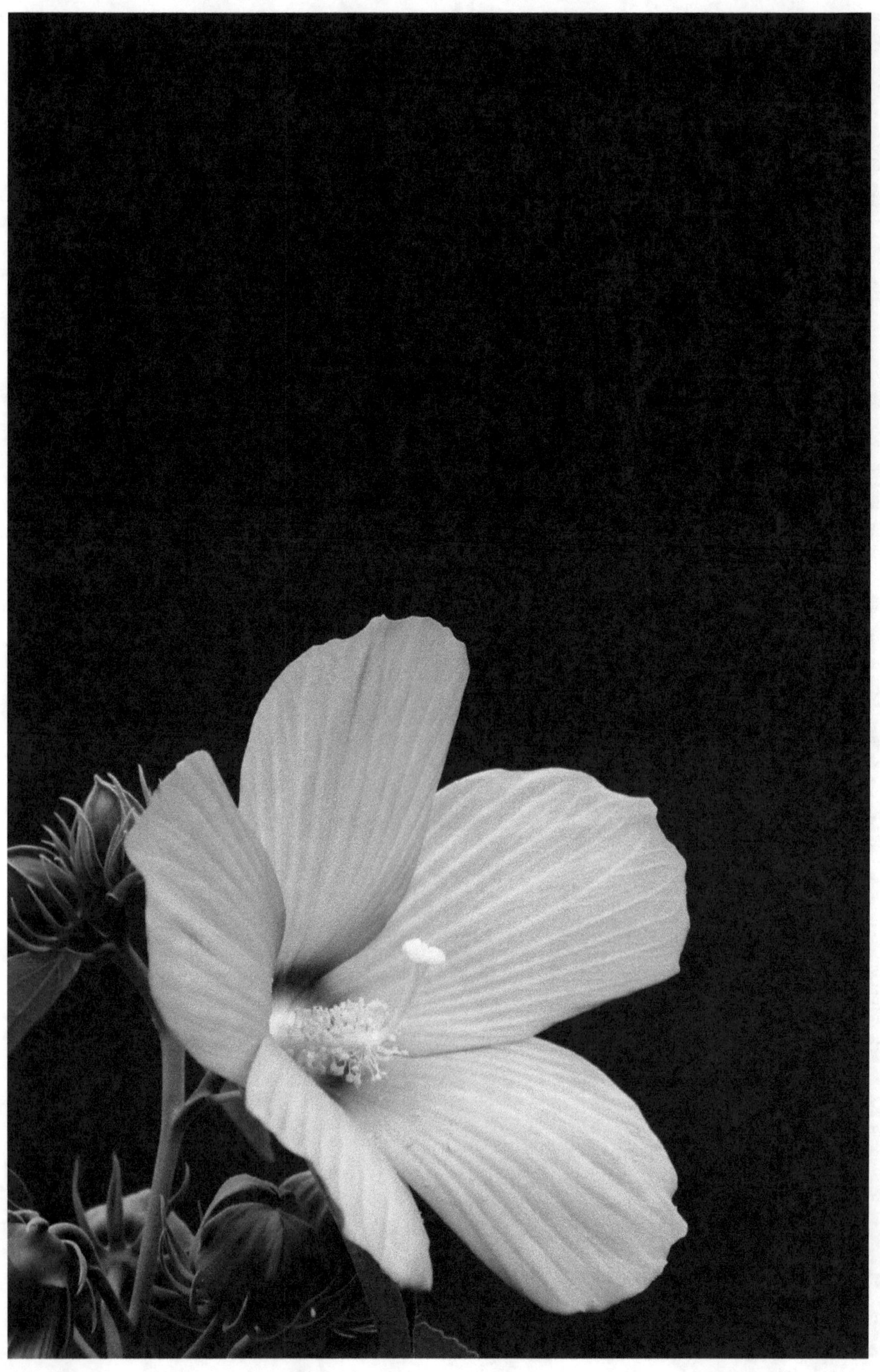

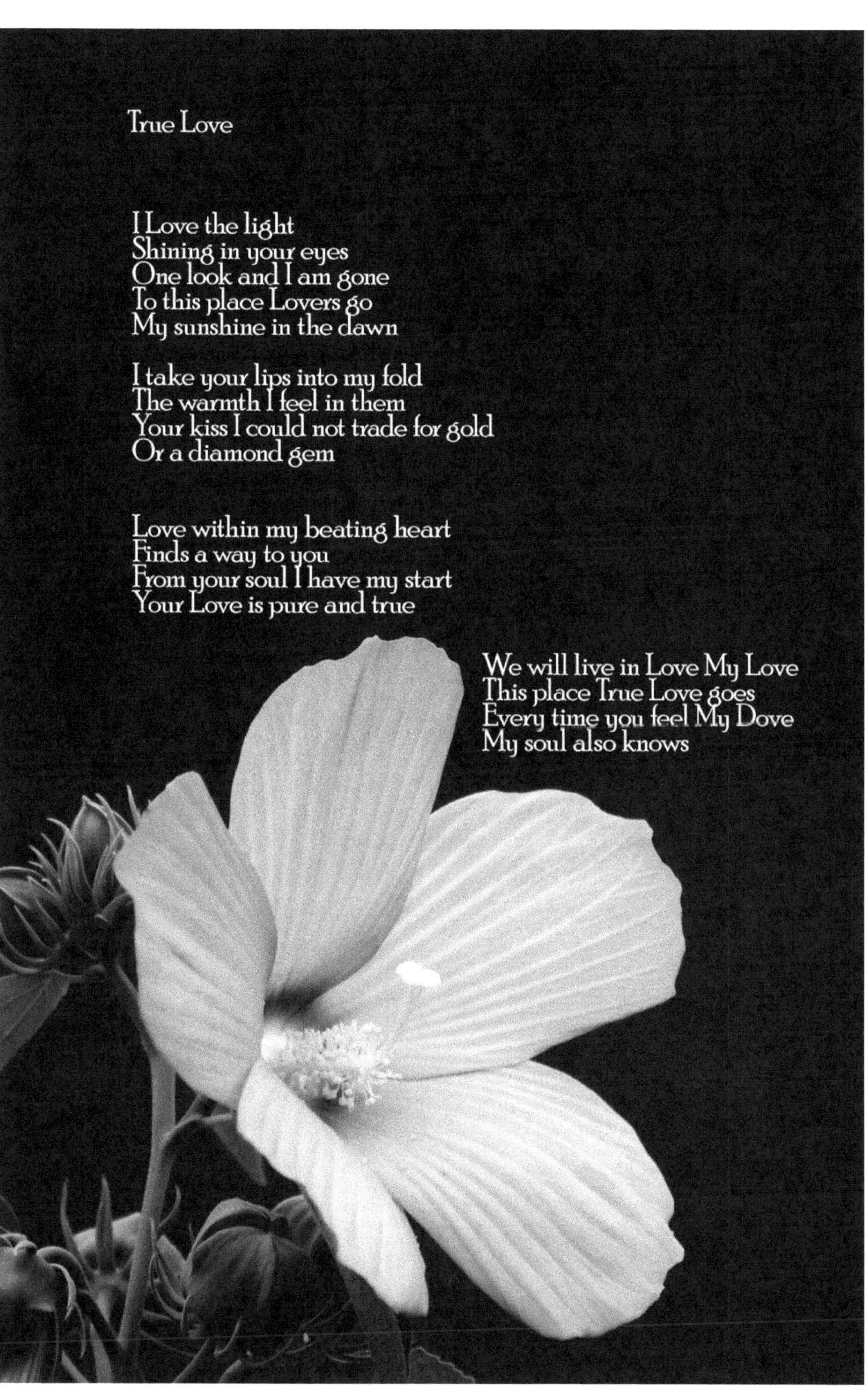

True Love

I Love the light
Shining in your eyes
One look and I am gone
To this place Lovers go
My sunshine in the dawn

I take your lips into my fold
The warmth I feel in them
Your kiss I could not trade for gold
Or a diamond gem

Love within my beating heart
Finds a way to you
From your soul I have my start
Your Love is pure and true

We will live in Love My Love
This place True Love goes
Every time you feel My Dove
My soul also knows

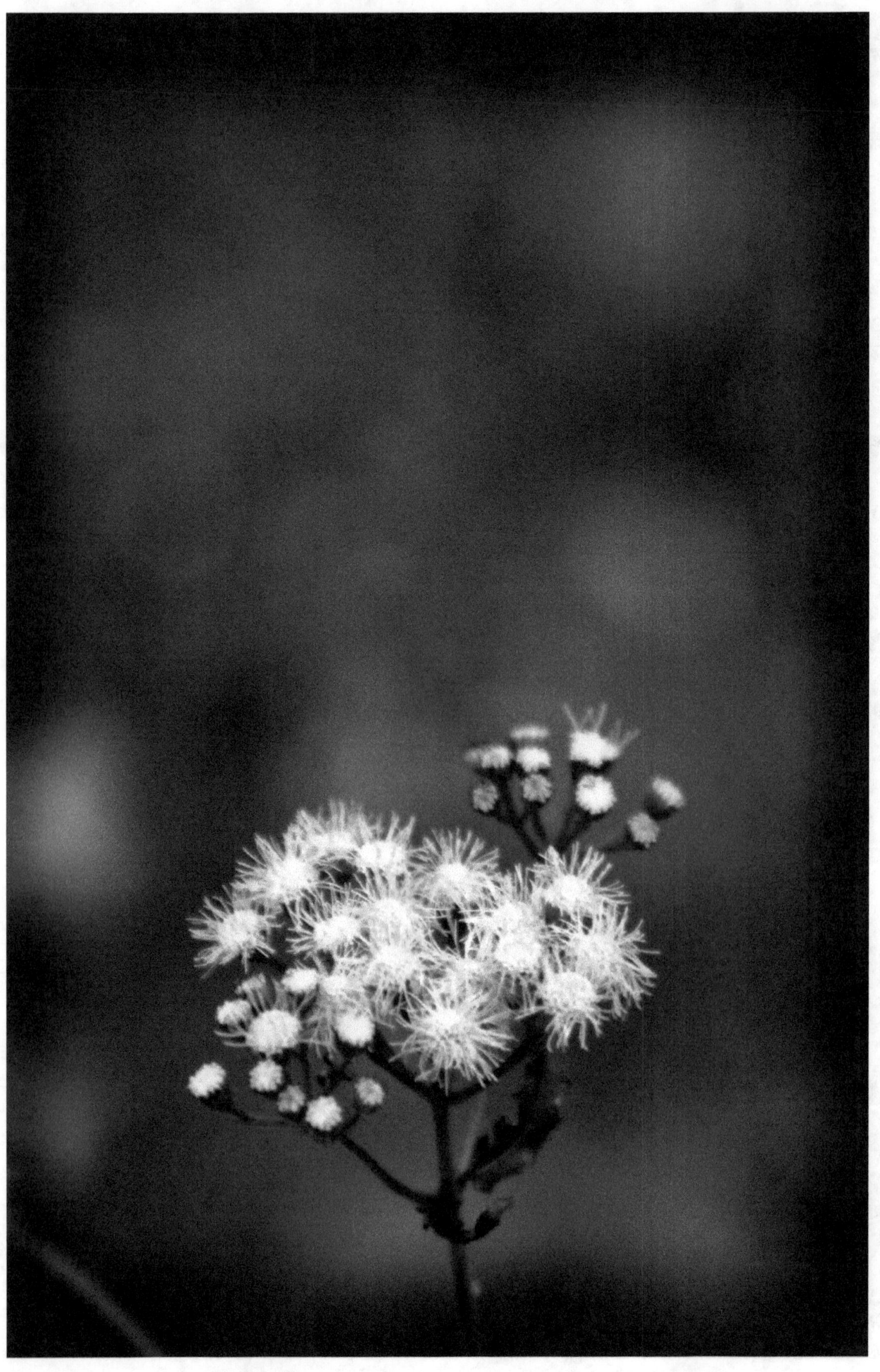

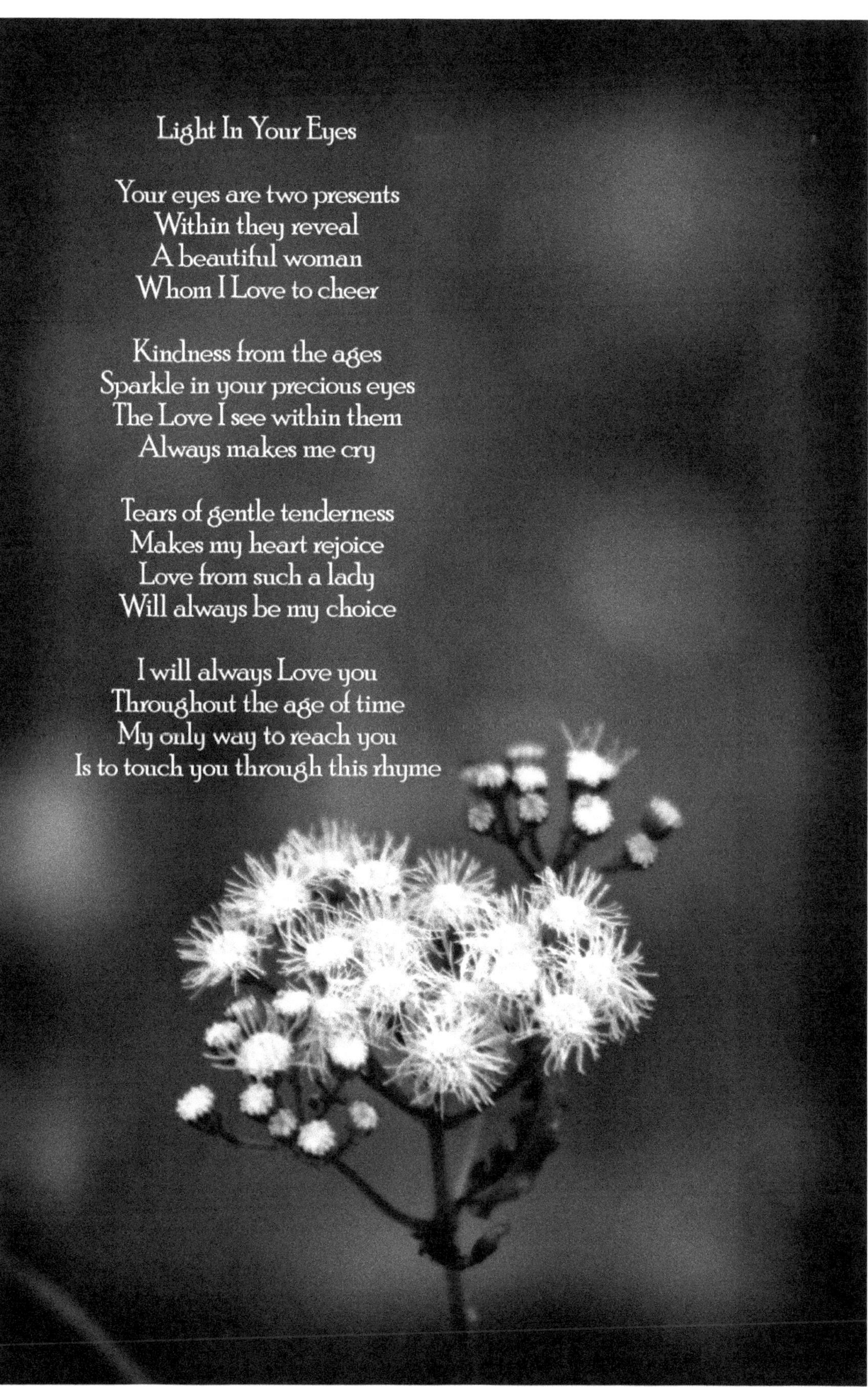

Light In Your Eyes

Your eyes are two presents
Within they reveal
A beautiful woman
Whom I Love to cheer

Kindness from the ages
Sparkle in your precious eyes
The Love I see within them
Always makes me cry

Tears of gentle tenderness
Makes my heart rejoice
Love from such a lady
Will always be my choice

I will always Love you
Throughout the age of time
My only way to reach you
Is to touch you through this rhyme

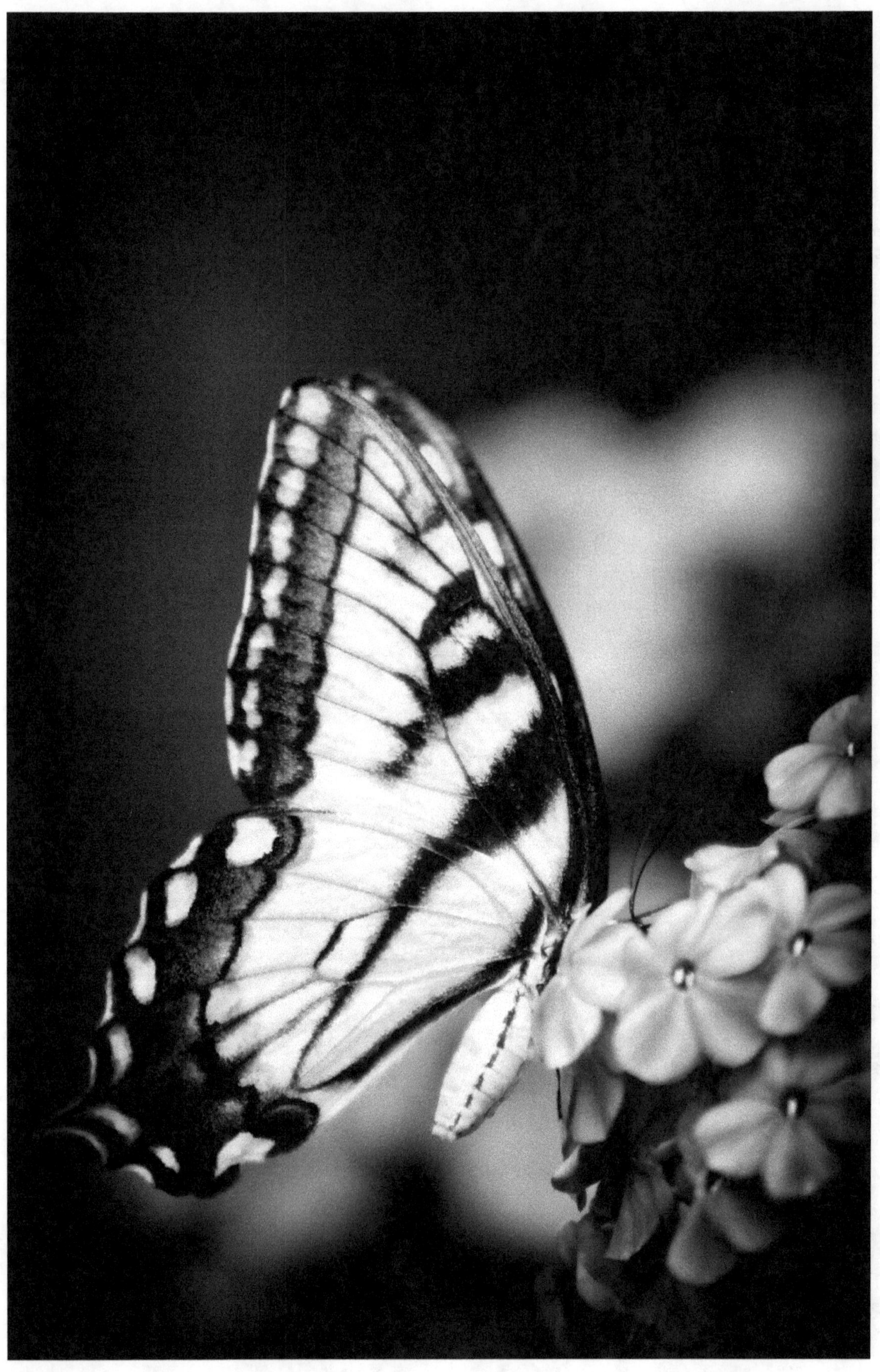

My Valentine

Your breasts ~ Are like clusters of fruit
Your stature is the palm
I cling to you My Valentine ~ And I sing your psalm
I hold your fruit in my hands ~ Like grapes on the vine
And place them gently in my mouth ~ Tasting your best wine

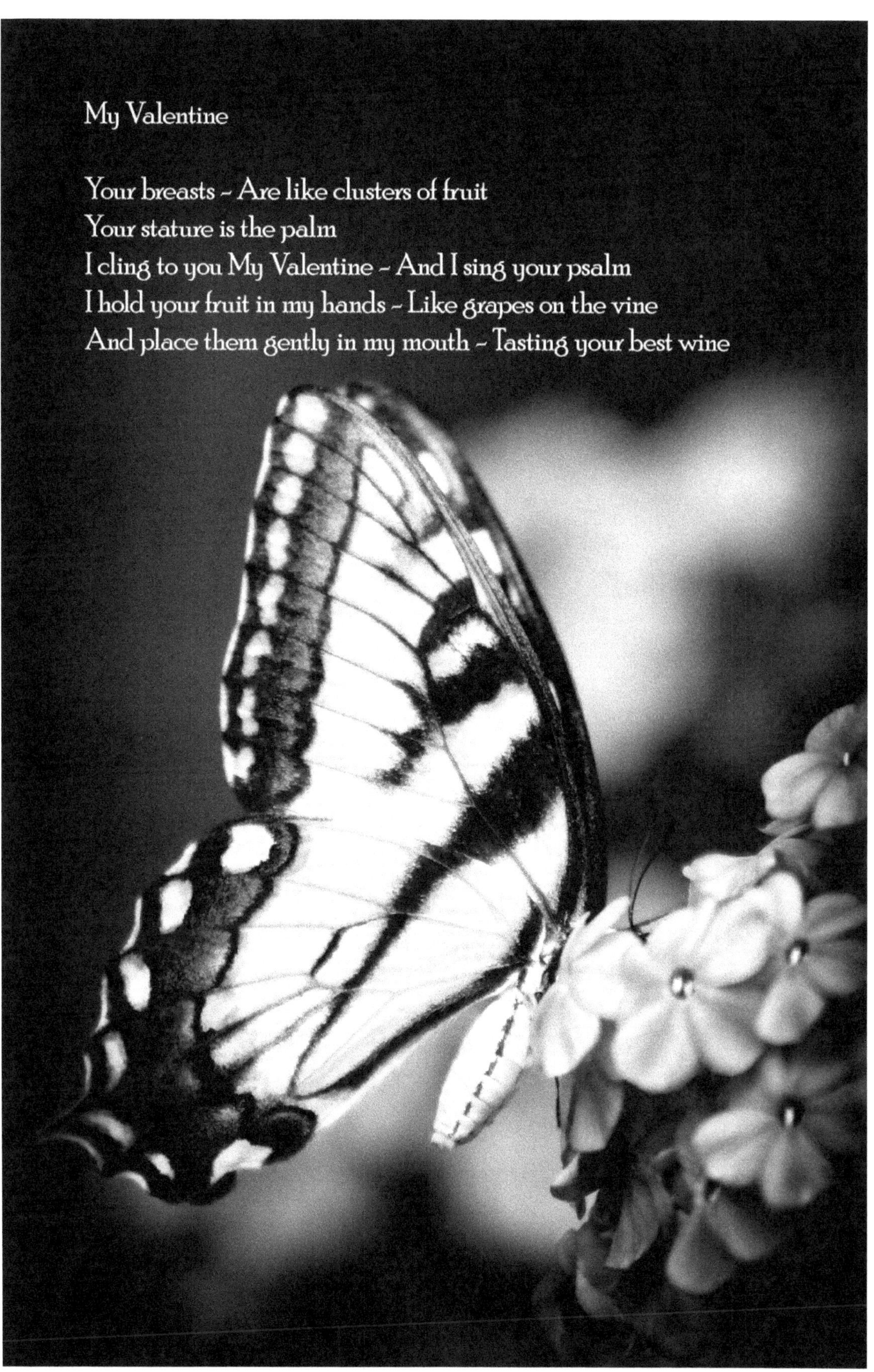

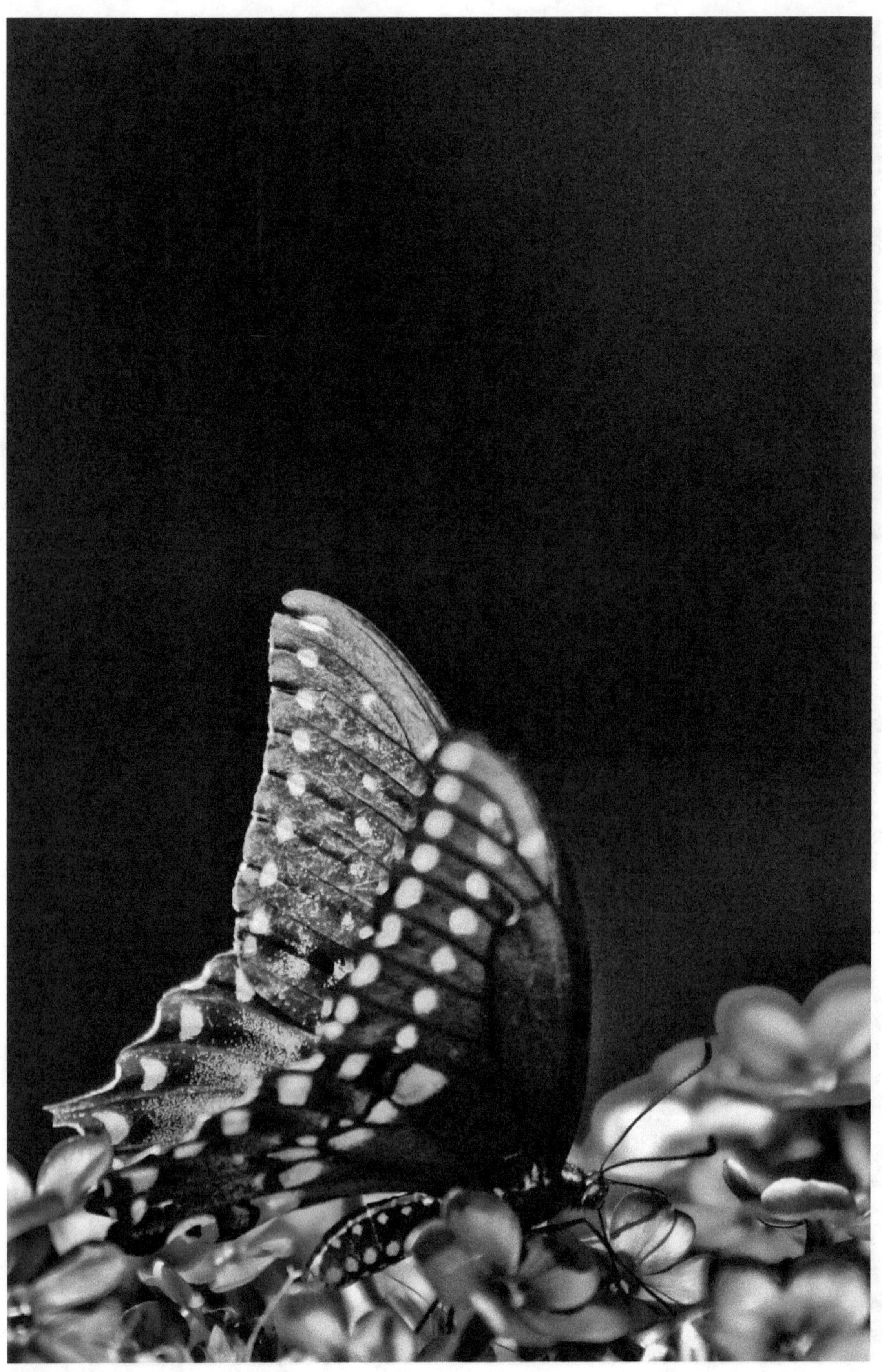

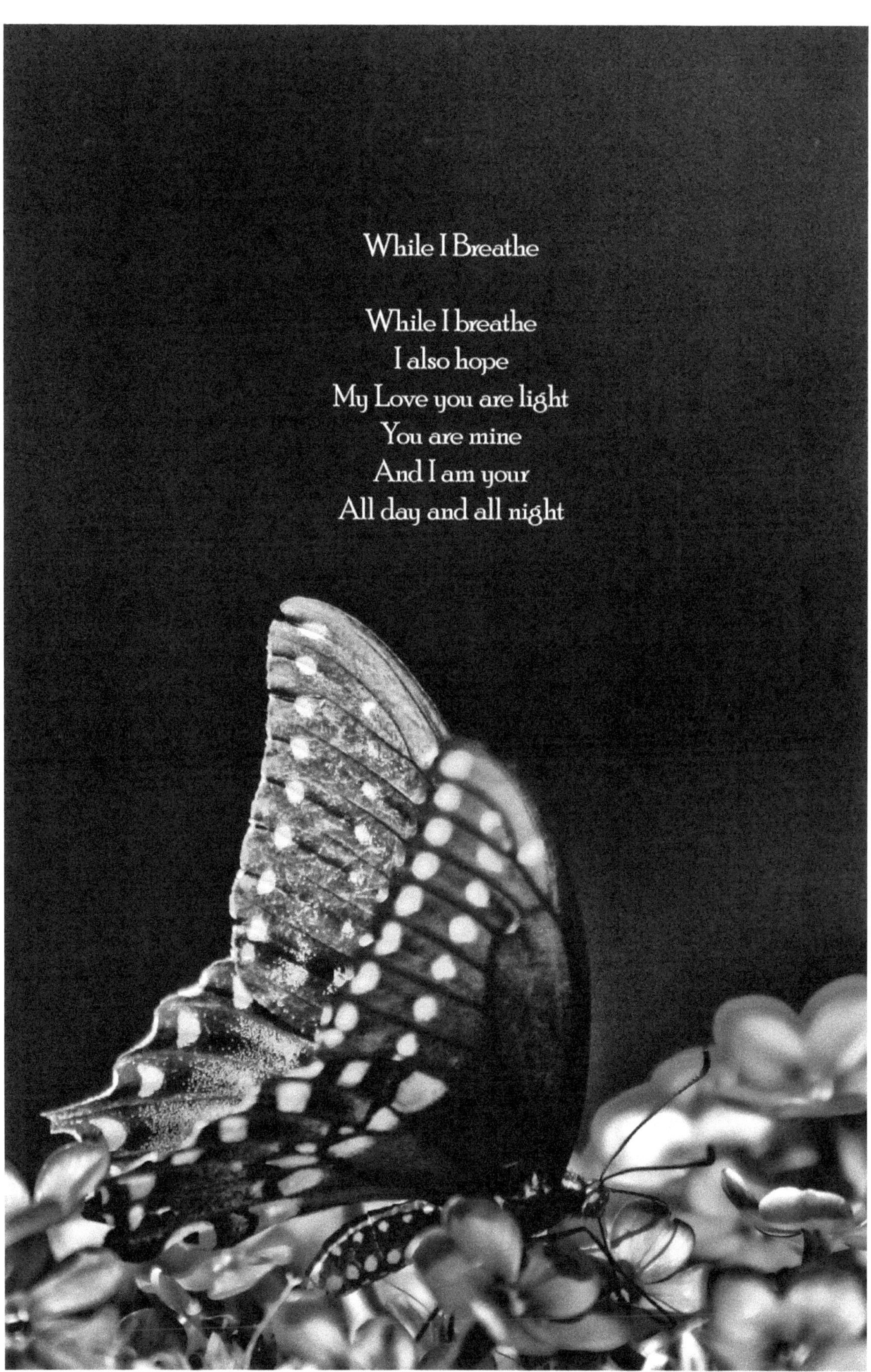

While I Breathe

While I breathe
I also hope
My Love you are light
You are mine
And I am your
All day and all night

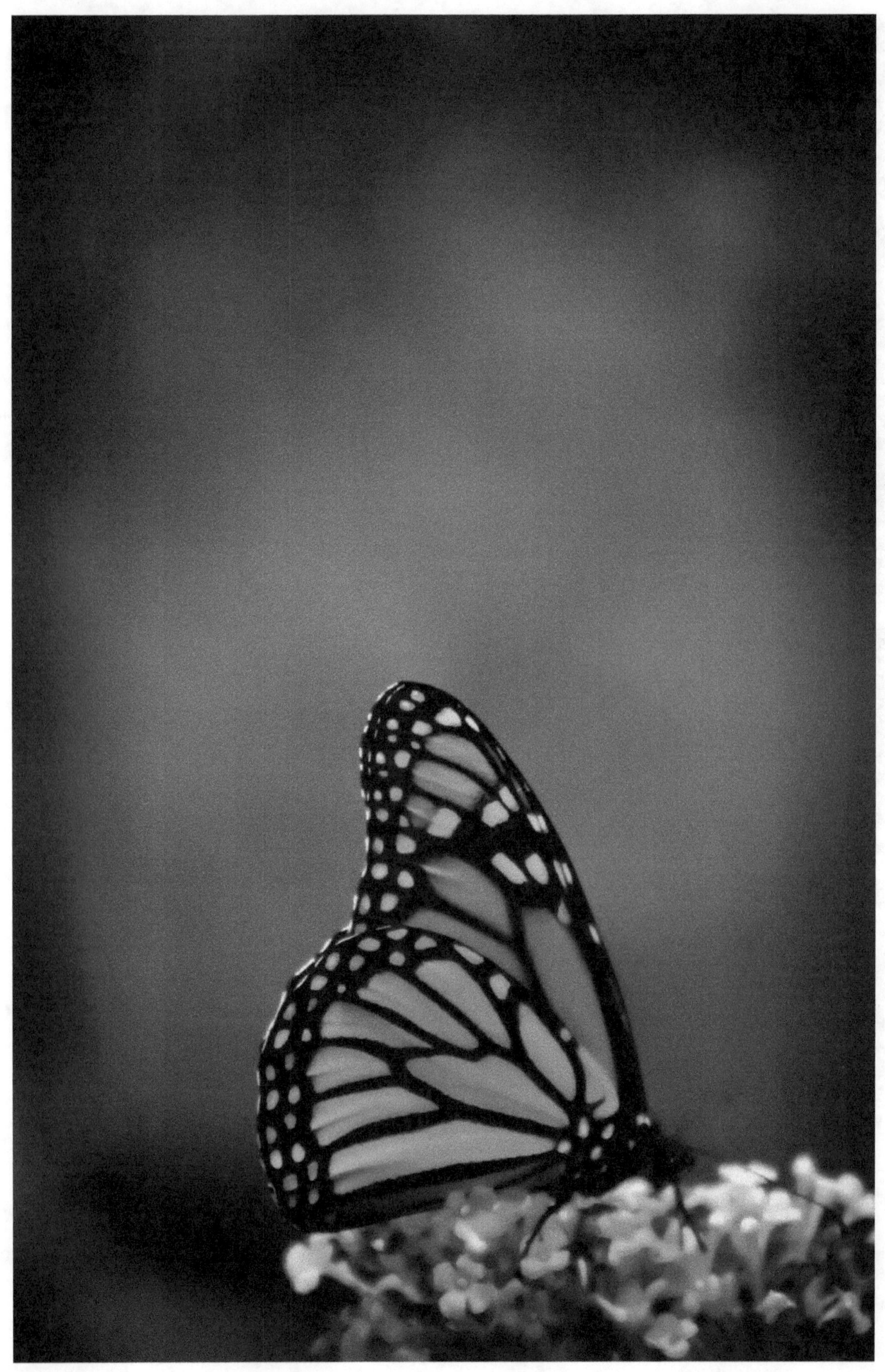

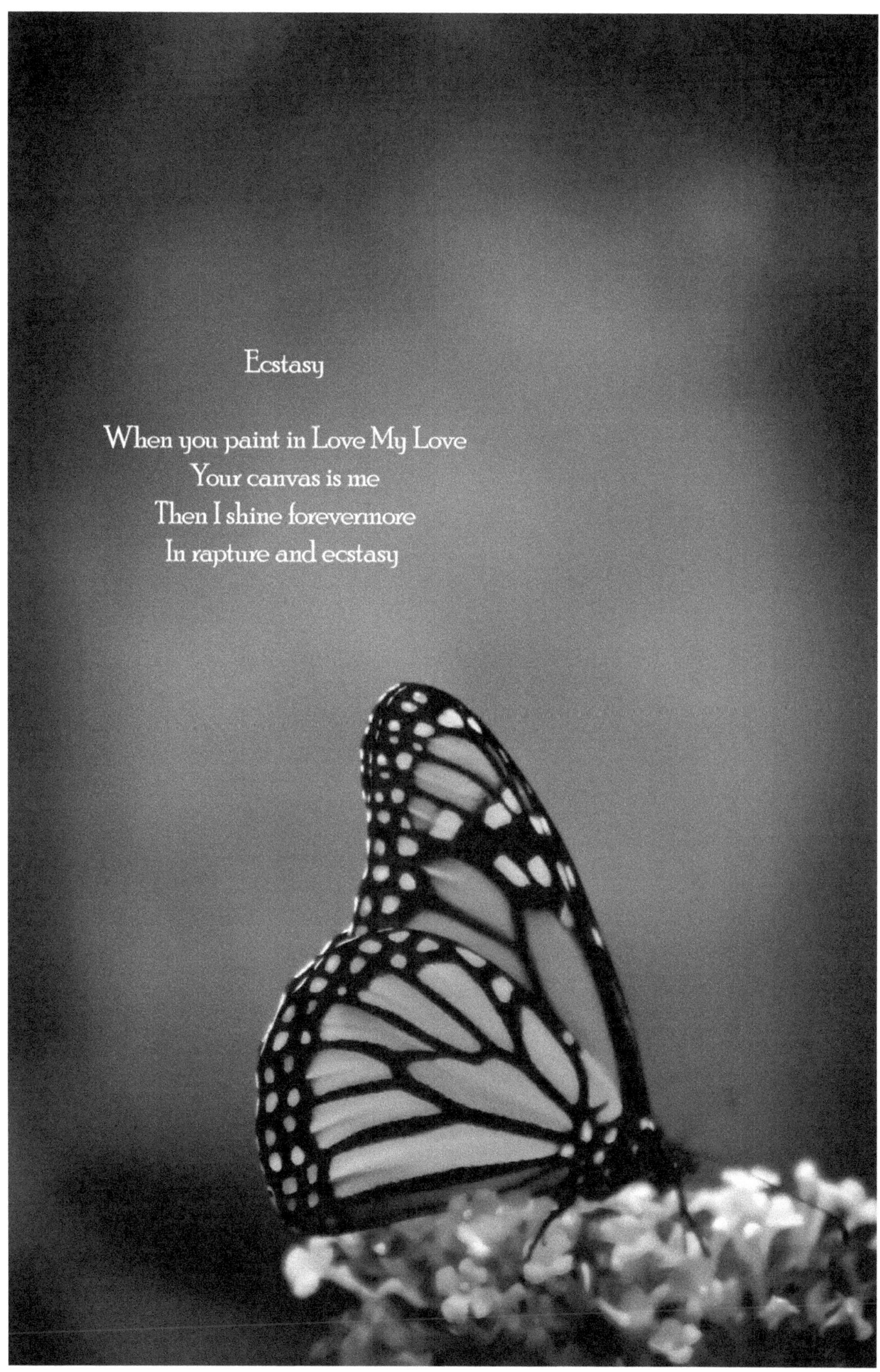

Ecstasy

When you paint in Love My Love
Your canvas is me
Then I shine forevermore
In rapture and ecstasy

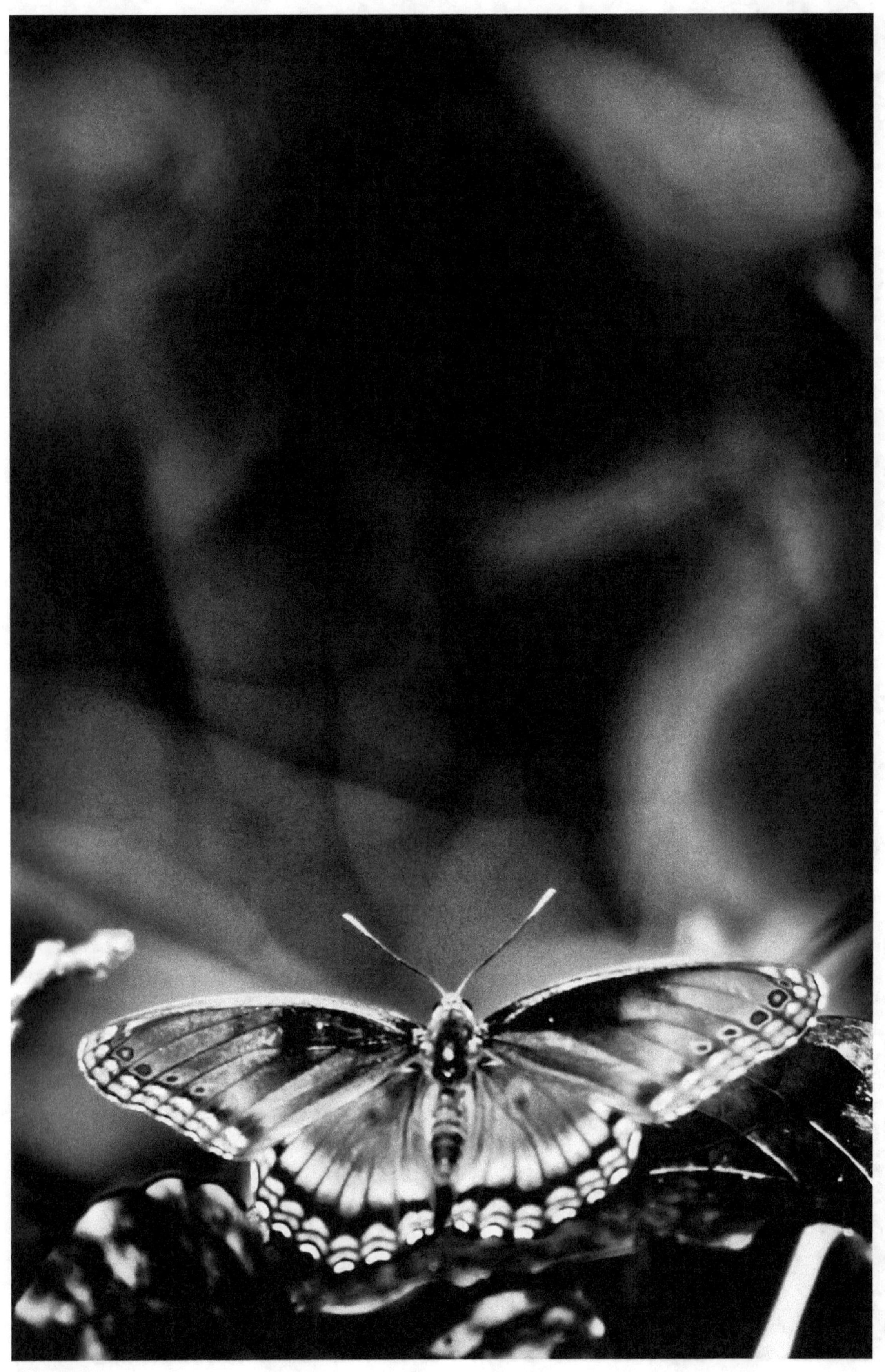

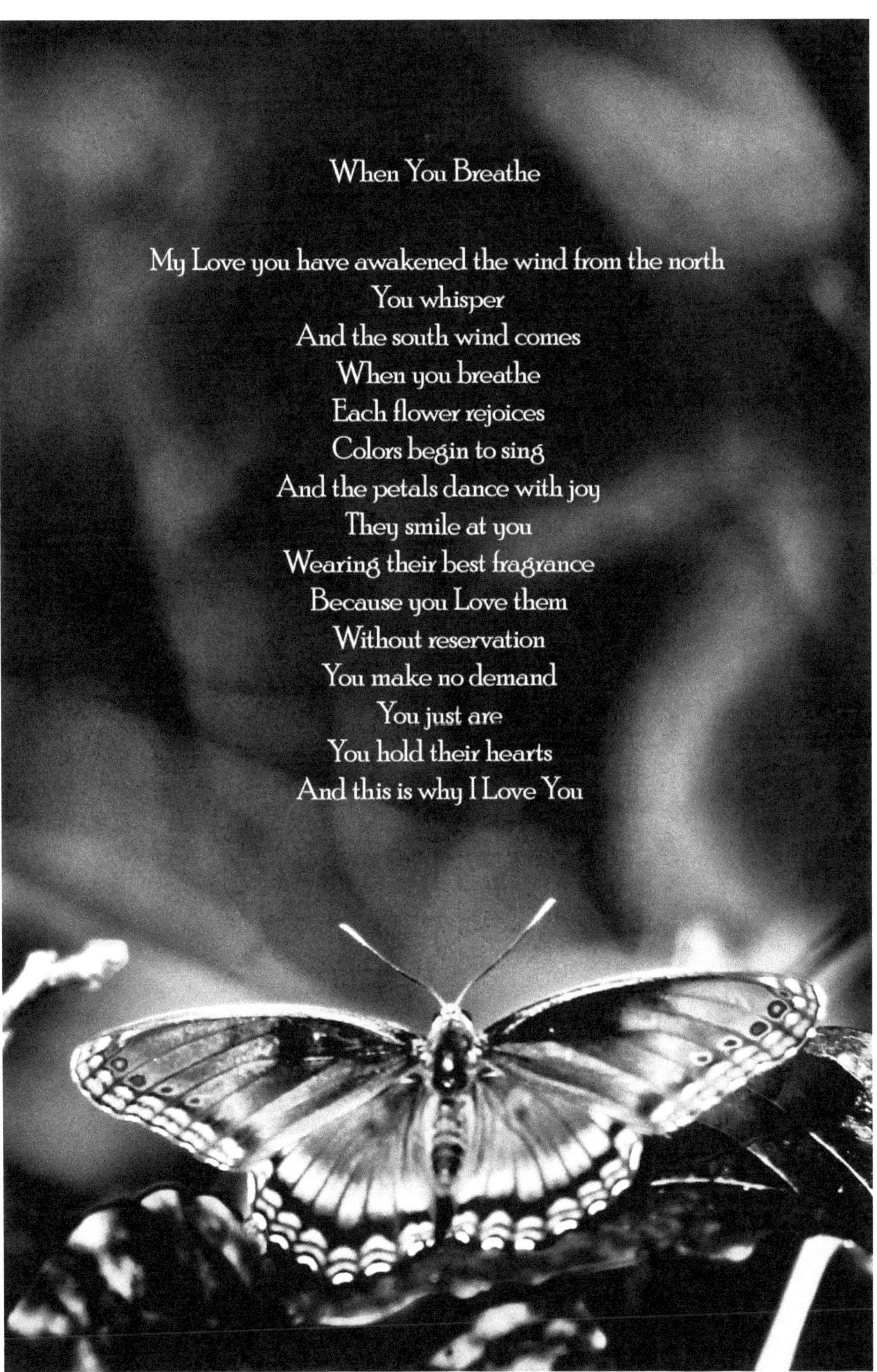

When You Breathe

My Love you have awakened the wind from the north
You whisper
And the south wind comes
When you breathe
Each flower rejoices
Colors begin to sing
And the petals dance with joy
They smile at you
Wearing their best fragrance
Because you Love them
Without reservation
You make no demand
You just are
You hold their hearts
And this is why I Love You

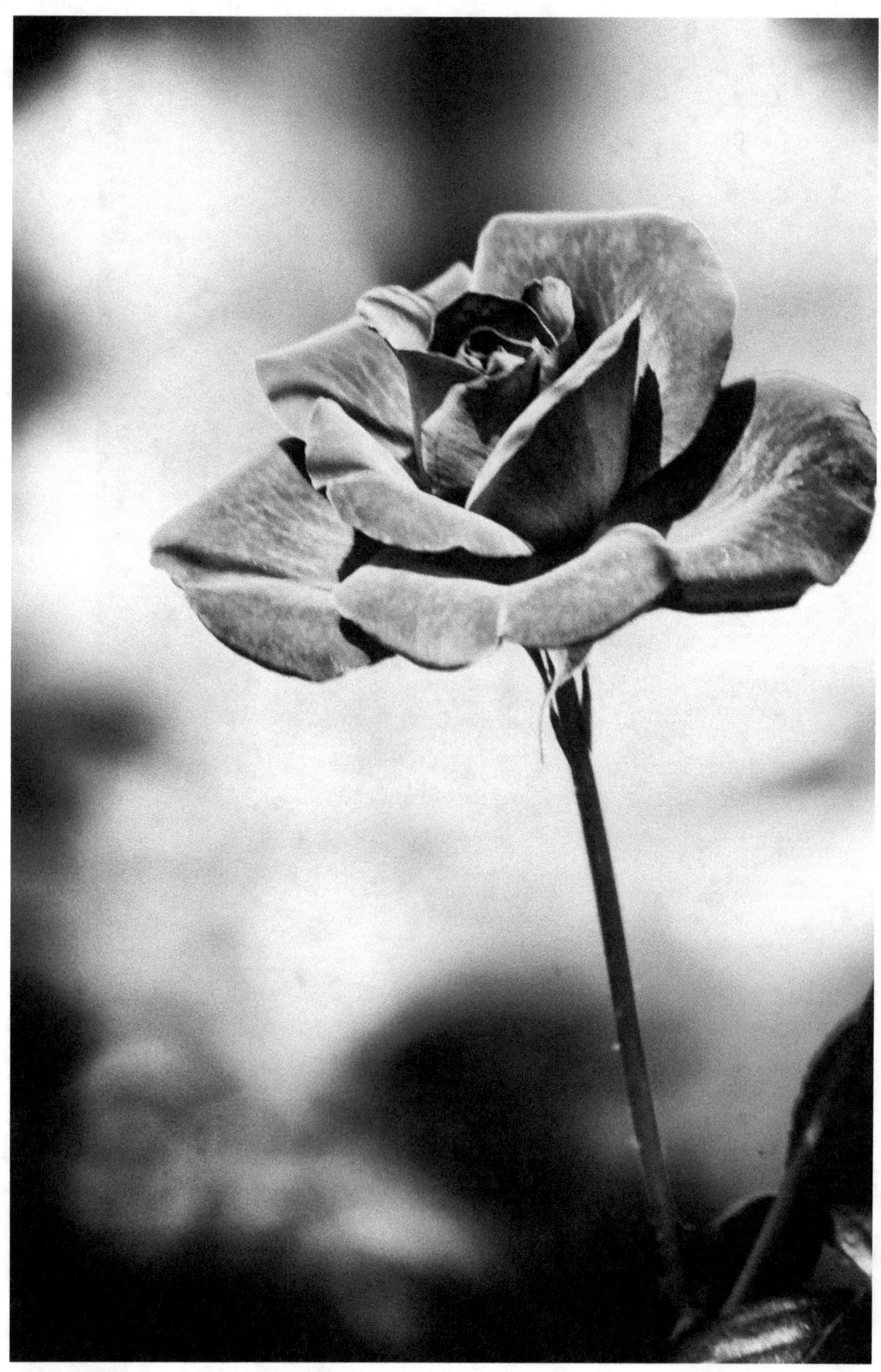

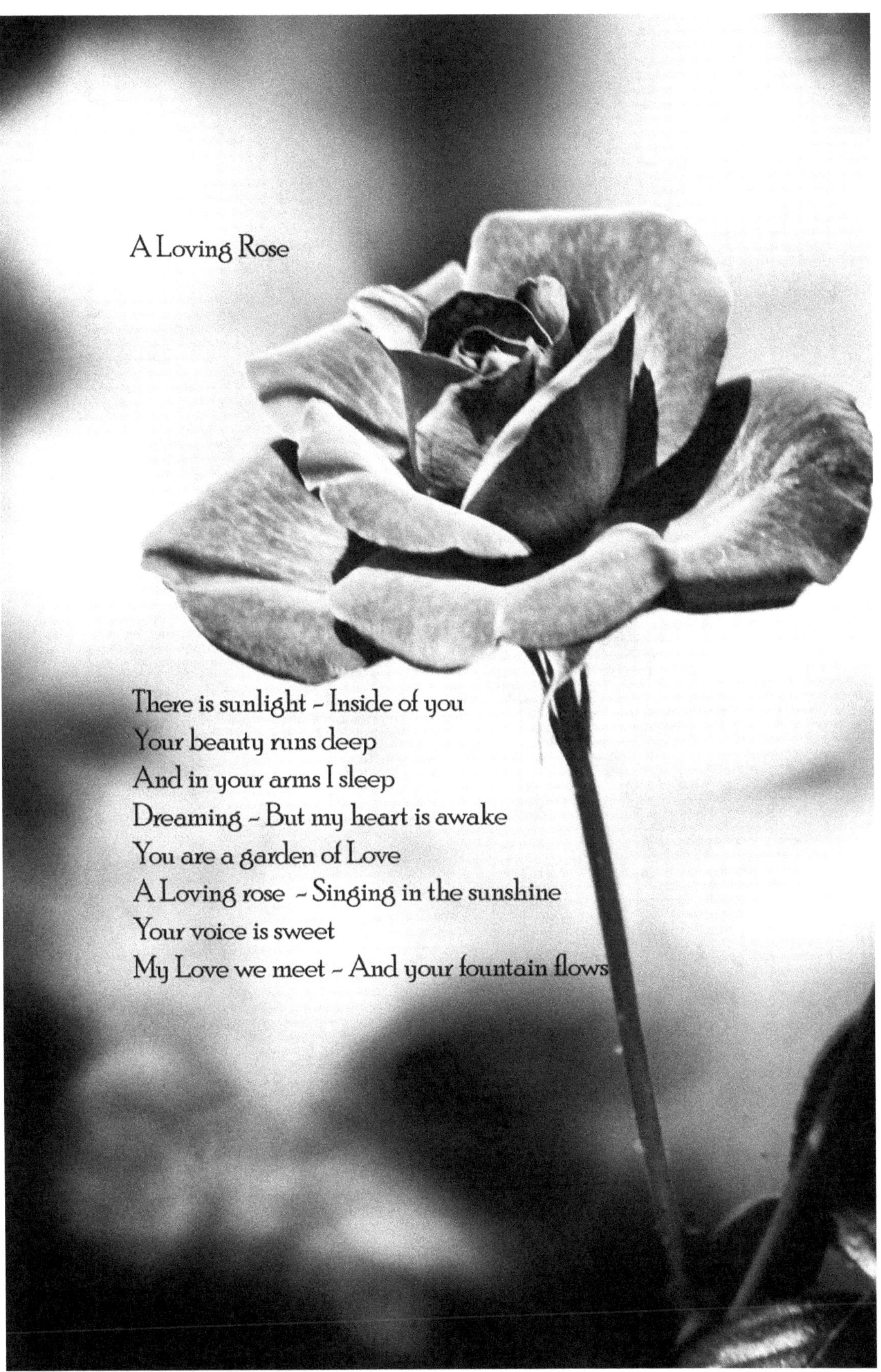

A Loving Rose

There is sunlight - Inside of you
Your beauty runs deep
And in your arms I sleep
Dreaming - But my heart is awake
You are a garden of Love
A Loving rose - Singing in the sunshine
Your voice is sweet
My Love we meet - And your fountain flows

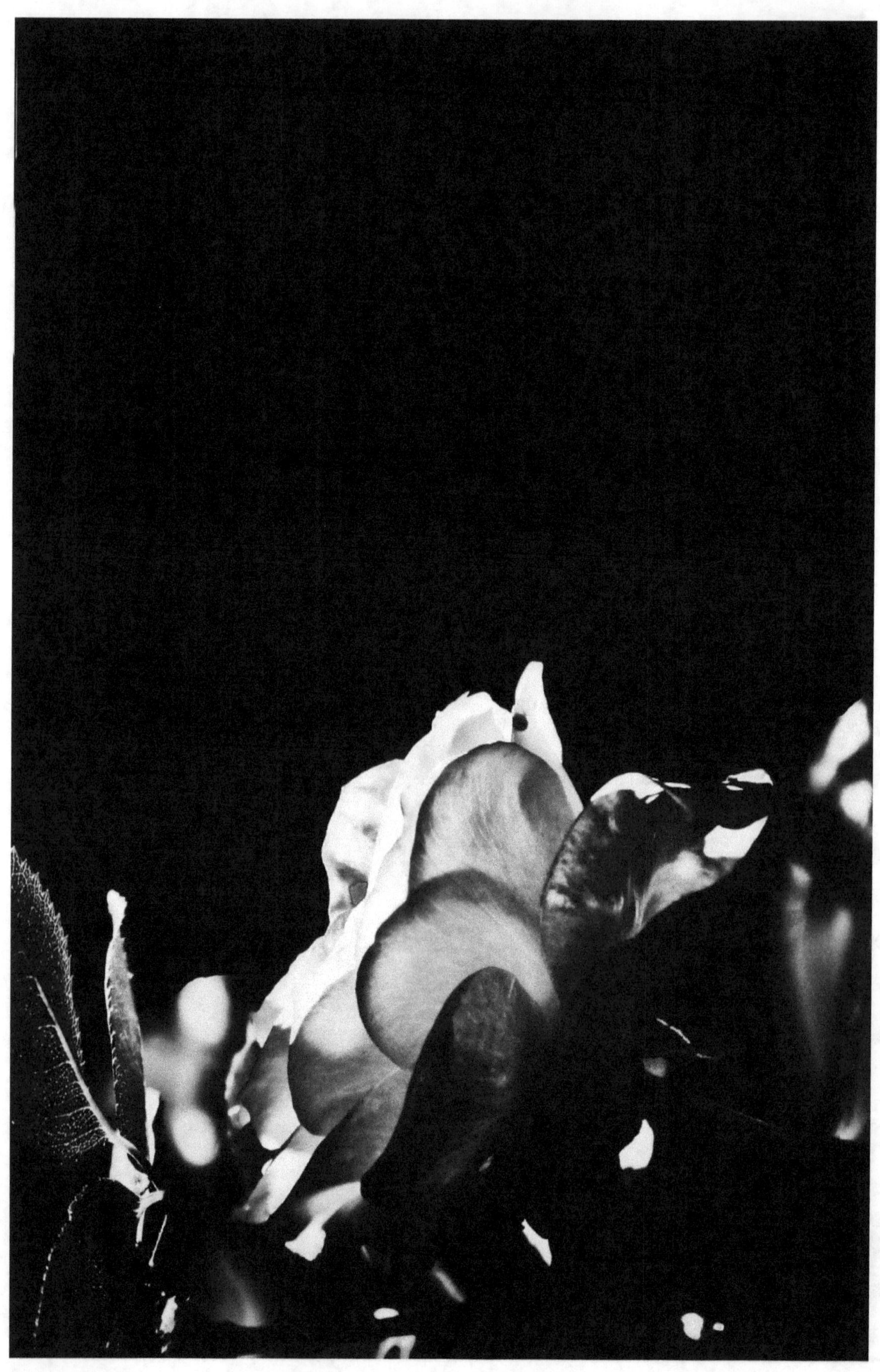

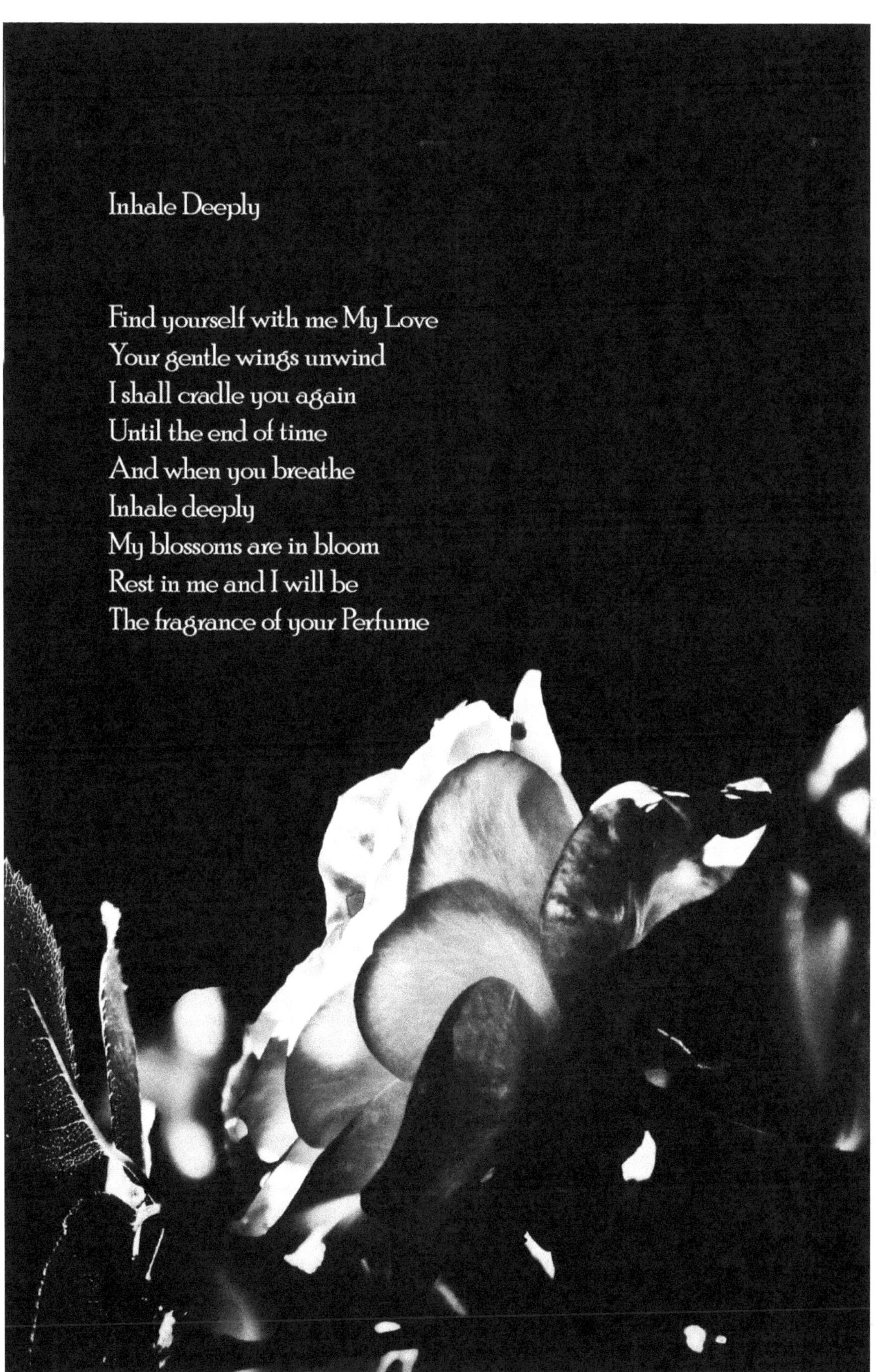

Inhale Deeply

Find yourself with me My Love
Your gentle wings unwind
I shall cradle you again
Until the end of time
And when you breathe
Inhale deeply
My blossoms are in bloom
Rest in me and I will be
The fragrance of your Perfume

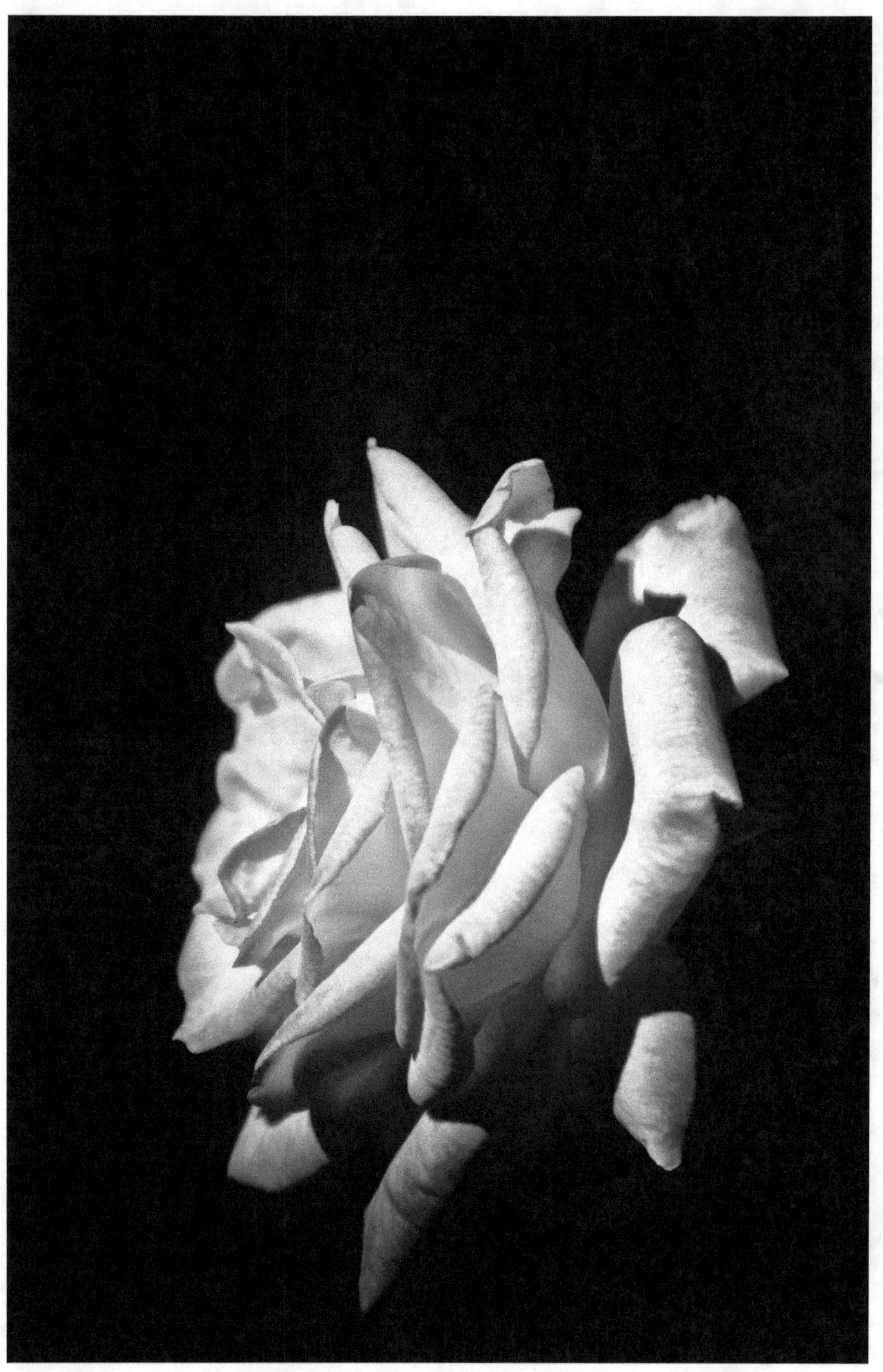

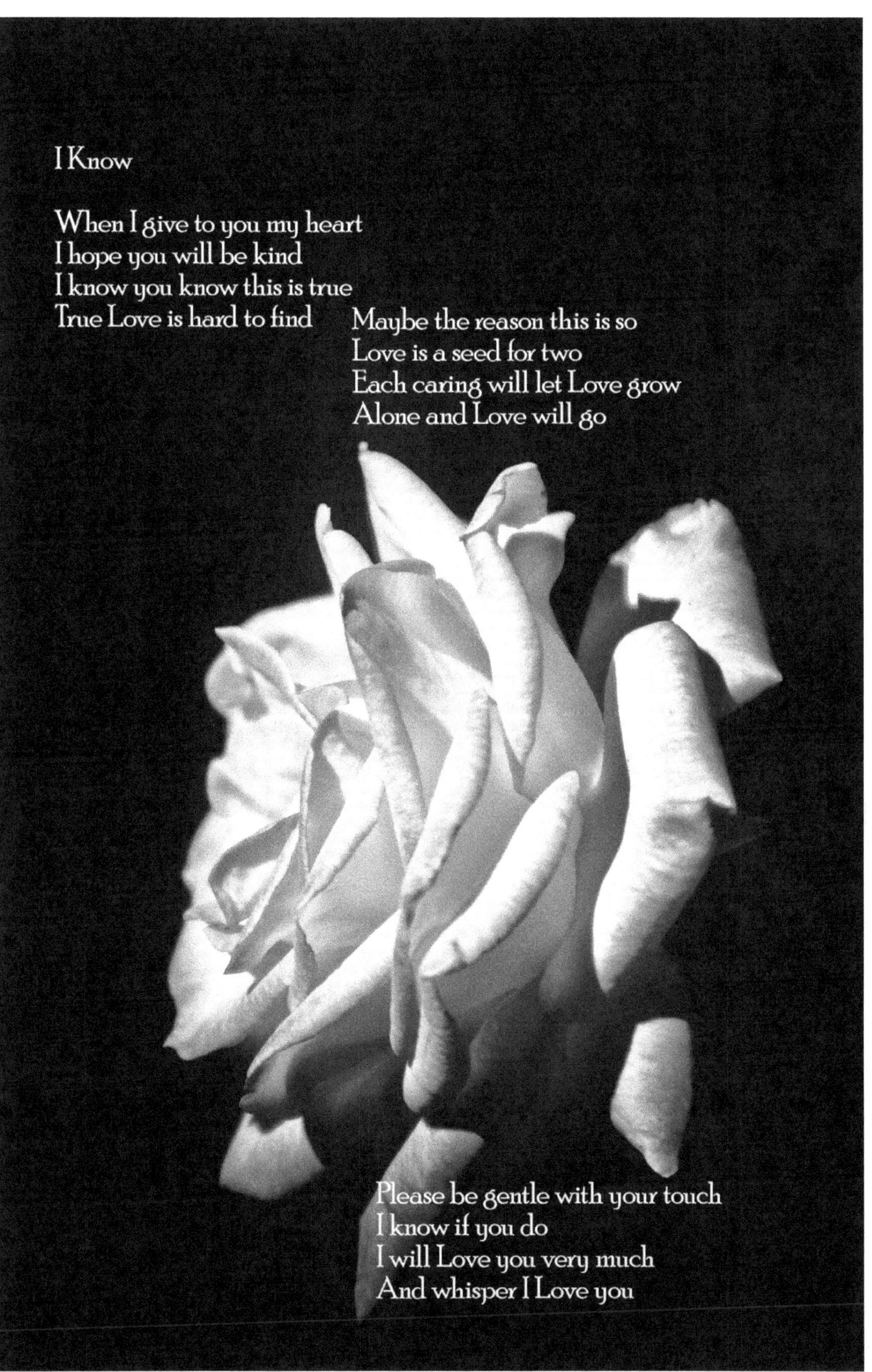

I Know

When I give to you my heart
I hope you will be kind
I know you know this is true
True Love is hard to find

Maybe the reason this is so
Love is a seed for two
Each caring will let Love grow
Alone and Love will go

Please be gentle with your touch
I know if you do
I will Love you very much
And whisper I Love you

Where Love And Life Are Ours

Your whispers of Love
Fly across the stars
Dance with me on the Milky Way
Where Love and Life are ours

The universe fills your eyes
Sunshine is your name
I Love You my heart cries
I will never be the same

Your eyes fill my soul
Cascading in rivers of Light
My Love you make the night time whole
With a billion stars at night

Shimmering colors bathe my world
As you look on me
All their facets I can see
You are beautiful and free

Dreaming now is all I know
Among the golden stars
Until your home with me My Love
Where Love and Life are ours

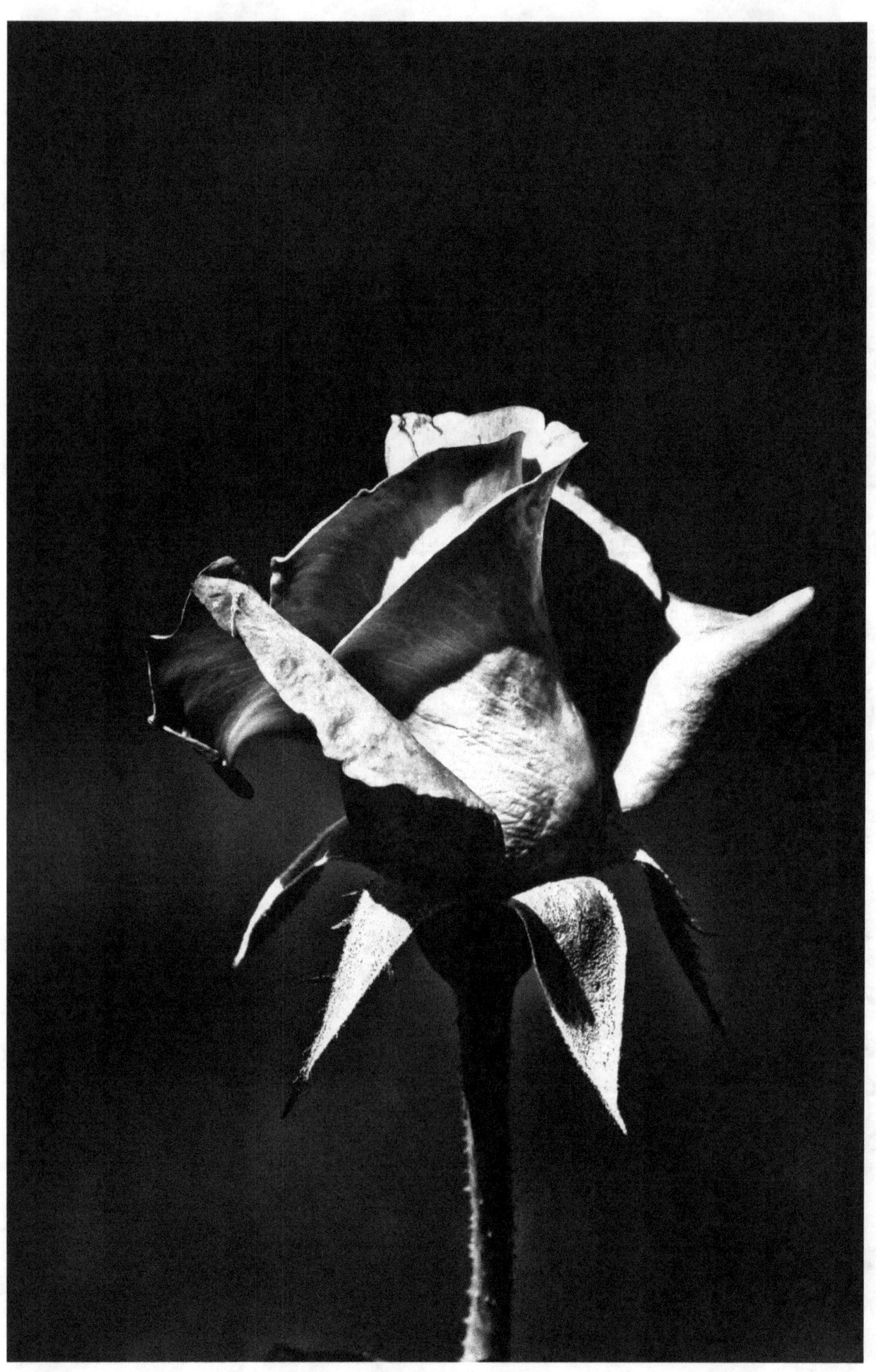

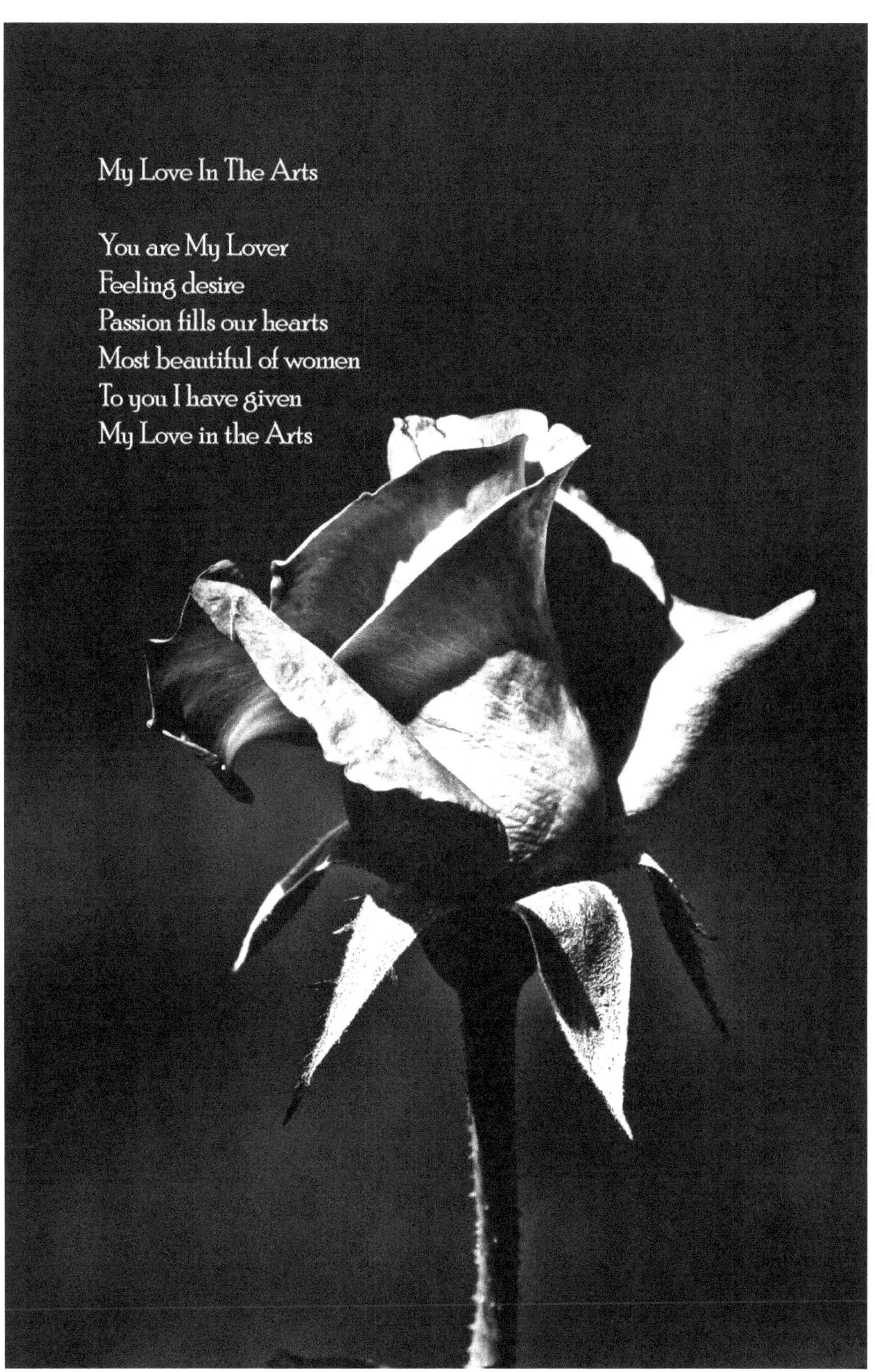
My Love In The Arts
You are My Lover
Feeling desire
Passion fills our hearts
Most beautiful of women
To you I have given
My Love in the Arts

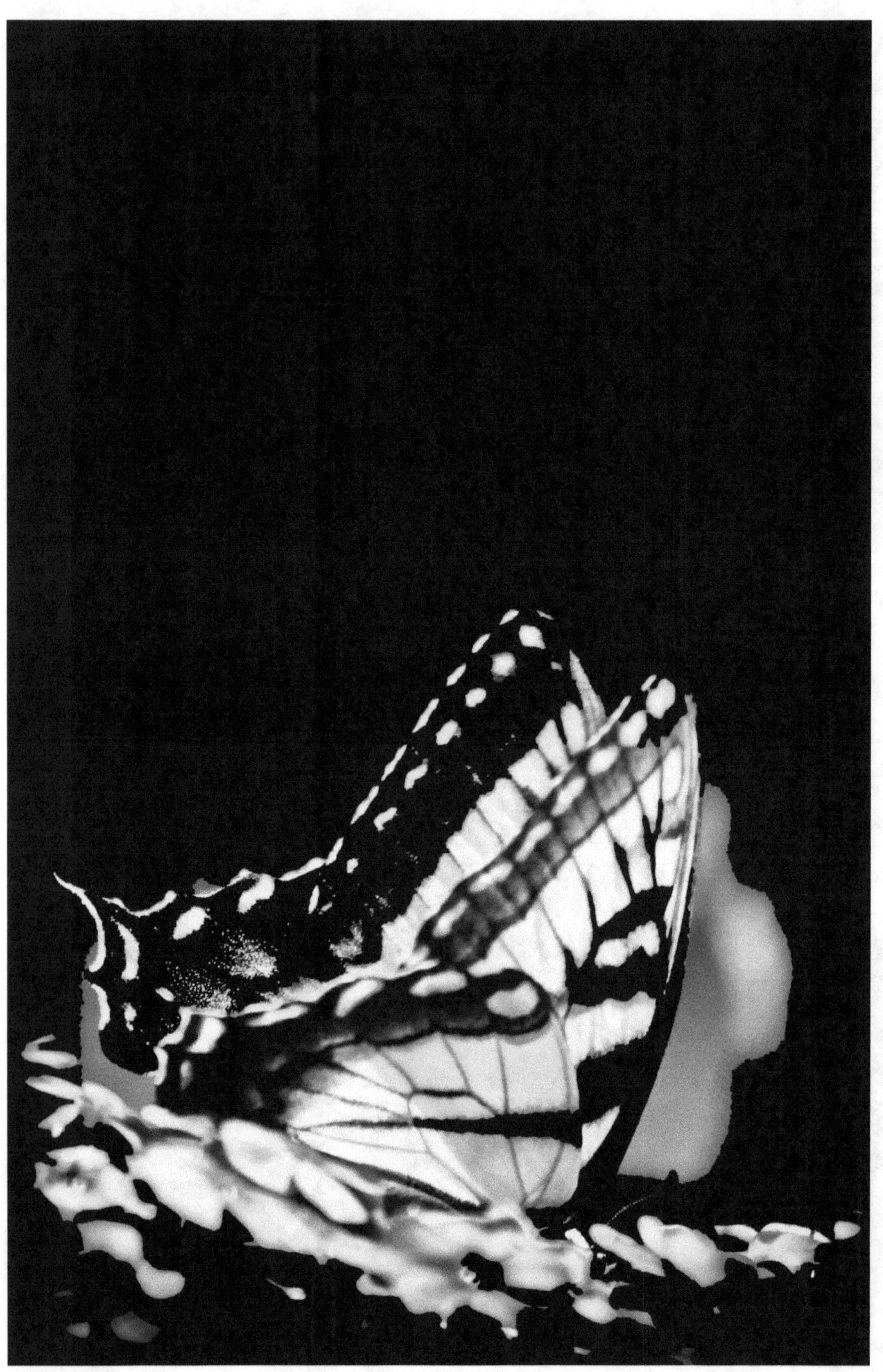

We Love On Butterflies

We Love each other on butterflies

Nothing below us only sky
Entwine we float without a care

Loving each other everywhere

My Love we Love on butterflies

In your joy you make me cry
For you my dear I will die

Our chance to Love on butterflies

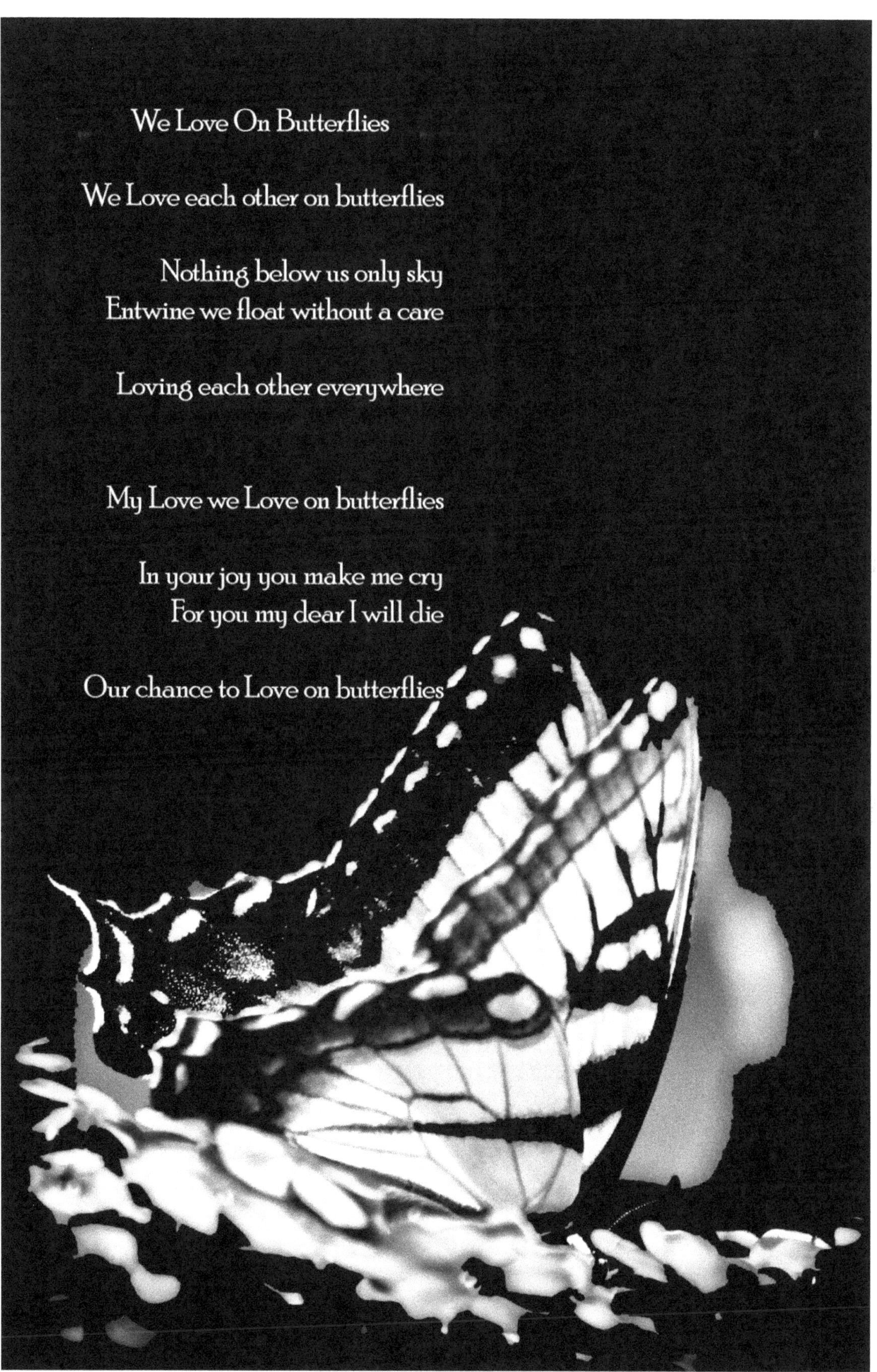

Dr. Claus combines his love of poetry, photography, and nature to create art.
His published works include:

A Gift of Love
Parsifal
Love Poems 101
Poems Of Love
To Thee I Sing
The Promise
The Poetess
Daughter Of Kings
When You Breathe
My Love Whispers
Inhale Deeply
My Lover
Clair de Lune Serenade
My Gentle Butterfly
The Poetess (Aquarelle)
The Poetess (Luz Celestial)
The Promise (Aquarelle)
The Promise (Luz Celestial)
My Lover (Aquarelle)
To Thee I Sing (Aquarelle)
To Thee I Sing (Luz Celestial)
Inhale Deeply (Aquarelle)
My Love Whispers (Aquarelle)
My Love Whispers (Luz Celestial)
The Keeper Of The Stones
When You Breathe (Aquarelle)
Daughter Of Kings (Aquarelle)
Medley Mole Meets Buddy Rabbit
Poems

www.ingramcontent.com/pod-product-compliance
Lightning Source LLC
LaVergne TN
LVHW061242100826
845148LV00008B/1009
* 9 7 8 1 6 1 4 9 7 0 5 0 7 *